# SUSTAINING DISTANCE TRAINING

## Integrating Learning Technologies into the Fabric of the Enterprise

Zane L. Berge
Editor

JOSSEY-BASS
A Wiley Company
San Francisco

Jossey-Bass books and products are available through most bookstores. To contact Jossey-Bass directly, call (888) 378-2537, fax to (800) 605-2665, or visit our website at www.josseybass.com.

Substantial discounts on bulk quantities of Jossey-Bass books are available to corporations, professional associations, and other organizations. For details and discount information, contact the special sales department at Jossey-Bass.

TCF Manufactured in the United States of America on Lyons Falls Turin Book. This paper is acid-free and 100 percent totally chlorine-free.

**Library of Congress Cataloging-in-Publication Data**

Sustaining distance training : integrating learning technologies
  into the fabric of the enterprise / by Zane L. Berge, editor.—
    1st ed.
    p. cm.— (The Jossey-Bass business & management series)
    Includes bibliographical references and index.
    ISBN 0-7879-5331-8
    1. Employees—Training of. 2. Distance education. 3.
Employees—Training of—United States—Case studies. 4. Distance
education—United States—Case studies. I. Berge, Zane L. II.
Title. III. Series.
HF5549.5.T7 S83 2000
658.3'124—dc21                                        00-009882
FIRST EDITION
*HB Printing*    10 9 8 7 6 5 4 3 2 1

THE JOSSEY-BASS BUSINESS & MANAGEMENT SERIES

# CONTENTS

## PART THREE: SETTING COMPETITIVE STANDARDS

# FIGURES, TABLES & EXHIBITS

## Figures

# Tables

# Exhibits

# PREFACE

Over the past decade and a half, I have been interested in technology-enhanced learning, especially learning at a distance. I have reviewed hundreds of cases in which technology has been used to accomplish training and education at a distance, and been involved in creating distance learning in the organizations where I have been employed or where I have consulted. I have noticed some patterns and commonalties that I believe will be useful to everyone involved in such endeavors. With this in mind, I wanted to explore in a more systematic way the question: *How do organizations sustain efforts in distance training when their goals are more than conducting isolated or sporadic distance training events?* I wanted to build a model or framework that describes the essential elements for organizations in which distance training and education has become a part of the enterprise's profile, and I wanted to supply the reader with multiple cases to illustrate a plausible theory that would help the readers relate to their organization.

In a book I coedited with Deborah Schreiber, *Distance Training: How Innovative Organizations Are Using Technology to Maximize Learning and Meet Business Objectives* (Jossey-Bass, 1998), Dr. Schreiber proposed the concept of *organizational technology capability* and related it to distance training. The concept described an organization's degree of technological sophistication—that is, the level of maturity or capabilities at which technology is applied to distance learning to meet business needs. Selection of cases for that book was based on factors other than the organization's stage of technological capability, and, not surprisingly, the organizations described fell across a wide range. While comparing and contrasting the cases used for that book, I gained insights that served to pilot my thinking as I developed the tentative framework for this study. Along with this effort, in Berge and Smith (2000) I also explored the relationship of change management, strategic planning, and project management and how these philosophies and related activities may affect the implementation of distance training and education within an organization.

Using the framework derived from this prior work as background, I wanted to understand, investigate, and explain to the readers of this book the way that organizations that have integrated distance training across their enterprise to meet their business needs have done so. To do this, I needed to identify organizations in which training at a distance is a normal event, not sporadic or separate from mainstream training. I wanted to analyze the context in which institutionalized distance training is occurring and develop a model that synthesized the significance of strategic planning in sustaining distance training and the importance of change management in the process that these organizations used to reach the higher levels of organizational distance training capabilities.

## Purpose

The purpose of this book is to disseminate a plausible model or framework for sustaining distance training and to describe the essential elements in that model with multiple cases to illustrate and help the readers' understanding. The cases have been selected as examples of organizations in which distance training is integrated into their business strategic plans. Each case summarizes the organizational obstacles encountered as well as the pitfalls and limitations that were overcome in meeting business goals and objectives through distance training.

## Audience

The intended readers of this book include organizational managers, performance consulting professionals, and practitioners charged with the training functions in corporations, nonprofit organizations, and government agencies. Such readers should use this book mainly to analyze how others have successfully integrated and sustained distance training in their organizations, including the pitfalls that were overcome in meeting business problems and opportunities through distance education.

Additionally, this book may be used as a primary textbook for students and professionals studying to enter the distance training field. As a text, this book is most suitable for courses in business management, government training, and college graduate classes in these and other areas such as education. Students should use this book to analyze case studies in distance training and discuss various perspectives on alternative solutions to the business problem the organization has identified.

## How This Book Is Organized

After reviewing the initial contributed drafts, I found it convenient for discussion to organize the book into these areas:

- Distance training helping to meet the challenge of uncommon organizational change
- Setting the competitive standards through distance training and education
- Achieving organizational goals using sustained distance training

Later in this Preface, there is a summary table for each of the three sections of case studies that allows the reader to determine at a glance which cases may be the most useful in the immediate circumstances.

Additionally, in the first two chapters, I set the context of distance training and education and explore various perspectives affecting distance training, ranging from project management to strategic planning. The last chapter suggests a few ideas for further research and summarizes the linking processes that managers use to plan and implement sustained distance training. The Appendix discusses the research methodology used in answering the research question. The Glossary is provided to help readers with terms that may be unfamiliar to them.

### Distance Training Helping to Meet the Challenge of Uncommon Organizational Change

Short of bankruptcy, there may be no business event that serves as a more imperative catalyst for change than a corporate merger. The cultural context in which people work is made clear when a merger juxtaposes different cultures and challenges everyone to change and grow. Another type of tumultuous change can come from a mandate—whether from a government authority or from the organization's chief executive. The cultural and organizational changes necessary to deal with these events are explored in this section of the book, with the emphasis on distance training and education.

To open the discussion of specific cases, *James B. Ellsworth* and *Luciano J. Iorizzo Jr.* explain in Chapter Three that designing—and even implementing—

## TABLE P.1. ORGANIZATIONS MEETING THE CHALLENGE OF UNCOMMON ORGANIZATIONAL CHANGE.

| Chapter | Organization | Business Product or Service | Headquarters Location | Approximate Number of Trainees | Percentage of Organization Budget Used for Training | Geographic Training Area | Distance Learning Tools Used |
|---|---|---|---|---|---|---|---|
| 3 | U.S. Army Intelligence Corps | Military training | Fort Huachuca, Arizona | 3,000 active and reserve soldiers | 100 | Worldwide | • World Wide Web<br>• Print |
| 4 | SBC Communications | Telecommunications | San Antonio, Texas | 120,000 | 2.1 (of payroll) | Worldwide | • Instructor-led classrooms<br>• Videoconferencing<br>• Desktop computer-based training (CBT) |
| 5 | MCI WorldCom | Telecommunications | Clinton, Mississippi; Atlanta, Georgia | NA | NA | United States and Canada | • Web-based training (WBT) |
| 6 | U.S. General Accounting Office | Evaluation of any and all federal government spending | Washington, D.C. | 4,500 | NA | Nationwide | • Videoconferencing<br>• Instructional television<br>• Online (e-mail)<br>• CBT |
| 7 | Réseau INTERACTION Network | Consulting firm: helping people train, learn, work, and manage at a distance | Ottawa, Ontario | Fluid workforce: 20–60 per year | NA | Mainly North America | • Audio conferencing<br>• Web-based technologies<br>• Desktop video-conferencing |
| 8 | U.S. Internal Revenue Service | Tax administration | Washington, D.C. | 105,000 | 1.3 | Nationwide | • Interactive video tele-training<br>• Online courses |

virtually anything involving emerging technology is relatively easy, but the rush to get on the bandwagon often means that action gets taken in such a hurry that the realities of organizational change are largely ignored. The *U.S. Army* overcame this challenge while embracing distance training to address a paradox: an increased requirement for career-long learning, coupled with diminished ability to spare soldiers from their duties and fund their travel to resident courses. This chapter describes the strategy that guided a major Army training institution's implementation and administration of distance training—offering guidelines and lessons learned for educational institutions beginning similar journeys.

In Chapter Four, *Natalie S. Friend* and *Tere Lyn Hepple* describe the challenges encountered in the process of merging the training programs of *SBC Communications's* Southwestern Bell and Pacific Bell regions. Each regional telecommunications training organization operated extensive distance learning programs with both classroom and desktop technologies. Identifying areas for maximizing efficiencies throughout the merged training organizations uncovered valuable insights related to buy-in, processes, selection, design, expertise, tools, systems, scheduling, deployment, facilitation, and support for distance learning. A key merger initiative was to reduce training expenses by using alternatives to traditional instructor-led training, and the chapter discusses this "alternative media" initiative in some depth. Identifying and measuring savings for each course strongly justified use of distance learning. The alternative media initiative was successful in saving the corporation millions of dollars and training hours.

Chapter Five takes up the story of how *MCI WorldCom* supported its 1998 merger by integrating the training groups from both companies to form the MCI WorldCom University, or MWU. The case study, by *Chris Treanor* and *Jessica Page Irwin*, is an account of how this new company used distance learning to prepare MCI WorldCom Business Markets employees to implement the company's slogan and literally "Open the World for Business." It details the strategies and programs that were implemented to accomplish this task, and provides guidelines (based on MWU's four-phase training strategy) to accomplish the following goals:

- Communicate a shared vision for training.
- Create a training infrastructure (or platform) that is scalable, portable, and redundant.
- Build training and use existing resources to meet the needs of the audience.
- Find delivery methods that have an impact on the company's training.
- Promote the program and motivate students to participate.

In Chapter Six, *Jo L. Longnecker* discusses organizational support for distance learning within a strategic framework, including the factors needed to implement and promote distance learning and the resource allocations required, through lessons learned at the *U.S. General Accounting Office* (GAO). A mandate to use technology and distance learning resulted in a dramatic organizational change in the GAO's training and educational efforts, including how it worked to attract trainers and facilitators to use the required technologies. Also outlined in this chapter is the hands-on "train the trainer" program and other measures GAO developed to strengthen instructors' confidence and skill.

*Daniel L. Larocque* and *Noël Thomas* devote Chapter Seven to *Réseau INTER-ACTION Network* (RIN), a company that was created in 1980 with the intent of supporting clients' efforts to learn, work, and manage at a distance. RIN's corporate structure is based on the premise of a spherical virtual organization, and RIN provides most of its services remotely, using a constant flow of short-term, project-based contributors. This fluid workforce makes it essential to bring people on board quickly, so that each new contributor becomes an integral part of a high-impact, short-term, project-based, distance team. To cope with its with many challenges, RIN adopted the concepts of just-in-time and just-enough training. In essence, permanent staff and contributors are trained when needed on values and skills necessary to meet the client's objectives. This model has proven to be successful for both staff and company, as it avoids information overload and yet allows for quick, practical results.

Over the past decade, the *Internal Revenue Service* has been grappling with continual and revolutionary organizational change. In Chapter Eight, *Teva J. Scheer* describes a case where this all-consuming transformation has served both as the backdrop for the IRS's creation of a distance learning system and as its catalyst. Continued growth of nontraditional course offerings (satellite teletraining, online and CD-ROM courses, electronic performance support systems) is seen as critical if the IRS is to provide all the training necessary to prepare employees for their new jobs in a reengineered IRS. The IRS has learned that an organization must expect and be patient with the natural learning curve necessary to establish a high-quality distance learning system.

## Setting Competitive Standards Through Distance Training and Education

We have entered the Knowledge Age, in which the new economy requires a continuously learning workforce. It is with this in mind that the organizations described in this section not only meet the challenge of their competition but set the standards in the marketplace.

In Chapter Nine, the process of strategic planning is discussed in the context of a partnership between the *UAW-DaimlerChrysler National Training Center* and *Michigan State University* for the purpose of creating an online distance learning program and providing UAW-represented workers at DaimlerChrysler with expanded learning opportunities. *Joseph R. Codde, Rhonda K. Egidio, Karyn J. Boatwright, Jack E. Zahn,* and *Raymond J. Czarnik* explain how strategic planning allows the organization to map out a program that both benefits its members and accomplishes its mission. This chapter is a practical description of strategic planning at both the organizational and programmatic levels, along with the resultant action steps.

*First Union National Bank,* the nation's sixth-largest bank holding company (with branch banking throughout the East Coast and services throughout the nation and the world), has developed an extensive satellite training delivery network. In Chapter Ten, *Sherry H. Latten, J. Michael Davis,* and *Neel Stallings* describe how First Union has broadened its system, originally used for informational broadcasts, to fully embrace the concept of distance learning. The authors describe the steps in this migration and present a case study of a highly successful program.

*Joan Conway Dessinger* and *Larry Conley* explain the *FORDSTAR network* in Chapter Eleven. FORDSTAR is a combination data-digital-video network, and Ford chose this approach to technology-based distance learning for its dealerships to meet four business needs related to training—increased speed, reach, interactivity, and reduced variability. FORDSTAR's infrastructure funding was generated by cost savings while FORDSTAR's ongoing operations funding of distance training comes in part from dealers and in part from the company. Although classroom training continues to play an important role in hands-on and skill-building training, technology-based distance learning now accounts for approximately 92 percent of the 700,499 courses that are completed annually by dealership employees.

In Chapter Twelve, *Greg V. Michalski* focuses on Web-based training in product time-to-market (TTM) at *Nortel Networks.* This effort serves as an example of sustaining distance learning by assessing user learning expectations concurrent with the development of Web-based instruction. The results of user surveys profiling user demographics, expectations, and rationales for engaging in Web-based TTM training are also presented, in the context of the sustainability of Web-based training and instruction. Overall results and lessons learned are discussed in terms of emerging business realities and the role of Web-based instruction in organizational change.

In Chapter Thirteen, *John E. May* and *Jan A. de Jong* describe *Cap Gemini Ernst & Young,* one of the leading European management consulting and IT services firms, which was recently declared European Company of the Year by the European Business Press Federation. Cap Gemini Ernst & Young Education & Training is a unit that started about thirty years ago as an institute to train the firm's own employees. Nowadays, 70 percent of the unit's turnover is generated by external customers. This chapter focuses on the lessons the organization learned with coaching in a distance learning environment.

## TABLE P.2. ORGANIZATIONS SETTING COMPETITIVE STANDARDS THROUGH SUSTAINED DISTANCE TRAINING.

| Chapter | Organization | Business Product or Service | Headquarters Location | Approximate Number of Trainees | Percentage of Organization Budget Used for Training | Geographic Training Area | Distance Learning Tools Used |
|---|---|---|---|---|---|---|---|
| 9 | UAW-Daimler Chrysler | Auto industry | Detroit, Michigan | 77,000 | NA | Nationwide | • Internet<br>• World Wide Web |
| 10 | First Union | Financial services | Charlotte, North Carolina | 70,000 | NA | Primarily Eastern U.S. and California | • Satellite<br>• Multimedia, intranet, and EPSS also used; not discussed here |

| | Company | Industry | Location | Employees | Locations | Methods |
|---|---|---|---|---|---|---|
| 11 | FORDSTAR | Automotive | Dearborn, Michigan | 215,000 | NA | North America (United States, Canada, Mexico) | • Interactive Videoconferencing<br>• CD ROM multimedia<br>• Instructor-led classrooms |
| 12 | Nortel | Telecommunications | Brampton, Ontario | 13,000 | 3 | North America | • Web audio and video streaming |
| 13 | Cap Gemini | Management consulting and computer services | Paris, France | 38,000 | 3 | Europe | • Web-based videoconferencing |
| 14 | Hewlett-Packard | Internet; computer | California | 16,000 | NA | San Francisco Bay Area | • Synchronous and asynchronous virtual classroom<br>• CBT accessed via the Web<br>• Interactive CD-ROM |

High-tech corporations increasingly face the issue of ensuring that knowledge workers have access to resources that will help them stay abreast of technological change while controlling the cost of sales, while the knowledge workers face the issue of finding time to keep up with the flood of information about technological change. Chapter Fourteen, by *Alice Branch, Amy Lyon,* and *Sarah C. Porten,* looks at how one organization within *Hewlett-Packard* approached the combined effect of these challenges to corporation and employee. Hewlett-Packard developed the Site Information & Learning Centers in Silicon Valley through a strategy that sought to ensure that alternative, technology-based learning resources be integrated into the fabric of employee training and development. After an analysis of its employee and business constituency, the group developed and implemented a plan that allowed the company to provide high-quality technical training "any time, any place." Over time, SILC dramatically altered the strategic plans of its parent organization for the delivery of training.

## Achieving Organizational Goals Using Sustained Distance Training

As the global economy changes the way business is transacted and as technology contributes more and more to that change, the competition for markets and customers continues to be a significant challenge. Distance training and education is looked upon as a way of investing in people throughout the organization, thereby adding value in the achievement of organizational goals. Increased benefits are derived from such things as a more widespread exposure to nationally and internationally recognized experts both inside and outside the organization. Reductions in cost areas such as time-to-market, travel expenditures, time spent in training, and opportunity costs of lost productivity also directly affect the productivity, quality, and access of employees in the organization.

Chapter Fifteen, by *Barbara Polhamus, Anita M. Farel,* and *Tim Stephens,* presents the case study of a distance learning approach to data skills training for the public health workforce. Web-based training provides an effective and economic means for staff to advance their skills while continuing to meet their professional responsibilities. The project known as *Enhancing Data Utilization Skills through Information Technology (EDUSIT)* trains public health professionals in state and local health departments in the southern regions of the United States to collect, analyze, and interpret data through a year-long Web-based course. The course is offered through the Department of Maternal and Child Health in the *School of Public Health at the University of North Carolina at Chapel Hill* in collaboration with the school's Center for Distance Learning. This chapter describes the organizational and management systems involved in delivering the course, and examines selected features for motivating participants.

*Barry Howard*, director of learning technology at *NYNEX*, a large telecommunication company (now a part of Bell Atlantic), devotes Chapter Sixteen to the challenges the company faced when it created an enterprise-wide, multi-tooled approach to implementing distance learning during the 1990s. By 1997 approximately one-third of the courses for existing employees were being delivered through some form of technology. A significant portion of the training department's work had moved out of the traditional classroom. That meant that the support systems that were traditionally relied on for forecasting, scheduling, evaluating, and so on were no longer as dependable to provide the kind of command and control required while the training volumes and training budgets fluctuated constantly. This chapter focuses on the new tools and management processes the company developed for training at a distance.

*Mary Jane (Molly) Wankel* devotes Chapter Seventeen to a discussion of how the U.S. Postal Service trains its workforce, which is one of the nation's largest and most widely distributed. The challenge in providing such training is threefold: cost, limited resources, and consistent message. Distance learning efforts at the Postal Service—initiated in 1986 and expanded over the years—play an integral role in meeting Postal Service business goals by providing employees with training at their job sites when they need it. Since 1995, using distance learning to address business needs has led to greater operational efficiency, profitability instead of recurring losses, unprecedented stability in postage rates, record levels of first-class mail performance, stricter standards for priority mail and first class mail, and greater customer satisfaction.

In Chapter Eighteen, *Rory McGreal* introduces *TeleEducation NB* (TENB), an innovative program in distributed distance education in the small Canadian province of New Brunswick. TENB is a network of networks with more than seventy distributed learning sites, connected by an audiographic teleconferencing system using either telephone lines or the Internet. In addition, the network supports computer-mediated conferencing and two Web sites. The chapter discusses the problems TENB has encountered and provides a list of recommendations.

The *American Red Cross* relies on approximately 33,000 paid employees and 1.3 million volunteers to carry out its mission. In Chapter Nineteen *Nadine E. Rogers* and *Sandra L. Becker* discuss the successes and challenges associated with implementing distance learning in a not-for-profit environment. The current strategy is to provide learning opportunities by use of the most efficient and effective methods that will meet the needs of individual users, and involves both satellite-based interactive television and the American Red Cross intranet. In part, this requires a culture shift for the entire organization and an understanding of the technology requirements as well as of the organization's culture and socialization as it relates to learning. The chapter also describes the continued focus on

## TABLE P.3.  ORGANIZATIONS ACHIEVING THEIR GOALS USING SUSTAINED DISTANCE TRAINING.

| Chapter | Organization | Business Product or Service | Headquarters Location | Approximate Number of Trainees | Percentage of Organization Budget Used for Training | Geographic Training Area | Distance Learning Tools Used |
|---|---|---|---|---|---|---|---|
| 15 | EDUSIT | Public health education | Chapel Hill, North Carolina | 40 | Under federal grant | Thirteen southern U.S. states | • WBT |
| 16 | NYNEX | Telecommunications | New York | 100,000 | N/A | Northeast | • Business television<br>• Videoconference<br>• Audiographics<br>• CBT<br>• WBT<br>• Electronic performance support-system (EPSS)<br>• In-person delivery |
| 17 | U.S. Postal Service | Mail and package delivery | Washington, D.C. | 800,000 | Less than 2 | Nationwide | • Audiographics<br>• Satellite<br>• Public Broadcasting System<br>• Videotapes<br>• CD-ROM<br>• WBT<br>• Performance support |
| 18 | TeleEducation NB | Online course development and delivery | Fredericton, New Brunswick | 28 | 10 | Mainly New Brunswick | • Audiographics<br>• Teleconferencing<br>• Web |
| 19 | American Red Cross | Disaster relief and emergency prevention, preparation, and response | Washington, D.C. | Over 1.3 million | 2 at each unit level | Mainland United States | • Internet and intranet<br>• Interactive television (satellite-based) |

understanding how the workforce wants to learn and how to provide the right learning opportunities.

## Acknowledgments

I would like to acknowledge the reviewers of this book: Myk Garn, Barry Howard, and Mick Mortlock. I greatly appreciate their time and valuable suggestions.

*Baltimore, Maryland*                                                    Zane L. Berge
*September 2000*

# THE AUTHORS

**ZANE L. BERGE** is director of the University of Maryland, Baltimore County (UMBC), Training Systems graduate program. Before joining the faculty at UMBC, Berge founded the Center for Teaching and Technology at George-town University. He consults and conducts research internationally in distance education. He is widely published in the field of computer-mediated communication used for teaching and learning. Most notable are seven books: the three-volume *Computer-Mediated Communication and the Online Classroom* (1995) and the four-volume *Wired Together: Computer Mediated Communication in the K12 Classroom* (1998). His most recent work, coedited with Dr. Deborah Schreiber, is the award-winning *Distance Training: How Innovative Organizations Are Using Technology to Maximize Learning and Meet Business Objectives* (Jossey-Bass, 1998). E-mail: berge@umbc.edu.

**Sandra L. Becker** is currently manager of performance improvement in the management and executive training function at the American Red Cross. She is responsible for overseeing the execution of performance analyses and the design and implementation of performance improvement interventions. She is currently pursuing a doctoral degree in human resources development at George Washington University. One of her main emphases during recent years has been on leveraging training technology, including one-way video, two-way audio satellite delivery with a viewer response keypad system and intranet technology. E-mail: BeckerS@usa.redcross.org

**Karyn J. Boatwright** is assistant professor of psychology at Kalamazoo College in Kalamazoo, Michigan. She earned both her M.A. degree (1986) in counseling and her Ph.D. degree (1998) in counseling psychology at Michigan State University. Boatwright's main research activities have focused on the role of gender in influencing workers' preferences for leadership styles and in identifying variables related to college students' leadership and educational aspirations. E-mail: karynb@kzoo.edu

**Alice Branch** is currently operations manager for the Internet Hosted Services business in Hewlett-Packard's Customer Education Division. She has worked for HP for nineteen years, and has assumed numerous roles in various divisions. From April 1995 to April 1999, she was manager of the Regional Training Center's Site Information & Learning Centers and Education Research & Development function. She earned her B.A. in linguistics at the University of California, Davis; has done postgraduate work at Stanford University; and is currently working on her M.A. in human resources and organization development at the University of San Francisco. E-mail: BRANCH_ALICE/HP-MountainView_om1@cupom2.cup .hp.com

**Joseph R. Codde** is an assistant professor and coordinator of the Educational Technology Certificate Program in the College of Education at Michigan State University, East Lansing. He is also coordinator for the VITAL (Virtual Interactive Teaching And Learning) program at MSU. Codde received an M.A. degree (1991) in adult and continuing education and a doctorate (1997) in higher, adult, and lifelong education from MSU. He possesses twenty-five years of business experience and twelve years of teaching experience at the postsecondary level. He is also active in developing online distance education programs for education and business. *Jack E. Zahn* and *Raymond J. Czarnik*, both from the UAW-DaimlerChrysler National Training Center, were invaluable in writing this case study. E-mail: coddejos@pilot.msu.edu

**Larry Conley** is currently head of the Conley Consulting Group. He retired from Ford in January 2000, after thirty-six years with the company. During that time he completely revamped the company's internal training programs, besides establishing working relationships and a dedicated auto repair curriculum at sixty-two U.S. colleges. He was in charge of the distance training program described in Chapter Eleven. E-mail: lconleyccg@aol.com.

**J. Michael Davis,** assistant vice president and learning specialist of First University (First Union Bank's corporate university), has over twenty years' experience in delivering and developing training. As project manager of the Managing Human Resources Policies course, he draws on his three years of distance learning experience and total training knowledge to identify ongoing opportunities for course design improvements. E-mail: Michael.Davis4@firstunion.com

**Jan A. de Jong** is an educational psychologist and staff member of the School of Educational Sciences, Utrecht University, in The Netherlands. His main research interests are work-based learning, on-the-job training, and on-the-job coaching. He has published in *Human Resource Development Quarterly*, *Human Resource Development International*, the *International Journal of Educational Research*, the *International Journal of Training and Development*, the *Journal of Workplace Learning*, the *Leadership and Organization Development Journal*, and *Teachers and Teaching*. E-mail: j.dejong@ fss.uu.nl.

**Joan Conway Dessinger** is a performance consultant to business, industry, and education. In 1989 she founded the Lake Group, a performance consulting firm. She also teaches graduate courses in the Instructional Technology Department at Wayne State University, and has facilitated workshops for more than fifty state, national, and international conferences. She has authored or coauthored journal articles and professional books, including *Why Employees Do What They Do: Human Performance Technology in the Workplace* (ISPI, 1999) and *Distance Training: How Innovative Organizations Are Using Technology to Maximize Learning and Meet Business Objectives* (Jossey-Bass, 1998). E-mail: LakeGrp@aol.com.

**Rhonda K. Egidio** is a professor in the College of Education at Michigan State University, East Lansing. She earned both her M.A. degree (1976) in college student personnel and her Ph.D. degree (1986) in educational administration at Michigan State University. Egidio developed and offered the first online course at Michigan State University in 1995 on the future of education in a learning society. She is director of the VITAL (Virtual Interactive Teaching And Learning) program at MSU, which has been instrumental in training higher education faculty in the design and pedagogy of online learning. She also directs the REACH program (Rehabilitation Education And Change), which builds technology environments for continuing education and knowledge management. E-mail: egidio@ pilot.msu.edu

**James B. Ellsworth** joined the U.S. Naval War College's College of Continuing Education faculty in the summer of 2000, following over a decade of service as a trainer, training developer, and training evaluator with the U.S. Army's Armor and Intelligence Centers. Best known as a scholar and practitioner of educational change, with a focus on technology-enhanced learning environments, Dr. Ellsworth led the early infusion of Internet-based technologies into the Army's Military Intelligence curriculum, beginning in early 1995. He holds degrees from Clarkson University and Syracuse University, and has authored numerous publications including a book on educational change, is a frequent invited speaker on education systems for information-based society, and serves as managing editor for ISTOnline, a project to create a peer-reviewed annotated bibliography of scholarly educational resources on the Internet. He is an active member of several professional associations including AECT, ISPI, and AERA. E-mail: JBEllsworth@aol.com

**Anita M. Farel** has been on the faculty of the Department of Maternal and Child Health, School of Public Health at the University of North Carolina-Chapel Hill for fifteen years. She is the principal investigator for the Enhancing Data Utilization through Information Technology (EDUSIT) project. Through several cooperative agreements from the Health Resources and Services Administration, she has worked with state Title V programs to improve the ability of program staff to collect, analyze, and use data effectively. E-mail: Anita_Farel@UNC.EDU

**Natalie S. Friend** is an instructional design manager at the SBC Center for Learning, specializing in multimedia design. She earned an M.S. degree in instructional technology from the Rochester Institute of Technology in 1993 in Rochester, New York, and attends post-graduate courses at the University of North Texas in Denton. She develops self-paced and instructor-led training using a variety of media-based solutions. Presentations and writings include topics on business, education, and alternative delivery systems for the American Society of Training and Development (ASTD), Society for Technical Communication (STC), International Society of Performance Improvement (ISPI), and *Performance Improvement Quarterly*. E-mail: NF9094@txmail.sbc.com

**Tere Lyn Hepple** is project manager/instructional design with Frontline Group's TelCom Training Division. She earned a B.S.Ed. degree in secondary education/English and journalism from Baylor University in Waco, Texas, in 1992 and an M.S. degree in computer education and cognitive systems at the University of North Texas in Denton in 1998. Hepple is a member of the multimedia special interest groups in STC, ISPI, and ASTD. As associate editor at Stevens Publishing for *Occupational Health & Safety* magazine and *Workplace Ergonomics*, she specialized in training and human factors. E-mail: terelyn.hepple@home.com

**Barry Howard** is a member of QED Consulting, a New York–based organization that specializes in human resource change management and the transition to learning technology, and an adjunct professor in computer science at Baruch College in New York City. He has also taught college-level management and marketing courses using two-way video for the Center for Distance Learning (State University of New York). In recent years, he has spoken at most of the major training conferences in the United States. He has written articles for a number of training publications, and is often quoted by the media on electronic education, strategic outsourcing, and computer training subjects. E-mail: barryhoward@ qedconsulting.com-

**Luciano J. Iorizzo Jr.** is chief of the Distance Learning Office, U.S. Army Military Intelligence Center, Fort Huachuca, Arizona. He leads Praxis, an initiative for the Military Intelligence Captains Career Course, to integrate a learning agent with a virtual tactical operations center to provide the benefits of synchronous collaboration when peers are unavailable. He holds a master's degree in instructional design, development, and evaluation from the School of Education at Syracuse University. He has coauthored a number of papers on distance learning over the last eleven years and continues to present at training and technology conferences. E-mail: iorizzol@huachuca-emh1.army.mil

**Jessica Page Irwin** is the team lead and senior instructional designer for MWU Training Technologies in Atlanta, Georgia, where she is responsible for closely aligning corporate training objectives and Web development. Jessica holds a bachelor of business administration degree in marketing from Baylor University, and served as a judge in the 1999 Internet and Multimedia Awards sponsored by Brandon-Hall.com. E-mail: Jessica.Page.Irwin@corp.go.com

**Daniel L. Larocque** is a consultant and project manager with Réseau INTERACTION Network Inc., specializing in distance education, work, and management. He has an Ed.M. in curriculum development (Harvard) and an M.A. in adult education with a focus in organizational development (Toronto). He is particularly interested in maximizing individual and group experiences at a distance, making them both efficient and rewarding. He has published various articles and learning support materials, one of which was awarded a national prize for best support material. E-mail: danilaro@village.ca

**Sherry H. Latten,** vice president and distance learning coordinator of First University (First Union's corporate university), has delivered, developed, managed, and consulted on numerous Instructional Design projects during her eight years in training with First Union National Bank. She currently consults with First University instructional designers on both satellite and videoconferencing courses. E-mail: sherry.latten1@firstunion.com

**Jo L. Longnecker** is an organizational effectiveness consultant at the MITRE Corporation in McLean, Virginia. She earned an M.A. degree in Spanish at San Diego State University, and an M.A. degree in human resource development from George Washington University, Washington, D.C. She is currently enrolled in a doctoral program concentrating on organizational development and leadership at George Washington University. She has presented at numerous national and international technology and distance learning conferences. She maintains academic affiliations in human resource development and currently serves on the Advisory Council to Marymount University for graduate curriculum in human resources. She has taught at Georgetown University, San Diego State University, and the World Bank. She is a member of the American Society for Training and Development, and the International Society for Performance Instruction. E-mail: jlongnec@mitre.org

**Amy Lyon** is currently the application support specialist for Hewlett-Packard's Bay Area Regional Training Center. With over fifteen years of professional experience, Amy has worked in the Learning Center since its inception five years ago. She has managed all aspects of the Learning Center business, has developed internal delivery solutions, and has extensively evaluated launching and tracking systems. She is also a member of an internal Learning Center Co-op. E-mail: amy_lyon@hp.com

**John E. May** is responsible for Distance Learning in the Cap Gemini Ernst & Young Benelux organization. He started his career in 1987 at Cap Gemini Ernst & Young, working on several projects in the Information and Communication Technology, from the design to realization of information systems. He transferred from ICT consultancy to Education & Training in 1990, starting as a teacher and coach and developing into an educational consultant. In this role he served several projects from management of educational development projects to educational consultancy in supporting reorganizations of customer ICT departments. Since 1998 he has adopted the distance learning program, Virtual Classroom, from the research and development department and is responsible for its implementation and transformation to a true e-learning environment. E-mail: John.May@ capgemini.nl

**Rory McGreal** is executive director of TeleEducation New Brunswick, a provincewide distance education and training network. As the principal leader of the TeleCampus initiative, he is responsible for creating an online Virtual Campus with courses available on the World Wide Web. McGreal's main interests focus on the implementation and development of distributed learning systems. He has written articles and book chapters on distributed learning environments, the economic development role of distance education, Web course design, and other related subjects. He is the lead author of *Learning on the Web*, an online instruction guide for teachers. E-mail: rory@teleeducation.nb.ca

**Greg V. Michalski** is a program development associate in Training Evaluation Services at ACT, an independent educational research and testing organization. He holds multiple advanced degrees including an M.S. (Virginia Polytechnic Institute and State University), an M.A. in educational leadership and human resource development (Western Michigan University), and a Ph.D. in education (University of Ottawa). He has also authored a range of academic and professional manuscripts, presentations, and articles. His current interests include Web-based learning and instruction (WBLI), evaluation and stakeholder diversity issues in training, and education assessment and evaluation. E-mail: michalsg@act.org

**Barbara Polhamus** works on the development of distance training at the Centers for Disease Control and Prevention. She previously was director and served on the faculty for the Enhancing Data Utilization Skills through Information Technology (EDUSIT) project at the University of North Carolina, School of Public Health, Department of Maternal and Child Health (MCH). She has worked in the MCH field for the past fifteen years and has extensive experience working with data used by MCH programs. E-mail: bpolhamus@cdc.gov

**Sarah C. Porten** is currently a member of the e-learning team at HP's Global Learning for Performance organization. Her main role is to define key strategies in e-learning infrastructures supporting "anywhere, anytime" access to knowledge and learning. Sarah received her M.A. degree in instructional design and technology from San Jose State University. She has published "Guidelines for Evaluating Self-Paced Courses" in B. Hall (Ed.), *Web-Based Training Cookbook* (Wiley, 1997). E-mail sarah_porten@hp.com

**Nadine E. Rogers** is currently the research project manager in the Health, Safety, and Community Services evaluation unit at the American Red Cross, where she is responsible for the design and implementation of studies that examine the effectiveness of technology for health-related educational products and services. She is currently pursuing a doctorate in public health education at Johns Hopkins University, School of Hygiene & Public Health. E-mail: RogersN@ usa.redcross.org

**Teva J. Scheer** is a curriculum manager with the Internal Revenue Service's Learning and Education Organization, responsible for development and delivery of the nationwide training curriculum for the agency's education specialists and instructors. In 1997, the Government Training Council awarded Scheer its annual award for outstanding course design projects for her development of the Curriculum for Education Professionals and Faculty. In 1999, Creative Training Techniques International recognized her as Outstanding Government Trainer of the Year. E-mail: tscheer@carbon.cudenver.edu

**Neel Stallings** is a vice president in the New Leadership College of First University, First Union's corporate university. She led the design and delivery of the Leadership College's first interactive satellite program, "Managing Human Resources Policies," in 1997. As a result, she won the prestigious Business Leadership Award in 1999 for "developing and maintaining technology to support effective human performance throughout First Union." E-mail: Neel.Stallings1@firstunion.com

**Tim Stephens** is director of the Public Health Training Center at the University of North Carolina School of Public Health. He holds an undergraduate degree from the University of Warwick (England) and a master's in communications from the University of North Carolina. He has conducted numerous studies of the educational needs of the public health workforce in North Carolina, the United States, and abroad, as well as assessing the ability of distance education to meet these needs. E-mail: tim.stephens@nexted.com

**Noël Thomas** is president and CEO of Réseau INTERACTION Network, Inc. and founder of The Electronic Village, a distance management and community support and education network. He has a master's degree in social work. He has been an organizational consultant for over twenty years, mainly in the field of distance education and distance management. He is also a driving force in Internet-delivered basic literacy projects and models of distance delivery of services to children in remote areas. He has taught at the college and university levels and has lectured and published extensively on the proper use of technologies in human relationships. E-mail: noelthom@village.ca.

**Chris Treanor** is a senior knowledge systems developer for MCI WorldCom Technology Solutions in Atlanta, with particular expertise in application and technology testing, instructional development, and interactive media design. He is currently working toward his Ph.D. in Instructional Technology from Georgia State University, and is an active member in the Society of Organizational Learning and ISPI (International Society of Performance Improvement). E-mail: ctreanor@virtualteamsinc.com.

**Mary Jane (Molly) Wankel,** a training development specialist for the U.S. Postal Service, has twenty-five years' experience in managing and implementing training programs. She has served as president of local chapters of the International Society for Performance Improvement (ISPI) and the American Society for Training and Development and is still a local and international member of both organizations. She has presented twice at the international conference for ISPI and has written papers for and delivered presentations to numerous organizations. E-mail: Molly.Wankel@windwalker.com

PART ONE

# INTRODUCTION

# CHAPTER ONE

# THE CONTEXT OF DISTANCE TRAINING

## Predicting Change

### Zane L. Berge

It does not take a fortune-teller to predict a future full of change for each of us. The world is changing and much of this is due to advances in technology. Technology that is changing the landscape of society in general is also a catalyst for shifting the delivery of training and education (Hawkins, 1999).

The trend in the United States is that instructor-led, presentation-style training is down and the delivery of technologically mediated training is increasing. About 25–30 percent of total training is now delivered using *alternative delivery systems*—systems other than stand-up, in-person delivery—with projections showing significant growth in the next five years (Bassi & Van Buren, 1998). Technology-based training is projected to represent 55 percent of all training by 2002, up from 21 percent in 1998. Web-based training, a growing component of technology-based training, is expected to expand from $197 million in 1997 to $5.5 billion by 2002, representing an explosive growth of 95 percent annually (Moe, Bailey, & Lau, 1999).

My goal in the chapter following this one is to present a framework for linking several perspectives found by various people in an organization who want to effectively and efficiently deliver training and education at a distance. Before describing the framework itself, this chapter will set the model in context. I will identify shifts in the economy that act as a catalyst for new roles, responsibilities, and expectations of instructors and learners that are concomitant with the changes in the economy (Berge, 1996, 1998c), and also describe a few key concepts that act as foundation for the model to follow.

## Distance Training and Education

*Distance education* has many definitions. In this book it means organized, formal training and education in which the learner is separated from the resources that are useful in learning the stated instructional goals. In distance education one resource that is most often remote from the learner is the instructor. Typically, it is the geographical separation of student from the instructor that has been the defining characteristic of distance education. While this may be a useful distinction, the separation from other resources and sources of information is also important—especially if a learning environment is designed for collaboration among students who are not physically near each other. The terms *distance training, distance instruction,* and *distance education* are used throughout the book to indicate an emphasis on what is done by the sponsoring organization and instructor. *Distributed learning* and *distance learning* are used to indicate an emphasis on what the learner does. "Distance education" is believed by some to carry pejorative baggage for many persons reading or hearing the term, but I have rejected that notion.

## What to Expect from the Nature of Training and Education in the Workplace

I strongly believe that there must be a direct and clear link between training and the solving of a business problem (Berge & Smith, 2000; Feretic, 1999; Schreiber & Berge, 1998). This is true whether the training is done at a distance or not. Training should be just-in-time and just-enough. When training is delivered as close to the time that it is to be used by the trainee as possible, its relevancy is increased and the student's motivation to learn is often raised. Designing just-enough training takes into account what each individual already knows and therefore does not have to learn, and also what the person will do with new knowledge and skills. This way only the skills and content that are necessary to sufficiently improve job performance need to be mastered.

*Training* has to do with the learners' acquiring knowledge, skills, and attitudes that are useful to them immediately to improve performance on the job. *Education,* on the other hand, by definition is just-in-case and not just-in-time. And, if you think about it, there is no such thing as "just enough education." Education deals with the acquisition of knowledge, skills, and attitudes too, but not necessarily for immediate improvement of performance on the job. Education is concerned with improving future job performance or simply promoting personal growth—with little to do with performance now or ever. These are important goals, but it must be remembered that just-in-case learning is often forgotten before it is needed or used.

There is an emerging emphasis on lifelong learning and the broadening of the philosophical underpinnings that guide the transfer of knowledge and the construction of knowledge. This chapter describes some of the concepts that form the foundations of sustained training and education.

Technology used for training and instruction can act as a catalyst to cause the people charged with training and education to rethink the whole teaching and learning process. People engaged with technology are shaping and reshaping training, education, and learning. Teamwork continues to permeate all aspects of the workplace. Exploration of the characteristics of the adult learner and the benefits and pitfalls of distance education can help shape activities and methods used in training and education. Finally, the way training is viewed by the organization providing it—either as an expense or as an investment—and the factors affecting the new economy all have an impact on sustaining training and education at a distance.

## Teamwork

There is probably as much written today about teamwork, cooperative learning, collaboration, and similar concepts as anything else in education and management. This book does not focus on teamwork in depth, but much of the analysis, design, development, implementation, and evaluation of training and education at a distance is done by people working together to leverage their individual expertise.

Collaboration is an important part of teamwork. *Collaboration* indicates that two or more people are synergistically working together toward a common goal. Thus collaboration is distinguished from cooperation in that individuals can cooperate if mutually beneficial to each of them without doing more than reaching each of their own individual goals. Teams of learners emphasize collaboration and interactive learning. These are some of the benefits of collaborating and teamwork (AQP, 1998):

• Diversity across people brings together different skills and knowledge. By combining diversity and commitment, the team will increase the probability of successful results by engaging a wider range of highly competent, energized, and willing individuals.

- Many people working together can accomplish a bigger goal or achieve something otherwise not possible. "The whole is greater than the sum of the parts" rings especially true here.

- There is a greater likelihood of the solution being generally accepted because various members of the system are included in the collaborative process and will help to sell the solution to those who were not directly involved.

- Individuals will gain knowledge and skills to apply in the future, increasing career flexibility and marketability.

- The work leads to personal development that includes self-discovery and understanding of others.

- Relationships tend to expand and deepen.

- There is an increased sense of meaningful contribution.

- It's just plain fun.

## Lifelong Learning

The emergence of technological changes and the knowledge-based organization is rapidly changing the way lifelong learning is generally perceived. The concept of a stable career with a single employer after high school or college is all but gone in the global world of today's business. Professionals and workers find little, if any, job security—regardless of their effort and performance. These days, the only route to employment security is what one knows and the flexibility one has in solving problems that the employer finds necessary to solve. This requires the acquisition of new knowledge, skills, and attitudes on a continual basis. The world that challenges us tomorrow will require every person to approach every job as an opportunity to increase their skills and knowledge. A career grows through successful accomplishment in several jobs and continuous lifelong learning.

## The Adult Learner

Malcolm Knowles (Knowles, Holton, & Swanson, 1998) conceives the adult student as moving from dependency on an instructor to being a self-directed learner. This is significantly opposed to the concept of a learner as necessarily dependent on an instructor who takes full responsibility for deciding what is to be learned, how it is to be learned, and when it is to be learned. Thus a tenet of adult learning is that adults have a strong desire for self-directed learning.

Somewhat related to this is the concept of readiness to learn. Learners are no longer assumed to be ready to learn whenever and whatever is decided by others.

Knowles emphasized that the adult is ready to learn when there is a pressing need, desire, or problem to solve. Therefore, a learning environment designed for adults should be created to promote learning and facilitate that learning using authentic problems and cases.

Historically, instruction has been designed as if the experiences of the learner have little or no value nor input to current learning. Instruction under this assumption relies on the teacher, writer, or other expert source to transmit knowledge to the learner. More recent conceptions of the adult learner value *experiential learning* as a source for knowledge for the learner and peers. Rather than direct instruction methods, there is an emphasis on such methods as laboratory work, problem solving, case studies, and discussion. Adult learning, under these assumptions, serves to increase life-related or work-related experiences and thus it should increase a person's competencies (Rothwell & Cookson, 1997).

## Training as a Cost Versus Training as an Investment

Leading-edge companies are starting to see that that a well-educated and well-trained workforce is a competitive advantage in the global workplace. The move to a learning organization is a move toward all organization members taking responsibility for their own learning. The new emphasis helps employees to handle a variety of jobs and unpredictable problems (ES Revitalization Project, n.d.). The perception of training is changing from a cost center to a business investment. Along with this shift comes the realization that investment opportunities have expectations of returns associated with them (Kobulnicky, 1999). For instance, Motorola calculates that every $1 spent on training equates to $30 in productivity improvements within three years (Moe, Bailey, & Lau, 1999).

# Two Paradigms in Training and Education

Training and education can be conveniently thought of in terms of two basic types. One type is concerned with instruction, the other with construction. The first deals with the transmission of knowledge, the second with transformation.

## Information Transmission

When instruction is the main concern, the key assumption is that it is possible to transmit a significant body of fixed information to students. This pipeline approach, or the "push" delivery of preconceived knowledge, manifests itself in training in approaches that are didactic, instructor-directed, often linear, recipe-type, and workbook focused. This is referred to in the literature as *instructor-centered*, because the focus is on what the teacher does in selection of the content and in the teaching methods used to get a specific outcome from the students. The philosophers and psychologists most often linked with this kind of behaviorism include Ivan Pavlov, John Watson, Edward Thorndike, B. F. Skinner, and more recently Robert Gagne, Benjamin Bloom, and Robert Mager.

## Transformation

The second category in which training and education can be placed focuses more on the activities of the learner. Training under this approach is more tentative and flexible; it is approached from multiple perspectives, experiential, project-based, and holistic—what is often referred to as *learner-centered*. Through the processes of assimilation and accommodation, old concepts are adapted and altered to fit a new but logical framework (Bentley, 1993). The resulting outcomes are not always completely predictable. Joyce and Weil (1996) state that if students learn within a discipline it is not so they will know exactly that discipline as known by others, but rather to help them create a way of framing the problem to be solved as is customary for that discipline.

Over the last five or six decades, instructional design theory has developed and incorporated principles of cognition. *Cognition* here refers to what a person knows, as opposed to only how a person behaves. The term *constructivism* covers a wide range of beliefs about cognition (Jonassen, 1991). Traditional (cognitive) constructivists, who most often cite John Dewey, Jean Piaget, Jerome Bruner, and more recently John Seely Brown, Howard Gardner, and Howard Rheingold as sources of their reasoning, emphasize individual thinking and the individual's own construction of meaning out of their experiences and perceptions.

A community of learners will often influence each individual member's learning through interpersonal interaction. When people work together, a synergy may be created that causes a team to be more effective than would be indicated by the sum of the individual members' efforts. One reason may be that the production of knowledge of value to others rather than only for personal achievement demonstrates strong engagement of the learner (Scardamalia, 1997) with the learning group. Many constructivist educators incorporate ideas regarding culture and social learning in their designs of the learning environment, with antecedents from several sources including Lev Vygotsky (1962, 1978), Albert Bandura (1971, 1997), and Allan Collins (1991). *Social constructivism* marries a constructivist's strong focus of the dynamic nature of knowledge with an interactionist's focus on creating understanding through requiring learners to explain, elaborate, and defend the position they hold. Participants interact by interpreting, evaluating, and critiquing peers' comments and by sharing information. It is possible to significantly improve much of the training and education that is done through such a learner-centered, collaborative, social, constructivist approach.

## Benefits and Pitfalls of Distance Education

Most readers of this book are aware of the benefits of distance training and education. The pitfalls may be harder to spot from a distance.

### Benefits

Cost savings such as lower travel expenses and less time away from the workplace are perhaps the most often cited potential benefits, and they're often persuasive in themselves. Here, I will merely mention two other benefits:

*Training that is just-in-time and not just-in-case is more relevant to employees.* Technology-based training enables companies to provide their employees with consistent, timely training tailored to the learner regardless of where the participants are located. Often training is mandated by a state or federal agency, or by executives in an organization. Even governmental agencies are making fundamental changes in their business practices so they can survive in the new economy of the twenty-first century (ES Revitalization Project, n.d.). Training that is mandated can be moved toward a just-in-time approach rather than offered haphazardly and just-in-case. Certainly, such training can be more just-enough in nature.

*Individualized training is more effective than a one-size-fits-all approach.* Some technology-based training programs employ pre-training diagnostic studies to determine a learner's areas of strength and weakness and customize the learning in a very efficient and effective way. This "just-for-me" learning becomes practical through technology-enhanced learning.

### Pitfalls

There are dozens of identified barriers to distance education (Berge, 1998a). Obstacles to online teaching and learning can be situational, epistemological, philosophical, psychological, pedagogical, technical, social, or cultural (for example, see Espinoza, Whatley, & Cartwright, 1996; Galusha, n.d.; Garland, 1993; Kaye & Rumble, 1991; Lewis & Romiszowski, 1996; Sherritt, 1992; Sherry, 1996; Shklanka, 1990; Spodick, 1996).

- "Faceless" teaching
- Fear of the imminent replacement of instructors by technology
- Organizational culture
- Lack of an adequate time frame to implement online courses
- Lack of independent learning skills among the students
- High cost of materials and material development
- Increased time required for both online contacts and preparation of materials and activities
- Resistance to change
- Lack of technological assistance

Some of the barriers are worth addressing in more detail here:

*Technology-mediated teaching and learning is more work for both instructor and participants.* My experience has shown that the preparation of technology-mediated instruction may take two to three times longer than in-person instruction. For the instructor, there is often a need to work with a team to develop learning materials suitable for the new medium. Interaction with students usually takes longer if it is computer-mediated than if it involves live videoconferencing. If text-based computer conferencing (the most prevalent form on the Internet today) is used, it takes the students a great deal of time to read and write responses in asynchronous or real-time discussion—more time than they would ordinarily have spent in training sessions.

*There is a tendency on the part of some learners to procrastinate.* My experience is that for some students, "any-time learning" becomes "no-time learning" because they have not developed the skills to structure and manage their own time. Asynchronous training and learning are some of the fastest-growing forms. Because there is no set time for students to get together for class and learning activities can be deferred, some learners report procrastinating and having difficulty staying on track (Brown, LeMay, & Bursten, 1997; Kubala, 1998). Most study guides will suggest strongly that learners guard against such procrastination. Most people who drop or fail online courses do so because they can't develop the habit of logging in regularly to see what is going on and to keep in touch with their teammates when involved in group learning.

## New Roles and Responsibilities for a New Economy

There are mega-trends affecting training and education: globalization, technology, outsourcing, consolidation, demographics, and branding (Moe, Bailey, & Lau, 1999). Table 1.1 illustrates a few of the major trends.

These shifts play out in training and education as shown in Table 1.2.

## TABLE 1.1. SHIFTS IN THE ECONOMY.

| Old Economy | New Economy |
| --- | --- |
| Individual skills acquired | Lifelong learning |
| Labor versus management | Teams |
| Business versus environment | Encourages ecologically sound growth |
| Security | Risk taking |
| Monopolies | Competition |
| Plant and equipment | Intellectual property |
| National | Global |
| Status quo | Speed, change |
| Top-down | Distributed |

## TABLE 1.2. SHIFTS IN TRAINING AND EDUCATION.

| Old Economy | New Economy |
| --- | --- |
| Four-year degree | Forty-year degree |
| Training as cost center | Training as competitive advantage |
| Learner mobility | Content mobility |
| Correspondence and video | High-tech multimedia centers |
| One size fits all | Tailored programs |
| Geographic institutions | Brand name university; celebrity professors |
| Just in case | Just in time |
| Isolated learning | Virtual learning communities |

It is with these shifts in mind that Tobin (1998), in *The Knowledge-Enabled Organization,* concludes that traditional training no longer works:

> Too often, the training group insists on large development budgets and long development cycles to develop and deliver programs that meet their professional standards. When this happens, business leaders often hire external consultants and trainers who can deliver more timely and less costly training. The shame of this common occurrence is that it does not upset the training group, which feels that if they can't "do it right"—according to their professional standards—they are better off not doing it at all. Then the same training people wonder why the company's business leaders feel their group is unresponsive to the company's needs [p. 13].

Today's organizational focus needs to be on learning, not training, in meeting business goals in the competitive environment. Table 1.3 outlines the new roles.

## TABLE 1.3. CHANGES IN LEARNER AND INSTRUCTOR ROLES.

| | |
|---|---|
| **Changing Learners' Roles** | • From learners as passive receptacles for hand-me-down knowledge to learners as constructing their own knowledge<br>• Learners become adept at complex problem-solving activities rather than just memorizing facts<br>• More activities in which learners refine their own questions and search for answers<br>• More collaborative and cooperative assignments with learners working as group members; group interaction significantly increased<br>• Increased multicultural awareness<br>• Independent, self-motivated managers of their own time<br>• Discussion of learners' own work in the classroom<br>• Emphasis on knowledge use rather than observation of the teacher's expert performance or learning just to pass the test<br>• Emphasis on acquiring learning strategies (both individually and collaboratively)<br>• Significantly expanded access to resources |
| **Changing Instructors' Roles** | • Instructors' role changing from oracle and lecturer to consultant, guide, and resource provider<br>• Instructors become expert questioners rather than providers of answers<br>• Instructor provides structure to student work, encouraging self-direction<br>• From a solitary instructor to a member of a learning team (reduces isolation sometimes experienced by instructors)<br>• From instructor having total autonomy to activities that can be broadly assessed<br>• From total control of the teaching environment to sharing with the participants as fellow learner<br>• More emphasis on sensitivity to student's learning styles<br>• Instructor-learner hierarchy is broken down |

The move to a knowledge-based organization—a *learning organization*, as Senge (1990, 1994) and others (for example, Lewis & Romiszowski, 1996) would call it—is a move toward all students' taking responsibility for their own learning. The new emphasis helps employees accomplish a variety of jobs and solve unpredictable problems (ES Revitalization Project, n.d.). No longer will an instructor-centered approach to training allow the organization to remain competitive in today's workplace.

CHAPTER TWO

# A FRAMEWORK FOR SUSTAINING DISTANCE TRAINING

Zane L. Berge

To try to have a distance education plan without a business plan, or vice versa, is to have neither.

My purpose is to present a framework for distance training and education that links several perspectives within an organization. It is important to place this framework within the broader context discussed in Chapter One, where the goal was to spell out the factors and assumptions underlying this view of distance education. What I would like to do here is suggest that there are stages or levels of technological and other capabilities within the organization with regard to technology-enhanced learning and distance education.

I believe managers in successful organizations are effective at managing projects and programs, and I also believe that much of the overall planning at a strategic level is well done. Given that, once managers become aware of the different levels of technological maturity, and aware of the relationship among project management, program management, and strategic planning, a better understanding may be gained concerning the need for change management to link these elements used in solving business problems or taking advantage of missing critical opportunities.

## Changing Expectations

It is becoming clear that changes in society and the marketplace demand changes in the workplace—including a shift in the focus of distance training and education from instructing to learning. What is not as clear to most people is that the development of enterprise-wide capabilities for sustaining distance training and education takes continuous effort to link project management, program management, change management, and strategic planning. It is also important to realize that these changes affect the expectations, roles, and responsibilities of instructors, learners, and managers as the organization builds capacity for technologically enhanced learning of mission-critical problems.

### Organizational Learning

Opportunities to learn are implicit in every new set of tasks or processes a person engages in. Learning events are approached differently by novice and expert performers. By definition, novice performers behave and think differently from expert performers. Experts often have a wider range of experiences from which to draw and access to a learning circle of peers, with all their stored knowledge, on whose expertise they can the call when problem solving and troubleshooting. We talk in terms of learning and growth as a person gains this experience within a field of practice or study.

Organizations are similar to individuals in that they also engage in new tasks and the implementation of new processes, so they are not static in terms of their experiences and the accumulation of new knowledge. The decision within an organization to conduct training at a distance represents a set of new tasks and processes to be organized and implemented, often with a significant reallocation of resources.

When an organization decides to offer a distance training event or program, this effort is often approached from a project management perspective. As the level of the organization's experience with, and capability for, distance training grows (that is, as distance training becomes institutionalized), it becomes useful to think both in terms of program management for the individual events and also in terms of how to manage the organizational change that the introduction of technologically mediated training often engenders.

At some point, the level of change effort needed to ensure the continuation of training at a distance diminishes, as reliance shifts from a focus on organizational changes to the inclusion of distance delivery of training in the strategic planning process. As distance training becomes part of organizational culture, there is a shift in emphasis to include both individual events and continuous improvement of distance training and education. Distance education becomes part of the organization's profile—that is, simply how the organization does business (Berge & Smith, 2000).

There are many sound models for both project management and strategic planning in organizations. My goal in this book is to suggest that there are more than one or two appropriate models for the implementation and management of distance training and education activities. In fact, it is better to use models you have or are establishing in your organization for project and program management and for strategic planning—recognizing that your organization may be reestablishing these models in light of the changing focus of e-business. My point is only that the models used here are generic and each organization will have its own refined processes and techniques for each.

Program management and strategic planning will be described to the extent they have an impact on the distance training delivery process. In other words, I will speak generically to significant issues involving distance training and education that are common to any program management and strategic planning model. Should your business needs be such that increasing the organization's capabilities to deliver distance training and education makes sense, you will find this chapter especially useful. The overarching plan in this chapter is to present a model that will help you identify links between your program management and your strategic planning processes. The emphasis of this book is clearly on distance training and education as a pathway to achieving identified organizational goals.

## Stages of Technological Maturity in an Organization

When considering the distance delivery of education and training and viewing the organization collectively, it is useful to think of stages that the enterprise goes through that are analogous to the learning processes of maturing individuals. A brief model that describes stages of organizational maturity, or capabilities, with regard to the delivery of distance education (Schreiber, 1998b) might look like this:

- Stage 1: Separate or sporadic distance learning events occur in the organization.
- Stage 2: The organization's technological capability and infrastructure can support distance learning events. When distance education events occur, they are replicated through an interdisciplinary team that responds to staff and management needs and makes recommendations regarding the organization and management of distance learning among the workforce.

- Stage 3: The organization has established a distance learning policy, procedures are in place, and planning occurs. This means that a stable and predictable process is in place to facilitate the identification and selection of content and of technology to deliver distance training.
- Stage 4: Distance training and learning have been institutionalized in the organization as characterized by policy, communication, and practice that are aligned so that business objectives are being addressed. The business unit has established a distance education identity and conducts systematic assessment of distance training events from an organizational perspective.

Let me remind you that *distance training* is used here to signal what the organization and instructors do, while *distance learning* indicates what the learner does. Of course, these stages represent points along a continuum; the capability stages an organization moves through are neither linear nor discrete. While it is convenient to describe an organization as generally being at a particular stage, this does not mean the absence of elements from earlier stages, nor does it mean that all units within the organization are at that same stage. Schreiber (1998b) concludes: "As an organization evolves from a level of immaturity to a level of sophistication in its application and utilization of technology to deliver distance learning, it experiences a point of transition that is pivotal to its evolutionary progress. This stage of corporate development is defined by the establishment of organizational policy and procedure regarding distance and distributed education and training" (p. 12).

This chapter focuses on planning and managing distance education as it might fit within these various stages of organizational capability for distance education. In general, success early in Stage 1 is characterized by the use of effective project management processes. Later, in late Stage 1 and in Stage 2, the emphasis shifts to program management. In late Stage 2 and Stage 3, along with the continuation of program management, a goodly amount of organizational development and cultural change efforts are necessary to sustain distance education implementation and use at the organizational level. Stage 4 in an organization's distance delivery capability relies on effective strategic planning to guide cultural change and resource reallocation for success and on the ability to link program planning and perspectives to organizational strategic planning and perspectives.

As you read this chapter, keep in mind that there are often two levels of analysis. There are activities, processes, and work at the program level, such as evaluation and marketing. There are also these same functions at a higher, organizational level.

Maximizing the use of technology to deliver distance and distributed learning is a process not dissimilar to the reengineering that redefines roles and responsibilities in an organization (that is, provoking cultural and organizational change). Concurrent with attaining the various levels of maturity in understanding the organization's use of technology in the service of distance training is the organization's maturity in the use of management systems and tools.

Not all organizations, perhaps not even most organizations, consciously strive toward a goal of achieving a higher stage of technology use or the highest stage of integrating distance education as part of the way business is conducted. There is nothing wrong with an organization's distance education being a series of events, or one or more separate programs. Program implementation initially relies on sound project management, and regardless of whether the organization changes to a more integrated stage of distance training or not, solid program planning and management will always be a key to effective and efficient program presentation.

## Project Management in Distance Education

Early in an organization's attempts to implement distance education, project management tools and techniques help structure distance training (Formby & Ostrander, 1997) within good business practices. Organizational focus is on designing, developing, and implementing a successful program for the first time. Even if an in-person training program is ongoing, it is usually useful to approach the conversion of that program to distance delivery from a project orientation. Concern for logistically supporting instructors and students, marketing the program within the organization, and evaluating the program can be left to subsequent implementations.

The Project Management Institute defines a project as a "temporary endeavor undertaken to create a unique product or service" (Duncan, 1996, p. 4). A project has a beginning and an end. It is performed by people, constrained by limited resources, and planned, executed, and controlled. It is not the purpose here to describe in detail a particular project management approach or model; suffice it to say that within each phase of project management there are activities, methods, tools, and formats reflecting whatever techniques the project management team has expertise in and chooses to use. Examples include a feasibility study, risk analysis, decisions about the scope of the project, a work breakdown structure, resource allocation and reallocation, and scheduling—all at the program level.

Projects also function to facilitate organizational learning and to inform organizational strategy. Project groups can help develop new interorganizational relationships and new learning opportunities within the organization (Systemic Reform, 1994, p. 3). Projects can carry learning between the top and the bottom of the organization, and laterally across the organization, with experienced project managers often playing a key role in successful distance education planning. There is an interdisciplinary element to projects that can help distribute learning opportunities throughout the organization. At the same time, there are barriers to these types of efforts. Overcoming barriers to interdisciplinary and interdepartmental efforts is critical to successful implementation and institutionalization of distance education. Managers, educators, and technologists must all assist in the evolution of the organization into a sophisticated user of technology.

Project management as a practice provides a rigorous discipline for getting results. Schaffer and Thomson (1992) distinguish between *activity-centered* and *results-centered* programs and recommend introducing innovations in increments to support specific performance goals. With tangible results available, managers and employees can enjoy their successes and build their confidence and skill for continued improvements. Schaffer and Thomson also recommend using each project to test new ways of managing, measuring, and organizing for results. Marrying long-term goals with short-term projects can help turn strategy into reality.

To the extent that targeted distance education projects align with the business of the organization, a project can mature into an ongoing program. It is useful at that point to view these programmatic distance education activities in the context of program monitoring and management.

## Program Management

Rothwell and Cookson (1997) present what they call their "Lifelong Education Program Planning (LEPP) Model." It consists of four quadrants and lists the significant factors in each:

1. Exercising Professional Responsibility
   - Work effectively
   - Magnify roles of lifelong education
   - Enact a sense of ethical responsibility
   - Articulate a working philosophy
2. Engaging Relevant Contexts
   - Appraise situation external to organization
   - Appraise situation internal to organization
   - Accommodate the characteristics of adults
   - Assess needs and negotiate stakeholders' interests
3. Designing the Program
   - Set goals and objectives
   - Plan process and outcome evaluation

- Designate learning procedures
- Formulate instructional design
4. Managing Administrative Aspects
- Plan promotion and marketing
- Plan recruitment and retention strategies
- Plan instructor selection, supervision, and training
- Determine financial responsibility

This model is explained and illustrated at length in the Rothwell and Cookson work. Some of the aspects in quadrants 1 and 2 are discussed in the first chapter in this book: the changing roles of professionals in the field, lifelong learning, and the principles of adult learning. Some areas in quadrants 3 and 4 are of particular interest in distance training and education and appear frequently in the case studies appearing later in the book, so I will develop them in more detail in this chapter. The Rothwell and Cookson model is a comprehensive framework that allows for convenient discussion here.

Operationally, the delivery of distance education requires different resources than those needed for face-to-face teaching and often requires a greater initial investment in equipment and infrastructure. As courses taught at a distance are usually designed and produced to fit the organization's available technology, they may require extensive written lesson notes, individual exercises and practice by students, or the scripting of computer code. High-quality distance training demands more planning and the development of materials and delivery methods beyond usual skills of most individuals. Thus teamwork is necessary and is common among managers, instructional designers, support staff, and course delivery experts. The instructor or trainer usually changes roles, becoming a content specialist and collaborator instead of an independent course preparation and delivery expert. If distance education, and technology-enhanced learning generally, is to make a sustained improvement in the workplace, both in the in-person classroom and at a distance, these changes in roles—and the pooling of expertise in development teams—must be encouraged at an operational level.

## Support Services for Learners

Learners' (and instructors') convenient access to the Internet or the firm's own intranet and other technology used in the delivery system for training are critical for the success of distance learning programs. Instructors have a right to expect that participants will come to distance learning experiences prepared to study effectively at a distance. This means that a certain standard of instructional and logistical support must be provided to the participants. The support team could develop such materials as a student handbook, a preliminary screening survey, or even a mini-course that would help ensure that learners acquire appropriate study and learning skills and understand their rights and responsibilities in a distance learning course. Online communities and mentoring have been developed as a significant way to promote learner success.

## Support Services for Instructors

Technical support is critical to the success of teaching and learning at a distance. Instructors who ask, "How do I teach with this technology?" or "In what ways will the use of technology change the nature of my instruction?" should be offered training in the use of the delivery technologies and in redesigning their instructional materials and processes as quickly as possible. An achievable goal is to make delivery technologies transparent to students' learning—as the whiteboard or the overhead projector have become in a place-based classroom. Opportunities for instructors' skills and competencies and instructional system development services need to be provided, too. Instructors have a right to look to support services to assist their efforts in the implementation of distance education.

## Administrative Support

Program leadership can be a controversial point. Should the organization decide to hire a director of technology-enhanced or distance learning, or reassign a member of an existing training or human resources department to those duties? While a director of distance learning activities can often supply necessary leadership and a skill set that may not be available within the organization, the cost justification for such a hire in the initial implementation of distance training may be lacking. However if one person can be hired to take the lead in promoting distance training and to concentrate their efforts on overcoming obstacles, that may be the most practical solution.

Organizations rarely have the budget to hire someone immediately, and compromises are frequently made in this area. It has been my experience that reassignment of executives usually does not work in the early stages of distance education programs because the available personnel lack expertise regarding the focus on e-learning, and it can be preferable to proceed on a decentralized basis at first. As the maturity level of the organization rises and more distributed learning programs are successful, it makes more sense to consider appointing a dedicated leader to direct these efforts—and at that point the choices are much broader, as the organization is apt to have both the budget support for a new hire and a pool of in-house expertise that could be tapped for reassignment.

## Program Evaluation

The evaluation of distance education programs should include specific components that relate to the technology-mediated delivery, separate and apart from the more traditional methods that rate the instructor's performance and the perceived worth of the content delivered. These components should also include a role for learners as participants in their own evaluation, in the determination of ways their learning should be assessed, the frequency of evaluation, distribution of evaluation results, and input into the ways in which longitudinal studies could be conducted to assess changes over time that could be attributed to the change in delivery technology and instructors' teaching methods. Instructors' and learners' perceptions of the delivery system and the desirability of participation in similarly delivered courses should also be collected.

## Increased Organizational Maturity Means Cultural Change

Rogers's (1995) work provided a foundation for diffusion of innovation theory, which underlies the principles of change management. His work provides organizational principles for the types and rates of adoption of an innovation (early adopters or innovators, middle adopters or opinion leaders, late adopters or laggards). Rogers's work also describes predictable patterns of adoption (the S-curve) that have implications for the development of time lines, the reallocation of resources, and other logistical considerations. As Grundy and Grundy (n.d.) explain, "Not everyone adopts innovations at the same rate. Rather, people adopt in a time sequence that classifies them into five ideal categories. Those categories, with their associated descriptions, are Innovators (venturesome), Early Adopters (respectable), Early Majority (deliberate), Late Majority (skeptical), and Laggards (traditional). These five categories of adopters form a bell-shaped frequency curve. If the frequency curve is converted to a cumulative curve showing adopter distribution, we then get a classical, S-shaped curve" (n.p.).

Awareness of these predictable patterns can help managers avoid rash actions and decisions in the name of getting results quickly. Change management for distance education capitalizes on involving the early adopters in well-planned and supported strategic projects such as pilot tests of new uses of technology. It also

includes consideration of adoption rates when planning large capital or other resource expenditures, planning the sequencing and locations of early projects, and
planning ways to overcome barriers throughout the entire process.

Knowledge of change management theory helps by focusing on human nature as a business consideration and also provides sensible guidelines for managing
the human side of technological innovation. Surry (1997) cites problems with the
diffusion and widespread use of instructional technologies that arise because the
many factors that influence adoption of innovations are ignored. In distance training, these factors may include instructors' lack of comfort with the nature of
teaching and learning in distance environments, lack of trust among different
departments with different expertise, lack of skill with technologies, lack of organizational resources, or poor learning design. These and other factors that influence adoption must be identified—and dealing with them included in planning
—so persons charged with implementation and planning can explain, predict, and
account for issues that facilitate or impede an acceptance of the innovation within
the organization.

Assuming there is a identifiable business reason for an organization to integrate distance training and education across the organization, there are management processes and tools that go beyond those identified with program
management that can significantly help such integration. As an organization's
distance training and education move to Stage 3 and Stage 4, elements that
may engender organizational change are present. Along with a strategic planning
process, there are management processes such as budgeting, infrastructure development and maintenance, communication, workforce development, and policy-
making that are used to change the fabric of the organization in desired ways.

One key to the success of initiatives in the integration and implementation
technology-enhanced learning and distance education is the support of the organization's top leaders. These leaders should exhibit enthusiasm for, champion, and
allocate resources to these programs while encouraging and rewarding instructor
and interdepartmental cooperation. The champions of distance education early in
the maturity of the organization must be change agents and innovators, and at the
same time attend to aligning programs with business planning. As organizational
capabilities grow, and as more executives and others throughout the organization
gain experience in using distance education, these competing demands are spread
more and more widely in the enterprise. Such leadership can build credibility for
distance education and training, maintain organizational currency in the field, and
gather support and partners inside and outside the organization.

The most important function of organizational leadership may be to create a
shared vision that includes widespread input and support from the instructors and

managers, articulates a clear training or educational purpose, has validity for all stakeholders, and reflects the broader mission of the organization. Both top-down and bottom-up support is needed for successful, sustained distance training and education at the higher stages of organizational capability. In addition to the establishment of a vision, leaders link strategic planning and specific program implementation and monitoring using such tools as budgeting, infrastructure development, communication, workforce development, and policy revision.

## Strategic Planning for Distance Training and Education

Strategic planning strives to answer the questions, Where are we now? Where are we going? How are we going to get there? In general, strategic planning activities often include

- Integrating actions with the organizational mission and vision
- Following guiding beliefs and principles
- Using external environmental scan
- Using internal organizational strengths

Strategic planning delineates the conditions or constraints of the organization as they are derived from its mission, goals, values, and priorities. Powers (1992) defines *strategic alignment* as the "systematic arrangement of crucial business systems behind a common purpose" and lists the following strategic alignment model components: mission, values, aims and goals, objectives, job roles, selection, expectations, tools, training, feedback, rewards, and financial and other management systems for quality performance (p. 258). At some point, organizations must take the time to establish a "big picture" showing how implementing distance training may change the organization and how it will fit within the organization, asking many questions up front to address issues such as need, cost savings, audiences, technical requirements, infrastructure, resources, communication, incentives, and support (Wagner, 1992).

The strategic planning team should assess organizational readiness by looking at factors such as the number and locations of potential users, projected demand for distance delivery, and technology's perceived value within the organization—to managers and to trainers and the learners themselves (Wagner, 1992). Other factors requiring consideration might be the prerequisite skill sets of learners and trainers, the barriers to the accessibility of distance education, the way major changes (if any) are distracting employees and resources, and so on. Once it is determined that the organization has a true need for distance training and education as a business solution, the strategic planning process must be connected to the end users and implementers (Berge & Schrum, 1998).

Noblitt (1997) notes that "top-down folks" are charged with administrative or organizational duties concerned with infrastructure, while "bottom-up people" are charged with instructional duties and meeting the demands for time and resources to get their projects and programs successfully implemented. Though there is a deep mutual dependency, both ends serve different roles. The top-down program advocate relies on upwelling success stories to justify larger investments in technology; the bottom-up project advocate needs administrative support and a well-conceived and reliable working environment for successful implementation of innovative concepts (pp. 38–39). Noblitt also calls for a *context-sensitive* implementation plan, meaning that everyone must work together on setting priorities. For distance education and training, this means that end users (trainers and learners) and strategic planners (executive management) work together with sensitivity to the internal and external environment and plan how changes caused by the new program can be smoothly integrated, with the involvement of all stakeholders, into the mission and vision of the organization (Vazquez-Abad & Winer, 1992).

## Creating the Environment

Another goal of strategic planning is to create and define the internal and external organizational environment—with its boundaries and parameters—in which learners learn, instructors instruct, and the organization competes. The challenge is to gather data and case studies, to analyze information, and to decide on an implementation plan that has a high possibility of success while avoiding expensive pitfalls. Although all parts of the strategic planning process are necessary, it is especially important to pay attention to those areas that affect the implementation and conduct of distance training and education as seen from the organizational perspective.

## Integration with the Institutional Mission

The highest priority should be given to the integration of plans for technology-enhanced training into the overall strategic plan of the organization. For example, making explicit how distance education programs fit within the mission of the enterprise comes first, before any major resource allocation should be expected.

*Resources Inventory.* An important first step is to take an inventory of available resources such as the existing hardware, software, distance delivery technologies, and technical and instructor support staff, and to identify any technology-enhanced learning projects that are already occurring anywhere in the organization. Indicators of resources capacity (for example, length of time instructors have to wait to get assistance in lesson design or technology support, and the availability of expertise represented by an instructional technology support unit) might also be included. Armed with a current organizational inventory, planners are then in a position to judge what existing space, facilities, equipment, and staff a program could use and what reallocation of resources and materials from within may be required.

***Financial and Market Assessment.*** A thorough review of strategic financial planning and opportunity costs should be made, designed to answer these questions:

- What financial advantage is there to the organization to offer distance education and training?
- Are an adequate number of qualified instructors and trainers available who are willing to teach using alternative delivery systems for the program?
- What is the cost of the additional equipment, infrastructure, and staff needed for developing the distance education course?
- Can the organization afford to boost spending enough to cover the inevitable increase in course-development costs entailed by a move from in-person to technology-enhanced courses?

Once the analyses are made, the distance education and training program needs to be compared to other resource allocation opportunities and the potential for each to achieve the organization's economic goals.

## Evaluation of Standards and Roles

Strategic planning can help establish a timetable for the roll-out of specific courses and programs. Organizational quality standards must be held consistent, regardless of the delivery system employed or the location of the participants. For example, approval for the training curriculum can generally follow the same established organizational procedure whether classes are delivered in person, through technology-enhanced formats, or entirely at a distance.

Programs can be developed that recognize the increasingly diverse ways in which instructors and learners interact with subject matter and each other. The standards of accountability for student accomplishment do not change simply because the instruction is mediated by technology. However, it should be noted that changes often do occur in the instructional methods used in technology-enhanced courses.

Distance training often serves as a catalyst for the adoption of learner-centered approaches to instruction (Berge, 1998b). As a result, a significant commitment to distance coursework often evolves into a commitment to significant changes in the roles of students, instructors and trainers, and the organization itself, even while holding the quality of the instruction stable. The impact of this paradigm shift on instructors and learners can be measured, as can the amount of time distance programs may take to gain acceptance. Instructors and learners must understand that quality instruction is of primary importance to the success of all technology-enhanced learning initiatives, and that instructional design is more significant than the types of technology used.

Figure 2.1 illustrates a model of distance training and education within an organization. On the left-hand side, labeled *Program Perspective*, are the needed elements for managing and monitoring a training or education event or program at a distance. On the right-hand side, labeled *Organizational Perspective*, are the

## FIGURE 2.1. LINKING AN ORGANIZATIONAL PERSPECTIVE WITH A PROGRAM PERSPECTIVE: USING PROJECT AND PROGRAM MANAGEMENT, TOOLS FOR CHANGE, AND STRATEGIC PLANNING.

| PROGRAM PERSPECTIVE | | ORGANIZATIONAL PERSPECTIVE |
|---|---|---|
| PROJECT AND PROGRAM MANAGEMENT | TOOLS FOR CHANGE | STRATEGIC PLANNING |
| Exercising Professional Responsibility | Budget | Integration with the Organizational Mission and Vision |
| Engaging Relevant Contexts | Infrastructure | Guiding Beliefs and Principles |
| Designing the Program | Communication | External Environmental Scan |
| Managing Administrative Aspects | Workforce Development | Internal Organizational Strengths |
| | Policy | |

elements of organizational planning. The last chapter in this book picks up on the "tools for change" that link these two perspectives.

## Conclusion

In the organization that has distance education and training as part of its profile, the key to sustaining technology-based learning at a distance is strategic planning. The transition from earlier stages of maturity, or capability, with regard to training and education involves a cultural change. A project management approach is useful in stages where distance education can be viewed as an event, or when programs that have been ongoing are transformed to delivery at a distance.

Change management and strategic planning both value individual projects as a way to pilot test, implement, and manage change. Program monitoring and evaluation are critical once the initial implementation has been done and any substantial organizational changes are made. To develop the capabilities and level of maturity beyond that needed for the delivery of isolated events or programs requires organizational development and a change in the way distance training and education are thought about in the organization. Some of the tools that leaders use to manage change include budgeting, infrastructure, communication, workforce development, and policy.

The further into Stage 4 the organization moves—that is, the greater the integration of distance education into its mission, the more use there is of management support systems such as forecasting, evaluating, tracking, and delivery, and the better the incentive systems are aligned with goals and the delivery system within the organization—the better the chances are for continuous improvement of distance training and education. A time comes when the level of distance training and education efforts within the organization meets any and all needs for training. People inside the organization no longer think in terms of moving toward technology-enhanced learning. Rather, these activities and programs become an accepted part of how business is done, while the focus of attention within the organization moves to other areas of competitive advantage that are at less mature stages. Distance training and education becomes transparent and sustained.

PART TWO

# MEETING THE CHALLENGE OF UNCOMMON ORGANIZATIONAL CHANGE

# CHAPTER THREE

# DISTANCE TRAINING AT THE U.S. ARMY INTELLIGENCE CENTER

## Surviving Implementation

James B. Ellsworth, Luciano J. Iorizzo Jr.

The U.S. Army is embracing distance training as a means to reconcile a paradox. Today's soldiers face an increased requirement for career-long learning —resulting from rapid technical change and ever-shifting international threats— coupled with the diminished ability of their units to spare them for travel to resident courses. Yet at the same time, the Army's institutional training structure—like most current educational systems—is built around resident schooling, restricting its ability to meet the challenge. Transforming such an organizational environment into one that integrates and supports nonresident instruction is a major obstacle to sustaining a distance training program past initial implementation.

Designing and implementing a distance training program is relatively easy. The "bandwagon effect" is a powerful ally of emerging technology (Sachs, 1999, p. 76). After all, "everybody" is using it—it's in the news, even the scholarly press, all the time—so if *we* don't "do something" (in a hurry), people think, "they" will get ahead of us! Unfortunately, the workforce is often told to do something in *such* a hurry that the realities of organizational change are largely ignored. Stakeholders—who will be expected to integrate nonresident offerings with the resident curriculum and provide the same standard of instruction over a new medium—may not be consulted or trained. Infrastructure upgrades may not be launched in time. Administrative changes to assess and track distant students' progress or to evaluate program effectiveness may be overlooked.

In this environment of hype, much of the change agent role involves moderating the process so that planning can occur and infrastructure can be built. Recognizing this, Army distance training programs like the one at the Intelligence Center—which in its present form really started in late 1994—have adopted an incremental approach. This chapter describes the sustainment problem and the strategy that the Intelligence Center adopted to address it—offering guidelines and lessons learned for institutions beginning similar journeys.

## Business Problem Statement

Change research has taught us much about facilitating successful—and lasting—innovation. The change agent must consider needs surrounding the innovation itself, the people or agencies responsible for its success, the process for managing its implementation and sustainment, and the clients it is intended to serve. Conditions in the change environment that favor innovation must also be assessed, along with the causes of present or potential resistance, and the change strategy adjusted accordingly (Ellsworth, 2000).

As the fledgling distance training program moves toward full integration with its institution's operations, our experience suggests that certain concerns are particularly salient. Some are bottom-up issues: those resulting from inadequate attention to the concerns of those who must make distance training work in day-to-day practice. Others are top-down issues, where decision makers' needs were not adequately met.

Among the former, addressing the personal and psychological causes of resistance to change is just as critical as providing the hardware and software to support it. Likewise, "technological barriers for resistance" (Zaltman & Duncan, 1977, p. 80)—where the skills to make the innovation work neither exist nor are provided during the change process—are another frequent cause of failure at this level.

Unfortunately for the poorly planned program, just when the effects of these problems are peaking, the top-down issues that were initially held in abeyance can deliver a knockout punch. Many well-intentioned programs, their efforts focused on development of effective distance training products, are caught entirely unprepared when management begins to want demonstrable benefit: return on investment (ROI) justifying the resources they committed. Conflicting requirements often compel the change agent to act as both innovator (to produce significant, measurable results in a timely fashion) and caretaker (to minimize resistance by attending to stakeholder needs and concerns).

# Population Served or Targeted

The Intelligence Center workforce trains soldiers and leaders of the Army's Military Intelligence Corps (one discipline within the total force) to meet the intelligence collection and processing requirements of the Army and its units in the field, and to act as partners in the strategic intelligence arena. This statement identifies the three key subpopulations targeted by our distance training sustainment strategy: stakeholders within the Center's own workforce, the soldiers they train, and the units employing those soldiers following graduation.

## Stakeholders

The Intelligence Center's decision makers and workforce must be considered as part of our extended audience, because their commitment is essential to success. In this sense, decision makers' needs are best understood in terms of information requirements. Workforce needs may be expressed in terms of employee tendency toward caretaker versus innovator roles, or in terms of the support (both cognitive and affective) an employee requires when directed to participate in change.

## Soldiers

The Intelligence Center offers nearly a hundred resident courses; about 25 percent of these (mostly midcareer courses) are targeted to use some form of distance training as a prerequisite to attendance. This translates into about fifteen hundred active duty soldiers annually, plus others who have completed resident courses and require follow-on support and mentoring. Students on active duty are of either gender, some single and others married. Their ages range from the mid-twenties to early forties. Nearly half own a personal computer. Most have some college, and many officers hold a master's. They may be located anywhere in the world. Potentially comparable numbers of reserve component soldiers with similar demographics must also be trained and mentored; most of these will be located within the United States.

## Units

Individual soldiers are assigned to a given unit. Each unit has a mission that bears on the most critical competencies its soldiers must have mastered. In support of their missions, units conduct both individual and collective training. Units are a key part of our target population—distinct from the soldiers assigned to them—on two grounds. First, their missions require collective training, which usually cannot be conducted in residence; second, those missions may require additional individual training on competencies not required of all soldiers in similar jobs.

## Outcomes Desired

To avoid the bandwagon effect noted earlier, the Intelligence Center initially focused desired outcomes on paving the way for change. Our emphasis shifted to production and institutionalization outcomes after this foundation was well established.

### Preparatory and Foundational Outcomes

*Establish the need.* Among the first foundational outcomes was establishing the need for distance training in the eyes of our own stakeholders. As experienced practitioners, the Intelligence Center's faculty and staff had grown up professionally in the traditional system of periodic resident instruction. This made many skeptical of change—especially since, despite dwindling resources, students continued to be brought to the institution for the same courses that had always been required.

*Provide the workforce with necessary competencies.* While it was clear that the existing system wasn't working as well as it used to, this realization created a harried atmosphere in which all felt compelled to work harder and to "do more with less." This posed a problem for another foundational objective: providing the workforce with the competencies—including knowledge of nonresident pedagogy—to make effective use of distance training across the curriculum. The typical top-down approach of mandatory training sessions was likely to backfire, with personnel who already felt stretched to the limit interpreting it as yet another administrative burden.

*Obtain grassroots buy-in.* Recognizing this as fertile ground for resistance, we identified obtaining grassroots buy-in as another critical outcome. This is distinct from establishing the need, in that faculty and staff can accept distance training as necessary for the institution while remaining opposed due to personal concerns—or merely unconvinced that it is appropriate for *them.* The change literature offers many examples where inattention to this issue produced only superficial adoption: even the chief executive will probably fail in sustaining a program that is disliked by those responsible for its day-to-day operation (Ellsworth, 1998, p. 131).

*Establish distance training as faculty partner, not competitor.* Inadequately addressing stakeholders' personal concerns was mentioned before as a common cause of failure. Although such concerns can simply be a by-product of the workplace overload described earlier, they frequently result from a perception that distance training is being introduced as a replacement for face-to-face instruction. Consequently, another key foundational goal at the Intelligence Center was establishing distance training as a partner for the resident schoolhouse—a tool to help its faculty and staff accomplish objectives important to them, rather than a threat to their jobs or status.

*Modernize the supporting infrastructure.* Finally, although we have emphasized the preceding outcomes because they are more often overlooked, the fact remains that current technology and infrastructure *must* be widely available early on if distance training is to survive. In 1994, many Army training units were still using 286-generation computers, and instructors—unless they had "real computers" at home—might never have used Windows. This presented an impossible environment in which to prepare the workforce to develop and use multimedia and hypermedia—so a final early outcome was modernization of the institution's technology and infrastructure.

## Production and Institutionalization Outcomes

*Meet the needs of the force.* Perhaps most obviously, a central outcome is meeting the needs of soldiers and units. For decades, these needs revolved around a monolithic adversary in a relatively well-known environment. Today, we are challenged to prepare soldiers for an environment where uncertainty prevails. Similar requirements are also present in corporate training and civilian education, leading to the current emphasis on critical thinking and problem-solving (for example, Tucker, Gunn, & Lapan, 1998).

Traditional instructional systems design models effectively replicate training involving consistent tasks, conditions, and standards; at issue is how to train for settings where tasks, conditions, and standards are variable—and sometimes unknown. To this end, the Intelligence Center chose to explore constructivist learning theory as a means to develop the competencies required for the Information Age environment.

*Educate the workforce.* Constructivism is a radical shift for Army training, so we introduced change incrementally. Our strategy required that the Center's workforce be familiarized with constructivist pedagogy and its relationship to the ill-defined problem sets and demand for reflective practice associated with information-based society. Thus workforce development remained a key outcome at this stage.

*Validate the program.* Our intent was to institutionalize an adaptive learning model that will help soldiers to be better thinkers, able to generalize at the competency level and be comfortable when faced with the unknown. Consequently, we also identified rigorous validation of the materials produced (an important component of decision makers' concept of ROI) as a key desired outcome. To this end, we tested the hypothesis that learning can occur when soldiers use constructivist courseware.

*Facilitate lifelong learning.* The next desired outcome was creation of an effective environment for lifelong professional development. Soldiers' careers may span twenty to thirty years, during which they must not only stay current but also advance in competence. The schoolhouse must facilitate this growth at a distance, as time available for resident instruction is limited. This raises a number of concerns about curriculum, courseware version control, record keeping, administration, assessment, and mentoring—and no one product or tool addresses all these issues (Curtin, 1998).

*Efficiently deliver instruction worldwide.* The size and geographic distribution of the population to be served implies a final desired outcome of efficient delivery. We selected the Internet for these purposes based on our experience with other projects, which suggests that it will yield efficiencies not possible with print, CD-ROM or DVD, video-teletraining, or resident instruction alone (Jackson, Lorenc, & Iorizzo, 1997).

## Description of Management Processes

We emplaced two sets of management processes to guide our efforts. The first, "executive" set carries out the program's intent and facilitates progress toward its desired outcomes. The second, "evaluative" set monitors that progress, ensuring that formative data is available to guide decision making.

### Executive Management Processes

This section focuses on the processes guiding the distance training program after its initial implementation, but one of the key lessons of our experience is the importance of the foundation established prior to and during implementation in facilitating its survival. Thus we will briefly discuss the processes enabling foundational outcomes before proceeding to those associated with institutionalization.

***Executive Processes During Implementation.*** We established the need for distance training through a top-down focus on the changes shaping the organization's environment and the needs of its customers. Building needed competencies among the workforce was approached more indirectly. Rather than try to simultaneously achieve this and persuade the skeptics of distance training's value, the Center formed a *Tiger Team* (an ad hoc task force), representing the key stakeholder groups and composed of individuals who already understood the technology and believed in its potential.

The process promoting instructor buy-in was even more discreet, using Tiger Team members' relationships with their previous units to leverage the confidence and trust they enjoyed among their colleagues. Much was also achieved simply by listening to what instructors were trying to do with their courses—and offering situated examples of how distance training could serve those ends. This process also strengthened the perception of distance training as a partner rather than a competitor for resident instruction. Finally, modernization drove technology and infrastructure enhancements down from the top until they were seen to be widely available to the trainers themselves.

***Executive Processes During Institutionalization.*** Aside from marketing and funding (essential for any effort), a mature distance training program must at the most basic level address "pipes," content, and the process of putting the content on the pipes. *Pipes* include networking infrastructure, hardware, and software. Often, distance training programs must rely on another organization for these needs, requiring an extensive coordination process.

*Content* encompasses all of the processes involved in producing conventional instruction. However, a distance training program must also address the workforce's ability to produce courseware that effectively facilitates learning in a distributed environment. Sometimes called "putting content on the pipes," the distribution process is one of the mature program's greatest challenges: until distance training is infused throughout the organization, there will be varying degrees of technological and attitudinal readiness among the subpopulations it serves.

To meet these requirements and facilitate the production and institutionalization outcomes presented in the preceding section, we emplaced several new executive processes during this phase. Integration with the organizational mission was signaled by the publication of *Intelligence Training XXI: Ready Now* (U.S. Army Intelligence Center, 1997). Infrastructure implications of new distance training policy were identified and acted upon based on equipment and bandwidth projections.

Staffing was accomplished largely by reallocating personnel with baseline competencies and developing their skills in areas the program required. Courseware authoring was taught in contracted or in-house workshops, while a local university provided courses on constructivist learning theory and instructional design/technology skills. An extensive marketing campaign was also undertaken to establish the value of the product in the eyes of decision makers and—just as important—to convey that value to the workforce in personally meaningful and rewarding ways.

Finally, the transition to full-fledged production and delivery—including the requirement to integrate administration and tracking of student progress with the institution's resident system—required another round of technology selection and acquisition. This process is characteristic of a Stage 3 organization as defined in this volume's organizing framework. At the Intelligence Center, it was guided by our previous experience (Turcotte, Ellis, & Iorizzo, 1994) and the requirement that soldiers be able to access courseware at little or no cost. Internet-based delivery met this last requirement, with Asymetrix Librarian chosen for administration and tracking.

## Evaluative Management Processes

Evaluation and assessment was a focus throughout our efforts, to provide decision makers and other stakeholders with the evidence that their investments of resources and time were producing returns. During implementation, we tracked progress on foundational—generally affective—outcomes qualitatively through observation, interviews, and document analysis.

During institutionalization (Stages 3 and 4 of the organizing framework), the focus shifted to quantitative processes. New products being brought on-line are subjected to formative evaluation and subsequent summative validation. These data will ultimately be compared with performance improvement data already collected by the Intelligence Center's evaluation program for resident instruction of the same content.

Content distribution is tracked by identifying all servers that store training materials and analyzing their log files, which are consolidated monthly to generate usage reports. These reports allow decision makers to assess the extent to which products are meeting customers' needs, and to track which customers are using a given product.

Combined with cost data—for development and distribution of distance training versus direct and indirect costs of resident instruction—results from these evaluations will eventually be used to provide ROI measures such as cost comparisons associated with a given performance gain for a specified number of soldiers. Tracking product usage may even enable consideration of *opportunity savings*—that is, the calculation of the amount saved as a result of a given number of soldiers staying on the job rather than being absent from their duty positions for the time that resident schooling would require.

## Outcomes Attained and Lessons Learned

The outcomes sought during implementation did in fact play the preparatory role for which they were intended—although several missteps offer lessons that are also worth relating. Without this foundation, sustaining the Intelligence Center's distance training program would have been considerably more difficult as several of the conditions for lasting change (see Ely, 1990) might not have been in place. The first part of this section will thus focus on the successes and lessons of these efforts, while the second part will present a similar analysis of our current initiatives.

### Preparatory and Foundational Outcomes: Successes and Lessons Learned

*Establish the need.* We selected a top-down approach to establish the need for distance training partly to show the commitment of top-level administrators—see Ely's last three "conditions for change" (1990, pp. 301–302)—and partly because the staff and faculty were already aware of the challenges driving this need. Our task was merely to reiterate these challenges and show them how distance training could help.

*Provide the workforce with necessary competencies.* The "train the trainer" approach used to develop distance training competencies was less successful. We selected a short duration for the Tiger Team, knowing that teams with greater longevity can become seen as independent entities—at which point members may lose their standing as colleagues in the eyes of their former organizations (Ellsworth, 1995, p. 141). Unfortunately, we misjudged the response of overburdened units directed to provide personnel for even a temporary organization. Many of those contributed were already scheduled to retire or change jobs, defeating our intent that they ultimately return to their units. Some organizations resisted contributing the best-suited individuals, considering their skills critical to their own missions.

*Obtain grassroots buy-in.* Despite this limited success, drawing personnel from the workforce played an important role in securing buy-in to the distance training concept. Conversations of Tiger Team members with colleagues in their former units diffused personally relevant applications of distance training technologies throughout the faculty and staff—who were often receptive to people still seen as coworkers.

If, for example, a member visited instructors who taught a block on a particular region of the world, he would locate the Web addresses of media resources on those countries, or of the Army Area Handbooks describing them. Should the conversation turn to a desire to provide students with more up-to-date, authentic resources, the member would chime in with, "Say, have you seen . . . on the Web?" and frequently within the week we would receive a call from the instructors' unit requesting help tying those resources into the course.

We owed some of this success to the "Systemic Change" movement (which recognizes educational settings as complex systems composed of interrelated elements). This literature emphasizes that all key stakeholder groups should be actively involved throughout the change process and their concerns addressed, so participants can "spend more professional energies paving new paths for learning rather than in waging battles for survival" in a system suddenly alien to their needs (Miller, 1992, p. 62).

*Establish distance training as faculty partner, not competitor.* A key result of these methods was confidence among the workforce that distance training was not a threat to their jobs or status. By presenting our Stage 1 and 2 products as tools for resident instruction, we emphasized that the faculty remained the central resource— and that distance training was a "force multiplier" for them. By calling to mind the historically successful Army Correspondence Course Program as an early form of nonresident instruction, we also reduced the perception of distance training as an alien concept.

*Modernize the supporting infrastructure.* The modernization process was another important success of our early efforts. Instructors and developers in some units almost instantly received state-of-the-art hardware and connectivity to support distance training integration; within two years, such technology was generally available. A network that was built to support mainframe-based e-mail was upgraded to the level necessary for Internet-based distance training. The Intelligence Center even pilot-tested Asynchronous Transfer Mode (ATM) technology as its standards first took shape.

Driving technology down through the hierarchy also succeeded in two key ways. First, ensuring a relatively uniform hardware and software standard through all levels of the organization allowed support activities to focus on a single "typical configuration" (Windows 95, Office 97, Toolbook II Instructor, and so on) rather than having to support instructors and developers with that configuration along with administrators still using Windows 3.1x and Office 4.2. Second, it removed the incentive for administrators to reallocate equipment their subordinates received to organizational needs unrelated to distance training, and it ensured that both the faculty and staff *and* their supporting administration had the technology to implement the program.

## Production and Institutionalization Outcomes:
## Successes and Lessons Learned .

*Meet the needs of the force. Intelligence Training XXI: Ready Now* articulated a vision that relied heavily on distance training. Among its goals was development of a Military Intelligence "Schoolhouse Without Walls" to facilitate seamless support of professional development across resident training and operational assignments.

Following its publication, the training organization for each Military Intelligence discipline conducted a "cradle to grave" analysis of the competencies their soldiers require throughout a career. This process yielded a matrix indicating how and when soldiers would be trained in each competency. Especially at midcareer, distance training requirements were often specified as prerequisites for resident instruction.

These matrices were consolidated in 1998 with results from a needs assessment survey of Military Intelligence leaders in the field to produce a "one to *n* list" prioritizing the competencies to be supported with distance training products. Together with *Intelligence Training XXI: Ready Now,* this list represented the strategic plan for our distance training program. Today's Distance Learning Office began where the Tiger Team left off, establishing distance training policy for the institution and overseeing execution of this plan—but maintaining infrastructure remained in the hands of the information management organization. At this stage, although the content to be produced and the sequence of its production were clearly defined, courseware development, validation, and delivery remained ambiguous.

*Educate the workforce.* Workforce development presented two significant obstacles: adopting constructivist pedagogy, and authoring for the distance learning environment. The first challenge presented itself when the development team members were asked to assimilate a learning model that was the antithesis of their traditional training development backgrounds. Simultaneously, at a broader level, other stakeholders—from senior leaders to students—were being asked to make the same transition.

Fortunately, although some resistance did arise, it was reduced by the intuitive similarity between constructivist learning environments and the rapidly changing, ill-structured problem domains in which today's soldier must be able to function. Just as soldiers build experience and expertise on the job—through performance (and feedback) under varied conditions—this cycle is rapidly repeated in the simulated job environment during constructivist learning. It is this contextualized experience that enables learners to create their own constructs that they can apply to new, unfamiliar situations.

While our developers readily accepted the second (authoring) challenge, our choice of constructivist design again proved problematic. Templates in the authoring software—which normally would have facilitated a more rapid transition to production—were of limited use in building scenario-based training. Here, the long-term focus of our workforce development strategy (involving university courses in educational psychology and technology) also fell short for the near term. Production could not wait for several semesters before the development team mastered the necessary skills; thus we used in-house workshops to establish these prerequisites and address developers' resistance to working outside the comfort zone of expository design. Ultimately, this anxiety subsided when the first developer made a breakthrough in a prototype lesson: team members realized that they could build constructivist courseware, and began to see themselves as innovators. This confidence should grow as developers' university-based educational and technology coursework adds new tools and understanding to their repertoire.

*Validate the program.* Our initial validation effort had a twofold purpose: to test the hypothesis that constructivist learning theory could form the basis for effective Internet-based courseware in a military environment, and to establish and test the validation strategy to be used in the future. The lesson selected (on completion of a report describing chronic failures or possible design defects in electronic equipment) employed a constructivist approach by simulating the authentic environment (Figure 3.1) within which this report is completed, where the soldier had access to the necessary information, references, and materials.

Multiple versions of the lesson presented distinct but similar scenarios, requiring the soldier to obtain corresponding information through different references during each trial. Test questions based on the completion procedure were cross-checked against copies of the completed report, to validate the test as an indicator of actual task performance. Fifty soldiers participated, completing one to three trials. Several problems were encountered, resulting in modifications of the original validation plan for subsequent iterations (Brush, 2000).

First, randomization of lesson versions through the trials can yield very low numbers of participants in any given cell during analysis: the benefits of methodological rigor must be balanced against the geometrically larger number of participants required for statistical power. Second, reliability of the data gathered declined substantially in the third trial, when boredom and gaming were evident: this suggested that validation should be restricted to two trials and/or that successive trials should be conducted on different days. Third, test items and distracters must be checked by individuals other than developers, and exercises should be scored by at least two individuals to guard against possible bias.

Despite these limitations, the validation process was a qualified success. One version of the lesson validated, exhibiting high degrees of correlation (.794) and reliability (.852) between test scores and actual performance ratings based on the

## FIGURE 3.1. THE ENVIRONMENT FOR LESSON COMPLETION— CREATED WITH VIRTUAL REALITY MARKUP LANGUAGE.

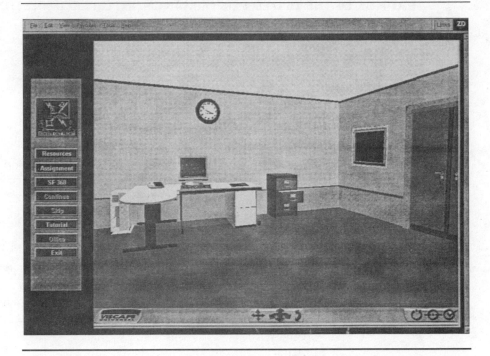

completed reports. Several other versions showed moderate correlations but fell short of the desired confidence level. (Figure 3.2 overlays the average score distributions for both measures for soldiers completing all three trials.) The average scores for actual performance (report completion) on *all* lesson versions during each of the three trials showed gains achieved through practice, although the gains in the third trial were not statistically significant (Brush, 2000, p. 2). This suggested that learning did occur through exposure to the constructivist learning environment. These results, coupled with adjustments to the validation strategy in response to the limitations noted here, contributed to the second validation purpose—establishing and testing a sound process for validating the Intelligence Center's distance training courseware.

*Facilitate lifelong learning.* While the length of time over which mentoring and lifelong learning occur imposes some delay in judging our success, indications so far are good. The constructivist approach seems especially suited to the characteristics and learning habits of the midcareer soldiers who make up our largest audience, and the validation results up to this point appear to support this conclusion.

**FIGURE 3.2. SIMILARITY BETWEEN DISTRIBUTIONS OF PERFORMANCE-BASED LESSON TEST SCORES AND EXPERT RATINGS OF THE TESTED PERFORMANCE (REPORT COMPLETION).**

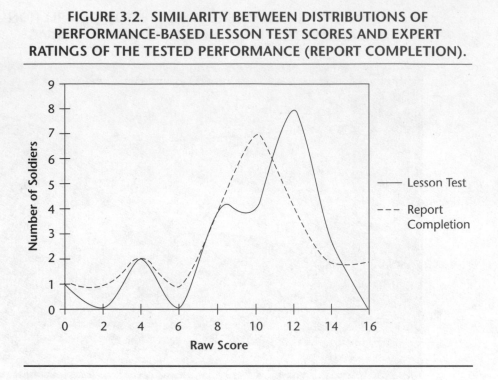

The software selected to administer our courseware and track student outcomes is in flux—Librarian giving way to Ingenium as Asymetrix became Click2Learn—but courseware version control, student registration, and record-keeping appear likely to be well supported. Compatibility issues with the mainframe-based record-keeping software that the Army uses in the resident schoolhouse remain an issue, but are being addressed.

Perhaps the greatest shortfall on this outcome remaining to be addressed is the absence of a telementoring environment, where novice and experienced practitioners can meet online to share best practices and lessons learned. The Internet has in many cases proven both effective and economical as a mentoring medium (Zellner, 1997, p. 50), and the Intelligence Center is now testing and refining a synchronous, virtual reality multi-user domain called the Virtual Tactical Operations Center (VTOC) to fill this role. Figure 3.3 illustrates this environment, which supports collaborative learning using an authentic simulation of a Tactical Operations Center incorporating a three-dimensional navigation tool, a two-dimensional map tool, and a chat tool.

*Efficiently deliver instruction worldwide.* A final note relating to outcomes at this stage concerns the process of aligning infrastructure (maintained by the Center's

### FIGURE 3.3. PARTICIPANTS GATHER IN THE VTOC FOR A TELEMENTORING SESSION.

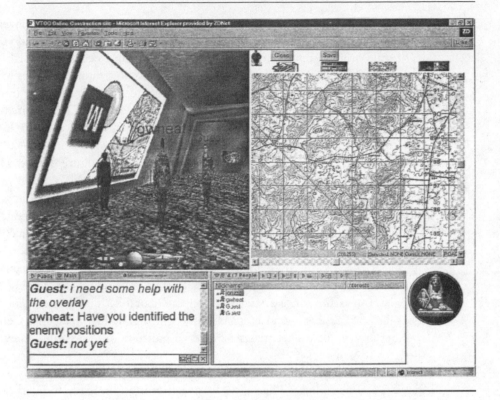

information management organization) with distance training policy (established by the Distance Learning Office). While the Intelligence Center has a fiber-optic infrastructure, this network primarily supported administrative communications such as e-mail. When the Distance Learning Office established courseware development and delivery—using the network—as a matter of policy, the demand for bandwidth in support of distance training quickly exceeded the capacity allocated by the typical network configuration. The resulting network-imposed delays intensified the stress of product development—and would ultimately impede delivery —yet the information management organization (whose customer service was measured in relation to e-mail and telephone services) considered bandwidth for instructional activities an ancillary requirement. Use of a network sniffer in support of a demand study ultimately helped establish a requirement to provide a minimum level of service, but this experience is illustrative of the confusion that can result when old measures of success meet new and unforeseen requirements.

## Discussion and Conclusion

We can draw several inferences from these experiences. At the broadest level, introduction of distance training is an instance of the change process and is subject to the principles governing organizational change. Recognizing this—and managing the process as a change effort—can overcome many obstacles to sustainment. It is also crucial to remember that distance training, like any innovation, succeeds—or fails—within the context of a larger system. It is not merely a matter of installing hardware and software and hooking it up to the Net: lasting success requires a coordinated package of complementary innovations—a "critical mass" to sustain it as part of the organization and its culture (Hall & Hord, 1987, p. 144; Hinnant & Oliva, 1997; Hirumi, 1995).

An equally key point is that this takes time. As Hall (1978) notes, change is a process, not an event (p. 1)—and reaching the stage where participant concerns can focus on the innovation's impact on student learning takes three to five years for most change efforts (Hall & Hord, 1987, p. 75). This timeline is supported by our experience. As the millennium dawns, distance training at the Intelligence Center enters its fifth year of incorporating the Internet and other emerging technologies. But its infusion as an integral component of the Military Intelligence soldier's lifelong learning—and as an established partner in the Intelligence Center's training strategy (characteristics of a Stage 4 organization)—was only achieved in the last two years.

In summary, implementation is not the end of the change process, only the beginning of a new phase. The successful program must be ready to build on the foundation it has established, with a clear vision and strong ties throughout the institution's culture and operations. It must be supported at the highest levels and given a footing equal to comparable functions from which to compete for resources. It must be prepared to deal with the affective dissonance between the Information Age paradigm it must embody and the investment its stakeholders are likely to have in their Industrial Age roots. It must balance the need for a long-term focus with the operational requirement not to delay action until the fruits of that focus appear, and weigh the legitimacy offered by methodological rigor with the pragmatism required by stakeholders who need to see results more than perfection. Sometimes it may have to accept limited success from a first effort—accompanied by a commitment to continuous improvement.

Finally, to extend our portrayal of a continuing process past the end of this chapter, we leave you not with a neatly tied-off ending but rather with a few words about our program's future. We believe that the potential for virtual communities of lifelong learning is one of distance training's most important offerings.

Yet while mentoring and co-mentoring are among the most effective tools for life-long professional development, the challenges are many—including fostering the conviction that the mentoring experience can be a two-way exchange—and encouraging the willingness to set aside traditional notions of professional hierarchy to make it so (Stansell, 1997, p. 142). This may prove especially difficult in a military environment—but perhaps in virtual reality ability can be made more visible and hierarchy less so, making such mutual interactions more feasible. The possibilities in other instructional settings are no less exciting.

CHAPTER FOUR

# LESSONS FROM MERGING SBC'S REGIONAL TELECOM TRAINING CENTERS

Natalie S. Friend, Tere Lyn Hepple

In 1997 when SBC Communications, Inc. (SBC) acquired Pacific Telesis, a number of corporation-wide initiatives emerged—to join infrastructures, combine resources, reduce operating expenses, and generate savings. The merger primarily affected operations in two regions:

- Pacific Bell region (California and Nevada)
- Southwestern Bell region (Missouri, Oklahoma, Kansas, Arkansas, and Texas)

Two initiatives transformed the distance training programs of SBC's regional training organizations: (1) merge each region's training efforts into one Center for Learning (CFL) curriculum, and (2) reorganize internal practices, delivery options, and infrastructures to meet clients' growing training needs. The CFL economized operations to help SBC meet the challenges of the Information Age, global market drivers, just-in-time training needs, and competition pressures in the telecommunications industry. This chapter discusses the CFL's success in terms of challenges overcome and savings and lessons learned from merging the CFL Pacific Bell and Southwestern Bell regions' computer-based and classroom distance training programs. Comparing regionally disparate programs reveals significant hurdles in organizational management. Resulting lessons learned pinpoint areas for the CFL to study for continued cost savings.

## What Is SBC?

SBC, one of the Baby Bells created after the 1984 breakup of AT&T, is a world-leading telecommunications corporation. SBC provides services including local telephone and wireless telephone service, Internet access, directories, media service, and data communications. After SBC and Pacific Telesis merged in 1997, operations grew to provide telecommunication services in widely dispersed regions:

- Southwestern Bell: Missouri, Oklahoma, Kansas, Arkansas, and Texas
- Cellular One: Massachusetts, Maryland, District of Columbia, Illinois, and New York
- SBC International: Mexico, Chile, South Korea, Taiwan, France, Israel, South Africa
- Pacific Telesis (Nevada Bell and Pacific Bell): Nevada and California

## What Is the Center for Learning?

At the time of the SBC–Pacific Telesis merger, the CFL was a separate incorporated subsidiary of SBC. Its performance consulting, instructional design, alternative media development, and instructional delivery staffs served SBC affiliate companies, mostly from San Ramon, California, and Irving, Texas. In 1998, SBC spent 2.1 percent of its payroll on training for more than 120,000 employees, most for wireline business and consumer groups and network, wireless, directory, and Internet business groups. In 1998, 15 percent of CFL training was delivered through alternative delivery methods—including computer-based training (CBT) and Web-delivered CBT (WBT) to the employee desktop, job aids, and classroom distance-training technologies (see Table 4.1).

This case study will focus on the learnings from the SBC–Pacific Telesis merger—learnings the CFL gained before completing later mergers with other regional Bell operating companies Southern New England Telecommunications (SNET) and Ameritech.

# TABLE 4.1. SBC CENTER FOR LEARNING (CFL) DISTANCE TRAINING TECHNOLOGIES SURVEY: 1997 AND 1998.

| Question | 1997 SBC CFL–Pacific Bell Region | 1997 SBC CFL–Southwestern Bell Region | 1998 SBC CFL–Combined Regions |
|---|---|---|---|
| *Program Description* | | | |
| 1. Number years DT and CBT used: | 7 DT; 13 CBT | 151.831 pt4 DT; 1 CBT | 8 DT; 14 CBT |
| 2. Technical delivery media (not including paper-based self-paced alternatives): | 1-way video, 2-way audio (broadcast quality); CD-ROM, LAN, and Web-based CBT, facilitated CBT; EPSS, video | 2-way audio, 2-way video (videoconferencing quality); limited vendor-developed CD-ROM and disk-based CBT and virtual reality; video, audiotapes | 1-way video, 2-way audio (broadcast quality), 2-way audio, 2-way video (video-conferencing quality); CD-ROM, LAN, and Web-based CBT, facilitated CBT; EPSS, video, audio |
| 3. Content and audiences: | PB region—Marketing, network, engineering, management, nonmanagement, executives, DT college courses and executive meetings | SW and CellularOne regions—Marketing, network, engineering, management, non-management, executives, DT college courses and executive meetings | PB, SW, and CellularOne regions—CFL Marketing, network, engineering, management, nonmanagement, executives, DT college courses and executive meetings |
| *Utilization* | | | |
| 1. Use of DT and CBT facilities: | DT, as much as expected; CBT, underutilized | DT, underutilized; CBT, NA | DT, underutilized; CBT, under-utilized |
| 2. Guidelines and standards for screening courses best suited for DT and CBT delivery: | No (process being designed) | No (process being designed) | Yes (Designer's Edge) |
| 3. Number of DT sites: | 25 | 14 | 36 |
| 4. Electronic alternative media as percent of total training (not including paper-based self-paced alternatives): | 12 | 2 | 15 |
| 5. Average class size: | 1–10 | 10 | 1–10 |
| *Support* | | | |
| 1. Specified competencies for designers and instructors: | DT, NA; CBT, Yes | DT, No; CBT, No | DT, No; CBT, Yes |
| 2. Specialized training provided for designers or instructors: | Yes, designers (formal and mentoring); No, instructors | No, designers; Yes, instructors (informal) | Yes, Designers; No, instructors |

*Instructional Effectiveness*

| | | | |
|---|---|---|---|
| 1. Evaluations completed on instructional effectiveness: | Yes (Levels 1 and 2) | Yes (Levels 1 and 2) | Yes (Levels 1 and 2) |
| 2. Student impression of instructional effectiveness: | Medium-High | High | Medium-High |

*Design*

| | | | |
|---|---|---|---|
| 1. Developers of DT and CBT courses: | Designers, vendors, team and individual | Designers, instructors, vendors, team and individual | Designers, vendors, team and individual |
| 2. DT and CBT courses developed by specified department: | DT, Yes; CBT, No | DT, No; CBT, No | DT, No; CBT, No |
| 3. Guidelines, templates, procedures used to develop DT and CBT courses: | DT, being developed; CBT, Yes | DT, No; CBT, NA | DT, No; CBT, Yes |
| 4. Average length of DT and CBT courses: | DT, 4 hours to 1 day; CBT, 1/5 to 1 hour | DT, 1 to 3 days; CBT, 1 hour | DT, 1 day; CBT, 1 hour |

*Future*

| | | | |
|---|---|---|---|
| 1. Future DT and CBT plans: | Pacific Bell and Southwestern Bell Regions merge DT curricula via connected networks, add response pads by 8/98, plan to have LAN and Web-delivered CBT available in SW by late 1998 to early 1999. | | Pacific Bell and Southwestern Bell regions merge DT curricula via connected networks, add response pads in most sites, capture DT-specific Level I evaluation data via online starting now and for Level II over the next year, introduce a CFL DT Web page for CFL employee access, provide LAN and Web CBT available in SW by late 1999. |

*Note:* SBC Center for Learning information provided by managers William Pivirotto, David Schmid, Clay Musa, and Sharon Johnson. Additional information provided by SBC Center for Learning Operations and Human Resources departments.

*Source:* Adapted from Friend, N. S. (1999). Case study: Distance learning at the SBC Center for Learning. *Performance Improvement Quarterly 12*(4), 33–44.

## Business Problem and Desired Outcomes: Reach Merger Savings with Alternative Media

Working across time zones with widely varying systems, practices, and cultures challenged the merged SBC. Eliminating redundancies resulted in savings for the CFL and its SBC internal clients. However, staffing varied continuously through restructuring, job changes, outsourcing, and new hiring. As employee experience levels fluctuated, the need for faster, more effective, and more flexible training had never been greater.

The CFL was charged with combining newly acquired Pacific Bell Education and Training (now the Pacific Bell region) with the SBC's Center for Learning (now the Southwestern Bell region). This included merging curricula and reducing combined CFL operating budgets 15 percent by 1999—in just two and one-half years.

One way the CFL sought to reach merger savings goals was by making better use of alternatives to traditional instructor-led training. "Alternative media"—the CFL's term for these alternative delivery methods—included distance training technologies, paper- and computer-based self-paced training, and job aids. The CFL's Alternative Media initiative focused on two distance-training technologies:

- *Distance Training (DT)* is classroom training in which students learn at different locations from the instructor and training is delivered via broadcast television or videoconferencing.
- *Computer-Based Training (CBT)* is self-paced, self-scheduled training delivered via diskette, CD-ROM, LAN, intranet, or Web technology, with no planned interaction between students and an instructor (Friend, 1999).

Increasing use of alternative media to provide the desired savings involved shifting traditional classroom training to CBT or DT. To do this the CFL took the following steps:

- Prepared Southwestern Bell region clients and their systems for CBT delivery.
- Extended Pacific Bell region's already successful CBT infrastructure to Southwestern Bell region client groups.
- Extended Southwestern Bell region's interactive two-way audio and video teleconferencing infrastructure into Pacific Bell region's one-way broadcast system.
- Streamlined alternative media production by replacing some DT studio production staff with automated controls and by implementing standardized CBT templates and processes.

This strategy reduced CFL expenses and brought value to SBC client groups by delivering more training while saving them several hundred thousand dollars.

# Challenges of Merging Regional Alternative Media Programs

Merging the alternative media programs imposed challenges of technology, staffing, and organizational support of the two well-established companies.

## DT Programs

***Infrastructures and Technical Challenges.*** The two regions used different DT models. In the Pacific Bell region, broadcasts were produced according to TV standards with a production crew, so viewers saw what is comparable to commercial TV programming. Remote audience members could call in their questions and comments via telephone.

In the Southwestern Bell region, two-way transmission of audio and video was used for classes and meetings. The instructor could selectively communicate with remote sites and switch between the main camera, document camera, slide show, or videotape. Videoconferences originated in a classroom and did not require production support. Participants could share information via microphones, room cameras, document cameras, fax machines, and telephones. They could interact with the instructor individually and in groups.

The Pacific Bell region incorporated TV broadcast facilities from two studios and five lecture halls in San Ramon, California, to twenty-five sites. A DS3 fiber and coaxial network delivered one-way, broadcast-quality, full-motion video.

The Southwestern Bell region used a fractional T1 direct-connect network delivered two ways with remote sites networked to the hub in Irving, Texas. In addition to a classroom and auditorium, the Irving campus had two mobile units (camera-mounted TVs with videoconference control panels).

With industry standardization, CFL staff could increasingly optimize interconnectivity for its widely varying infrastructures. To operate as one network, the two regions were linked via an electronic bridge and CODEC, which translated audio and video signals into a common protocol over a network consisting of fiber optics, direct T1, and dial-up ISDN. Training could then originate from either region to all SBC sites.

The quality of one-way broadcasts in the Pacific Bell region was on a par with TV, while two-way transmissions originating in the Southwestern Bell region suffered from loss of signal and quality from video compression. Delay and "jerky" video made it difficult for students to concentrate, according to end-of-course surveys. These problems caused credibility issues that had to be overcome through consistency and reliability. The technical support staff improved systems and increased bandwidth to correct most audio and video quality problems.

*Instructor and Student Support.* The Pacific Bell region's program had a production studio staff to control audiovisual elements. In the Southwestern Bell region the instructor managed the controls, which was initially frustrating, user-*un*friendly, and intimidating for many trainers.

The technical staff instituted a simpler graphical user interface for Southwestern Bell region instructors. The interface used a touch-sensitive screen to control the camera, along with upgraded cameras that would follow the instructor. Also, another touch screen operated a keypad system, which controlled the slide show notes, quiz questions, remote site cameras, and data and voice from the student keypads. The keypad system reduced the need for remote site facilitation or camera control.

Student keypads were added in both regions to allow greater interaction. When a student pressed a call button, the instructor saw the caller's name, and could broadcast the call as the student spoke into a keypad microphone. If the instructor displayed a multiple-choice question, students could submit answers via the keypad. The instructor could display how many students responded for each choice, and give instructional remediation as needed. Greater use of this interface was expected as instructors saw how it enhanced distance classroom relations and as instructional designers were trained on the system and were assigned appropriate course projects.

*Organizational Acceptance.* Managers and executives who requested airtime to train their sales and technical employees drove the Pacific Bell region's DT program. People who came to broadcasts were proud of the fact that their company used such cutting-edge technology.

Pacific Telesis was providing much more than rudimentary training through DT, and pulled significant student days. Meanwhile, DT in the Southwestern Bell region had not gained the same acceptance. Initially, the Southwestern Bell region's DT facilities were used for executive briefings, meetings, and only a few courses. The loss-of-signal and image-quality problems established early poor experiences for students and managers using videoconferencing in DT classrooms and conference rooms.

*Outcomes Attained in DT.* As shown in Table 4.1, DT facilities after the merger totaled thirty-six across the Southwestern Bell and Pacific Bell and Cellular One regions. Twenty-two facilities had keypads and more than thirty in-house courses were delivered to employees via the DT network, not to mention a growing number of university courses. Approximately 9 percent of alternative media courses were DT delivered in 1998. Management did not expect a reduction in course length for DT, but the DT courses garnered savings by reaching more students at one time with fewer instructors.

The number of courses delivered via DT has increased slightly during the two and a half years of the merger initiative. In third quarter 1999, the CFL began to see more focus on the medium. In addition, university courses in business administration, engineering, and telecommunications have drawn students toward the CFL's DT program.

## CBT Programs

*Infrastructure and Technical Issues.* Before the merger, the use of CBT in the Southwestern Bell region was very limited. Merging infrastructures was a huge task, as the need for speed and file space grew faster than the time to merge and upgrade both networks. The Southwestern Bell region's network could not support LAN-delivered CBT. In addition, computer-managed instruction (CMI) tools were vendor-specific, and standards were not yet established to run CBT developed with multiple authoring applications. Without standardized end-user software and hardware for the entire enterprise, technical support for more than 120,000 employees using multiple operating systems became a major challenge. Supporting various platforms required hands-on work at each personal computer to install and then update software (for example, different Web browsers, plug-ins, and so on).

When the networks and intranet were ready in the Southwestern Bell region, the need for technical support increased dramatically. Once the system was deployed, there were capacity issues on servers used for courses delivered to large audiences in short delivery times. Load-balancing programs were developed to distribute the load automatically between multiple servers. Ongoing, the system has been continually monitored to adjust as needed. For example, stress tests for courses with large audiences have been done to ensure expected capacities can be handled.

*Client Acceptance.* In addition to technical challenges, initial resistance from Southwestern Bell region clients delayed the process. What they had was working and they did not see the advantages of making efforts to change. Therefore, many customers' workstations and networks did not have the minimum specifications to deliver network- or intranet-delivered CBT. When deployment began, many clients were not even familiar with how to use a browser or access network- and vendor-delivered CBT.

The CFL could not make clients want CBT, but could educate them on the benefits for their employees and budgets. Over the past two and a half years, the resistance to alternative media has slowly changed. This is seen through mass utilization of SBC's "Ethics in the Workplace" and "Code of Business Conduct" WBT programs and inclusion of instructor-facilitated CBT courses in the Southwestern Bell region's initial training for call centers.

***Platform and Content's Effect on Design.*** Because of the slow deployment of adequate desktops in the Southwestern Bell region, CFL designers had to produce an equivalent version in another format—such as paper-based—as well as the CBT version. This increased development time and costs. Greater deployment of new computers has been resolving this problem.

The extremely short timelines allotted for CBT development were complicated by unstable course content. New products demand new training material. Standard templates and reusable code have helped to address these issues of short design-development times. In addition, as designers became more skilled they were able to produce alternative media more quickly.

***Designer Support.*** The Pacific Bell region was staffed with experienced multimedia designers, but the Southwestern Bell region's staff had little design expertise and support. CBT use was limited to vendor-developed disk and CD-ROM programs in the Southwestern Bell region before the merger. The CFL considered this when it restructured to support the increased use of alternative media in the corporation. Staff, training, and support systems were added and the combined design group (called Instructional Design & Technology—ID&T) decentralized alternative media resources to the various curriculum design teams to help them develop their skills. An alternative media expert in each team mentored newer designers in multimedia design and development. All designers could receive training on multimedia design and DT. Experienced alternative media designers and graphic artists could receive training in advanced programming and Web development.

***CBT Program After Merger.*** Two and a half years after the 1997 merger, ten business groups used CBT. The biggest users were call centers. Typical content included customer service and sales skills (38 percent), technical skills (35 percent), and corporation-wide mandatory coverage topics such as ethics and business conduct. In 1997, CFL CBT was underutilized. However, as CBT student days jumped from two thousand in 1997 to eighteen thousand in 1998, utilization steadily increased.

Better tools were added to reduce alternative media development cycles. For authoring, experienced multimedia developers used object-oriented applications with development templates for quicker development of LAN- and intranet-delivered training. Models were updated to accommodate newer application versions and provide for faster development. Less experienced developers used a simpler CBT authoring tool, entering training content into a database application.

Once the CBT infrastructure was expanded many employees in the Southwestern Bell region were able to use LAN- and intranet-delivered CBT. As in the Pacific Bell region, students accessed LAN- and intranet-delivered training through Learning Manager (the CFL's computer-managed instruction application). For LAN-delivered training they chose a course from a list customized for their job title. The course downloaded to the user's workstation, where it resided while it was used. Associated paper-based references and job aids were available from the students' training coach or manager or via a fax-back process. For intranet-delivered training, students accessed CBT via a Web version of Learning Manager or through an individual URL.

The Standard Desktop organization supported the end-user workstations. CFL Operations staff supported the server hardware and software, and monitored the network for problems, and made adjustments to balance server loads.

## Outcomes Attained with the Alternative Media Initiative

Resulting savings justified the related challenges. Since the merger, the CFL has saved millions of dollars in operating expenses, student days, and headcount. It has shortened course lengths by an average of 50 percent for leader-led courses converted to CBT. Here are some examples of DT and CBT savings:

- "Ethics in the Workplace," a WBT program, trims approximately three hours of training time for each of tens of thousands of employees annually and eliminates instructor hours for delivery, saving hundreds of thousands of dollars every year.
- Pacific Bell's LAN-delivered "Call Waiting ID" CBT program trims approximately half an hour of training time for thousands of call center representatives annually and eliminates instructor hours for delivery, saving hundreds of thousands of dollars annually.
- Pacific Bell call center representative initial training, a facilitated CBT program, trims approximately eighty hours of training time for hundreds of

employees, reduces instructor hours for delivery, and standardizes content delivered. The program saved hundreds of thousands of dollars in 1999, and the same savings is expected annually.

- "ISDN Products," a one-day DT course, trimmed travel-related expenses for hundreds of students and saved thousands of dollars in 1999.

The CFL's merger initiatives emphasized that use of alternative media does have higher front-end costs for infrastructure and development. However, instructor, material reproduction, and training-related costs were eliminated for CBT courses and reduced greatly for DT and facilitated CBT courses. The out-of-pocket training costs per student were estimated at zero for CBT and at about 50 percent of former levels for DT programs and 70 percent of former levels for facilitated CBT. Such cost savings clearly show the alternative media initiative to be valuable.

## Lessons from Merging Alternative Media Programs

Besides these savings, organizational changes from combining alternative programs resulted in important lessons. The existing mature experiences and expertise of both regions' DT staffs and the Pacific Bell region's CBT teams were instrumental in merging DT programs and extending LAN- and intranet-based training to the Southwestern Bell region. Organizational changes such as reorganization, responsibility changes, outsourcing, and new employee hiring kept experience levels (within the CFL staff and the customer groups) ever changing.

Following are key learnings from the merger, common to both DT and CBT programs.

*Leadership buy-in and experience leads to better planning, teamwork, and support for better utilization of alternative delivery methods.* An early push from the CFL leadership to educate Southwestern Bell regional clients and internal teams about alternative media delivery and its deployment needs could have influenced earlier adoption of alternative media by some client groups. Initial adoption of classroom and desktop distance-training technologies was slow, due in part to limited internal experience with the approach—a common problem also experienced in the Pacific Bell region when it began to use alternative media.

As the CFL staff became more versed with alternative media options and benefits they became more effective advocates. CFL leadership learned that establishing awareness strategies for educating inexperienced leaders, teams, and clients is key to provide them with firsthand experience with multimedia applications. Once comfortable with new options, CFL teams and clients began to make better use of them for their solutions. Examples of awareness strategies included sharing the Pacific Bell region's hard data on the savings of training expenses and how just-in-time training at the desktop has been an advantage for call center managers, as well as showing how simple it is to use network-delivered CBT. This led to more aggressive selling of the benefits (for example, the cost savings and scheduling flexibility from just-in-time training options) and attempts to educate client groups about classroom and desktop distance training technologies.

*Get the right expertise.* While centralizing and filling staffs across regions, the CFL emphasized that highly specialized skills were required to manage, design, develop, implement, and support alternative media courses. If the course design required expertise with graphics, authoring, or programming, team members with these skills would ensure high-quality and timely completion of the project. For CBT, when experienced designers were not available, experienced contractors were used. In addition, as more than 50 percent of its designers were inexperienced with multimedia design, the CFL began to teach foundation multimedia skills as well as CFL-specific multimedia processes and policies.

The CFL has learned that project management of multimedia projects requires experience with all of the additional complexities of multimedia to avoid potential pitfalls and successfully meet the required set of time, quality, and financial expectations of CFL managers and clients. For example, when multimedia instructional designer Amy Rouse mentors designers new to CBT design and project management, she steps them through all the considerations that may affect success. Amy allows more or less time for a project depending on considerations illustrated in Table 4.2. It is crucial to account for these up front, so the project manager can communicate concerns, needs, and progress to the client, make changes when needed and possible, and end up with a project that meets the client's time, quality, and financial expectations. Without planning, the project illustrated in Table 4.2 would have missed the schedule by an estimated 70 percent—it would have been late and over budget.

"Order Writing," an early post-merger CBT project led by an inexperienced CBT project manager, would have benefited from this kind of project planning. The project had team members in three different states to provide the subject matter expert (SME), designer, and author/developer needs of the project. And, although an industry-standard multimedia development ratio was used, the scope of the project changed in midstream. Without the project consideration estimates completed, the impact of these midstream changes on the project could not be accurately estimated. Adjusting the focus of the project was chaotic.

For DT delivery, expertise in the subject matter was the first big consideration. Second was competence with technology. In the Pacific Bell region, where studio support teams produced DT sessions, instructors needed only coaching in

### TABLE 4.2. PROJECT PLANNING DEVELOPMENT CONSIDERATIONS.

**Project RATE: CBT Project Management Consideration Estimates**

| Consideration | Factor | Consideration | Factor |
|---|---|---|---|
| • Product stability and completeness | 1 | • Content experience on team | 1.2 |
| | | • Authoring experience | .8 |
| • Information availability | 1.2 | • Storyboarder's experience with authoring models | 1.1 |
| • Inclusion of storyboarding in design | 1 | | |
| • Prototype approval included in process | .8 | • Team working at same location/not from each other | 1.3 |
| | | • Review process followed | 1 |
| • Availability of subject-matter experts | 1.3 | • Graphics expertise availability | 1 |
| • Effectiveness of reviews | 1 | • Ownership of project scheduling and deadlines | 1 |

*Scale:* highly experienced and controlled =.8, average = 1.0, no experience or control = 1.4

$1 \times 1.2 \times 1 \times .8 \times 1.3 \times 1 \times 1.2 \times .8 \times 1.1 \times 1.3 \times 1 \times 1 \times 1 = 1.71$

$$280 \text{ development hours/class hour}$$
$$\times 1.7$$
$$= 476 \text{ development hours/class hour}$$

on-camera presentation skills and rehearsal with course material. Instructors in the Southwestern Bell region attended a vendor workshop with hands-on practice using the DT classroom equipment.

The CFL learned that it was important to anticipate the incentives required to keep trained professionals on consulting, instructional, and support staffs. Considerations included compensation, benefits, and bonuses. Looking back, reorganization would address the workloads and growing expertise expected of the staff. It was also important to provide the infrastructures required to support and keep existing staff.

*Educate internal training staffs.* In the CFL, use of alternative media was a familiar concept for some people but a new one for others. The merger provided a perfect opportunity for CFL leadership to identify and fill the multimedia and instructional design skill gaps of their teams.

The CFL found that it was important for internal training teams to understand the concepts of alternative media and believe in the benefits. Introducing more specific alternative media concepts, benefits, and delivery options sooner would have aided earlier adoption of CBT in the Southwestern Bell region.

It was also critical to ensure that the required skill sets were present—and, if the skills were not present, to provide them—in the functional areas of analysis, consulting, design, development, delivery, evaluation, scheduling, operations, and support. This was addressed at the CFL in varying degrees in these different areas.

For example, some instructors feared alternative media technology would replace their jobs. Some also believed that training was becoming more impersonal. Educating these instructors about how alternative media would free them to focus on hands-on training, and less on lecture, slowly started to show progress. It was also important to explain that using one instructor to reach more students via DT or delivering content in a self-paced CBT format allows the CFL to allocate instructors to new courses.

Also important was that training provided for the CFL's internal personnel addressed the audience needs and was developed with the same instructional integrity as training provided for the CFL's clients—including analysis, objectives, practice, and testing. For example, CFL performance consultants needed to suggest the right delivery type and media attributes for each client's performance needs. Therefore, training for consultants should have addressed specifics of each CFL delivery method (instructor-led or alternative media) and media attributes (interaction, sound, animation, video). If a suggested alternative media delivery did not meet audience needs, that client would probably not readily adopt future suggestions of alternative media solutions.

*Educate clients.* Educating clients about alternative media involves transforming their paradigms of training—what it is, how it can be delivered, when it is needed, and what performance and business problems it can solve. CFL teams learned this with bringing CBT options to clients in the Southwestern Bell region. "A variety of development tools are needed to solve clients' performance needs," explained Amy Rouse. Moreover, the CFL found that it was essential that clients were familiar and comfortable with the options available for them. "We need to develop the client and sell what this product can do," noted Bill Pivirotto, DT technical operations manager in the Pacific Bell region.

If alternative media was an appropriate solution, CFL personnel doing the needs analysis would clarify its advantages and characteristics. This should involve demonstrations or evaluation and savings reports from successful projects. It also should involve building on partnerships with corporate communications groups to share success stories of alternative media usage, savings, and mass appeal.

The CFL learned that educating new alternative media students involved managing the comfort level of students. DT students must be prepared to expect different time zones' meal breaks and different audio or visual quality from the other region's transmission pipe. CBT students must be given training on how to access and operate courseware, along with technical support and uninterrupted time to complete training.

*Clients' successful experience, acceptance, and readiness drive utilization.* Many of the CFL's clients still believed that CBT and DT were less reliable than traditional classroom delivery. Any equipment failure (for example, inability to access courseware, limited audio communication with an instructor from a remote site, and so on), even if not the fault or within the control of the CFL to resolve, would taint clients' future desire to use alternative media solutions. They did not understand that if a network goes down, so does the training application, as Sharon Johnson, ID&T area manager, explained.

Most DT problems dealt with audio or visual quality and timely delivery of the correct materials to distant sites. For example, students in remote sites of one class were able to hear and interact with the instructor, but did not receive class handouts in time for the class. The instructor had to delay the class to fax the materials to the remote site facilitator, who then had to reproduce them for the students.

Similarly for CBT, early difficulties with accessing courseware slowed its adoption in the Southwestern Bell region. Things did improve for both DT and CBT, but negative experiences with alternative media have greatly reduced requests for alternative delivery options.

Utilization was also greatly influenced by the clients' technical and financial readiness to incorporate alternative media methods into their infrastructures. Many DT classroom sites were already set up, but additional sites would have made instructor-led DT more accessible for more employees. Many desktops were upgraded to support LAN- and intranet-delivered CBT, but those employees without computers still had no access to CBT. One solution that was initiated was to establish walk-up terminals and DT viewing sites at client locations.

*Continually improve existing and new processes.* A key element of the CFL's plan to meet cost reduction goals was to evaluate and improve internal processes. Process improvement was one of the most effective methods for reducing expenses. As a result of the initiative, the distance and desktop technology groups of the alternative media program adopted the following tools and procedures:

- Customized CBT and DT templates, which decreased development times and employed sound instructional practices (objectives, practice, student interactions, and post-testing)
- Internal processes for quality assurance testing, deployment, and troubleshooting
- Certification, mentoring, and communication resources for designers on basic and advanced alternative media design and development
- Merged and still growing distance and desktop training infrastructures

The CFL ID&T group projected alternative media project management needs by analyzing designers' utilization. Reports identified analysis, design, and development tasks that required more time—identifying the issues that affect the bulk of the projects. By providing support (personnel, training, expertise, processes, and so on), the group found it could reduce development times.

*The amount of effort in terms of time, support, and money that is required to produce, deploy, and maintain alternative media projects varies in complexity.* As the CFL grew in experience, the ID&T staff identified various types of projects and their peculiarities of infrastructure, development, and support. They were then able to focus energy on issues and processes common to the bulk of the projects—to get the most bang for the buck. By continually learning from experience and researching distance training and desktop delivery options, the CFL reduced development times and operational support needs.

Process improvement teams continually evaluated the CFL's growing alternative media programs, implementing and improving design and development processes. The CFL reduced cycle times through use of templates, standards, common practices, and reused code. The operations support group was staffed to provide the testing, standards, and processes to reduce the test-to-deploy cycle time and plan for higher volumes of courses to be deployed.

*Select objectives and design courses specifically for the alternative media environment.* CFL teams learned that certain learning objectives are best suited to the alternative media learning environment. Moving from *pedagogical* (traditional instructor-centered) learning to *andragogical* (student-directed) learning required a paradigm shift.

For DT, the best courses were brief, with content heavy with concepts and policies and time-sensitive objectives appropriate for learning at a distance. Courses with hands-on practice that were shorter than two days worked best.

For CBT, the best courses combined visual, textual, and audio components—especially instruction on principles and processes. In these courses, animations, diagrams, narration, and text explanations provided high-level overviews as well as rich, robust explanations, demonstrations, and practice opportunities. This rule for content selection works for both CBT multimedia and video DT.

As CFL curricula were conjoined and converted, courses were made modular according to learning objectives. This simplified selection of cognitive-level course material for alternative media delivery.

*Be on your instructional design game and take full yet reasonable advantage of technology.* In 1998, the CFL redesigned a regular instructor-led lecture course for newly hired technicians into a DT course called "Essential Telephony." A pre-test and post-test were added to measure learning, as well as an icebreaker to introduce students to each other and to the jargon they needed to know. Also added were programmed notes to fill in, section review quizzes, lesson review crossword puzzles to enhance group competition, video vignettes about various technologies, and answer keys for each quiz and exercise. To cue instructor sequencing, the presentation slides were revamped to include all the important bullet points. Also added were review questions and puzzles, better graphics, photos, and animated diagrams. However, too much required activity can undermine a distance trainer's need for flexibility.

For example, the programmed notes were designed to keep students on task but became distracting, time-consuming, and inflexible. Because of this most programmed notes will be replaced with strategically placed questions. From this experience CFL designers learned to use well-chunked material and appropriate instructional strategies, to suggest ways to enhance student interactivity, and to allow flexibility for the instructor through design.

*Effective analysis and design are key for instructionally successful alternative media courses.* Media and method must match audience needs and performance objectives. New CBT courseware for consumer call center curricula were one highly successful example. Some courseware was developed to be facilitated by an instructor as part of an instructor-led training program. The advantage of including facilitated CBT in an instructor-led course was that CBT content would be delivered consistently for all students in all classes. For this program, the design strategy also allowed for additional time for on-the-job practice. The facilitator provided role-playing practice on customer contact skills both in the classroom and on the job.

The courseware in these curricula was created with the simpler database–authoring tool mentioned earlier. The CFL ID&T staff continually evaluates new technology to enhance courseware products and increase their effectiveness. The CFL employs each authoring application according to its strengths, project design needs, and team skill sets.

*Plan for deployment and technical support needs.* "The worst thing you can do is to put technology out there that does not work properly," explained Sharon Johnson. Experienced technical support staffs and management ensure successful deployment of alternative media delivery methods.

In 1996–1997 (before the SBC–Pacific Telesis merger), 8 percent of SBC employees completed a CBT diskette version of the traditionally instructor-led "Ethics in the Workplace" course. This program had a rough start:

- Thousands of questions and desktop problems arose for this new delivery method.
- Various materials distribution and internal billing processes needed to be accommodated.
- Many employees were not given specified time to complete the training.
- Seventy-six percent of CBT students were interrupted while working at their desk (Friend, 1997).

After this experience, the CFL reevaluated how CBT would be best delivered. Merged Operations teams decided to deliver the CBT through the LAN and intranet. They decided it would solve some of the previous user problems in the Southwestern Bell region, it was a logical option for experienced CBT audiences in the

Pacific Bell region, and it would yield greater savings than disk-delivered CBT. In 1998, the CBT version was redesigned as WBT for access via the CFL intranet. The new delivery method was easier for students to access, use, and return to over multiple sessions. It also provided managers with tools to track completion.

Operations also established the CFL Help Desk to answer learners' questions about using the intranet and accessing the Learning Manager CMI to complete LAN- and Web-delivered CBT courses. The Help Desk initially received about five hundred calls per day and now receives an average of just fifty calls per day.

Ongoing changes in the technology and changes in clients' hardware and software continued to require Operations support. Therefore, appropriate staffing was essential. Alternative media support staffs needed to be highly capable as well as extremely customer focused and responsive. They needed to continually stretch the capability of the technology and be able to foresee and resolve problems before they happened. They also needed to clearly define roles and document and refine their work processes.

## Lessons from Merging DT Programs

Linking and upgrading disparate DT networks involved much more than technical troubleshooting. All areas were under examination to determine how to streamline, upgrade, or merge them for best advantage.

*Be creative in designing and scheduling lengthy courses.* Flexible, creative solutions are required to accommodate regional learner outlooks, content, and delivery differences. Scheduling has been especially difficult across time zones that have different start, break, and end times.

Traditional instructor-led courses ranged from half a day to twelve weeks, with many running three to five days. The CFL excluded long courses from adaptation to DT altogether. However, to realize training savings and take advantage of the DT network, concept-heavy lectures could have been delivered in prerequisite DT courses. The previously discussed DT course called "Essential Telephony" took place over two eight-hour days. Many technicians were hands-on, kinesthetic learners who found it difficult to sit in a DT classroom watching a TV screen for two full days in a row. Holding DT sessions in short (up to four-hour) sessions over several days or on a weekly schedule would have accommodated their learning styles while simplifying the task of scheduling for multiple time zones.

For example, before attending highly technical courses requiring hands-on practice in fiber optics, technicians could attend DT courses that taught the conceptual portions of how the systems work. After completing the prerequisite, the target audience could travel to the CFL campus lab for the performance-based portion of the course. This setup requires course redesign but would cut the face-to-face time in half. Another option would be to use portable lab equipment or the portable DT equipment to take the performance-based exercises to the students. These proposals have failed so far as the network organization firmly believes that these high-demand technical courses should stay the way everyone has taken them for decades. Creative proposals are being reconsidered, however, in light of new mergers and business initiatives involving widely dispersed audiences.

*Instructional support should include management of instructor comfort as the DT environment changes.* DT instructors who are uncomfortable with the medium tend to become "talking heads" or phantom voices behind their presentation slides. DT support personnel should duplicate the classroom as much as possible. If the instructor normally wanders among students, the room and camera should be configured so that the instructor can wander forward among students in the host site.

Because of increased instructor responsibilities and limelight, rehearsal is critical. For one course, the CFL scheduled a combination live train-the-trainer and field trial class in several remote sites and placed the print order for the course materials at the same time. Given this time frame, the instructor did not have a chance to practice with the revised materials and the result was less than desired. Practice time is important, as viewers have high expectations for what they see on the screen when they are in a DT environment. The instructional sequence must be second nature for the instructor before attempting to deliver the course via DT.

Initially, the instructor's control panels in the Southwestern Bell region's DT classrooms resembled an airplane cockpit. The control panel requires trainers to be a "one-man-band" as they operate the panel and teach the class at the same time. This was upgraded to a friendlier graphical user interface. Instructor orientation to DT was changed to include a demonstration of how to operate the control panel, along with practice on videotape and constructive feedback.

*Reduce reliance on remote site facilitators.* To maintain remote site facilitation across the country, the DT network relied on administrative support staffs in the field organizations. Site coordinators were not CFL employees, they were administrative staff for the client organizations and they had other responsibilities and demands that often took precedence over site facilitation. This effect was seen when the field reduced headcount and fewer people were available to handle greater workloads. For example:

- A course began at 8 A.M., but the site facilitator did not arrive until 8 A.M. to unlock the room, turn the lights and equipment on, and coordinate with the host site technical staff.
- Security personnel, uninformed of facilitation and class schedules, turned away students.

- Course materials arrived in the mailroom early enough for a class, but were not distributed to the classroom before the start of class because mailroom staff was uninformed.

The CFL took steps to address these issues including installation of sophisticated remote control equipment to perform every setup task except physically turning on the power and bringing in the handouts. Site facilitators have better training, checklists, and backup procedures. Instructors, previously accustomed to centralized material distribution staff setting up classrooms, identify a facilitator or student volunteer to manage handouts.

## Lessons from Growing the CBT Program

CBT-specific learnings relate to the rapid growth of LAN- and intranet-delivered CBT into the Southwestern Bell region. In addition, development and tracking of alternative media reports generated key development and utilization findings.

*Keep control of IT systems and support functions.* The CFL learned that centralization can enable the CFL to manage support functions without depending on dispersed Information Technology (IT) departments in the numerous client groups. This was critical for scheduling upgrades and maintenance and meeting minimum hardware and software requirements. Since the CFL's client groups were supported by many different IT groups, CFL Operations had hurdles in how software upgrades would be done, what image (combinations of applications, settings, versions, and so on) would be on each computer, and how and when new versions would be disseminated. For example, specifications to access and operate WBT included a specific brand and version of Web browser. Students who operated computers with incompatible browsers had problems.

Centralized support would ensure fewer problems with user access and operation and less rework for operations and development teams. Centralization was key not only to maintain successful operation and production of quality CBT products, but also to keep pace with technology advances.

*Any CBT course with a seat time of less than one hour requires the same programming, testing, and deployment time as a one-hour or longer CBT course.* Tracking the progress of CBT utilization and improving CFL processes uncovered this lesson. In addition to reevaluating the design ratios being used, how those hours were utilized had to be broken down—how much time was actually required to complete each of the tasks. "What we learned was that any alternative media product of one hour or less takes close to two hundred hours to develop, test, and deploy unless it is a spin off from another course," Sharon Johnson explained. If it takes two hundred hours to develop a one-hour CBT, it will *not* take only one hundred hours for a half-hour CBT; it will still take two hundred hours. Clients must be taught that design of such CBT programs does take more time, but the savings are in deployment. Some of the CFL's most successful CBT programs were the Pacific Bell region's call center continuation training courses that were one hour or less—because employees could access them directly from their own desks. When training thousands of employees, the savings for clients from short, easily accessible programs were immense.

*CBT projects are driven by a range of design, development, and support requirements.* A number of considerations arise for each CBT project to meet client and learner needs, including SME availability, content stability, and familiarity with user platforms. Merger adjustments to the budget, staffing, and infrastructure presented additional challenges for new CBT projects.

A recent mandatory-coverage course on telecommunications regulations in the Pacific Bell region is an example of the importance of identifying project considerations and risks up front. Although ID&T managers had planned for the project to be developed in six weeks and had started development, the due date for the project was moved up overnight. Due to a regulatory decision, ID&T found itself with four days left to develop, test, and deploy a Web-based training package—instead of the planned six weeks. The design team was able to lock up subject-matter experts to determine content, program the course in a day and a half, and test and deploy the course to twelve thousand users overnight. All users were then trained within one week. Without a desktop alternative media product this could not have been accomplished—a leader-led course could not have been fielded in the time allowed. The solution did create its own additional challenges—CFL Operations had to add five new servers to handle the load and then develop load-balancing techniques, again overnight. This was a real-life stress test for CFL teams and actually, although painful, it provided very good data for future planning directions.

## Future Directions

The lessons learned from the alternative media merger initiative will help CFL teams address larger, global audiences as technology gets better and better. Integrating two training organizations of this size provided an opportunity to choose best practices—from the two companies and from outside organizations—and establish them in the new conjoined organization. In two and a half years, many lessons were learned and in the end, merger savings reports show that the CFL saved millions of student hours and millions of dollars.

The challenges of merging two training organizations of this magnitude also provided planning baselines for future mergers. SNET has already benefited, as SNET's alternative media programs were integrated with the CFL's after merging with SBC in 1998. SNET brought twenty years of alternative media experiences to the CFL. In 1997, before the merger, approximately 9 percent of SNET's training was alternative media, including broadcast-quality video to twenty-nine remote sites and several CBT courses. SNET's DT and CBT alternative media programming grew after the merger with SBC.

Changes from merging the SBC and Ameritech are expected to be equally successful in reducing training expenses. The SBC-Ameritech merger in late 1999 nearly doubled the size of the corporation to more than 200,000 employees. Combined with SBC's aggressive business initiatives, there will be tremendous training opportunities. Within 2000, SBC anticipates

- Greatly increased emphasis on data communications and broadband services
- Entry into the long-distance market
- Selling products and services in markets outside SBC's regions
- Restructuring the organization in the Southwestern Bell and Pacific Bell regions
- Continued merger integration of Ameritech and SBC infrastructures
- Standardization among regional operations

These initiatives will bring rapid changes at a massive scale.

SBC's training organization must continually evolve to keep pace with business initiatives and industry changes. Training will need to help prepare employees for future policy, infrastructure, budget, and staffing changes. Learnings from merging the Pacific Bell and Southwestern Bell regions' alternative media programs make a strong business case for the value of alternative media. Alternative-media distance-training technologies will continue to play a key role in reducing training expenses and improving the training of employees throughout the corporation.

CHAPTER 5

# THE WORLD IS OFFICIALLY OPEN FOR BUSINESS

## How MCI WorldCom Used the Corporate Intranet to Train a New-Era Communications Company

Chris Treanor, Jessica Page Irwin

In September 1998, the newly merged MCI WorldCom announced, "The world is officially open for business." This merger created a communications company that provided customers around the world with a full set of communications services over its own "local-to-global-to-local" network.

Today, MCI WorldCom owns and operates its own network in cities across the United States and around the world. The company's assets allow its customers to combine voice and data traffic from local U.S. and international locations onto one seamless, end-to-end network.

- MCI WorldCom serves millions of U.S. businesses and consumers with a fully integrated package of long distance, local (available from more than a hundred U.S. markets), data, Internet, and other communications services.
- The company has developed the most reliable and widely deployed Internet network through UUNET, as well as networking and hosting solutions. The powerful UUNET backbone supports speeds ranging from 28.8 Kbps to OC-12 and provides local access from more than a thousand locations worldwide.
- Globally, MCI WorldCom has established itself as a local, facilities-based competitor in fifteen countries outside the United States, with high-capacity connectivity to more than 38,000 buildings linked to the rest of the company's network via transcontinental and transoceanic cables.

The case study presented in this chapter is a firsthand account of how distance learning techniques helped prepare MCI WorldCom Business Markets employees to "Open the World for Business." It will detail the strategies and programs that we implemented to accomplish this task.

## A History of Two Companies

Both WorldCom and MCI had extensive training programs prior to the merger. WorldCom Training focused on traditional leader-led training delivered from classrooms at the Jackson, Mississippi, headquarters and at remote locations across the country. The bulk of the group's efforts involved presentation materials and fax-on-demand services. Content from WorldCom Training focused mainly on sales and skills-based subjects, including orientation and new hire training, regional sales programs, and professional development programs for managers. The training team was a small but experienced group serving a relatively large audience; it had limited experience with distance learning.

MCI also focused on traditional leader-led learning at its Atlanta-based training headquarters, but had begun expanding its curriculum with distance learning in 1995. Early initiatives included a variety of training options using videoconferencing, CD-ROM, and downloadable computer-based modules, or CBTs.

In 1997, MCI's training organization launched its first state-of-the-art training Web site. It featured online registration for traditional classroom training, descriptions for all MCI courses, and interactive online training modules. Content for online training focused on mainly the products and services offered by MCI, but there were also some courses teaching basic systems tools, sales skills, and generic industry knowledge.

## MCI WorldCom University

In September 1998, the merger of MCI and WorldCom integrated these two groups, who formed the new MCI WorldCom University, or MWU. This team combines the efforts of experienced trainers and course developers and proven sales leaders from throughout the combined company.

### Business Problem Statement

The newly formed MWU was given the task of preparing the combined legacy-MCI and legacy-WorldCom employees to support a new era of customers. This meant that we had to create a consistent message focused on the combined company's new strategy. Supporting this effort required training on completely redefined products, specifications, services, pricing, and business, as well as providing employees with the tools to master this new environment.

## Population Served and Targeted

To accomplish all this, we first had to analyze our new audience. The core audience was made up of the very professionals who would have to implement MCI WorldCom's new strategy. Analysis showed that approximately two-thirds of this group were sales representatives (64 percent) who supported all types of local, regional, national, and global customers. The remainder were service and sales support representatives (21 percent) and technical service representatives (15 percent) dedicated to serving MCI WorldCom customers and sales representatives. We also knew that the majority of our audience needed basic telephony, data communications, or systems training (67 percent), while the remainder had to be brought current on the latest industry applications and advanced communications specifications.

This was a difficult audience to understand and reach, as they all had differing skill sets, customers, and quota requirements. An added challenge was that these employees were located at branches and field offices all across the country.

The following examples represent typical MWU students for the purposes of this case study:

*Nancy the New Hire*

Experience:            0 – 6 months

Training Needs:        Nancy joined WorldCom as her first job after leaving
                       school. She needs to learn the ropes of telephony and
                       quickly get up to speed on MCI WorldCom's new com-
                       munications strategy. Nancy has no previous experience
                       with computer- or Web-based training.

Access Method:         Connected to the Denver branch LAN via a standard lap-
                       top, which she shares with nine other members of her team.

*Tomas the Sales Rep*

Experience:            1 – 2 years

Training Needs:        Tomas has been successfully selling voice products to mid-
                       size WorldCom customers for over a year. Following the
                       merger, he will be able to sell data products as well, which

will give him enormous opportunities to increase his sales base. Tomas has no previous experience with computer- or Web-based training.

Access Method:        Dial-up access using a standard laptop at 28.8 Kbps via a proxy server from various remote locations.

### Suzy the Sales and Service Support Specialist

Experience:           1–2 years

Training Needs:       Suzy has been working with MCI for over a year support- ing the sales force in Order Entry and Implementation. She needs to understand the new tools available since the merger, and also the basic nuts and bolts of core services (long distance, local, access) products sold by the sales reps she supports. Suzy has some previous experience with computer-based systems training.

Access Method:        LAN access from corporate headquarters in Clinton, Mississippi.

### Daniel the Data Guru

Experience:           2–6 years

Training Needs:       Daniel has been with MCI for years, always in the top 5 percent of the sales force. He already has a thorough understanding of telephony and data communications strategies, and knows former MCI products inside and out. He needs to get up to speed on the fundamental differences between new MCI WorldCom products and services and the legacy-MCI suite he has been selling for years. Daniel has some experience with Web-based product training.

Access Method:        Dial-up access from a standard laptop at 28.8 Kbps from various remote locations.

### Taylor the Tech

Experience:           2–4 years

Training Needs:       Taylor has been a technical support representative for MCI for years, supporting high-end data communications applications. He needs to understand the differences in the combined platform, and also what new resources are available so he can discern how his new offerings and opportunities will affect each of his customers. Taylor also strives to continually improve his communications expertise, and often finds he needs to quickly get up to speed on advanced networking and support concepts to stay one step ahead of his increasingly intelligent IT customers. Taylor has extensive experience with Web-based technical and industry training.

Access Method:       LAN access from branch in Southfield, Michigan.

## Outcomes Desired

The legacy-WorldCom and legacy-MCI training managers began by working together to determine exactly what needed to be accomplished. Based on an intensive training needs assessment, content review, and direction from MCI WorldCom executives, the following four items were deemed most critical to MWU's success:

1. Gain executive and segment support for training, create awareness of the program, and develop a support structure to motivate students to complete training.
2. Teach the core components of MCI WorldCom's new products, services, and systems using a combination of new courses and existing applications, and create a means of tracking student progress.
3. Find an effective delivery method that would make sure all segments of the audience have access to the right tools to successfully perform their job requirements.
4. Create a flexible and reliable training platform (or infrastructure) that will be easy to maintain and update.

## Description of Management Processes

MCI WorldCom had the technological core and infrastructure to support the new training model, but people resources, time factors, and budgetary constraints provided major challenges to overcome in implementing the new strategy.

*Resource Strengths*

- Experienced and talented team of trainers, content experts, instructional designers, and programmers
- One of the most reliable and widely deployed intranets in the world

- Established intranet training Web site and delivery medium
- Solid basis for technology infrastructure and support
- New and impressive content that fits core audience needs
- Existing training resources that may meet some audience needs

*Resource Constraints*

- Extremely limited budget for training
- Geographically dispersed target audience
- Limited development time and staff

## MWU Training Strategy

MWU set out to achieve these objectives with a four-phase training strategy that gave us a structure to accomplish the following goals:

- Communicate MWU's shared vision for training and gather support from key players.
- Create a training infrastructure (or platform) that was scalable, portable, and redundant.
- Build training and use existing resources to meet the needs of our audience.
- Find effective delivery methods for our training.
- Promote the program and motivate students to participate.

Figure 5.1 illustrates this strategy.

### FIGURE 5.1. MWU TRAINING STATEGY.

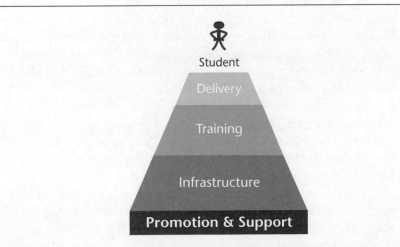

## Tactic 1: Promotion and Support

The foundation for ensuring MWU's success was promotion and support. The MWU management team knew that if the effort were to succeed, it would be necessary to get executives excited about the vision for training before, during, and after the rollout of the training program.

*Step 1: Win Initial Support.* Due to MCI WorldCom's existing resource strengths and constraints, getting execs excited about distance learning as an alternative to classroom training actually proved to be relatively simple. This was, in large part, thanks to the fact that we had an exceptionally powerful intranet and training Web site already in place. But it can also be attributed to the excitement and momentum that prevailed at the time of the merger, when MCI WorldCom executives were keen to use state-of-the-art techniques to streamline training processes and accomplish business goals.

*Step 2: Involve Segments in the Process.* After gaining the initial buy-in of key executives, we worked to build relationships with the *segments,* that is, the influential leaders in the sales, service, and technical channels that made up our target audience. Working with segment leaders helped us ensure that our program would include all the elements that students needed to accomplish their objectives, and also gave those leaders some stake in the game so that they would help us make sure that students knew about it. It's a simple truth; you can have the best training in the world, but it won't get anywhere if your audience doesn't know that it exists or how it will help them do their jobs.

To illustrate the importance of segment support, let's revisit Tomas the Sales Rep. As you recall, Tomas had been successfully selling voice products to midsize WorldCom customers for over a year. The merger will add data products to his offerings, which gives him enormous opportunities to increase his sales base. The sales segment leaders knew that product training would be a critical element to get reps like Tomas ready to sell data, and worked with us to create the MWU Data Certification program. Data Certification was a collection of Web-based training courses that certain job levels were required to complete before they were allowed to sell MCI WorldCom's new data products. Sales managers then tracked the progress via the MWU Web site to ensure that individual reps were certified before selling MCI WorldCom's products.

The dual motivators of direction from segment leaders and compensatory need combined to ensure that MWU's Data Certification program was a huge success.

*Step 3: Promote Using Existing Resources.* The final piece to Tactic 1 was promotion. Through alliances with Marketing Communications and Product Marketing, MWU was able to make sure that training was a vital piece of the merger rollout. It was included in all print and Web materials, and it had a significant role in train-the-facilitator sessions preparing the professionals in the field who would be supporting our key audience. We were able to directly communicate with the people who influence our end users, and this made all the difference in getting students to the Web to make this rollout a success.

## Tactic 2: The Platform

Now let's return to the predevelopment phase. Once we had the support of MCI WorldCom executives, we had to define our training vision. It began with something that any small group assigned a huge project will be able to relate to: *maximizing technology resources*. Since we didn't have the resources (or the budget) to train the entire sales, service, and technical force in face-to-face sessions, we had to find ways to integrate technology-based solutions to optimize training design, development, and delivery.

Luckily, the MWU Training Technologies Team had been working since August 1997 to prepare the platform, infrastructure, and staff to meet just such a challenge. Our goal was to create a platform that was scalable, portable, redundant, and based on open systems and standards. The following paragraphs will expand on these characteristics and what they meant to MCI WorldCom University.

*Scalability.* Scalability is crucial to any strategy as it applies to the technology infrastructure. For MWU, *scalability* meant that our platform had to be flexible enough to facilitate training for a large and growing audience. We wound up with a software infrastructure that can support an audience of a hundred students— or a hundred thousand students. As our audience grows, we will simply upgrade hardware and bandwidth to support larger numbers of visitors.

*Access and Portability.* MCI WorldCom's network capabilities and hardware and software standardization policies have had an important role in our success. For example, because MCI WorldCom policy dictates the access package (currently Internet Explorer 4.0), we know that 100 percent of our audience will access our training using the same browser. Therefore, we were able to build and test the Web site and training knowing exactly how it would work for every student that visited the site. Also, our needs analysis research found that in some locations, certain job levels of students would share computers (like Nancy the New

Hire). We had students like Nancy in mind when we built the system, adding features that allow access to be driven by each student's personal profile, or user name and password. This lets students complete coursework from any computer, anywhere in the world, as long as they can reach the corporate intranet.

The need to standardize led to one of the great battles between the systems teams of the two legacy companies. The WorldCom organization had built its Web-based applications and tools to be viewed with the Netscape browser, while MCI had built all applications—including the training Web site—for Internet Explorer. Both companies had made a perfectly reasonable decision to specialize; corporate applications are designed for an internal audience and are delivered behind a firewall. That means that the company traditionally dictates how the audience accesses applications, and using a standard browser simplifies development and minimizes duplicate development. Obviously, the outcome of this issue was of great import to both teams.

Luckily for us (as legacy-MCI staffers), the MCI WorldCom IT group authorized the IE browser that we were already prepared to support. If it had gone the other way (or if the new IT group had decided to support both browsers), we would have had to design our new applications to meet the needs of the new access method, or methods. We could have coped with either decision, but the chosen course simplified our workload a great deal.

*Redundancy.*  We knew that a major advantage of Web-based training was continuous access, or training that is available 24 hours a day, 365 days a year. It was very important to guarantee access to training without downtime. By working with best-of-breed hardware vendors, we were able to purchase the right equipment to meet this challenge and succeed.

*Open System and Open Standard.*  Whether you're in business or academia, you've doubtless been approached by many vendors selling the "latest and greatest" software or training systems—systems that they claim will be the answer to all of your training needs. MWU's situation was no different, and many vendors have visited us over the years we've been building and sustaining our distance learning platform. Unfortunately, many of these vendors were selling applications that looked great but were built with proprietary tools or on proprietary hardware. For us, *proprietary* means that the system is difficult to maintain, update, and modify. From a business perspective, proprietary systems are very costly for two reasons: dependence on the vendor to customize the application, and dependence on the few employees who hold the very specific skill set needed to maintain it. In other words, it is nearly impossible to find the permanent or contract help necessary to customize and maintain the system over time.

By using open system and open standard hardware and software not tied to a vendor, MWU is able to easily find the talent and tools to build, configure, and customize training applications to meet changing business needs. Establishing a platform that was scalable, portable, redundant, and based on open systems and standards gave us the building blocks for everything that would follow. This infrastructure provided the flexibility and power to support just about any method of delivery that would meet our student needs.

## Tactic 3: Training

The merger of two very prominent companies determined our content, which had to be tailored to the specific needs of our complex audience. It had to be dramatic enough to capture their attention, and it had to be created very, very quickly. So we began planning even before the proverbial ink was dry on the contract.

*Step 1: Determine Training Specifications.* Both companies already had strong learning emphasis, and training was an integral part of the overall strategy. Our task was to support this strategy by determining a training solution that could reach a large audience, minimize the need to budget for travel or training facilities costs, and be developed in less than ten weeks from start to finish. The instructional design process also had to include specifications for

- Full 24x7 availability
- Access to educational media and technology not dependent on location or budget
- Ease of use, user friendliness, and growth potential of the interfaces
- Promotion of better understanding of communications standards and technologies
- Cost-effective training

We quickly began mapping out our strategy to best balance the resources available and the needs of the student audience. Except in limited high-priority and high-profile areas, traditional classroom learning wasn't an option and didn't meet the specifications of the program.

*Step 2: Evaluate Training Options.* The technology-based training solutions at our disposal included high-quality streaming video (live and on-demand), live multicasting, interactive classrooms, self-contained Web-based training modules, animation, audio, and interactive performance analysis tools. There were also a variety of existing courses and third-party vendor applications that seemed likely to be useful. It was up to MWU to determine which of these existing resources would meet the needs of the audience.

We had to keep in mind that the majority of our students would be totally new to distance learning, and they would *all* be totally new to MCI WorldCom's portfolio of composite products. One of our first ideas was to launch state-of-the-art live multimedia sessions via our media server to transmit training simultaneously to students in all areas of the country via the intranet. We had been building this capability for some time, and it seemed like a wonderful way to personalize the sessions and cut down on development time. Unfortunately, it quickly became clear that too large a percentage of our audience accessed the intranet via 28.8 Kbps dial-up modems that would make the process painfully slow. So our whiz-bang solution wasn't an option.

The restrictions of dial-up access also eliminated the possibility of store-and-forward video that, like live streaming, would have offered the added benefit of personally introducing the field staff to their new product managers and subject matter experts by way of their monitor screens.

***Step 3: Develop New Applications.*** It seemed the best solution would be straight Web-based training using HTML authoring and dynamic graphic design. Applying principles of instructional design and development, we developed this overview as an example of typical product training course delivered via the Internet or corporate intranet:

| | |
|---|---|
| *Course Home* | The course home page should include an introduction and links to essential course features including course objectives, course outline, and tips for taking Web-based training. |
| *Modules and Sections* | Course content is split into modules and sections of modules that include objectives and mastery quizzes to reinforce content retention and prepare the student for the final exam. |
| *Glossary* | Each course includes a terms glossary with detailed definitions for difficult terms and phrases. |
| *Summary* | Complex course content is summarized to ensure that the critical points are reinforced before the student attempts the final exam. |
| *Final Exam* | Randomized testing is derived from a larger pool of questions in our database. The final exam gives immediate feedback on content retention through scoring and |

remediation with specific directions on needed review based on incorrect answers.

*Optional Multimedia*     Multimedia such as audio and video are used for more advanced topics to allow subject matter experts to explain complicated theories and strategies in detail.

***Step 4: Maximize Existing Resources.*** In addition to training on new products, our training needs analysis also illuminated a number of other requirements. For these, MWU took a hard look at its existing resources to determine what might fit the bill.

• *Basic Training.* MCI had already been supporting a third-party Web-based training application that was designed in 1997 to train sales reps whose customers were small and medium-sized businesses. After an exhaustive review and update by a joint team of legacy-WorldCom and legacy-MCI trainers, this application was enhanced to apply to a general audience and meet basic training needs for telephony, data, and Internet knowledge. This basic training was an ideal solution for meeting the needs of Nancy the New Hire and helping Tomas the Sales Rep to learn the basics of data to expand his customer base.

• *Generic Industry Training.* The MCI training group also had a store of third-party video training on complex communications concepts such as communications protocols and Internetworking. Careful review showed that these videos would be of great service to more advanced reps, but the process of checking out, shipping, viewing, and returning videos was cumbersome and expensive. We had Taylor the Tech in mind when converting these videos to streaming media for supplementary online training.

• *Systems Training.* The final distance learning component that passed review was a computer-based training application designed to teach skills and hands-on use of many of the legacy-MCI systems that would continue to be used after the merger. Suzy the Sales Support Rep is a perfect example of this group of employees, who were able to master the tools available to support Order Entry, Implementation, and Billing Support in a very short time thanks to these online systems modules.

The combination of new product training with enhancements of existing courses created a complete solution that was ready to go. Next, we simply had to determine how to give students access to the program.

## Tactic 4: Effective Delivery

The legacy-MCI organization already had a Web site that was chosen to serve as training's launch pad for basic Web-based training and traditional leader-led course listings and descriptions. So as we merged with our WorldCom counterparts and doubled our audience, we looked to develop a delivery method that would allow all segments of the target population to quickly and easily find the information they needed. It also had to provide a means of tracking our progress so we could learn from our successes and failures.

*Step 1: Analyze Access and Use.* So once again we were back to determining how to maximize our meager resources by making technology work for us—the most efficient way to sustain our new distance learning program. We began by asking the following questions:

- What types of student interactions are captured regularly in the database?
- What sorts of student interactions can be mined from other databases?
- What functionality depends on the database for success?
- How will the solution integrate this information?
- How can we use tracked information to promote and support other areas of the curriculum?

*Step 2: Capture Data.* Our first tactic was to capture data from students when they visited the Web site. In fact, this was the cornerstone of our new Web interface, and was based on what we called the *Student Profile*. Before first-time visitors could enter the site, they were required to complete a brief profile that captured all the basic user information (name, SSN, segment, and so on). Once we have this information, we can then identify specific students every time they visit the site and guide them to a career path specifically designed for their job profile. And because MWU training tracks online course completions by the students as they successfully complete the final exam, the database holds complete records of every student's progress.

*Step 3: Mine Data from Other Sources.* In addition to the training information that we could collect directly from students, we set out to incorporate additional records from other areas of the company that, when combined with MWU's data, would offer a more complete picture of each student's progress. In technology circles, this tactic is known as *data mining*, and incorporates a number of push/pull strategies for collecting records from other databases.

We quickly worked to forge alliances with the other organizations that housed student data, such as the legacy-MCI human resources and corporate training registration system. We also worked to collect training records and information from the legacy-WorldCom organization, but discovered that no established data warehousing system was in place to provide us with a history of legacy-WorldCom student training. We formed alliances to show a full transcript as well as a hierarchy of employees for reporting purposes.

The data gathered from these alliances helped us provide more than just a record of each student's Web-based training progress. The Web site could now house a complete history of MWU training that isn't tracked using randomized testing (such as classroom training or interactive distance learning sessions delivered via NetMeeting and Farsite). It also provided complete records of training that originated from other groups, such as Human Resources.

We wanted to take our reporting to the next level by incorporating corporate revenue, compensation, and reporting systems—but that would have to wait until the new company structure was more fully integrated in the months following the merger.

***Step 4: Implement a Data-Driven Web Interface.*** Once we knew what types of data would be collected via our data capturing and data mining tactics, we set out to determine how to best use that information to enhance the student learning experience. First, we determined what we wanted to accomplish with the site's prime real estate: the home page. We realized that we needed to accomplish the following minimum tasks:

- Give students a clear career path.
- Recommend and promote training based on job segment.
- Promote a feeling of progress and accomplishment.
- Inform students of new and enhanced courses and programs.
- Provide a quick and easy way for students to locate the information they need.

Based on these objectives, the home page was designed to include data-driven records that were pushed to the student on each visit. These included a tally of the last five courses completed and corresponding scores, a personalized career path of courses determined by job segment that rotated as progress was made in the curriculum, and a link to each student's personal transcript. The home page also incorporated dynamic convenience features such as a course search activated by keyword and a running marquee for headlines and news that links directly to the latest MWU courses, services, and offerings.

## Outcomes Attained, Successes, Failures, and Words of Advice

The most important bit of advice that we can share is to build your infrastructure. Our strategy to access the power of the corporate intranet to accomplish our business goals was within our grasp precisely because of this structure; a structure that we had built up during the year prior to merger. Our goals included (and still include):

- Communicating and garnering support for our shared vision of training
- Driving down costs through efficiency
- Sharing core data across the enterprise
- Exploiting emerging technologies—again, using them only as a tool to meet field needs
- Integrating functionality, processes, and systems to create a total learning experience
- Developing applications that operate across functions instead of reinventing the wheel

Your platform must be scalable enough to grow into new technologies, and be based on open systems and open standards. It must be portable, and the architecture should be able to run from multiple locations all over the world. And the most obvious but most often overlooked requirement: redundancy, redundancy, and redundancy—that's the only way you'll ever get close to true 24x7 availability with zero downtime. If you follow these tips, you will be able to grow your program as needed, hire from a deeper pool of technical talent, and focus your efforts on how to customize applications for your own changing business needs.

CHAPTER SIX

# ATTRACTING, TRAINING, AND RETAINING INSTRUCTORS FOR DISTANCE LEARNING AT THE U.S. GENERAL ACCOUNTING OFFICE

Jo L. Longnecker

This chapter discusses the organizational support for distance training and education from a strategic framework of resources, budget, technological infrastructure, staffing, policies, and rewards and recognition at the U.S. General Accounting Office (GAO). The collaboration of individuals within technology and training functions is essential to successful distance training efforts and is woven throughout the discussion. Beyond that, the chapter highlights the challenges and means of assisting instructors' transition to successfully deliver technology-mediated courses. A specific program example is provided to illustrate how the GAO attracted, trained, and retained instructors for a briefings course delivered through online and teletraining formats. The author was closely involved with many aspects of the distance training programs discussed here and draws primarily from her experiences for this chapter.

## A Mandate to Use Technology

With the increased need for trainers and facilitators using technology-mediated material, the U.S. General Accounting Office confronted the challenge and developed an effective approach to attract, train, and retain a cadre of technologically skilled trainers and facilitators. The agency faced limited training and travel funds and resolved to expand the use of existing and new technologies to address the organization's continuous demands for training and education. It was clear that a comprehensive program to train instructors to deliver technology-mediated training was needed to meet business objectives.

The videoconferencing (two-way audio and two-way compressed video) capability was introduced at the GAO in 1992 to link headquarters and regional office locations across the continental United States. Almost immediately, senior managers, technologists, and instructional designers with an interest in technology looked to expand the use of the technology within the organization consistent with the pace with the rest of the world. In 1995 GAO underwent a 25 percent reduction in budget and a parallel reduction in staff. These reductions reinforced the need to make the most efficient use of monetary and human resources possible. At that point, interest in technology escalated. In 1997, the GAO Strategic Plan set forth the operational goals the agency could reasonably expect to achieve over the ensuing two years. Top management identified an increase in the use of technology for business solutions as one of the four overall performance objectives for the agency (see Figure 6.1).

In emphasizing the use of technology, GAO cited the potential for maintaining productivity to offset the agency's reductions in staff. Among several technological improvements, videoconferencing was highlighted as an important resource linking headquarters to regional offices. In addition, the report indicated the need to increase the capabilities of the Local Area Network (LAN) and Wide Area Network for Internet and intranet usage, paving the way for online activities.

GAO administrators were highly motivated to increase the use of technology and expand the portfolio of training options available to meet agency objectives in providing high-quality, timely training to staff at headquarters or regional offices. An interest in these two motivating factors merged advantageously and,

## FIGURE 6.1. GAO'S 1997 ORGANIZATIONAL GOALS.

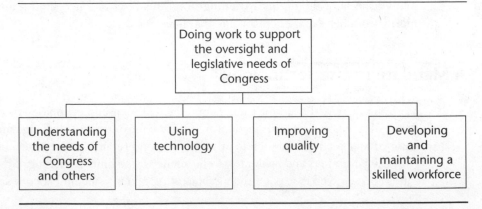

as outlined in this discussion, GAO's distance learning evolved both intentionally and unintentionally toward establishing the agency as a leading governmental provider in technology-mediated learning.

## Translating Technology to Distance Learning

Although distance learning was not the agency's original objective for using the existing videoconferencing equipment, videoconferencing steadily gained importance as an effective means of providing training and meeting business objectives. The Training Institute (GAO's performance and learning organization) determined that distance learning was an opportune use of existing technologies for educational purposes.

The Office of Information Management and Communication (OIMC) provided technical expertise and resources for the agency. OIMC both purchased and maintained the hardware and software for the agency's videoconferencing and telecommunications efforts. With occasional upgrades to the system over time, OIMC (in partnership with the Training Institute) enhanced the videoconferencing capability and functionality to meet the technical demands of delivering live educational programs to linked remote locations. The Training Institute benefited from the increased technical capabilities and began working with OIMC to increase user capacity for educational purposes. The collaboration of several technically oriented professional staff members (IT, instructional designers, telecommunications technicians) was essential in supporting the design, development, and delivery of high-quality distance learning.

## Background

The GAO is the investigative arm of Congress. Charged with examining matters relating to the receipt and disbursement of public funds, GAO performs audits and evaluations of government programs and activities. The GAO was established by the Budget and Accounting Act of 1921 (31 U.S.C. 702) to independently audit government agencies. Over the years, Congress has expanded GAO's audit authority, adding new responsibilities and duties and strengthening GAO's ability to perform independently.

GAO is committed to developing and maintaining a skilled workforce that can function as an independent government auditing organization. Ongoing training and education for geographically dispersed staff continues to challenge the agency in new ways—during times of rapid change, and fewer resources—distance learning has indeed contributed to the organization's business objectives.

## The Role of GAO Auditors and Evaluators

The GAO evaluator (line staff) audits and evaluates the full spectrum of government programs and activities. The evaluator and audit staff are the prime resource for completing GAO's mission in providing unbiased information that supports Congress in carrying out its legislative responsibilities. These responsibilities require that staff have expertise in a variety of disciplines: accounting, law, public and business administration, economics, the social and physical sciences, and others. The GAO offers a wide range of products to communicate the results of its work—testimony, oral briefings, and written reports. Evaluators develop specialized experience and a detailed level of knowledge to conduct their work.

## Training and Education Requirements for Evaluators

Training and education are highly valued and supported within the organization. GAO requires evaluators to receive eighty hours of continuing professional education requirements over a two-year period as prescribed in the *Government Auditing Standards*. GAO's Training Institute is responsible for providing significant training and educational opportunities for all staff. In 1997, for example, the institute provided about 78 percent of the evaluator training in-house.

The Training Institute has a skilled team of instructional designers, computer specialists, and graphic artists. They design, develop, and deliver management and professional development curricula as well as technology-related courses using both traditional and innovative instructional methodologies and delivery formats.

## Who Teaches Distance Learning?

The technical experts selected from GAO's internal evaluator community possess the highest credibility to conduct the agency's professional development efforts. The principal instructors for distance learning and technology-mediated training have predominantly come from the evaluator ranks, often pairing with trainers from the Training Institute. The agency wishes to attract, train, and retain as skilled distance training instructors those individuals who are already prominent and effective in GAO classrooms, who have an interest and ability to work with technology-mediated systems, and who are willing to experiment with innovative educational deliveries.

## Organizational Support for Distance Learning

The GAO ensured its strategic commitment to distance learning through the allocation of technical and financial resources, technological infrastructure, staffing, policies, and awards and recognition (see Table 6.1).

**TABLE 6.1. STRATEGIC ORGANIZATIONAL SUPPORT FOR DISTANCE LEARNING AT GAO.**

| Staffing Resources | Technological Commitments* | Infrastructure | Contributors | Rewards and Policies | Recognition |
|---|---|---|---|---|---|
| *Technical Support* <br>• OIMC–Telecommunications <br>• Technicians <br>• OIMC and Training Institute staff | *Training Institute* <br>• Up to seven staff members on projects (rotating assignments) | *Equipment and Upgrades* <br>• Computers <br>• TV monitors <br>• Satellite links <br>• Phone lines (T-1 and ISDN) <br>• Videoconferencing system <br>• CD-ROM | *Videoconferencing User Group* <br>• Best Practices Subcommittee—lessons learned shared GAO-wide | • GAO Strategic Plan <br>• Agency Objectives: "Using Technology" | • Assistant Comptroller General Award for Videoconferencing and Teletraining (for OIMC and Training Institute) |
| *User Support* <br>• Training for Technicians <br>• Troubleshooting | *Telecommunication Branch* <br>• Up to one staff member and two contractors on projects (on call) | *Software* <br>• CBT <br>• Freelance <br>• PowerPoint <br>• CC:Mail <br>• LAN | *Teletraining Team* <br>• Instructional designers <br>• Subject matter experts <br>• Graphic designers <br>• Technician <br>• Administrative staff | Revised Job Management Processes <br><br>Rollout of Windows 95 and Office 97 | • Director's Award for Aggressive and Smart Use of Technology (for Training Institute) |
| *Training* <br>• Designing, developing, and delivering teletraining <br>• GAO Videoconferencing Technical Guide (1996) | *Computer Support* <br>• Up to three staff members on projects (intermittent) | | *Others in Training Institute* <br>• Instructional technologist <br>• Consultants <br>• Administrative staff | Aggressive and smart use of technology | • Comptroller General's Award for Job Processes Team |
| *Teletraining Guide* <br>• Video Teletraining: A Guide to Design, Development, and Use (1995) | *Evaluators and Line Support* <br>• Up to three staff members on projects (intermittent; a rotating assignment) | | • Instructors <br>• Editors | Consider distance learning strategies in all instructional designs | • Comptroller General's Award for Revised Job Processes |
| | *Traditional budget figures not available. | | *Evaluators:* <br>• Instructors <br>• Subject matter experts | | • Promotions |

# Development of Technological Infrastructure

The agency is committed to increase the use of technology to support its educational efforts. This philosophy is apparent in GAO's learning and performance organization, which emphasizes learning with the actual technology that staff members use in audit and evaluation work. Integrated in the business processes are software applications, the network and e-mail, Internet, intranet, and compressed video. Also linked is the reliance on technology hardware such as the videoconferencing system, satellite links, ISDN lines, T1 lines, CD-ROM, and so on. When the principal hardware and software were installed for videoconferencing at headquarters and remote locations, distance learning applications were not yet implemented. Swiftly, OIMC added auxiliary TV monitors, cameras, special lighting, and microphones to improve the system's capability—and as a by-product improved the quality of instructional delivery. The Telecommunications Branch maintained the equipment and upgraded the technological interfaces resulting in faster, clearer videoconference and teletraining transmission. This branch provided the technical support to launch the new technology-based training. The Training Institute invested in developing the technological skills and experience of its staff to expand their training repertoire. Moreover, OIMC cooperated with the Institute to deliver technology-mediated training through these various means.

Currently enhanced services for learners include access to GAO's intranet for internal training information, quarterly schedules, registration, prerequisites, dates, duration, and the number of continuing professional education opportunities available.

# Initial Efforts in Distance Learning

The agency used communication links to launch educational programs via satellite link for instructional television (ITV). Live and videotaped ITV courses were synchronously delivered to multiple locations at headquarters via satellite, a service provided through the University of Maryland's School of Engineering. ITV has a very extensive curriculum to draw from, and GAO's program administrator had to carefully investigate the quality and efficacy of the various programs and presenters. Quarterly publications to which GAO subscribed identified a broad range of professional and technical courses for educational broadcasts. Available programs featured highly recognized authors from well-known organizations. At the average cost of approximately $16.29 per participant (per class), ITV was a very affordable training option.

ITV, however, did not offer specific courses that dealt with the evaluator community's professional challenges in mission-critical areas such as data collection, problem analysis, and framing of recommendations. GAO had an extensive in-house curriculum to address these specific training needs. The videoconferencing system was initially the logical technology of choice for limited offerings of technology-mediated learning targeted for the evaluator.

As mentioned earlier, GAO evaluators and staff administrators became familiar with the videoconferencing system and its capabilities, and usage increased rapidly for nontraining activities within the first couple of years. Educational activities on the videoconferencing system, however, evolved more slowly as the Training Institute and OIMC learned to work more effectively with both the new technology and the human factors involved in training and education efforts. Assistance from professional instructional designers and developers for successful distance learning via videoconferencing was imperative. At the time, the dedicated staff of instructional designers had yet to gain significant knowledge, skill, and experience to develop distance learning. Notwithstanding this situation, the educational resources manager in the Training Institute was extremely involved in distance learning on a national level, and she began to plant seeds of interest that eventually led to many of the successful endeavors discussed later in this chapter.

Gradually, the interest in innovative learning methodologies excited the curiosity of a small cadre of instructional designers and technical and nontechnical staff. They were eager to meet the training and educational needs of the agency's geographically dispersed population. They were challenged to design, develop, and deliver teletraining (two-way audio, two-way compressed video) to address those needs. The Training Institute piloted and delivered much-needed professional development courses for evaluators in this manner, among them several writing skills courses, a statistics course, a compliance auditing course, a writing testimony course, and evidence, fraud awareness, and presentation skills courses.

## 1994–1999 Distance Learning Efforts

GAO has experienced both successes and setbacks in its distance learning efforts over the past five years. The agency's initial efforts maximized the use of the videoconferencing system for teletraining point-to-point or multipoint sessions (involving several sites simultaneously). Less extensively, the agency also used the ITV capability for education and training. Additional early efforts included distributed learning and computer-based training. Online learning using e-mail and a document-sharing capability that relied on instructor-led interaction were launched in 1997 and 1998. Both online efforts were delivered in an asynchronous, sequential time frame, and conducted with local or geographically dispersed participants. More recently, GAO has offered self-paced computer-based training on the desktop through CD-ROM. Technological capabilities have increased every year. In 1998, for example, the agency converted to Windows 95 and Office 97 and provided self-paced computer-based training and instructional television (ITV) programs to meet over twelve thousand completed training events (many individuals completed more than one class). These various distance training strategies increased the learning opportunities, and training was more learner-focused (rather than instructor-focused) and more readily accessible than in the past.

## Educating the Instructors

Early in GAO's distance learning efforts, a pilot delivery of a statistics course using the videoconferencing system was not fully successful in meeting learner needs. A contributing factor was the instructor's lack of familiarity with specific techniques required in this new medium. He was a wonderful instructor, one who made statistics come alive—but he was also a "walker" and very animated, which doesn't work in less than real-time video. In other words, relying on techniques used in a traditional classroom setting was not effective. Unequivocal evaluation feedback following the class indicated that participants were frustrated with his inability to work within the system. This input resulted in a more systematic approach to the design and delivery of teletraining efforts through the Training Institute. Instructional designers and trainers were asked to build on their solid instructional systems design (ISD) backgrounds and incorporate the elements of successful distance learning in future educational endeavors.

The agency sponsored attendance at distance learning conferences and training courses on a limited basis for key instructional designers and technical staff supporting the effort. Expert practitioners were brought in-house to deliver workshops and presentations on successful distance learning techniques used in education, industry, and government. Instructional designers, instructors, and facilitators from across the organization attended these sessions (some of which were delivered over the videoconferencing system, replicating actual teletraining sessions). The director of the Training Institute, Anne Kalvin Klein, videotaped a strong message preceding the training emphasizing the importance of this innovative use of technology in meeting the agency's training and educational needs. In addition, the GAO sponsored the Training Institute's publication of *Video Teletraining: A Guide to Design, Development, and Use* (1995), highlighting techniques and strategies to help course designers, course managers, instructors, and others adapt to the requirements of teletraining. See http://www.gao.gov/special.pubs/publist.htm for an online copy of this publication.

## Technical Resources

GAO supported the training of selected staff in work units and regional offices to operate and track the videoconferencing sessions across the country. OIMC staff wrote and distributed *GAO's Video Conferencing Technical Guide* (1996) with instructions to operate the equipment. The technical guide identified common technical problems and incorporated troubleshooting solutions to resolve minor audio and video glitches. OIMC also provided knowledgeable on-call technicians to handle unexpected technical difficulties. This resource proved invaluable during teletraining sessions and minimized the downtime experienced during technical difficulties.

***Integration of Technical and Human Resources.*** GAO also began a Video Conference (VTC) User Group Best Practices Subcommittee, representing users from all parts of the agency including regional offices. This group identified and promoted the most effective uses of videoconferencing, including teletraining. The group recognized numerous opportunities to promote best practices across the organization by working with two different target groups: current VTC users who would benefit from improved techniques, and current non-users whose sense of intimidation needed to be eased. The group also agreed not only to show people how to do things (technologically) but also to help them see what (objectively) videoconferencing could accomplish for them. Moreover, they collected and distributed relevant articles, shared successes, and worked through challenges as the functionality of the hardware and software increased in sophistication and complexity. Due to this group's efforts, best practices were incorporated in numerous applications across the organization, not least of which was teletraining. This group's efforts contributed greatly to the demystifying of technology-mediated learning. Many of the early students in teletraining classes were already seasoned videoconference users.

***Hiring the Right People.*** The Training Institute hired an expert instructional technologist with extensive knowledge and experience in distance learning efforts. The manager of educational resources was tasked to develop educational opportunities using alternative delivery formats for all employees. Under her direction GAO implemented a multimedia learning center, multimedia distributed training, instructional television, computer-based training, and teletraining. In later years, as interest and expertise in technology increased among the staff, she guided the in-house development of online learning by coaching instructional designers in the development, implementation, and evaluation of writing and presentation skills courses.

The task of developing distance learning at GAO was enormously daunting given the very limited budget and staffing devoted to its implementation. In the early 1990s distance learning efforts were understood and supported by a few pioneers. But challenge and opportunity were no strangers, and by the mid-1990s GAO's distance learning efforts received national attention through publications and presentations by Training Institute managers and staff at several national and international distance learning and technology conferences. GAO's Learning Center was cited for excellence in the federal government by the Office of Personnel Management.

***Establishing the Teletraining Team.*** The Training Institute director recognized that few if any of the instructional designers had a background or consuming interest in distance learning. When the opportunity to work with this new instructional format was advertised, a limited number volunteered for the assignment. The director needed instructional designers with strong ISD skills and selected a core team to promote the design, development, implementation, and evaluation of teletraining. The original team of five consisted of an assistant director, an instructional designer with experience in video production, two administrative staffers to provide technical and production assistance with course delivery, and one staff member to provide administrative support and technical backup for the team. The team's leader came with extensive experience in public access television and some knowledge of distance learning programs. It's fair to say that technology-mediated learning was fairly new to all members of the team. Other members of the Training Institute contributed greatly to various components of the teletraining implementation by providing expertise in graphics design, instructional technologies, subject matter expertise, movement, and sound. These attributes contributed to the broader technology-mediated training developed later.

Specialized technical training was provided to the technical and production assistants to understand and operate all aspects of the videoconferencing system. The team also relied on technical staff, including operations and production personnel and systems engineers.

## Using Technology: Impact and Change

Teletraining is an interactive medium for broadcasting live instructors or guest speakers to off-site locations with a significant reduction in travel costs for trainers or participants. The cost of conducting point-to-point teletraining (at a rate of

$30 per hour) is nominal compared with instructor or participant travel costs. The cost of multipoint teletraining is still reasonably inexpensive at a starting rate of $60 per hour or more depending on the number of additional sites participating. In 1998 the Training Institute continued to deliver several courses through tele-training (typically in point-to-point sessions):

- Awareness of Fraud and Wrongdoing
- Better Briefings (a presentation skills course)
- Writing Testimony (broadcasting management briefings)

In preceding years, a variety of other courses were delivered in this format. In addition, videotaped programs of training courses and conferences were offered at headquarters. For example, Congressional Relations Update was delivered as a single live video teletraining presentation to headquarters staff and was followed by multiple video-based classes. Approximately eight hundred headquarters and regional office staff members viewed these classes at a cost of about $1.40 per participant. The 1998 *Annual Training and Education Report* explains that it would have cost more than $50 per participant if all presentations had been live; thus, GAO realized savings of more than $38,000.

### TABLE 6.2. COMPARISON OF DISTANCE TRAINING COSTS VERSUS TRADITIONAL CLASSROOM TRAINING.

| *Distance Training* | | | *Traditional Training* | | |
|---|---|---|---|---|---|
| Distance Training Source | Average Cost per Participant* | Class Duration | Classroom Presenter | Average Cost per Participant* | Class Duration |
| ITV | $16.29 | 1–4 hours | Executive panel (3) | $50 | 2 hours |
| Teletraining | $30.00 | 6 hours | Senior manager (1) | $40 | 8 hours |
| Online | $10.00 | 6 hours | Midcareer instructors (2) | $55 | 8 hours |
| Self-Paced CBT | $12.21 | 6 hours | Junior instructor (1) | $20 | 8 hours |
| Videotape | $ 1.40 | 2 hours | | | |

*Actual delivery costs (does not include course development costs)

## Goals Achieved and Consequent Cost Benefits

In 1998 the mandate to use technology was the impetus for expanding GAO's delivery of high-quality training through economical means by using videoconferencing, teletraining, videotaped programs, instructional television, CD-ROM, computer-based training, and online learning. The increased cost-efficiency of training continues to be a vital guiding principle in achieving the Training Institute's business objectives. GAO's *Annual Training and Education Report* (1998) indicates that the Training Institute undertook several initiatives to train staff in a cost-effective manner:

• Purchasing commercial off-the-shelf computer-based training
• Increasing the use of teletraining and video technology
• Providing additional self-paced training courses
• Training additional GAO instructors to provide on-site instruction

By using commercial off-the-shelf computer-based training to train GAO staff, the Training Institute achieved the savings it had estimated in 1997. The report estimates that staff received training at a greatly reduced cost—about $150,000 rather than the estimated $1 million that the same training would have cost if it had been delivered in the classroom. The report goes on to say that using computer-based training allowed GAO staff to tailor the learning to their needs, at the appropriate time, and from the convenient location of their own desktops. This shift toward learner-focused training offered each participant increased control and autonomy in the learning process.

Beginning in October and ending in December 1998, the agency successfully distributed new personal computer systems and rolled out Microsoft Windows 95 and Office 97 software to virtually all staff members. The development and support of alternative training delivery enormously increased the agency's ability to train staff during the rapid transition to new hardware and software. The success of the effort was achieved through the collaboration and partnership of GAO management, the Office of Information Management and Communications, the Training Institute, the divisions, and the regional and staff offices.

## Awards and Recognition

By 1997, the combined efforts of the Office of Information Management and Communications and the Training Institute were measurable and worthy of organizational recognition. They developed the TI-OIMC Award, *To Celebrate the Partnership*. Select members of both organizations received joint recognition for their contributions in support of video teletraining and videoconferencing projects. Other recognition at higher levels of the agency were awarded teams and individuals who incorporated distance learning into their program implementation and organizational change efforts.

### Rewarding Aggressive and Smart Use of Technology

That same year, the Training Institute defined for itself the agency priority to use technology by prescribing the "aggressive and smart use of technology" in delivering learning products and services. A technology team was appointed by the director to articulate specific objectives for individual staff members in the Training Institute and to include these criteria in performance measures. These performance measures led to a much greater emphasis on the increased development of technology-mediated training. That year, five staff members received awards for their "aggressive and smart use of technology" by developing various innovative technology-mediated approaches to the agency's plethora of training and development activities. Although distance learning was not the preferred mode of training for the agency (some learners were averse to technology), positive reinforcement at the policy level resulted in the advancement of instructional designers who implemented the program. By 1998, an array of technological delivery strategies were taking hold in nearly every corner of the curriculum and this was strongly encouraged and reinforced through rewards, recognition, and promotions.

## Addressing the Obstacles

Embedded in GAO's culture is an almost instinctive response to look at opportunities to improve and capitalize on less successful efforts. What the agency has learned through many trials and tribulations may one day enrich the folklore of distance learning efforts. In the following pages we will discuss some of the obstacles, challenges, successes, and failures that enhance the GAO story and make it real.

## Organizational Challenges

The distance training effort at GAO developed during fiscally challenging times. Federal cutbacks resulted in agency downsizing, organizational restructuring, and reduced budgets and staffing. Nevertheless, the interest and motivation to launch distance learning persisted and succeeded. In some ways, distance training was needed then more than ever—it opened the doors to a world of technical, managerial, and professional development that had been unknown and untapped. The successful launch of distance training relied on the innovation and collaboration of several staff members to resolve the dilemma of limited resources (talent and dollars), and prevail over the natural organizational resistance to use new and unfamiliar technologies (including some resistance from the Training Institute itself).

***Strategy to Address Resistance.*** The team mapped out a strategy to market their services and promote the feasibility of distance training at GAO. The team first met with program managers in the Training Institute, and subsequently with the instructional designers from each branch to market their services and demonstrate some of the techniques used in teletraining. They also met with human resource managers and training coordinators across agency divisions and from regional offices to encourage registration in distance training programs. They developed a briefing and marketing information packet that explained the characteristics of an online seminar, described what participants are expected to do, and listed the online learning opportunities available. Most meetings were held in a teletraining session to illustrate the technology and its capabilities. The team inserted themselves into the project plan for all instructional design efforts and provided consultation where needed. This effort met with mixed success.

The Training Institute's director articulated her support for distance learning and clarified the importance of taking advantage of technology-mediated learning methodologies wherever possible. In her "State of the Institute" address of 1997, she emphasized the importance of using technology in realizing the Institute's mission. One solution was to increase the design, development, and delivery of technology-mediated learning as a means of meeting the enormous training demands.

***Instructor Resistance.*** The distance learning approach surfaced several obstacles that had to be overcome to attract instructors to deliver training in this new format. Instructors opposed to distance learning raised the following objections and difficulties:

- Less reinforcement value of online discussions compared to face-to-face interaction
- Lack of familiarity with advanced features of the technologies
- Need to develop instructor presentation skills using the technology
- Increased time commitment
- Need for incentives to reward line instructor's time toward training deliveries
- Skepticism about the new approach (within a traditional corporate culture)
- Fear of failure

Trainers (line evaluators, contractors, and institute staff) perceived their classroom days were over. They had relished the role of "sage on the stage" and were reluctant to relinquish that gratifying identity. With technology perceived as the enemy of human interaction and spontaneity, many felt the joys of interacting with peers and colleagues would rapidly decline in this new medium—reminiscent of the "high tech, low touch" theory. They struggled to envision the possibilities of building positive educational relationships online or through videoconferencing.

## Dealing with Instructor Concerns

To launch their services within the Training Institute, the Teletraining Team had to consider and address the resistance to change from instructional designers, trainers, and facilitators to learning experiences that depart from traditional stand-up classroom training. The task of overcoming the psychological and technological fears of trainers was addressed in a variety of ways. The institute's instructional designers and course managers developed sophisticated train-the-trainer sessions for instructors and facilitators with hands-on experience. These sessions included a number of valuable features:

- Actual online interaction replicating the online session
- Practice sessions using the videoconferencing system or other technologies
- Samples of evaluation feedback from online learning participants
- Instructor Supplement for conducting distance learning (specific to course)
- Videotaped teletraining sessions to experience and learn from
- Template to track online interaction and participation by activities (see Exhibit 6.1)

### EXHIBIT 6.1. BETTER BRIEFINGS ONLINE
### INSTRUCTOR-PARTICIPANT TRACKING SHEET.

| Daily Activities | | Participant 1 | | Participant 2 | |
|---|---|---|---|---|---|
| | | Review | Comment | Review | Comment |
| Part 1 | Introduction Workshop Goals Discussion Other | | | | |

The instructor should interact with all participants in Part 1 by responding to their intros and their workshop goals, and respond to questions they might have. Encourage class participants to provide feedback to one another online. Ask to hear from someone if they haven't been active.

| Daily Activities | | Participant 1 | | Participant 2 | |
|---|---|---|---|---|---|
| Part 2 | Discussion Purpose Goals Objectives Discussion Other | | | | |
| Part 3 | Organization Structure Draft Other | | | | |
| *Evaluations* | | | | | |

*Note:* Instructors should use this form as a self-check that they have read or commented on each participant's work and have received an evaluation from all participants.

## Capitalizing on Lessons Learned

It is useful to discuss real examples to gain a better understanding of GAO's distance learning efforts. The Better Briefings course was converted from a traditional classroom delivery to a technology-mediated delivery in 1998. The revised course was designed and delivered in two stages to increase the potential for success. In the first stage, the training was delivered via e-mail over a ten-day period, incorporating instructor-led discussion and participant interaction with manageable assignments building on the previous day's content. The design team benefited from the "lessons learned" in previous less successful online courses. As a result of those

**EXHIBIT 6.1.** (*continued*)

| Participant 3 | | Participant 4 | | Participant 5 | |
|---|---|---|---|---|---|
| Review | Comment | Review | Comment | Review | Comment |
| | | | | | |
| | | | | | |
| | | | | | |
| | | | | | |

efforts, they pre-tested the implementation (from various perspectives—evaluating content flow, transitions, style, and language), reviewed the technical instructions with experienced instructors, developed accurate and realistic time frames for learning segments, and created a participant tracking template before pilot testing the first session. The initial pilot tests were very successful because this effort

- Relied on instructors who were skilled with the technology and learning format
- Tested the learner-instructor interaction with prototypical participants and instructors with varying degrees of technical skills
- Maintained a low participant/instructor ratio—eight to one (or less)
- Used a technology that was widely familiar to all participants and instructors

- Matched the delivery method to the way participants work on actual assignments
- Acknowledged the innovation and experimentation with candor to all involved
- Included humor and a friendly conversational manner within the instructional materials and online discussions

## Observations and Feedback from Learners

The online format required a friendly, almost chatty, casual manner to encourage learner participation and interaction. This style was observed in all the online learning courses. Instructors were immediately attracted to the relaxed, conversational approach of online discussions. Participants were often more candid using this medium than in the normal classroom, where participation for some might be quite minimal. Extraverts and introverts participated on a more even playing field, in that the "air time" was equally available to all. In this manner, the learner-focused model relied heavily on the wisdom and experience of the participants to jointly instruct and participate. Instructors reported receiving numerous follow-up e-mail messages after the completion of the course, thanking them for the personalized feedback and for introducing them to the new learning experience. Even those participants whose technical skills were weak said they would attend future distance training programs and would recommend them to others.

Post-course evaluations indicated a highly favorable response (4.7 on a scale of 1 to 5, with 5 being highly favorable) to the learning medium, activities, and meeting the objectives of the course. It was my experience that participants in this course would often e-mail me afterward to tell me how much they enjoyed the course, elaborating on the value-added aspects of flexibility to work at their own pace, location (desktop), and schedule, and the benefit of learner-specific feedback.

## Attracting, Training, and Retaining Instructors

Despite the overwhelming success achieved in the pilot tests, few volunteered to teach the various distance training courses populating the Training Institute curriculum. The high demand to deliver much-needed training to staff across the country became a forceful impetus for the conversion of traditional classroom-style deliveries to technology-mediated ones. The Teletraining Team and the design team for Better Briefings resolved to develop a Train-the-Trainer program to strengthen the confidence and skill of their instructor pool to meet the delivery goals of the agency. The design team confronted the instructors' obstacles and overcame them by

- Developing incentives
- Creating a detailed instructor guide that walked instructors through the entire delivery process
- Delivering Train-the-Trainer sessions using the technologies required to deliver the courses
- Rewarding those who participated in the design, delivery, and implementation
- Conducting detailed evaluation feedback with participants and instructors following delivery
- Learning from mistakes

These interventions supported the culture change that was indeed occurring as a result of GAO's commitment to deliver technologically mediated training. In addition, the efforts mentioned earlier were organizational mechanisms and reinforcements that encouraged folks to give it a try by providing specific life lines of support that were tried and tested. In a culture where risks are discouraged and competence is highly prized (so making mistakes is troublesome), the team attempted to resolve the mysteries of distance training. Even though funds to support the Training Institute's own staff's training and development were minimal during a few lean years, support for those developing their technology skills was made available. Distance training was considered mission critical for both the agency and the institute.

There were strategic incentives to use technology-mediated processes for both training and the implementation of business processes. Key instructional designers who developed and promulgated technology-enhanced training were representing GAO at national and international distance education conferences. They gained recognition within the agency and in the public arena as well. Adele Suchinsky Ewing was recognized by the International Society for Performance Instruction for her involvement in writing *GAO's Video Teletraining: A Guide to Design, Development, and Use* (1995). The author was asked to present on the topics of designing, developing, and delivering distance training for classes at Johns Hopkins Graduate School of Business and the University of Wisconsin Continuing Education for Human Resources Managers. A few staff members were promoted within a couple of years, largely for their technological savvy and contribution to mission-critical training and business processes.

## Desired Outcomes

Facilitators and instructors within the Training Institute and across the GAO began to request "one-on-one" coaching sessions from members of the teletraining team to improve their distance training skills. Seemingly overnight, senior executives wanted to increase their use of technology and distance learning applications to aid in their effective communication of a broad spectrum of reengineered business processes without delay or distortion. Distance training had penetrated the agency at the highest levels. A new comptroller general whose technical skills were ahead of many of his senior staff hastened the executives' motivations toward technological innovation to meet business objectives. At this writing, his short tenure has already quickly focused on innovative uses of technology-enhanced business processes and training.

## Unexpected Rewards

As an unexpected reward across the agency, the distance training instructors and facilitators were among the most widely respected, technologically skilled staff at GAO. Using technology was more than a passing fad. Individuals with knowledge and experience in distance learning efforts were in high demand to support a variety of organizational initiatives and priorities. For example, in 1998 a seasoned distance learning facilitator developed a group performance feedback session for a director with her regional offices in a teletraining format (for three separate locations). In 1997 a synchronous multipoint "Town Hall" meeting was conducted across the country (involving nearly two hundred people) relying on a recognized distance learning facilitator for technical and facilitation support. This particular facilitator intervened to influence the quality of oral and visual communications and overall effectiveness of that session. Feedback from the participants following the session indicated that suggested techniques (humor included) resulted in a noticeably more successful "Town Hall" meeting than previous unsupported efforts.

In 1996, the Job Process Re-engineering Team (a cross-divisional team) received the agency's Continuous Improvement Award for designing and implementing a standardized job process for GAO's evaluation work. This team worked with the assistant comptroller general of OIMC and other senior executives to communicate and train staff in these new job processes via distance learning technologies. Distance training had become a part of the executive lexicon, and technology-mediated learning for business solutions became a strong consideration, if not an expectation.

## Final Summary

Strategic planning at the organizational level to align resources, infrastructure, staffing, budget, policies, and rewards and recognition are necessary links to sustain distance training efforts. From this broad perspective, the collaboration between offices such as the Training Institute and the Telecommunications Branch of the Office of Information Management and Communication are essential to achieve successful technology-mediated learning. Funding to upgrade hardware and software is critical to acquire cutting-edge technologies that expand the training and learning opportunities in a time-critical, competitive business environment (this includes government and nonprofit companies). Furthermore, favorable outcomes for the pioneers who build new skills and test new technologies that strategically support business objectives creates the business case for continued investment and support. Finally, there must be a willingness to take risks, make a few mistakes, and learn from them. At GAO, drawing from lessons learned is a general characteristic in the culture that bodes well for the future of distance training and education.

As GAO develops its priorities for the new millennium, the comptroller general and the director of the Training Institute emphasize that distance training will clearly play a continuing and important role in the future. The agency's policies, rewards, technical resources, budget, staffing, and infrastructure will continue to support and encourage technology-mediated learning. The Training Institute's objectives include increasing staff knowledge of enhanced delivery technologies and expanding their use to deliver training, support performance, and disseminate information to learners through more efficient and convenient means. There is now a reliance on technology and an articulated expectation that distance learning is part of the way to do business at GAO.

CHAPTER SEVEN

# MAKING IT WORK IN A NONTRADITIONAL ORGANIZATION

## Distance Training at Réseau INTERACTION Network

Daniel L. Larocque, Noël Thomas

This chapter describes how the training dynamics of a small corporation evolved in the last twenty years. The corporation in question may seem atypical for two reasons: most services are provided remotely and staffing is mostly through short-term contract work with a constant flow of staff arrivals and departures. Nonetheless, its experiences provide useful insights for more mainstream organizations.

## Helping People at a Distance

Réseau INTERACTION Network (RIN) was created in 1980 with a focus on helping clients learn, work, and manage at a distance. It shows clients how to train and learn, resolve daily issues, hold meetings, supervise work and budgets, complete and look over time sheets, and do individual counseling or coaching when the participants cannot get together face to face or prefer not to do so.

RIN helps clients tame the notion of distance in four ways:

- *Analysis:* This function centers on front-end needs analysis to better understand how an organization works and how best it could integrate communicating at a distance.

- *Instructional Design:* RIN may also suggest distance learning as part of a solution and then support clients with the instructional design process.
- *Implementation:* In some cases, clients ask RIN to help with the implementation of a program. At this point, RIN develops learning packages, that is, Web-based modules with presentations, activities, and assessments along with a technical help desk and a mentor accessible by e-mail, phone, and fax. RIN may also facilitate training sessions or train future facilitators to deliver a given content using a variety of technologies including audioconferencing, videoconferencing, Web-based media, or a mix thereof.
- *Evaluation:* In some cases, clients want their processes evaluated to uncover what works best and what does not.

RIN is a one-stop service for integrating communication at a distance. Some clients want all four functions in the service agreement, while others will only need to focus on one or another (as when an organization has already conducted its own analysis and asks RIN to help solely with the instructional design process). Project sizes vary. Smaller organizations may work with one consultant or a team of two or three. Larger multiyear projects may take a team numbering in the dozens. Because project sizes vary so much, RIN must always have access to a pool of highly motivated individuals ready to take on a given contract. As an example, RIN once agreed to put together a Web-based literacy program, evaluate the results, and recommend the means for wide-scale implementation. In total, more than fifty people worked on the project over the course of a year; only six were permanent RIN staff.

Even when the end goal is to help clients communicate at a distance, contributors to the project may themselves need training on communicating at a distance. For example, a project may need experienced researchers, instructional designers, or content specialists. RIN tends to find that individuals often have the content skills needed to do the job but lack experience in working at a distance. They must be introduced to the processes and tools used so that they, in turn, can participate in a team that will help clients be introduced to these processes and tools.

## What's in a Name?

The concepts of *network* and *interaction* have been part of the name of the company from the beginning to emphasize the basic tenet: human progress is based on groups of people (networks) working together (interaction) as a community of interest in a humanized and humanizing environment (see http://village.ca/eng/ under Company for a detailed mission and value statement). The community of interest is usually geographically dispersed, giving rise to the need for mediated communication. Clients and project contributors (that is, contract-based staff) are often in Canada but also in the United States, Europe, and Northern Africa. Most of the work is accomplished through telephone-based technology and the many tools of the Internet.

## The VHQ Principle

Most companies eloquently state their support for customer service and quality products—while remaining fundamentally profit centered. RIN addresses its mandate somewhat differently by asserting its Very High Quality (VHQ) principle as the central driving force. RIN has no financial or growth objectives. Instead, its finality is full customer satisfaction through VHQ services, with the proven result that profits then happen naturally.

## A Spherical Virtual Organization

To further emphasize the client-centered approach practiced by RIN, its organizational chart gives top priority and power to the client—the client is literally the center of RIN's universe.

Initially, RIN used a traditional top-down chart to illustrate its line of authority. Another iteration reversed the chart by showing clients at the top and the president at the bottom. It became clear that any such linear representation was incongruous with RIN's approach and practices. Figure 7.1 shows the latest RIN representation of how it sees itself as a spherical virtual organization (Miles & Snow, 1995). After the client, front-line staff represents the next most important layer. It is followed by project management, which is itself supported by the outside layer, corporate management. The layers are separated by porous boundaries (illustrated with dotted lines) that allow for reciprocal influence.

Three main types of influence are recognized and encouraged to flow through boundaries:

- New outside knowledge such as new products, new ideas, new ways of doing
- New inside knowledge, emerging from need identification or evaluation processes
- Movement of staff and contributors between layers

This last influence is a major departure from traditional corporations. In a spherical virtual organization such as RIN, staff move to and fro between the front line and project management or even between corporate management and the front line with many persons filling multiple roles on multiple projects simultaneously.

## FIGURE 7.1. RIN: A SPHERICAL VIRTUAL ORGANIZATION.

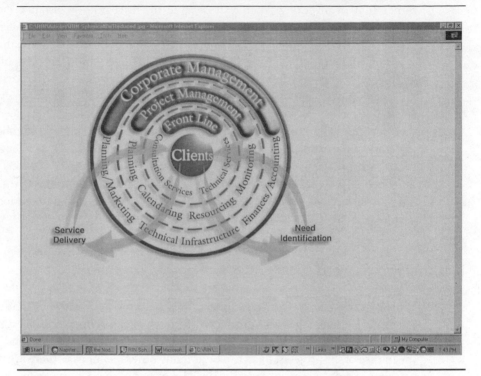

Two iterative forces drive transactions through the porous boundaries between layers. One focuses on delivery and one on need identification. The delivery force typically starts with corporate and project management and zooms into the client layer. Delivery activities include implementation, tracking, and evaluation. The need identification force typically flows in the opposite direction. It starts with clients and front-line staff moving toward forecasting, corporate planning, and positioning. However, all layers influence both processes.

## Business Problem Statement

RIN has always worked remotely, bypassing second-wave, assembly line practices to adopt third-wave work distribution practices and global village behaviors (Toffler, 1980). As a result, RIN has never had to move from face-to-face training (which it basically never did) to the new construct of distance training (which it has done since its foundation). Thus, unlike most companies, RIN hasn't faced the challenge of integrating the principles and practices of distance education but rather that of inventing—before it became mainstream—a distance delivery model. The company has had to establish and improve practices (also called protocols), clearly define policies, and find ways to implement and evaluate them.

The challenge of choosing and formalizing a delivery model is compounded by the reality of a very fluid workforce. In a spherical virtual organization, there are few employees and many outside contractors, which RIN refers to as *contributors*. While pride in the work and in RIN is anticipated, company allegiance is neither encouraged nor expected. With people coming and going all the time, it is also impossible to schedule regular staff orientation or training. The challenge is to create corporately well-adjusted and highly productive high-impact teams made up of people who have varying degrees of ease with communicating at a distance, have never met, will probably never meet, and will never all gather in one location at the same time.

## Population Served

With a head office in Ottawa, Canada, RIN had to cope with work that is provided in two languages and distributed through four permanent offices: two in the Ottawa area, one in Toronto, and one in the Montreal area. Depending on the nature of the projects, there can be as many other locations as there are people working. Contributors have worked for RIN from an island in the Pacific, a small community in eastern Quebec, a cottage in Florida, and assorted home offices in Toronto and other urban centers in Canada and the United States. Staffing levels vary from six to fifty, working part-time or full-time, with people joining and leaving depending on project schedules.

As is suggested by RIN's corporate chart, staff is assigned, or hired on contract, to work within one of three main layers:

- *Front Line:* This layer is composed predominantly of outside contributors with a few permanent staff. It is responsible for both consulting services (that is, content analysis, research, instructional design, and so on) and technical services (Web design and construction, intranets, streamed audio and video production, and so on).
- *Project Management:* This layer is composed of both permanent staff and outside contributors. It is responsible for overseeing the implementation of projects: training new contributors, developing calendars of deliverables, monitoring delivery.
- *Corporate Management:* The outside layer of the circle is composed predominantly of permanent staff, with occasional support from contributors. On one hand it

collects data from clients and the front line to identify needs and then conduct forecasting, planning, and marketing strategies. On the other, it oversees the overall delivery of services; it tracks calendars, deliverables, and budgets, and conducts both formative and summative evaluations.

For RIN to succeed, each person needs to learn at a distance how to work at a distance. Everyone involved needs the technical skills to manipulate a variety of technologies (e-mail and Web, fax, audioconferencing, desktop videoconferencing) and, most important, the facilitation, self-management, and participatory skills required to work as a member of a team that works at a distance. For example, in the recent Web-based literacy project, three individuals were hired because of their extensive research skills. They were thousands of kilometers apart, in three different time zones. They had various experiences with working at a distance, from very little (that is, a beginner on the Internet with no knowledge of intranets and no audioconference or videoconference experience) to a moderate comfort level (that is, at ease with e-mail and audioconferencing but no experience with intranets or desktop videoconferencing). All three had to quickly learn how to function with each other at a distance, with the variety of means used, so that their knowledge of research could be applied to the contract at hand.

## Outcomes Desired

RIN and contributors have a list of related training expectations. RIN's perspective is centered on the ability to work and produce the required results. Its desired training outcomes are corporate in nature. Contributors focus on knowledge and skills. Their desired training outcomes are more personal.

### Outcomes for RIN

All in all, RIN needs to provide training activities to ensure that its VHQ principle is understood and applied to all projects. To do so, training seeks to accomplish the following goals:

- Integrate new staff to a project and its objectives.
- Develop team cohesiveness among strangers working remotely and demonstrate how to sustain healthy group dynamics at a distance.
- Introduce and socialize contributors to RIN values, client-centeredness, and conceptual framework.
- Develop skills for contributors to produce results, on time and on budget, using RIN technologies and principles.

- Ultimately maintain RIN's high level of client satisfaction and corporate reputation.

In essence, the major training challenge at RIN is to keep everybody and everything in sync, both ideologically and logistically, both locally and remotely, and with both regular staff and short-term contract employees.

Faced with this challenge, RIN adopted (or borrowed from assembly line jargon) the concepts of just-in-time and just-enough training. Staff and contributors are trained when needed on values and skills necessary to meet the client's objectives. This is done through individual or small group interaction and involves both formal sessions and informal mentoring. For example, during the first meeting of the design team for the literacy project, thirty minutes was set aside so that content experts (literacy practitioners) could be introduced to the project's intranet (Exhibit 7.1). The intranet included computer conferences to share ideas, a virtual

## EXHIBIT 7.1.  SAMPLE PROJECT MANAGEMENT INTRANET.

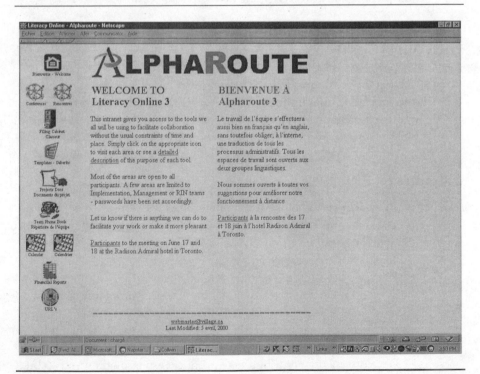

filing cabinet to store documents, a calendar, a team address book, and other useful features. It also had a variety of quality control tools, such as electronic timesheets where contributors submitted a daily overview of the work they achieved. The intranet had essential tools for communicating and managing the project at a distance.

Those hired to work on the project needed to quickly learn how to use the required tools. The training occurred mainly at a distance and employed a mix of Web access and the telephone or desktop videoconferencing.

Interestingly, the basic training model at RIN (just-in-time and just-enough) has not really changed over twenty years. Technological evolution has allowed RIN to do more now in a distance mode than was possible two decades ago by using party lines, 300-baud modems, and 32K (not MB!) machines. RIN's real advancement has been mostly in the harmonization and formalization of policy and training processes.

## Outcomes for Contributors

What does the adoption of just-in-time and just-enough training mean for contributors? Borrowing from the work of Lebel (1989), RIN believes it means contributors are ready for the contract at hand on four different levels of preparedness: cognitive, metacognitive, socio-management, and emotional preparedness. These four levels dictate both how the model is applied and the outcomes sought.

1. *In terms of cognitive preparedness (the how-to skills), contributors need to know how to manipulate a variety of technologies used at RIN.* While a contributor is negotiating the details of a contract, we complete an assessment of skills required. Contributors are then initiated to the necessary technical environment. This process includes most of the following: e-mail (including file attachments), advanced Web features (which may include installing and using plug-ins for audio and video streaming), using the project's intranet (which includes reading and leaving messages in conferences, leaving and retrieving files from our virtual filing cabinet, consulting online project documents, filling out an online calendar of events, filling out time sheets or project updates electronically), using presentation software, dialing in to an audioconference, using online software for synchronous meetings (includes desktop videoconferencing, file sharing and collaboration, and to a lesser extent a white board and a chat room).

2. *Metacognitive preparedness focuses on the transfer of skills to situations outside the training sessions.* As they work at a distance, contributors will all encounter unanticipated events (that is, a Web page freezing on the screen or questions from clients about technological options). Although they have access to technical and management support, they must be able to adapt and transfer learned skills to a variety of

situations so that they are able to function somewhat independently and become mentors for client groups.

3. *Although contributors often work in physical isolation, RIN emphasizes the importance of teamwork and thus the need to work on socio-management preparedness.* Members of a team must create and sustain a healthy group dynamic even when lacking the visual feedback they are used to in face-to-face meetings. In many cases, contributors have to learn how to communicate consistently, how to maintain a dialogue, how to lead a discussion (synchronously and asynchronously) or how to participate actively under someone else's leadership, and how to debate, disagree, and resolve conflicts at a distance.

4. *Finally, contributors need to be emotionally prepared.* They need to feel secure in the task to be accomplished. Contributors are hired because of their knowledge and skills in certain areas of expertise, for example, specialized content (basic literacy, advanced nursing, high-speed metal machining), research, instructional design, or graphic design. The appropriation of technology and the transfer to working at a distance must not threaten their abilities. It must enhance their feeling of self-worth; it must add excitement given that their knowledge and skills are crossing time and space boundaries.

## Description of Processes

To achieve the desired outcomes using its just-in-time and just-enough training model, RIN has had to elucidate and apply a number of training processes. Some of these are still being tested, as RIN moves to ensure a greater harmony between its mission, values, and training model. To use the conceptual matrix Berge introduces in Chapter Two, RIN is entering and gradually consolidating its Stage 4.

### Documentation to Describe and Prescribe

As in many small organizations, RIN evolves organically depending on opportunities and pressure points. Policy statements are used as commonsense guides and are introduced gradually, initially orally and, when accepted, in writing. Practices evolve over many years and eventually get written down as the company's preferred modus operandi. RIN's training policy and practices have followed this evolutionary administrative process.

The training policy at RIN simply states that contributors must be provided with the training required for successful performance of their duties. It is assumed that both contract and regular staff will assume full responsibility for their professional competence. As noted, RIN's training activities thus focus more on the transmission of RIN's values, the development of skills to meet client needs, and the ability to operate in a distance environment.

## Training Practices

The following are some of the regular training practices at RIN. The intensity of each event varies of course with the nature and size of the project. Every practice is organized and implemented at a distance.

1. *For each project, there is a launch event with client participation.* This event facilitates and accelerates team building and cohesiveness, at least for those people available when a project is initially launched. The process involves a visioning exercise where participants, clients, contributors, and management share their own value system and wishes for the project. RIN's value system is introduced, mostly implicitly, by way of the visioning exercise. In one project, a core group of seven met via audioconferencing. The facilitator (RIN staff) asked the group to visualize what the result of the project would look like: "What do you see people doing in five years? How are they using your Web learning site?" The group then described what they saw. The ideas were put together, summarized, harmonized, and used as the basis of a vision document. The draft document was distributed via the virtual filing cabinet. Members of the core group had a chance to download it, read and annotate it, and then met once again by audioconference to revise the document and finalize it. For many in the group, it was the first time they had gone into an intranet, had used a virtual filing cabinet, and had participated in an audioconference.

2. *For each project, there is a closure event with client participation.* The focus here is on evaluation of both product and process. There is also an important celebratory component to this event—which is gratifying by itself and is also useful to maintain ongoing synergy as many contributors may work again with RIN. In one project, contributors met in three sites with videoconferencing equipment. After an official opening and a thirty-minute review of the project, refreshments were served and participants were encouraged to play with the cameras and to call upon team members in other sites for a virtual handshake and a verbal chat. More than ninety minutes passed; participants were still sharing their successes, their mishaps, their discoveries.

3. *For each staff there is individual or group training on tools used to deliver services or manage the delivery of services.* Training uses audioconferencing with NetMeeting support. NetMeeting is a desktop, Web-based videoconferencing system that allows participants to see and speak to each other, to share a document and collaborate on revisions live on the computer screen, and to send drawings using a white board or even to chat if need be.

4. *Ad hoc just-in-time training events will often occur during team meetings.* Project managers are encouraged to deal with training issues on the spot, if it can be done effectively for the benefit of all. These events typically last five to twenty minutes. During a recent meeting, a contributor asked how she could share a document and point to two problem areas. Deadlines were tight and she wanted a quick response. Instantly, the team was told to get on the Internet. Once there, the facilitator, along with more experienced contributors, did a step-by-step overview of the sharing and collaborating functions of NetMeeting. The document was used as a case study. Within twenty minutes, everyone had a working knowledge of NetMeeting—and the document had been revised as needed at the same time.

5. *All contributors produce daily online descriptive time sheets.* Beyond providing billing and project progress information to managers and clients, this allows project managers to monitor individual performance and provide mentoring or additional training when warranted. This is also a good location to identify training gaps.

Each project has an intranet with links to company practices on bureaucratic necessities like expense accounts and other routine matters. A Quality Assurance process helps identify patterns of recurring problems and prescribe further training. Project managers and technical support staff are always available for individual mentoring and handholding on any issue affecting the delivery of VHQ services.

As an additional training resource, RIN's president has summarized a number of best practices in what is called "Rapid Application Development (RAD) Practices at RIN." Influenced by the software industry (McConnell, 1996), this document provides words of wisdom about preferred practices, examples of classic mistakes (that is, adding new staff when a project is late under the misguided impression that more people will save the day), and explanations of the incremental delivery mechanism (such as a spiral process where multiple versions of projects are developed, smoke-tested, and presented to clients for adjustments).

## Appropriate Support Technologies

Of course, distance delivery depends on appropriate media. Since RIN has had to deploy the full gamut of Web-based technologies to meet the needs of its clients, it has easy access to these technologies to support its own internal needs. RIN's training uses the following tools:

- Audioconferencing using regular speakerphones or group conveners (we do not use IP telephony at this point as the technology is not sufficiently reliable and fluent).

- NetMeeting for synchronous document sharing, white-boarding, and general brainstorming. Video is provided when possible for purposes of humanizing the relationships.
- WebBoard is used for asynchronous communications through a flexible online conference system.
- RIN's corporate intranet and specific project intranets are used to share and store content documents using one or multiple Web servers, depending on feature requirements.
- RIN's in-house project management software allows monitoring of performance through daily time sheets.
- Streaming audio and video synchronized with Web presentations has been introduced as a vehicle for durable content.

While it is recognized that not all companies own the full spectrum of technologies, it is now relatively easy and inexpensive to purchase necessary access from outside suppliers, when required, with the goal of eventually developing in-house capacity as volume and comfort increase.

## Outcomes Attained

While perfection is an illusive target, RIN's training model and practices have met a certain amount of success. These outcomes are described under contributor and RIN points of view.

### The Contributors' Point of View

Nearly all contributors who have worked with RIN over the last twenty years want to do so again. Of all accomplishments, this one is the most significant as RIN has access to a wide pool of experienced professionals it has at least partially trained over the years. What factors can account for such a high rate of contributor satisfaction?

For one, the training environment is a safe space. Training is offered predominantly by "non-techies." Although technical support is available at any time during regular business hours, technical staff will not necessarily lead technical training sessions with contributors. Trainers are predominantly staff who have lived through the process of learning at a distance how to work at a distance. They are able to offer hints on how to make working at a distance a fun activity;

they offer anecdotes to support the creation of healthy group dynamics. There is little tech-talk and much sharing of war stories from the field—all can laugh . . . and learn.

Just-in-time and just-enough training at RIN also involve the concepts of ongoing coaching or mentoring; the integration of contributors with little knowledge of technologies and working at a distance is accomplished with the helping hand of those with more experience in a "your brother's keeper" mentality. New contributors are often intimidated by technologies and the idea of working at a distance. The trainers-cum-mentors are most able to allay these fears and provide the secure space needed to move from fear or intimidation to mastery. For instance, all project leaders are asked to support contributors when technical questions come up (that is, contributors are told to communicate with the project leader for any question). Depending on the size of the project and its calendar, project leaders may spend up to two or three hours a day answering questions on technical functions (such as how to access an audioconferencing bridge, how to send a document to multiple individuals all at once, how to convert files, and so on) and on process (such as how to handle a misinterpretation or a conflict at a distance, how to keep group members at a distance informed of developments, how to facilitate a meeting at a distance using audioconferencing or videoconferencing, and so on). Of course, the amount of time spent on coaching diminishes as contributors become comfortable with the tools and the processes. Training is integrated with the supervisory process so that time is spent productively.

Contributors also like the just-in-time and just-enough training model. Many contributors are self-employed or members of small firms. It is notoriously difficult for such individuals to take time off for training (it may be a hindrance for one person out of five hundred to take time off for training; it is often critically impossible when you are one of five employees or even the sole employee). The just-in-time and just-enough training model also ensures that contributors get the training they need, when they need it and want it, in a short amount of time (or most often in short intervals over one to three months). For instance, training may happen on the spot when needed (that is, the ad hoc events) or a fifteen- to thirty-minute session on a specific question will be scheduled so that the contributor feels comfortable and is able to go on with the job. In a world of increasing access to information, this delivery model lessens the occurrence of "data smog" (Shenk, 1997). That is, it avoids the confusion caused by having too much information in too little time or too much information too early in the process.

Contributors also relish the amount of learning achieved. Although initially skeptical, within hours contributors are able to list the skills they have learned and demonstrate their ability to apply these skills in various situations. Many will conspicuously use the jargon learned as an exhibit of their new-found knowledge and a source of pride. Overall, RIN's just-in-time and just-enough delivery allows contributors to develop a feeling of empowerment and to realize they are growing personally as they are working on a project.

## RIN's Point of View

Why has RIN chosen to train its staff at a distance using a just-in-time and a just-enough model? For one thing, the costs are kept low. Contributors supply their own space, basic equipment (computer, modem, telephone, fax, word-processing software), and Internet connectivity. In exchange, RIN pays for bridging and audio and Web server capacity and offers training and access to experts. Bridging costs are far lower than the costs of bringing together individuals from across the North American continent. Additionally, RIN's training is not curtailed by the one-shot approach. Training, with its important mentoring and supervisory components, occurs as often as needed, when needed.

The just-in-time and just-enough delivery model also generates quick results. Contributors are able to function in their team within hours of joining a project. Basic skills are addressed first (e-mailing, faxing, accessing the project's intranet and the group discussions), then other skills are added as needed. Moreover, as the name of the model suggests, it's at the right time and is just enough to allow contributors to function in a complete and fulfilling manner. The model ensures fast start-up and high productivity.

RIN is also pleased with the high satisfaction rate confirmed by contributors. It endorses the way the company works; it supports the company's reputation and its positive corporate image; it even lessens the burden of recruitment as most contributors offer to work with RIN on other projects. In the end, the model allows RIN to meet its mission and value statement and VHQ principle.

Finally, the ultimate clients, those receiving the product or service put forth by the team of core staff and contributors, also appreciate the impact of the training model. Most important, they are on the receiving end of a quality product or service. Moreover, the product or service is delivered on time and on budget. Finally, they work with a company that has good working relations, a high energy level, and a strong capacity for lateral thinking and creativity.

## Challenges and Questions

RIN's distance management approach and just-in-time and just-enough training model has not been without its challenges. Over the years, both contributors and RIN management have had to contend with various issues.

## The Contributors' Point of View

As a spherical virtual organization, RIN manages its work through project-based contracts. These projects typically last two to twelve months (some are renewed after twelve months but with a new direction, often necessitating new teams and new contracts). For any given contract, team members will be asked to be highly productive for a given number of weeks—they have to hit the ground running! Such work can produce heightened creativity bursts, but it also entails the risk of deliverable fatigue or even professional burnout.

Accepting a first contract with RIN may be intimidating. Contributors with limited experience at working at a distance have to quickly gain the knowledge to work with the rest of the team. One contributor once compared joining a RIN project as jumping on a train that will not slow down. This initial reaction is part of the reason why RIN provides the support for emotional and socio-management preparedness as well as cognitive and meta-cognitive preparedness. This may take the form of an asynchronous computer "Café"—a discussion group where teams share doubts and aspirations and describe past experiences and anecdotes—or even personal events like weddings, illnesses, holidays.

The initial intimidation may also lead to doubts about the contributor's capacity to work within a virtual team. In essence, there is a risk that contributors will question their professional expertise because they do not have the technical skills to match. Although it may be surprising, we have seen professional researchers and designers, people with more than thirty years' experience and many accolades, suddenly doubt their abilities because they have to transmit and use these skills at a distance. Project managers and other team members must regularly remind contributors of the reasons why they were hired, point to their recent acquisition of skills, and reinforce the sense of belonging within the team.

Finally, contributors sometimes feel isolated. Both synchronous conferences (audio and video) and the special events listed earlier (such as a new project launch) help diminish the feeling of isolation. Still, project managers must always be on the lookout and intervene when such a perception affects the contributor's self-confidence and productive capacity. A special how-are-you-doing telephone call can go a long way to boost sagging morale and humanize relationships by showing that people care.

## RIN's Point of View

While RIN's approach has endured over two decades, it is far from static. It has to adapt to ever-changing forces: client needs change, technology evolves, contributors come in as a steady stream of new faces or, should we say, new online personalities. RIN must address these challenges as they surface.

While forecasting is required, long-range corporate planning has moved from five-year plans to one-year and, in some instances, six-month plans. We have not been able to plan training content or calendars over the long term and are wondering if it is at all possible to set long-term training plans in our environment. Right now, we have set the stage and are providing resources for a cafeteria-style on-the-go training process, as opposed to a structured leisurely sit-down dinner. We are not certain if this difficulty in planning is due to our own foibles, in which case we should focus on a fix, or if it simply reflects an intrinsically unpredictable environment and is thus something we should accept and move on.

As part of its evaluation process, management must continuously assess what is needed in terms of training. It must then ensure immediate access to that training. A quick turnaround is both necessary and potentially perilous. For example, what is to be done when you have a limited number of core staff to offer the training, who are themselves assigned to project teams and have to meet their own deliverables, but who are confronted with multiple projects where multiple contributors have never worked at a distance? To allay some of the pressures, RIN now encourages the use of staggered project starts and staggered team starts within each project.

RIN has also come to understand the need for more detailed administrative procedures to control the quality of the output. While an ISO 9000 type of process would be overly stifling and a definite overkill in our situation, we still need quality assurance tools that will do a better job as feedback loops to training decisions.

Contributor training and performance evaluation go hand in hand. While we are quite good at training and providing regular reinforcement for a job well done, we have not provided structured feedback to contributors. We feel more feedback at contract termination with concrete suggestions for personal training would help the outside resource pool grow and provide even better services in the future.

As described earlier, RIN has two main types of teams at the front lines: the consulting services team and the technical services team. Most members of a typical consulting team have a background in social sciences and education, while members of a typical technical team have a background in science and technology. RIN must work at harmonizing these two working cultures, which tend to have their own ways of thinking or doing. For example, a consulting team often has a general idea as to what it would like to improve in a given technical environment. Members of this team can describe the desired end in a visual manner and with a holistic list of attributes. The technical team expects a much more detailed description along with a more linear, step-by-step illustration of the functions (that is, what happens first, then what, and then what next, and so on). Both groups can become frustrated: the consulting team believes the technical team is not listening; the technical team perceives the request as fuzzy and pie-in-the-sky.

Management must step in to clarify mutual expectations and ways of doing. In essence, management must bridge the gap between the teams and allow the discussions to continue. We have not yet been able to develop a training process that can rapidly merge consulting and technical team approaches.

Finally, RIN is continuously trying to improve the overall ease of communication. Since the work is physically decentralized over a continent, we do not have chance meetings at the water cooler or at the coffee machine. Ensuring the flow of information is a constant preoccupation. For example, teams need to be informed of strategic decisions and of new technological environments, functions, or improvements. When communication slows down, core staff or contributors may end up following their own path.

## Discussion

RIN's clients are trying to integrate distance education, training, or management into their operations. That need is their primary reason for approaching RIN in the first place. To adopt and sustain distance delivery, these organizations confront a number of issues. Depending on the circumstances, there might be an ideological question. Various echelons of the organization (board, administration, management, and so on) or sectors (human resources, finance, project implementation, and so on) disagree with the whole concept of working at a distance or with certain parts of it. If they adopt it, organizations have to integrate the notion of distance in their organizational culture. For others, there is a question of money (How much will this cost? Is it worth it?) or of technology (What do we need? Which is best? How often will it need to be updated?).

Since its inception as a spherical virtual organization, RIN has not really had to deal with these issues. RIN was created with the intent of working at a distance. While looking for the best adapted technology for the lowest price, de facto, it never questioned the need to invest in technologies or in the training of staff and contributors to work at a distance. However, RIN—and the many other businesses that are now starting as virtual organizations—must still address a number of issues to sustain the initial vision.

To respond to client needs, virtual organizations must quickly put together functional project teams—in a situation where some or even many of the team members may know little about communicating at a distance. When a firm of engineers wants to put together an advanced Web-based training package, it requires a team that includes, for example, both engineers and graphic designers. Similarly, the literacy project mentioned earlier required, among others, researchers, literacy practitioners, and graphic illustrators. The lead organization, in this case RIN, may be comfortable with the concept and its application; it must also ensure that all contributors who come on board for a project are comfortable with it as well.

Choosing appropriate technologies may be overwhelming at times. After all, virtual organizations are required to keep up. That being said, technologies should only be bought when they are proven to be useful, not simply because they are available. Fortunately, it is increasingly easier to purchase communication time from outside suppliers (say, one hour of audioconferencing time). By tracking use, organizations can quickly recognize which means are most convenient and can then decide to invest in in-house capacity (that is, buying an audioconferencing bridge outright).

Given the recent development of virtual organizations, we do not know how far they can go. Both the corporate model (spherical virtual organization) and the chosen training model ( just-in-time and just-enough) have produced desired outcomes for RIN. What will happen with the pressure on RIN to grow even more? Do these models apply whatever the size or rate of growth of a company? How big can a virtual organization be? How big can it become before the just-in-time and just-enough model fails? In essence, is there a breaking point and where is it located?

Part of the success of virtual organizations is linked to their flexibility. With RIN, contributors and clients both cite how pleased they are that the company can adapt and turn around quickly when there is a need to meet. As we saw earlier, however, RIN also needs to formalize certain processes to avoid unnecessary repetition and waste of time and energy. Virtual organizations thrive on the moment; they strive to answer training needs as they happen or within a very short time (often within hours at RIN). That being said, such organizations have to confront the dynamic tension created by the need to formalize certain processes and the requirement for flexibility inherent in their corporate model. What can and should be formalized to be most efficient? For example, could we formalize assessment procedures and access to text-based training resources without compromising our approach? On the other hand, what cannot or should not be formalized? Can such organizations formalize mentoring practices, ad hoc training events, one-to-one hand-holding—and still maintain a high degree of flexibility?

As with all spherical virtual organizations, it may come to discover that maintaining itself, its vision, and its approaches is both its greatest challenge and its most enduring source of excitement.

# CHAPTER EIGHT

# DISTANCE LEARNING AT THE IRS

## Supporting Organizational Change

Teva J. Scheer

A former IRS chief operating officer, Phil Brand, opened a speech to some employees in the early 1990s by advising them, "Seek change, not security. A boat in the harbor remains safe, but eventually its hull rots out."

Brand's warning was both fitting and prophetic. Just a few years later, Congress passed the IRS Restructuring and Reform Act (RRA 98), which required a total overhaul of the agency's mission and organizational structure. The existing national, regional, and district structure, organized by stovepipe functions such as auditing, collection, and returns processing, was to be scrapped. In its place, Congress mandated a new, cross-functional structure organized by customer populations such as large and midsize corporations, small businesses and self-employed taxpayers, and individual taxpayers. RRA 98 gave focus to downsizing and reorganization efforts that had actually begun early in the 1990s with a consolidation of regional and district offices.

Having spent decades in an agency whose culture and organizational structure were generally stable (the last major IRS reorganization occurred in the early 1950s), IRS employees in the 1990s have been launched into a profoundly turbulent period of continuous organizational transition and cultural change. In less than ten years, the number of regional offices has dropped from seven to four, and soon there will be none. The number of district offices has dropped from more than sixty to just thirty-three. Functional responsibilities, position descriptions, spans of control, reporting relationships—indeed, the agency's essential purpose and mission—all are changing, and there is no end in sight. Pushed by congressional mandate and technological developments, the IRS is about six years into a total transformation. With the flattening of the organization has come a loss in organizational position and prestige for many chiefs and managers, and a loss of security, clarity, and organizational trust for thousands of employees. There is a deep longing to return, if not to the past, then at least to some form of organizational stability. It is unlikely, however, that IRS employees will ever again experience a stable, unchanging organization like the one in which most of them grew up.

## The Problem

The IRS's experience with distance learning implementation can be thought of as a metaphor for the agency's larger organizational change. Since IRS functions and responsibilities are unique in the nation, the agency sponsors a huge internal training program in which technical employees are taught instructional techniques that are then used to teach the dozens of technical courses available to employees. Traditionally, the training process has been comfortable, easy to understand, valued highly by most employees, and based almost entirely on the traditional classroom model. Employees enjoyed traveling to other cities to attend classes and to meet their peers from other offices.

Over the past decade, as the agency organization began to change, so did the training process. In general, the increasing use of nontraditional training media has engendered the same kind of nostalgia for past days as has the changing organizational structure. Many employees feel that they haven't really been trained unless they attend a traditional classroom course. But just as IRS employees will have to adapt to a new culture of continual organizational change, so they will also have to adjust to a new paradigm for the IRS training program. Distance learning is here to stay.

In 1999, a strategic human resources team released projections of the scope of training design and delivery that would be necessary to support the reorganization during fiscal years (FY) 1999, 2000, and 2001. Table 8.1 depicts their conclusions concerning what the team called the training capacity gap. Readers will note a major increase in the identified shortfalls in instructors, support, and training space between FY 1999 and FY 2000. FY 2000 is the year that most of the new IRS divisions are expected to "stand up." During that year, thousands of employees will be reassigned to new jobs, creating a one-time shortage of training resources.

## TABLE 8.1. THE TRAINING CAPACITY GAP.

| Supply Element | Practical Internal Capacity | Identified Shortfall | | |
|---|---|---|---|---|
| | | FY 99 | FY 00 | FY 01 |
| Instructors | 1,325,000 hours/year | 150,000 | 585,000 | 365,000 |
| Delivery support | 344,000 hours/year | 61,000 | 123,000 | 7,000 |
| Developers | 167,000 hours/year | 17,000 | 28,000 | 3,000 |
| Training space | 69,000 classroom days/year | 7,000 | 33,000 | 18,000 |

A major category of solutions identified to address the capacity gap relate to increased use of alternative, nontraditional media. Expanded use of video tele-training would minimize travel time and expenses, allow top experts to reach many more students, and make the best use of talented instructors. Additional computer-based training and use of electronic performance support systems would reduce the requirement for formal classroom training, reducing demand for instructors, space, and delivery support, and cutting the travel budget.

Most organizational development models suggest that the process of change management proceeds through a set of rational steps, instituted at the top of an organization and unfolding through a series of planned phases and actions. Indeed, in the introduction to the distance learning case study volume that precedes this one, Deborah Schreiber proposes just such a model. She suggests that as an organization's distance learning program begins to mature, it typically forms an interdisciplinary steering team with executive leadership and representatives from information technology, network systems, broadcasting, communications, instructional design, and training or performance consulting. In the case of the IRS, a steering group was formed—but it had no power. It lacked executive membership, it had no representatives from network systems or corporate communications, and it addressed only satellite teletraining, not the other media. The impetus for distance learning arose and has generally remained at the middle levels of the organization. While there have been attempts to coordinate the agency's distance learning efforts, the various entities responsible for sponsoring online learning, employee performance support systems, and satellite teletraining are still largely independent.

The earliest IRS distance learning initiatives began in two separate departments starting in the late 1980s:

• *The IRS Studio,* whose initial mission was to produce informational videos, began a slow transition from video production to interactive video teletraining (IVT) when it began to rent satellite uplinks for periodic informational broadcasts.

In 1990, the studio established a pilot satellite network with downlink sites at fifteen IRS offices to test the concept of IVT.

• *The National Learning Center* (NLC), whose mission is to train technical computer personnel and end users on software, hardware, and data communications, began its distance learning efforts in 1987 with text-based self-study computer courses supported by online testing and individual trainee coaching over the phone.

The ongoing reorganization of the IRS human resources function, rather than consolidating distance learning leadership and policy, has further decentralized it. From 1995 until the middle of 1999, oversight and delivery of distance learning was in several separate offices, but at least they were all under the national Corporate Education Division umbrella; only the TV studio was located outside Corporate Education. As of October 1999, the television studio that produces agency IVT courses belongs to the Communications Division. The NLC now belongs to the chief information officer. The IVT Project Development Office, responsible for the nationwide IVT infrastructure for satellite delivery, and the Office of Performance Technology (OPT), responsible for development of online and computer-based performance support tools, belong to the director of human resource technologies. Finally, the General Business Institute (GBI), responsible for training distance learning course developers and instructors, particularly for the IVT medium, belongs to the national director of learning and education. Although the IVT Project Office, OPT, and GBI all fall under the human resources officer, they are separated by more intervening layers than they were before the reorganization.

This fractionalization of responsibility for the agency's distance learning policy and implementation was an unintended by-product of the agency's larger, long-range goal to embed all support functions within the new business units so that the support functions would be as close as possible to their new customers. However, the reorganization of these functions does render development of an overall distance learning strategy problematic.

In sum, the business problem is, How can an agency training program, which itself is attempting revolutionary changes, support and facilitate a much larger, all-encompassing transformation of the agency's culture and organization?

## The IRS Population and Culture

Between FY 1992 and the end of FY 1999, the IRS experienced a significant downsizing (from 136,804 to approximately 105,000 employees, or about 23 percent). As part of the ongoing reorganization, the agency has made a concerted effort to reduce the number of organizational layers and to increase the managers' spans of control. External hiring has been largely limited to temporary or seasonal clerical and paraprofessional help to process tax returns and answer taxpayer phone calls. As a result, our agency population has become older, and the average length of service in the agency has gone up. Our professional employees have tended to spend their entire careers within the agency. As the new century dawns, a sizable percentage of the full-time permanent employee group is within five to ten years of retirement eligibility.

It will probably not surprise the reader that the IRS is a traditional, conservative organization. The two mainstream occupations from which a majority of the agency's executives traditionally have emerged are *revenue agents*, or professional accountants responsible for audits and examinations, and *revenue officers,* responsible for collection of delinquent taxes. We live in a agency culture that values facts and figures, stability and rationality. Our traditional management style has been authoritarian, top-down, and detail-oriented. What may be more surprising than these stereotypes is that I believe no government agency more earnestly strives to do the right thing. Most managers and employees truly believe they have provided the best service possible to the American taxpayer, and most have been deeply hurt and embarrassed by the negative publicity our agency has received in the last few years. Internally, we have embraced the quality movement; we have worked hard at promoting diversity; we have forged a largely solid partnership with the National Treasury Employees Union; and we have tried to remain sensitive and open to employee concerns and feedback, albeit with mixed results. If there is one fault with our efforts, it may be that we take on too many "right things" at once, rendering the results less effective than we would wish.

One of the right things we are pursuing is to become a learning organization. As described by Peter Senge (1990) in *The Fifth Discipline,* a learning organization is one in which "people continually expand their capacity to create the results they truly desire, where new and expansive patterns of thinking are nurtured, where collective aspiration is set free, and where people are continually learning how to learn together." While our agency aspires to become a learning organization, we are having great difficulty in understanding exactly what that means and how we must go about transforming ourselves to achieve this goal. In particular, few individuals in our organization have thought about how much our culture will have to change for our agency to become one.

Before the IRS can become a learning organization, employees and managers will have to think of "learning" and "training" as processes that are embedded in daily activities and work tasks, not as formal, instructor-led training courses that occur in classroom isolation. Training modules and performance support systems will have to become just-in-time, available whenever the employees need them. In a learning organization, individual employees will be increasingly responsible for proactively identifying their own training needs, pursuing available training opportunities, and acquiring necessary job skills. Employees will have to embrace the concept of lifelong learning as discussed in Chapter One of this book.

In the top-down, authoritarian environment that characterizes the historical IRS culture, it has been considered management's responsibility, not the employee's, to identify and fill training needs. By extension, in the classroom, primary responsibility for a trainee's mastery of new material lies with the instructor, not the employee. Nontraditional training opportunities such as online self-study courses place a responsibility on trainees that goes against everything the IRS culture has taught them to expect in the training arena. This attitudinal issue compounds the challenge facing the agency's distance learning champions.

## IRS Distance Learning Accomplishments

In this case study, I have consciously focused on our problems and our remaining challenges because I thought they would be more instructive and useful to readers than our successes. But indeed, we have much to be proud of with our distance learning programs. We have come a long way in a very short time.

In just six years, the number of satellite informational and teletraining programs has increased by 1,750 percent—from 13 programs in 1993 to 241 in 1999. In the fiscal year ending September 1999, over eight hundred hours of total programming were provided to 17,996 trainees. Our one-way video, two-way audio infrastructure features approximately 130 downlink receiving sites in IRS field offices and one permanent uplink location in New Carrollton, Maryland, which houses two studios. Studio instructors communicate with distant trainees using a ONE TOUCH Viewer Response System. By FY 2002, we project that our network will include 230 downlink sites, bringing 95 percent of our employee population within commuting distance of a satellite classroom. Within the next two years, we will add a second channel of IVT broadcasting and increase the broadcast day from five to thirteen hours by offering multiple airings of programs across our six time zones (Puerto Rico to Hawaii). From its 1987 start providing computer trainees with text-based self-study courses, NLC had begun to purchase and provide off-the-shelf online courses by 1995. By 1999, NLC was offering 673 courses to employees at its intranet Web site. In addition to its online courses, the NLC also supports text-based self-instructional courses and courses on CD-ROM since many IRS employees still lack state-of-the-art computer equipment, Internet access, or computer expertise adequate to complete online courses. Excluding the continued classroom offerings, the NLC enrolled a total of 11,777 trainees in various courses during 1999.

OPT, formerly the Employee Performance Support Systems Institute, was founded in 1996 to develop in-house, custom-designed computer-based training (CBT) courses and help systems for internal customers. OPT produced its first CBT course, Bribery Awareness, in 1997. In 1999, it produced nine courses, and it also expanded its mission to create internal learning centers and knowledge management portals. Table 8.2 provides a summary of key distance learning statistics relating to course offerings, participants trained, and budgetary support of the various distance learning components. Compiling the table data was a major task. While we are experienced and thorough when it comes to creation and maintenance of taxpayer data, we are still in the early stages of creating a uniform Management Information System for our distance learning programs. Readers will note that there are gaps in Table 8.2. There was no single database where I could obtain the information. For some data elements, conflicting information was being maintained by two or more individuals in different offices, so that I was forced to choose which set of data seemed most credible. For other data elements, there simply was no information at all. The institutional memories of the various distance learning entities, and therefore the availability of historical data for early years, is completely dependent on how long the various responsible officials have held their current positions, as well as their personal interest in maintaining historical records. The database that contains trainee course evaluations is only two years old, so it is impossible to determine whether trainee evaluations of nontraditional courses have improved over time.

Since it was impossible to create a complete set of data for Table 8.2, I debated leaving the table out altogether. However, I decided that the table's gaps were per-

### TABLE 8.2. KEY IRS DISTANCE LEARNING STATISTICS.

|                              | FY 93  | FY 94  | FY 95  | FY 96   | FY 97  | FY 98  | FY 99  |
|------------------------------|--------|--------|--------|---------|--------|--------|--------|
| IVT programs conducted       | 10     | 43     | 36     | 36[1]   | 117    | 201    | 241    |
| Satellite participants       |        |        |        |         |        |        | 17,996 |
| Satellite network budget ($)[2] | $207K | $361K | $320K | —       | $1.4M  | $2.55M | $2.34M |
| NLC enrollments[3]           |        |        |        |         | 4,231  | 7,582  | 11,777 |
| NLC budget ($)               |        |        |        | $57K    | $119K  | $615K  | $963K  |
| OPT/CBT courses developed    |        |        |        |         | 1      | 2      | 9      |
| OPT budget ($)               |        |        |        |         | $477K  | $807K  | $1.3M  |

[1] Funding freeze precluded expansion plans.

[2] Includes hardware, telecom costs, course development, and delivery for IVT only; informational programs are not included. The FY 98 funds included system expansion that carried over into FY 99.

[3] Excludes computer classroom courses.

haps as instructive as its inclusions were. They illustrate our lack of consistent management information, which is a barrier to comprehensive evaluation of our distance learning program.

# Linking Organizational Management with Program Implementation

## Integration with the IRS Organizational Mission

While some agencies' distance learning organizations might find it difficult to attain full integration with the overall organizational mission, that is not the case at the IRS. The agency's all-consuming focus on reorganization has ensured that its distance learning components are fully engaged and integrated in the transitional strategic planning and implementation process. During the first three years of the new century, thousands of agency employees will either change jobs or will find their current duties substantially changed as the new IRS business divisions are established. The top priority for *all* the agency's training and education units is to ensure that new or revised training courses are available quickly, and that adequate numbers of well-qualified instructors are available to teach or facilitate those courses. Nontraditional training programs are seen as a critical component in closing the training capacity gap, which—through sheer anticipated volume—classroom courses cannot meet.

More than likely, the major reason that no IRS executive has stepped up to champion an overall distance learning program is that they all are consumed with the reorganization. That is not to say that executives responsible for the various training and education units do not value their distance learning programs, they do. But since the units actively involved in distance learning development (the NLC, the OPT, the IVT Project Office, GBI, and the TV Studio) are functioning and producing reasonably well within their separate spheres, there has not been a pressing need for the executive cadre to forge an overall distance learning strategy. The distance learning units, in their own way, continue to support the reorganization with design and delivery efforts. The good news is that distance learning efforts are fully integrated in support of the agency mission. The bad news is that each distance learning unit is left to develop its own priorities, policies, and operating procedures without regard to the other units.

In the IVT program area, the IVT Project Office has attempted to provide agencywide policies and coordination. The Project Office has been responsible for making the business case for the IVT infrastructure expansion. It has established liaisons with other agencies and companies who are also involved with IVT implementation. It has sponsored an internal IVT steering group that, as discussed earlier, lacks real power—but at least fosters some degree of communication. Unfortunately, since the Project Office is at the same organizational level as the other distance learning units, it has been difficult for the project manager to exercise IVT program leadership or to enforce agencywide policy. And while the project manager maintains communication with the National Learning Center personnel, his scope does not extend to policy development for online course delivery.

If our individual distance learning components are fully integrated with the larger organizational mission, then why should we care that they are not integrated with each other? Three issues arise:

• *Budget prioritization.* As can be seen from Table 8.2, the budget allocated to the agency's distance learning initiatives is significant. Each distance learning unit, within its own division, prepares annual budget justifications, tracks its own dollars, and answers to its own chain of command for its results. But there is no distance learning executive to consider such issues as the proper balance between these budgets or where distance learning funds can most effectively be spent in support of agency priorities.

• *Unclear division of responsibility.* Without overall coordination and leadership, the various distance learning units may inadvertently duplicate one another's efforts in some areas while allowing other tasks to fall through the cracks. This problem has been seen most clearly in the IVT area, where three of the distance learning entities have sponsored initiatives to help train IVT course developers and instructors' initiatives that have sometimes resulted in inconsistent guidance to their audience. Other IVT areas, most notably support of infrastructure maintenance in the field, have not received adequate attention from any of the distance learning entities.

• *Ad hoc media selection decisions.* In addition to the distance learning units discussed earlier in this chapter, the IRS Learning and Education Division and other divisions of the Human Resources Organization have several institutes that are responsible for developing managerial, tax-related, and other kinds of training courses. As these institutes venture into development of nontraditional courses, they find it difficult to determine which medium or combination of media will be most effective for any given training need and trainee population. This has led to development of some courses using inappropriate media, which has had an adverse impact on employee acceptance of nontraditional training opportunities in general. If there were stronger executive leadership, the advice and guidance given by the various distance learning units to agency course developers in other institutes could be more consistent.

## Management Support Systems: Budgetary Systems and Expenditures

Forecasting, evaluation, and tracking of distance learning courses are well integrated into the overall IRS training system. Early each summer, local offices are asked to canvas their managers and employees concerning projected training needs for the coming year. These needs are rolled up through a nationwide, automated database called the Administrative Corporate Education System, or ACES. Once the agency's executives make decisions about training priorities and funding levels, ACES is used to fund the courses and trainees that are above the funding cutoff line. ACES is used to capture budget allocations and expenditures relating to trainee and instructor travel, training supplies, contracts with external vendors, and IVT studio costs. ACES also contains the agency course catalog that describes the hundreds of existing IRS courses.

The online distance learning courses sponsored by the NLC and the IVT courses sponsored by all the various course development institutes are also contained in ACES files. As with classroom courses, delivery costs and trainee history records for distance learning courses are captured in ACES. The only IVT expenses not captured in ACES are for infrastructure expansion and satellite transmission costs, along with some of the development and course conversion costs funded by the IVT Project.

One problem with the ACES database is that it is not easy to isolate IVT and online course expenditures from other expenditures. Easily available reports are organized by sponsoring institute rather than by medium. Budgetary data are based on the IRS cost structure system, which also does not code expenditures by medium. For this reason, individual distance learning managers tend to keep their own historical files. Those were the data used to develop Table 8.2.

As the IVT delivery program has matured, the philosophy concerning the cost of programs has changed. During the early years, cost per student was not as important as student reaction to a program. The emphasis from the program sponsors' viewpoint was on learning how to use the new medium, not on cost containment. By the mid-1990s, however, the emphasis had changed. IVT programming can be enormously expensive, and questions had arisen concerning costs and relative benefits. The IVT Project Office instituted an approval process that required curriculum managers to complete a simple cost-benefit analysis form, which was submitted to the IVT Steering Group for review. In actuality, few if any courses were rejected by the Steering Group—the group was advisory only. However, the organizational message was clear: IVT costs should be minimized.

One initiative that was designed to reduce cost was the electronic classroom. When the TV Studio added a second set of studio and control rooms to its operation, it envisioned an instructor-controlled environment in which the IVT instructor would operate most of the studio equipment. Instructors would use the ONE TOUCH system to handle audio; they would use PowerPoint and a computer to build and display graphics in support of a course. They would even wear a sensor that would allow automatic cameras to follow their movements. With this model, studio crew support would be reduced from eight to ten down to one or two.

The instructor-controlled studio model has worked well for many organizations and agencies, including some whose case studies are profiled elsewhere in this book. So far, however, it has *not* worked well for the IRS. IRS courses are primarily taught by technical employees on the front line for whom teaching is a minor collateral duty. While a few "resident lead instructor" positions exist around the country, it would be impractical to maintain a full-time instructor cadre because of the large number of specialists needed to teach the hundreds of distinct courses. Typically, one of our part-time instructors may be brought in to the studio just once to teach an IVT class. Even when such instructors are given the opportunity to practice with the various studio tools available to them, they have consistently asked for crew support. The TV Studio philosophy has been that it is more important to put these part-time instructors at their ease in front of a camera and allow them to concentrate on their course content than to bring them up to speed on the IVT technology.

In addition to our part-time instructors' desires for crew support, another issue has driven a move away from an emphasis on producing IVT courses at the lowest cost possible. By 1999, executives up to the commissioner level were hearing loud and clear that managers and front-line trainees were disgusted with the poor quality of some IVT courses. Quality issues will be discussed in the next section of this chapter. The bottom line on budget issues at this point, however, is that cost concerns are not as important as program quality. We must meet customer standards for quality if IVT is to be an effective training tool in the organizational transition. While we will continue to struggle with the appropriate balance between cost and quality, finding the right balance between the two should be easier as we continue to gain experience and skill with IVT development and delivery.

## Management Support Systems: Program Evaluation and Development Issues

Evaluations of trainee reactions to courses, called Level 1 feedback, are collected on almost all IRS courses. Evaluations of trainee knowledge acquisition as a result of a course, called Level 2 feedback, are collected on selected courses. Historically, Level 2 evaluations have been used in some of our technical fields to make decisions about employee retention and placement. As a result, a decision to include a Level 2 knowledge test in any course is subject to union negotiation. Evaluations of trainee behavior change as a result of a course, called Level 3 feedback, are rare in the IRS.

Level 1 evaluation results for all IRS courses are contained in a database called ITEMS. During FY 99, there was one mandated evaluation form for all training classes, regardless of medium. The form included six questions that specifically related to IVT courses. For FY 2000, a separate evaluation form will be used for IVT courses, although the data will still be loaded and available from the ITEMS database. The ITEMS database is maintained by a contractor and available on the Internet. At any given point, it contains data on the current and the prior fiscal year. To conduct a historical analysis of evaluation results, it is necessary to obtain prior-year archives. ITEMS features several canned report formats available to course designers and training managers, but none of them are useful for evaluation of distance learning offerings. A program manager would either need to pull evaluation data for each individual course or obtain the raw ITEMS database to extract more useful information about distance learning offerings.

The quality of IVT courses varies as much as that of classroom courses, and so do the Level 1 IVT evaluations. In general, however, the ITEMS database documents that IVT courses are not rated as highly as classroom courses. One reason for the lower evaluations is the employees' continued preference for the classroom format. However, another reason is that many of the courses *have* been of low quality. Many satellite programs have been billed as IVT "training" that have actually been pure information sharing—lots of "talking heads" and little or no interaction and skills practice. The inexperience of new IVT course designers who must go through a natural learning curve has contributed to poor course quality. Another contributing factor has been the inadequate time frames allocated by many developers to design and produce their IVT projects.

## Management Support Systems: Training for IVT Course Developers

In 1996, the General Business Institute and the TV Studio, in partnership, developed and delivered a course called Train the Teletrainer. Although the original intention was to develop separate courses for IVT designers and IVT instructors, we quickly found that most of our IVT courses were one-time shots, due to the many tax law changes and continuing organizational changes that are a feature of our environment. The same individuals were involved in a course's development and delivery. Train the Teletrainer provided its students with knowledge and skills in both design and satellite instructional techniques. Participants were not allowed to enroll unless they had a live IVT development project in hand. After enrollment, they each received a self-study guide and course video with several lessons. As they completed each lesson, they were required to complete tasks related to the lesson content: They developed course objectives, a lesson script, accompanying student materials, and specifications for course visuals. After completing the various lessons and exercises, they were scheduled to come to the studio for an orientation and to practice delivering their draft course material. One unexpected by-product of the course was that it helped some participants to decide that IVT was not the proper medium for their material. While this decision meant that an expensive training experience would not be used, it also meant that course material that was unsuited to IVT delivery from the start would not be produced in that medium, which was a valid result in its own right.

A major problem with the teletrainer course was that, given the growing volume of new IVT development projects, the course could not be scheduled often enough to catch all the potential projects at the right point, so a lot of programs went forward without adequate coaching and feedback. Currently, an individual coaching process is evolving to take the place of the formal course. Both the TV Studio personnel and the General Business Institute are involved in this ad hoc coaching of individual IVT project teams. In addition to providing the teams an orientation to the studio and practice in front of the camera, the program includes coaching new IVT course designers on proper IVT design. Basic design techniques that new IVT developers are encouraged to follow include

- "Chunking" course content so that trainees are changing activities (discussions, studio lecture, Q&A, local exercises) every eight to twelve minutes
- Using short, drop-in video trigger tapes (B-rolls) to focus and elicit discussion
- Incorporating exercises, discussions, and case studies
- Using on-site distance facilitators

Typically, these distance facilitators are knowledgeable in the course subject matter, and are tapped in advance by the studio instructors to become part of the course delivery team. Distance facilitators can answer some trainee questions, run local breakout exercises and discussions, and act as the local eyes and ears for the studio instructors.

When it became clear that too many IVT course developers were continuing to produce informational, "talking head" programs rather than bona fide training courses, the General Business Institute developed a second course for IVT developers called Distance Facilitation Techniques for IVT Course Design and Delivery, which is conducted twice a year. The course begins with an introduction to distance learning and why the IRS is promoting it. It introduces trainees to the benefits of having distance facilitators at each downlink site during satellite-delivered IVT courses. The Distance Facilitation course is built around a series of exercises, using the TV studio facilities and simulated downlink sites created using rooms near the studio. Trainees take turns facilitating breakout exercises as part of a simulated broadcast. These future IVT course developers get to experience how the use of distance facilitators at each downlink site can exponentially increase trainee interaction and accountability.

Earlier in this chapter, I referred to the difficulty our course developers have had in trying to decide which medium or combination of media would be best to deliver new courses. In some cases, this confusion has led to an overreliance on the familiar classroom model, while in other cases, it has caused course developers to select an inappropriate or ineffective nontraditional medium. The Distance Facilitation course introduces course developers to a simple model they can use to walk through the process of media selection (see Figure 8.1). Since course developers both inside and outside the agency have found the model helpful, I have included it in this chapter. Keep in mind, however, that the process of media selection is not as straightforward as the model would suggest. The best solution is usually to use a combination of media whenever possible. Also, circumstances vary from organization to organization; for example, your organization may have other media that we do not. The bottom line in media selection is to be guided by this question: Given my content learning objectives and the characteristics of my trainee population, what media are available to me to maximize the effectiveness of the learning experience?

## Lessons Learned

I have truly enjoyed my involvement in the IRS distance learning program. I am convinced that nontraditional courses are the wave of the future; they seem to me to be indispensable tools for employees to acquire needed knowledge and skills exactly when they need them. If your organization is just starting out on its own distance learning journey, here are the lessons we have learned that I think will help you the most:

• Keep in mind that there is an inevitable learning curve through which all organizations must proceed as they develop a high-quality distance learning system. Be prepared for some bumps along the way, and expect that as you learn more and make your offerings more sophisticated, you will probably continue to look

## FIGURE 8.1.  TRAINING DESIGN AND DEVELOPMENT MEDIA SELECTION MODEL.

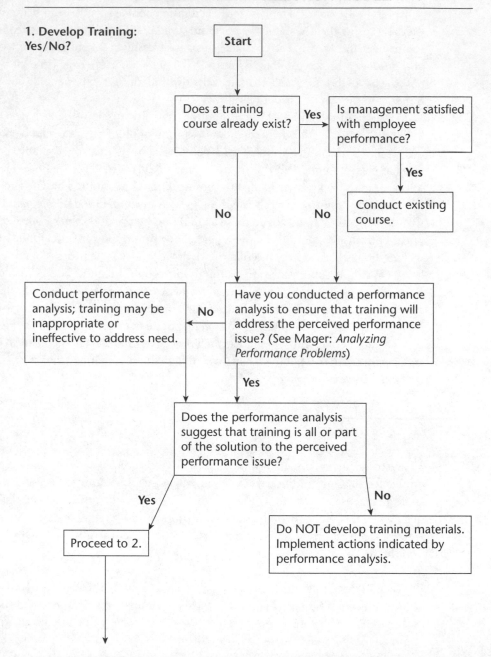

## 2. Media Selection

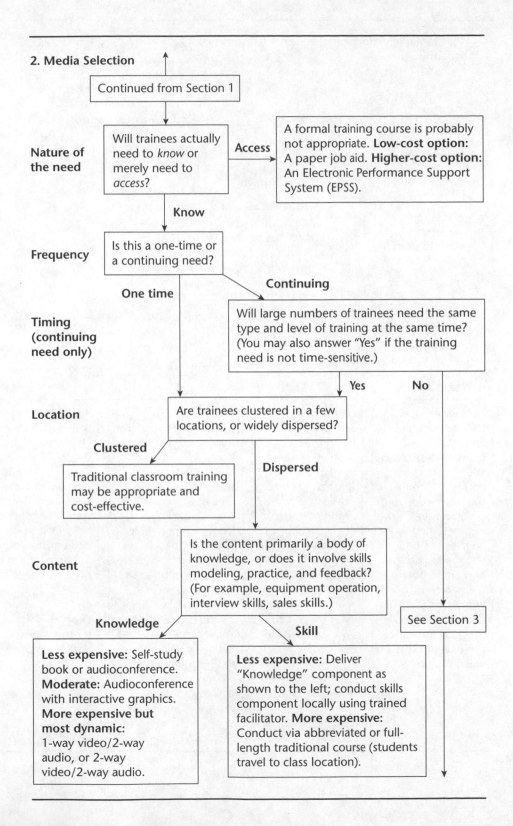

Continued from Section 1

**Nature of the need**

Will trainees actually need to *know* or merely need to *access*?

**Access** → A formal training course is probably not appropriate. **Low-cost option:** A paper job aid. **Higher-cost option:** An Electronic Performance Support System (EPSS).

**Know**

**Frequency**

Is this a one-time or a continuing need?

**One time**

**Continuing**

**Timing (continuing need only)**

Will large numbers of trainees need the same type and level of training at the same time? (You may also answer "Yes" if the training need is not time-sensitive.)

**Yes**  **No**

**Location**

Are trainees clustered in a few locations, or widely dispersed?

**Clustered**

Traditional classroom training may be appropriate and cost-effective.

**Dispersed**

**Content**

Is the content primarily a body of knowledge, or does it involve skills modeling, practice, and feedback? (For example, equipment operation, interview skills, sales skills.)

See Section 3

**Knowledge**

**Skill**

**Less expensive:** Self-study book or audioconference. **Moderate:** Audioconference with interactive graphics. **More expensive but most dynamic:** 1-way video/2-way audio, or 2-way video/2-way audio.

**Less expensive:** Deliver "Knowledge" component as shown to the left; conduct skills component locally using trained facilitator. **More expensive:** Conduct via abbreviated or full-length traditional course (students travel to class location).

## 3. Media Selection (continued)

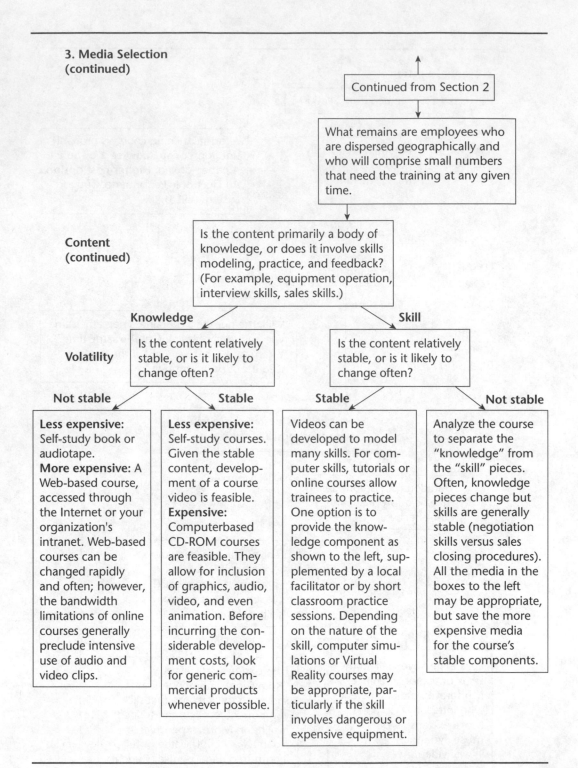

**Content (continued)**

**Volatility**

Continued from Section 2

What remains are employees who are dispersed geographically and who will comprise small numbers that need the training at any given time.

Is the content primarily a body of knowledge, or does it involve skills modeling, practice, and feedback? (For example, equipment operation, interview skills, sales skills.)

**Knowledge**

**Skill**

Is the content relatively stable, or is it likely to change often?

Is the content relatively stable, or is it likely to change often?

**Not stable**

**Stable**

**Stable**

**Not stable**

**Less expensive:** Self-study book or audiotape.
**More expensive:** A Web-based course, accessed through the Internet or your organization's intranet. Web-based courses can be changed rapidly and often; however, the bandwidth limitations of online courses generally preclude intensive use of audio and video clips.

**Less expensive:** Self-study courses. Given the stable content, development of a course video is feasible.
**Expensive:** Computerbased CD-ROM courses are feasible. They allow for inclusion of graphics, audio, video, and even animation. Before incurring the considerable development costs, look for generic commercial products whenever possible.

Videos can be developed to model many skills. For computer skills, tutorials or online courses allow trainees to practice. One option is to provide the knowledge component as shown to the left, supplemented by a local facilitator or by short classroom practice sessions. Depending on the nature of the skill, computer simulations or Virtual Reality courses may be appropriate, particularly if the skill involves dangerous or expensive equipment.

Analyze the course to separate the "knowledge" from the "skill" pieces. Often, knowledge pieces change but skills are generally stable (negotiation skills versus sales closing procedures). All the media in the boxes to the left may be appropriate, but save the more expensive media for the course's stable components.

back with some horror on your earlier products. But be tolerant of the learning process! I think distance learning development is a journey, not a destination.

- Likewise, it will probably take some time for the managers and employees in your organization to accept the new training media. Distance learning implementation is a major cultural change, and it will never happen as quickly as its champions hope or expect.

- Whenever possible, involve your end users and executive customers in the planning and design of your systems and training courses. You will gain their early buy-in, you will help to educate them about distance learning, and you will be able to give them better products than if you proceeded on your own.

- Make sure the hardware and software are there to support your new courses, and that they work well. For example, do not produce an Internet course if many of your employees lack easy Internet access, and do not incorporate audio and video if many of your employees are still limping along with 386 computers. Remember that customers will need your support and guidance in mastering the technology needed to complete distance learning courses. Make sure your products are as user-friendly as possible, and provide support systems for distant employees. Otherwise, your potential customers will walk away.

## Conclusion: Onward to Stage 4

In Chapter Two, Zane Berge proposes four stages of distance education implementation. In Stage 3, an organization has developed a distance learning policy, and a stable process is in place to facilitate the identification, development, and delivery of appropriate technology-delivered courses. In Stage 4, an organization's distance learning program has reached organizational maturity as an established, discrete business unit whose policies, communications, and practices support agencywide business objectives. I began my work on this chapter convinced that the IRS distance learning program had achieved Stage 4. As the chapter draft took shape, however, it became clear to me that although the IRS distance learning champions may aspire to Stage 4, we are still working through the tasks of Stage 3.

If the agency is to reach the fourth stage of distance learning implementation, the following actions would be helpful:

- *Creation of an overall distance learning focus to coordinate and prioritize individual projects, be they intranet-based, CD-ROM, IVT, or other forms of nontraditional training.* I am not suggesting that the agency should reverse the direction of its reorganization and unite all the distance learning entities into one centralized division. However, it *will* be necessary to establish a stronger matrix to link the distance learning functions and to begin true formulation of agencywide distance learning policy, strategy, and priorities. Most important, the distance learning program needs a champion at the executive level, someone who will make creation of an agency-wide distance learning program a true priority. It is simply not possible to achieve a unified program when its promoters are midlevel or below and are located in isolated pockets of the agency support structure.

The challenge is to create this kind of corporate distance learning focus without creating a cumbersome bureaucracy. Centralized management and coordination offer the agency certain benefits (quality control, overall strategic planning, centralized decisions on budgets and priorities). But creation of a centralized bureaucracy would more than likely slow down the process of project identification, development, and delivery. And potentially, a certain level of ownership, excitement, and individually motivated creativity could be lost.

  • *Establishment of a Management Information System (MIS) that facilitates analysis of the IRS distance learning program.* As the research for this chapter demonstrated, information about budget, programs, and program evaluation is scattered throughout the organization. No historical information exists for earlier than two to three years back. The existing information is not easily retrievable, nor is it uniform. A viable MIS should be able to provide easily retrievable data concerning existing courses by medium, employees trained by medium, dollars spent by medium, dollars spent per employee to train within each medium, and evaluation (quality) data by medium.

  • *An increased level of employee acceptance of nontraditional training will have to evolve.* Even after an organization's distance learning is well institutionalized and it has established a distance learning policy and programs that address business objectives, if the employees continue to disparage the results, the program cannot sustain itself at Stage 4.

At the IRS, our employees may not as yet be enthusiastic about distance learning courses, but the good news is that the general quality of our courses and instruction is certainly improving, and trainees are beginning to accept that some level of nontraditional training delivery is here to stay, even if they do still wish we'd just send them off to Cleveland or Philadelphia to be "trained" in a classroom.

Within our agency, I believe three factors will contribute to eventual employee acceptance of the distance learning programs:

1. Continued improvements in distance learning course quality. As developers of nontraditional courses become more sophisticated in the new media, courses will evolve from an overreliance on information sharing to training modules that feature more interaction and skills practice. The pattern will be one of continual and evolutionary improvement in course design and delivery.

2. The simple passage of additional time for employees to adjust to a new conception of continuous learning will increase acceptance of nontraditional training.
3. Turnover—the departure of the many employees nearing retirement, and their replacement by younger employees who take computers, video, and non-linear learning for granted—will complete the transition.

Musing in 1958 about the processes of education, Bent and McLean observed, "Although no single key to this puzzle [of teaching and learning] has been found, baffled but determined educators continue their quest." More than forty years later, these words aptly describe the sincere efforts of the IRS's distance learning staffs to provide high-quality course design and instruction to the agency's employees and managers. Their efforts to facilitate the agency's transition to a continuously evolving, learning organization will be a critical factor in the agency's larger organizational transition and, most important, in its quest to provide a respected and high-quality level of service to the nation's taxpayers.

PART THREE

# SETTING COMPETITIVE STANDARDS

CHAPTER NINE

# STRATEGIC PLANNING FOR AN ONLINE DISTANCE EDUCATION PROGRAM

## Driving Change Through Education at the UAW-DaimlerChrysler National Training Center

Joseph R. Codde, Rhonda K. Egidio, Karyn J. Boatwright, Jack E. Zahn, Raymond J. Czarnik

As a global society we are moving into the Knowledge Age, where we will live, work, and learn differently than we did in the Industrial Age. To cope with the inevitable changes, we will need continual learning, skill development, and knowledge acquisition (Irby, 1999). The economy of a global society requires a workforce that is knowledge driven, collaborative, and able to deal with an accelerating pace of change. Possession of these qualities becomes a source of competitive advantage for both individuals and organizations (Norris & Malloch, 1997), and is thus a central function for organizations desiring to be viable and renewable.

The UAW-DaimlerChrysler National Training Center (NTC), established in 1985 for UAW-represented workers at DaimlerChrysler, recognized this shift and began offering educational and employee assistance programs designed to develop a world-class workforce to lead DaimlerChrysler through the new century. The NTC also recognized that technology could aid it in reaching its target audience with distance education programs. Today, the UAW-DaimlerChrysler NTC directs approximately forty-six educational and work and family life programs in forty-four locations across the country and at its eight Regional Training Centers. The most recent offering is an online distance education program that will allow over 77,000 workers access to education programs online via the Internet and World Wide Web.

The past decade has been one of mergers and collaborations—but perhaps none more fundamental to successful leverage in the Knowledge Age than the fusion of business and education for shared goals. The strategic planning process described in this chapter is the result of a business-education partnership between the UAW-DaimlerChrysler National Training Center (NTC) and Michigan State University (MSU) whose purpose was to build a distance education program to foster perpetual learning and reach as much as possible of the NTC's target audience.

The NTC chose MSU as a partner because the school is a leader in the field of adult education, and especially in bringing the advantages of technology to adult learning environments. Since 1996, the MSU's Virtual Interactive Teaching And Learning (VITAL) Program has been instrumental in training higher education faculty across Michigan to create online courses and offer distance education programs exploring pedagogical issues in distance education and promoting principles of online instructional design.

## The Challenge

The challenge the NTC-MSU partnership faces—one it shares with many organizations in this changing world—is to find a way to provide lifelong educational opportunities for the greatest number of employees. Traditionally, training and educational programs have been limited to on-site workshops, correspondence courses, conferences, and conventions. With the advent of satellite television, larger groups of people had access, but these programs are still limited because the audience must be in a location where they can receive the signal. Clearly, education via satellite is not a viable option for many workers.

Fortunately, today's computer technology and the Internet make it possible to provide distance learning opportunities without regard to the location of the students. Additionally, distance education via computer meets the increasing demand for flexible, relevant education programs. This generates the opportunity for business and education to develop partnerships that capitalize on each other's strengths.

In 1997 MSU and the NTC began to take advantage of this opportunity to fuse business and education, creating a fresh vision and learning environment for DaimlerChrysler workers. To advance workers' value and opportunities in the new knowledge economy, the NTC and MSU are collaboratively and strategically designing a program that links the NTC organizational mission with a comprehensive online distance education program to promote lifelong learning without regard to geographic locations, time zones, or shift work.

## Strategic Planning

Achieving this creative solution requires a comprehensive strategic plan that addresses issues both at the organizational and programmatic level. This is a complex matter, and one where it is useful to consider Berge's insight (described in Chapter Two of this book) that organizations go through four stages in planning and managing distance education. In this case, the NTC has begun to enter Stage 4 — strategic planning to guide cultural change and resource reallocation. It accomplished Stage 3 through a policy and program that provided distance education to a limited number of employees through a satellite delivery program. But the planning team recognized that, with the rapid changes in technology, a more comprehensive program could be offered.

As Berge notes, "Stage 4 in an organization's distance delivery capability relies on effective strategic planning." Strategic planning for this project was deemed essential from the beginning. The planning process allowed us to explore various alternatives for employing the NTC's human and financial resources to best advantage. It also allowed the various providers associated with the project to better understand their role. Other benefits of the plan included a better understanding of the program, a higher level of communication and participation among stakeholders, and better decision making (Bryson, 1988). The plan also allowed for a systematic deployment of the program.

Strategic planning must begin at the organizational level, when an organization considers its mission and identifies an unmet need or gap between where it is and where it wants to be. This chapter describes the process we followed and the steps we took, as illustrated and summarized in Figure 9.1.

### Organizational Strategic Planning Steps

*Action Area 1: Create and charge a planning team.* The challenges of planning and implementing a large-scale distance education program require a planning team equipped to address important issues and to make decisions. Members of this team should include representatives from the organization's upper management, communications, technology, member services, and financial management areas. The NTC planning team consisted of representatives from the Tuition Assistance Plan, communications professional staff, regional center coordinators, technical training coordinators, multimedia service coordinators, and the educational resources administrator.

Once created, the planning team must develop an agenda that addresses the issues necessary to successfully accomplish the organization's mission. In this case,

## FIGURE 9.1. STRATEGIC PLANNING PROCESS: DEVELOPING THE NTC ONLINE DISTANCE EDUCATION PROGRAM.

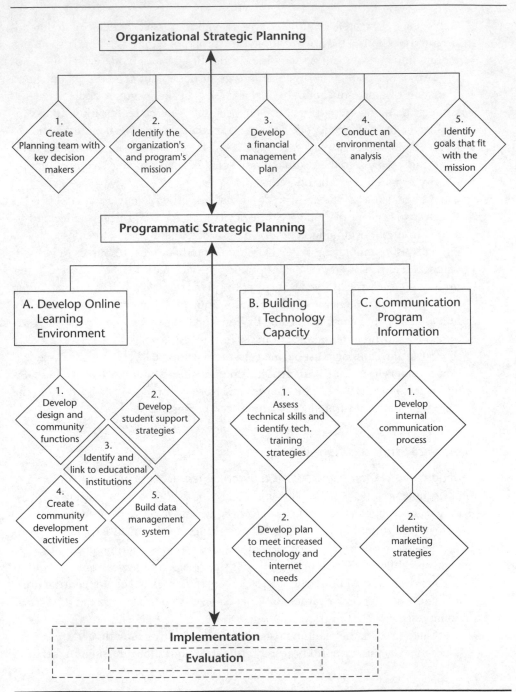

the NTC planning team's agenda included the following action items (Berge & Schrum, 1998):

- Respond to organizational mandates that identify needs and require solutions.
- Identify the purposes and goals of initiating and supporting a distance learning program offered through the NTC.
- Collect and summarize information on past and current distance education programs and the strategic plans of the organization.
- Evaluate strategies and technologies for delivering distance education programs (advantages, disadvantages, costs) and reach an agreement on which strategies and technologies will be used.
- Define what is needed to deliver technology-enhanced learning programs effectively, including equipment and facilities, skills and training, and policy development and culture change.
- Investigate successful models at other organizations.
- Estimate costs and resource commitments.
- Identify potential barriers to successful implementation of the recommended strategies and technologies and suggest how to manage these.
- Report findings and recommendations to senior decision makers.
- Define needs for stakeholders, members, and other potential participants.
- Identify and build collaborative relationships with outside providers and organizations that can aid in meeting the program's goals and objectives.

***Action Area 2: Identify the mission of the Online Distance Education Program.***
An important step in the strategic planning process is to develop a program mission that is consistent with the overall mission of the organization. This ensures that the activities related to and funded by the organization further the organization's goals and deserve the organization's expenditures.

In this case, as noted earlier, the mission of the online distance education program was to provide UAW-represented employees at DaimlerChrysler with lifelong educational opportunities that both enriched their lives and increased their value as employees. The goal was to provide an online distance education program and lifelong learning environment that encouraged participation and ensured access to the greatest number of people.

***Action Area 3: Conduct an environmental analysis.***  An environmental analysis is essential when planning a new large-scale program. This analysis looks at both the internal and external environment. The purpose of the internal analysis is to provide a better understanding of the organization's character, its offerings, and the available human resources. The external analysis provides information on the world in which it operates. Both are important as they give the organization, outside providers, and program partners a baseline view of the organization. From an organizational standpoint, breaking new ground without this understanding could lead to a disorganized program. In this case, essential points in analyzing the NTC and its environment included seven steps:

*Step 1: Identify important industry and organizational trends.* As competitive forces intensified in 1997, the UAW-DaimlerChrysler National Training Center's role as an engine for driving workplace change was brought into sharp focus. Assisted by favorable foreign exchange rates and quality products, Japanese automakers regained their market share. DaimlerChrysler's rivals among the U.S. Big Three improved quality of their products and introduced new vehicles that challenged DaimlerChrysler in its strongest market segments. Against such a backdrop, a highly trained, motivated UAW-DaimlerChrysler workforce became even more pivotal to sustaining the corporation's rebound in the mid-1990s. DaimlerChrysler had to have workers with the skills to keep pace with the ever-changing technology. Equally important, it had to have workers with attitudes that supported the new way of doing business, workers who could participate in workplace decision making and help keep the company up to speed. The UAW's commitment to preserve good jobs in America depended on workers' ability to adapt to such pervasive change.

*Step 2: Identify opportunities for training and education.* The NTC responded to the industry educational challenges by upgrading its programs and offering a variety of programs to meet members' needs. With many of its courses accredited by the American Council on Education, the NTC gained credibility as an institution that promoted higher learning while maintaining its traditional commitments to meeting the diverse training needs of workers. The training and education opportunities included GED completion programs, two- and four-year college-level programs, courses for personal interest, and specialized training programs.

*Step 3: Identify and overcome barriers to member participation in educational programs.* As an organization, the NTC focused on delivering educational programs to the membership. In the process, it identified numerous barriers that prevented many workers from participating in programs:

• Lack of time to participate due to shift work, job responsibilities, and home responsibilities
• Inconvenient schedules of current satellite distance education programs

- Inconvenient locations of program offerings
- Lack of confidence in their ability to participate in lifelong education or in their existing programs
- Lack of confidence in their ability to learn

By developing an online distance education program, many of these barriers were overcome, which allowed a greater number of people to participate. In a worker survey, the NTC discovered that 94 percent of respondents had access to the Internet either from their home or work locations, making an online distance education program a viable option.

*Step 4: Identify training and education problems and their potential solutions.* The largest problem the NTC faced was how to reach the greatest number of workers. Past programs required workers to attend a traditional classroom for face-to-face instruction or satellite broadcast programs. By taking advantage of current technology, including the Internet, the NTC was able to reach workers both on-site and in their homes.

*Step 5: Assess the potential business impact of the educational program.* The programs offered by the NTC, including distance education programs, focus on promoting the value of workers and ultimately the quality of DaimlerChrysler products. Although the direct impact that these programs would have on DaimlerChrysler would be difficult to measure, the program was deemed important in moving the company ahead in the next millennium.

*Step 6: Provide accountability for the use of NTC resources.* In the area of financial management and budgeting, accountability for spending is essential. Funding for programs is from a "Memorandum of Understanding" between the UAW and DaimlerChrysler that basically specified that DaimlerChrysler would make available funding at five cents per hour worked per worker. This is often referred to as the "nickel fund." The nickel fund is then used to pay tuition costs for UAW-represented workers, qualified dependents, and retirees.

*Step 7: Monitor changes in attitudes and perceptions related to training and education.* For programs to succeed at the NTC, the members must perceive these programs to be valuable and worthy of their participation. Through an aggressive evaluation program, the NTC monitors changes in attitudes and perceptions about various programs.

*Action Area 4: Identify program goals that fit with the organizational mission.*
Goals relate to specific items or activities that, once achieved, will aid in accomplishing the organizational mission. Goals should be framed as action items that direct project participants toward an end, the successful accomplishment of the organization's mission. Once goals have been set they require specific strategies to accomplish and should be articulated in the strategic plan. We shaped the goals for this program through collaborative participation between team members. This is the process we used to identify the primary goal outlined earlier, that of providing an online distance education program and lifelong learning environment that would encourage participation and ensure access to the greatest number of people.

*Action Area 5: Develop a financial management plan.* The budget is an important tool for use in the strategic planning process. In essence, the budget is a monetary expression of the strategic plan. Budgets should be formed using two distinct principles: policy and efficiency. At the policy level, the organization determines what programs to offer, what programs fit within the mission of the organization, and how much of the organization's resources should be allocated to each project. As a policy tool, the budget offers managers the opportunity to define the scope of selected programs and evaluate their benefits. When adding new programs without increasing revenue, an organization must make policy decisions on which programs offer the greatest benefit and value for those served and how resources are to be allocated (Bryce, 1987).

At the individual program level the principle of efficiency will influence budget formulation. Several specific questions need to be addressed here (Bryce, 1987): How much will the development of an online distance education program cost? What new equipment must be purchased? What will it cost to deliver the program on an ongoing basis? What will be the schedule of disbursements and expenditures over the life of the program?

## Programmatic Strategic Planning Steps

Programmatic strategic planning is an extension and expression of the organizational-level planning and reflects the organization's goals, financial planning, and environmental analysis. Strategic planning at this level is designed as a way to execute the strategies that enable the organization to meet its mission. This level surfaces as the organizational plan develops action areas that create the online distance education program. As the programmatic plan emerges, new specific function teams are created. In our case, the function teams working in this area included MSU VITAL learning environment designers along with vendor teams representing marketing, evaluation, media design, and technology—

hardware and Internet connectivity implementation and computer and Internet training.

**Program Strategic Planning Category A: Developing an Online Learning Environment.** The major visible outcome in this area is the actual Web site learning environment, LearnNTC.com. Rather than a corporate university, this is an online learning community center from which participants access links to educational institutions offering online courses leading to certificates and degrees, use support materials, and participate in community-building activities.

*Action Area 1: Develop design and community functions for the Web site.* This action area involves an interface between learning and technological design. In this specific case, the working teams discussed how the Web page would look and feel, what community objectives were desired, what kinds of support students needed, and what functions would facilitate students when selecting educational options. To expand the vision of what was possible in these areas, the teams searched the Internet for examples of best practices in design, function, user-friendliness, and visual appeal. We did not, however, want to be shortsighted and limit ourselves to the current state of the art. We wanted to set a standard for best practice by engaging in thoughtful and creative team processes.

In the pilot stage of the program, LearnNTC.com Web site development focused on six primary areas:

1. *Internet Learning Links.* This area involves three subsections: "Learning Online," which links to partner higher education institutions for the program; "More About the WWW," which includes links to sites that offer information on how to use the Internet and sites with free online workshops; and "Related Links," which features links to the NTC, UAW, and DaimlerChrysler Web sites among others of interest.
2. *Online Learning Tools.* This area was customized with support information and activities to promote readiness and success of our participants. A special feature in this area is an interactive readiness assessment and road rally that helps potential online learners reflect on their readiness in terms of technology capacity, Internet access, and personal learning traits that match the traits of successful online learners. Participants practice some essential skills necessary to be a successful online learner—sending an e-mail message with an attachment, contributing to a discussion and a chat room, and downloading a file. The road rally is an interactive online hunt that is fun as well as instructive. Participants receive a first question with a clue whose answer is located somewhere in the Online Learning area of the Web site. To correctly answer the

question, the participant will need to navigate and read through material in the area. When the first question is answered successfully, the participant gets the second question and a clue. The questions get progressively harder as participants' skills improve, helping them build self-confidence as well as specific knowledge.

3. *Tool Topics*. Web site information and learning tools initially covered the following areas:

Readiness
- Online Learner Assessment
- Online Learning Tools
- Road Rally

Success Strategies
- Motivation
- Time Management
- Study Skills

Self-Assessment
- Learning Styles

Written Communication
- Writing Strategy
- Writing Resources
- E-mail and Netiquette

Environment

4. *Frequently Asked Questions*. Participants can find answers to typical questions about tuition assistance, important dates, related policies and practices, and other program information in a well-developed FAQ area.

5. *Coming Soon / Contact Us*. The development of this program and Web site is a continuous process. In this area, participants can learn about the vision for the site and coming attractions.

6. *Community Area*. Participants are more likely to be successful if they are able to be part of a learning community. In this area, participants can share student stories and concerns in a discussion room, find contact information for other participants, and offer feedback on ways to improve our program, Web site, and community.

*Action Area 2: Develop student support strategies.* For NTC's overall learning online distance education program to succeed, individual participants needed to succeed. Because many participants were unfamiliar with learning online, a variety of student supports were developed to assist participants. These supports were offered online, face-to-face, and through mailings of useful resources. On the Learn-NTC.com Web site, support information was offered to help participants develop the student skills necessary for academic success—writing, time management, research, reading, etiquette, and motivation, among others. Additionally, a toll-free number was provided to enable participants to obtain direct information from a program coordinator.

*Action Area 3: Identify and link to educational institutions.* Participants were able to register for courses at any accredited institution, whether or not it was linked to the site. However, the site helped students select effective institutions by presenting links that NTC regarded as especially useful for its online students.

The linked schools were selected through a comprehensive application process. This process was deemed essential to the program, as member participants would be very limited in their knowledge for selecting institutions on their own. Through the application process, the NTC could select schools that met certain minimum criteria, assuring the participants that the linked schools offered programs that would meet their needs. A committee made up of representatives from the NTC and MSU reviewed the applications submitted and selected only those with credible programs. In selecting schools, the greatest emphasis was put on substance and range of course offerings and student support services. The review areas for selection covered a much broader range of factors, however—the committee considered the institution's Web site, accessibility and security, offerings of courses and programs online, history (including a history of online programs), accreditations, experience in providing educational services to the auto industry, technical capacity, and experience with tuition assistance programs. Reviewers also considered the number of students who had participated in and graduated from an online program, faculty expertise in teaching distance education courses, the support programs for distance education students, and the orientation programs offered to new distance education students.

*Action Area 4: Create community development activities.* In today's online learning environments, collaboration, shared goals, and teamwork are powerful forces (Palloff & Pratt, 1999). In this type of collaborative environment, the teacher serves as a facilitator of learning. However, many LearnNTC.com participants have completed high school under a model of learning in which the teacher was perceived to be the expert and was expected to disseminate knowledge. In an online community, learners can potentially construct knowledge from their collaborative experiences—but relatively few start out with the skills or mind-set to take full advantage of this opportunity.

The community environment of LearnNTC.com prepared participants for a new mode of learning. By taking part in readiness and community-building activities, participants rehearsed and prepared for their new student role in a safe, supportive environment.

*Action Area 5: Build data management systems.* Data management was incorporated into this learning environment for the purposes of customizing the environment to fit the individual, and collecting evaluation data. First, when learners arrived at the site, they were addressed by name and given notice of updates on the site since their previous visit as well as results of any group activity in which they had participated. Program developers, as an example of evaluative data collection, assessed which pages of the site were visited most frequently and how often on-site quizzes were taken.

**Program Strategy Category B: Building Technological Capacity.** When considering a technology-driven program, a very important step is to analyze an organization's present technology status, the skills of potential organization participants, and the organization's future needs. Then a specific plan for determining the technology resources to fill the gap between current capacity and needed capacity can be developed.

*Action Area 1: Assess technology skills and identify technology-training strategies.* In this case, the UAW membership that the NTC serves was surveyed to determine potential participants' technology skills and the degree to which they had computer access. Our results were surprisingly more positive than expected:

- *Computer access:* 68 percent had access to computers at home with only 11 percent not having access to any computer at home or work.
- *Computer readiness:* 86 percent of the respondents expressed comfort using computers and an interest in learning more about computers.
- *Keyboarding skills:* 72 percent of the membership felt somewhat or very comfortable with keyboarding skills.
- *Word processing skills:* 52 percent of the membership reported feeling somewhat or very comfortable with word processing software.
- *Internet access:* 67 percent of those with home computers reported personal access to the Internet and 94 percent reported Internet access from a computer they could use on their own time.
- *Internet readiness:* 91 percent of the membership showed enthusiasm for using the Internet.
- *Experience with Online Training:* 33 percent of the membership reported having used the Internet to take a class or training program.
- *Interest in Online Training:* 75 percent of the workforce expressed an interest in taking a course via the Internet through the NTC.

Once it was clear that there was sufficient interest for online learning, it was important to ensure that participants developed skills and tools for successfully handling the challenge. The environmental data analysis resulted in the conclusion that the target audience was moderately comfortable with computer basics but needed additional support to use the Internet and more specifically in developing online learning skills.

Three strategies were developed to meet the gap between current skills and necessary skills: online activities on how to use the Internet and learn online, technology training workshops at regional training centers and in plants, and technology helplines were located at regional training centers and in plants to provide telephone assistance.

*Action Area 2: Develop a plan to meet increased technology and Internet needs.* Even though the NTC had been very forward-thinking with technology, technological changes and increased demands with the new online learning program led NTC to conclude that it needed more. It decided to purchase new high-capacity computers and install these with high-speed Internet access in the regional training centers and at some plant locations.

### Program Strategy Category C: Communicating Program Information. This is a large-scale project involving many planning team members and a large audience, which makes effective communication essential.

*Action Area 1: Develop internal communication processes.* Collectively, there were over thirty people directly working on this program at the organizational and programmatic strategic planning levels. Providers from various states were part of the group, which meant that communication was a challenge. Two strategies to promote effective communication were implemented.

First, an online directory of all the team members was constructed at a Web site to ensure that all members had access to all pertinent contact information. Second, a project management Web site containing searchable functions and templates for entering objectives, action items, subtasks, responsible staff, status, and target dates was constructed. Every two weeks, via e-mail, project managers released progress reports to update planning team members on tasks completed, current status, and future actions. Occasional face-to-face meetings occurred when necessary for collaboration.

*Action Area 2: Identify Marketing Strategies.* The objectives of the marketing strategies were to generate awareness of the distance education program, educate the membership on the benefits of this program, motivate members to participate, and enroll members in the program. These objectives were linear—that is, with any given employee, each had to be accomplished before the next.

A number of internal marketing strategies were implemented to accomplish these objectives. Internal communication tools including an NTC publication, a separate announcement letter, a presentation at an NTC national conference, and visits to various plant locations informed members about the program. Once awareness was generated, a video was sent to all participants welcoming them to the program, showing the Web site, and describing the local support that they could expect. (Clips in the video included interviews with UAW members who had already had successful experiences with using the Internet for learning.) Finally, the Web site itself became a marketing tool by continuously adding new information and activities that benefited participants.

## Implementation and Evaluation

Strategic planning is defined as a disciplined effort to produce the decisions and actions that shape and guide the development of this program. Once a strategic plan has been developed, the plan then moves toward implementation, which includes ongoing review and evaluation. In this case, implementation began as a pilot project that allowed the NTC to offer the new online program to participants in the previous distance education program (which had been offered primarily via satellite and, later, fiber-optic systems). The review process began at the same time, with the goal of assessing the value of the program and the efficiency of the delivery mode. Essentially, we wanted to know as soon as possible if this program was of value to the participants, if it was working well, and if NTC resources were being wisely spent.

An evaluation program identifies the decisions that must be made and the program characteristics to be evaluated. These are the basic decisions that must be made:

- What is the purpose of the evaluation?
- Who will conduct the evaluation?
- What will be evaluated?
- What criteria will be used in the evaluation?
- What evidence will be appropriate?
- How will the evaluation be used for program improvement?

By first offering a pilot, we were able to evaluate the program for a number of purposes and to make improvements before redesigning and releasing the full program. For the purpose of program improvement, we chose to evaluate the ability of the program to be effectively fused into the infrastructure of the organization, and the effectiveness of the online and other strategies as they contribute to participant satisfaction and success. Everyone involved, but primarily the core team members of the NTC and MSU, evaluated the program formatively. The needs analysis and summative evaluation team included a professional program evaluator vendor to guide the soundness of the assessment and evaluation design.

If an innovation doesn't fuse smoothly then the program is apt to be side-tracked and success over time is difficult or totally impossible. The NTC has many systems, operations, and policies related to continuing education and many personnel who interface with this program in some way. The online learning option needed to fit with existing practices where that made sense—and to challenge those practices and surface new behaviors for the organization where necessary. The degree of fit or need for changes needed to be determined and all vested parties had to become part of creating the new environment that would support the new program.

Communication and involvement of relevant staff is key in integrating formative evaluation with continuous improvement of the pilot in readiness for a full program implementation. We used written surveys with our participants, direct phone calls, and a problem-discussion hot line to surface concerns relative to the program and host environment. Once concerns were evaluated, the appropriate staff was called together as a team to determine and implement a solution.

Infusing programs with technology often stimulates organizational review and change. For instance, we found that the NTC had always regarded online courses as similar to correspondence courses and therefore not eligible for tuition assistance. This turned out to be a problem in the context of the current program, but the small pilot group—about 120 people—made it feasible to explore the impact of changing this policy with numbers that were reasonable to manage. With additional information on the qualities of online learning, the organization realized that it would be desirable to change the policy and inform responsible staff of the new practice. The change was successfully made before the program opened up to the rest of the organization.

Another practice that surfaced in the evaluation of the new program was the process of applying for tuition assistance by filing a written application. The project team found that the process could be improved by putting the application online. Improvements that result from evaluation of an innovation often pervade beyond the scope of that particular project, and the tuition assistance application may prove to be such an improvement, with benefits extending beyond online courses to the whole NTC offering.

To evaluate for our second purpose—the effectiveness of online and other strategies as they contribute to participant satisfaction and success—evaluation strategies included needs assessment, satisfaction surveys, data collection, and focus groups.

A needs survey was conducted with a sample of 500 of the population of 77,000 UAW-represented workers. The survey was done by phone since this was deemed as a successful strategy from past experience with this organization. The phone survey took about twenty minutes to complete and included questions on the worker's interest and readiness in terms of technology access and computer and Internet skills. When the 120-member pilot group was selected, they completed a similar survey in written form.

At this phase in the project, we have not yet completed the pilot. Upon doing so, we will assess satisfaction with all aspects of the program including success with navigating and finding useful support in the online environment, ease of interfacing with organization policies and practices, usefulness of the video and other marketing strategies in terms of program awareness, and helpfulness of participating higher education institutions in all aspects of their student life.

Data on student participation in the program and satisfactory completion of courses will be maintained and continuously evaluated as will data on usage of individual areas within the LearnNTC.com Web site, the referral hot line, technology help services, local technology training, and problems that surface in any of these areas.

Upon completion of the initial pilot test, a second pilot test will be used to further evaluate the program. In this phase we will choose two or three plant locations. Although the program will be open to any UAW-DaimlerChrysler employee who may discover the program through modest internal marketing, the selected plants will receive more extensive marketing, on-site computer training, and more intensive support. Again the program will be evaluated and improved, applying the same purposes and strategies used in the initial pilot test. In the phase two pilot, extensive use will be made of focus groups. By having our sample from specific geographic sites, it will be possible to have more face-to-face contact for evaluative purposes. Eventually all plants and training locations will receive this focused attention and support as the program takes on full national capacity over a three-to-five-year period.

## Summary and Conclusion

To accomplish a distance education program that would reach the largest number of workers, the NTC and MSU collaborated to develop a strategic plan. That plan produced the decisions that shaped and guided the development of the online program and enabled the NTC to have a better understanding of the program, a higher level of communication and participation among stakeholders, an accommodation of divergent interests and values, and a process for orderly decision making.

Strategic planning took place on two separate levels: the organizational level and the programmatic level. At the organizational level, a planning team was created, the mission of the online distance education program was articulated, an environmental analysis was conducted, training and education problems and their potential solutions were identified, and a financial plan was developed. At the programmatic level, an online learning environment was designed, technological capacity was analyzed, and a plan for communicating program information was established.

The value of strategic planning is that it allows the organization to map out a program that benefits the organization's members and accomplishes the organization's mission. The strategic planning process and resulting strategic plan has enabled this program to go forward successfully. There are many examples of the benefits that result from careful strategic planning. This project can point to the following successes:

- Because the program was created with broad-based involvement of related departments within the NTC, the innovation is being integrated smoothly into the system of the organization.
- The pilot test surfaced problems with internal practices that could be resolved before releasing the program to the organization as a whole.
- Through discussions, teamwork, and problem solving the business and education partners developed a better sense of each other's culture and how to respect and blend the strengths of each.
- The quality of the program was enhanced by the successful inclusion of expert providers in marketing, Web site design, and evaluation.

The NTC recognized that DaimlerChrysler's employees were the organization's most important resource, and that having a knowledgeable workforce would be essential to ensure a successful shift into the Knowledge Age. Moreover, the NTC recognized that technology could enable DaimlerChrysler to reach workers through distance education on-line programs. Strategic planning was the primary tool that enabled the NTC and the UAW at DaimlerChrysler to reach their organizational goals.

CHAPTER TEN

# SUSTAINING DISTANCE EDUCATION AND TRAINING AT FIRST UNION

## Transitioning from the Classroom

Sherry H. Latten, J. Michael Davis, Neel Stallings

First Union National Bank, the nation's sixth-largest bank, has a branch network covering the Eastern seaboard and beyond. In the fast-paced and quickly changing financial industry, the bank must be able to provide real-time training to large numbers of employees spread across a geographically diverse area.

To ensure a highly skilled and competitive workforce, alternative training solutions had to be identified and implemented. An elegant solution was fashioned by using available First Union technology in satellite television delivery. With 2,400 viewing sites, First Union already had in place the most extensive satellite system in all of banking and its use for business television was commonplace. The transition from the classroom to distance education would be an evolutionary process, but the business was ready for new solutions.

## Key Business Drivers

Planning for distance education within First Union's First University began in the mid-1990s, with a more concentrated effort in 1997. As with many rapidly growing organizations, we faced increasing business challenges.

Our client base was quickly surpassing the existing training infrastructure. Mergers and organizational changes were creating an environment where key business decisions were being made faster than ever, leading to an increased demand for training as a result of new business strategies and processes. The need for training to reach growing numbers of participants, faster, and in their place of business was at an all-time high. We knew that traditional classroom training was not a possible solution for meeting the current business challenges because it cost too much and took too long to deliver.

- *Cost.* The cost to the business for having a majority of training delivered via the traditional classroom was high. If trainers were not on-site, clients had to fund travel budgets and assume the loss of productivity for travel time for participants. The alternative was to have trainers travel to participants and therefore potentially reduce the overall corporate training cost. The impact on the quality of life for our trainers, however, was tremendous. Knowing that one of First Union's key values was to encourage employees to balance work and family life, this was not an optimal solution.
- *Cycle times.* Implementation timelines for new business strategies and processes were becoming shorter. Between 1985 and 1999, First Union completed more than eighty acquisitions, growing to $253 billion in assets from ($16.6 billion). To achieve that growth, new initiatives were occurring faster than ever. Project timelines were accelerated to meet the growing demands. The impact on training: less time to build trainer expertise and less time to reach larger numbers of participants.

Distance education seemed an ideal solution for our business challenges. Not only did it address the current obstacles, it also offered new possibilities for our clients. It increased flexibility in scheduling and expanded the exposure to both internal and external experts.

## Learning Obstacles

Though cost and speed were two key business drivers, the traditional classroom also posed a series of learning obstacles in our ever-changing and rapidly growing environment. More often than not, required skill training was completed by having participants or trainers travel if an on-site solution was not available. For developmental training, on the other hand, access became a major learning obstacle.

Developmental training events such as leadership, communication skills, and personal growth courses were often viewed as optional and therefore more difficult to justify travel expenses if the course was not available on site. As a result, many employees lacked access to the high-quality training courses that were available to those in regional centers that could afford to employ trainers.

In addition to lack of access, we found that sites without trainers were creating their own developmental programs. Because of the varying skills and resources available to those developing the programs, inconsistencies and duplication of effort existed across the corporation. Where one employee found it easy to develop in an area, another employee had to be more assertive and take numerous additional steps to obtain the same knowledge. The learning opportunities were certainly inequitable, depending on location.

Satellite programming ensured a consistent message was provided to thousands more employees. First University was able to capitalize on the expertise across the corporation to develop core courses, while enabling states to focus solely on state-specific differences. Geographic location no longer made a difference to either the access to training or the quality.

## Target Audience

First University is the organization in First Union that supports the majority of training throughout the corporation. The overall population at First Union is in excess of seventy thousand, and a college structure enables us to target various segments of that population. Each college is focused on a different core business unit within the corporation with leadership development being centralized into one college. As a result, distance education course offerings can be targeted to specific job families.

## Outcomes Desired

In addition to overcoming the existing business challenges of cost, speed, and demand, we expected distance education to help us move beyond the boundaries imposed by traditional classroom training. As with any new endeavor, our expectations of distance education have passed through several key phases, and it seems clear that they will continue to evolve as we mature in our learnings. These are some of the key phases of the transition from the classroom to distance education:

- *Phase 1: Testing.* The expectation was focused on meeting operational business challenges such as cost and efficiency. During this phase, individual risk-takers tested distance education as a delivery method to overcome key business challenges. It is viewed as a secondary option relative to the traditional classroom.

- *Phase 2: Comparing.* The expectation begins to focus more on meeting learner and facilitator needs along with operational business needs. Rather than being a method that is primarily used by the risk-takers, it's a method being supported at an organizational level. In this phase, classroom and distance education are compared to one another without necessary emphasis on either medium's being appropriate for meeting differing needs. The perception begins to change from one where distance education is a secondary option to one that is comparable.
- *Phase 3: Exceeding.* The expectation is focused on exceeding traditional classroom goals in effectiveness, efficiency, and cost reduction. Infrastructure exists to support an ideal learning environment. Instead of comparing traditional classroom and distance education as interchangeable options, distance education is sought as an approach to meeting differing needs. The perception shifts from distance education's being a comparable method to its being the preferred method for specific needs.

Recognizing that the organization evolves through various phases of expectations, the key desired outcomes could be focused in several areas.

## Evolutionary Transition

Again, it is important to note that the origins of distance learning at First Union have been evolutionary rather than revolutionary. With the large number of outlets, most employees were well aware of the satellite system and virtually all had watched some programming; almost everyone tuned in to particularly newsworthy informational pieces or executive roundtables. All of these were studio produced and one-way, from the studio to the receiving site. The shift to satellite-delivered courses evolved out of a need to meet greater training demands, faster, better and cheaper. It was an idea that would require a complete paradigm shift in a culture where the current view was that classroom training was best and all other training failed in comparison. With the financial industry embroiled in a competition for survival of the fittest, we slowly began shifting mind-sets of trainers and participants to accept distance education as an optimal solution.

The evolution of training though satellite delivery began to develop around several key areas of advantages. The first area was the efficient manner that material could be delivered. It was not a large leap of logic to take the executive roundtable one step further by having an expert in a business area talking about methodology. As noted earlier, prior to the satellite option, this type of information dissemination was done in the old "dog and pony show" style, where the expert would make the rounds of the various business unit locations, repeating the same program for continuously new audiences.

## Efficiency and Effectiveness

Put the expert on a satellite broadcast, however, and everyone can tune in at the same time to hear the presentation. This is beneficial in two ways. All affected employees can hear the message at once, and the expert only needs to devote time once to the effort. Thus, the expert can increase span from the traditional classroom limits of 1:20 to as high as 1:200.

Consistency of message is another desired outcome. When the message is coming from a central location and at a single time, consistency is enhanced. The traveling dog and pony show was hampered by the length of time it took to get the message out. In today's fast-paced business world, critical information delivered in a timely fashion is the lifeblood of any organization.

Consistency has been a developmental issue at First Union's Employee Television Network (ETN) as well. ETN has sought from its origins to develop a brand for itself. This is essential to develop a share of mind with employees. Therefore, ETN has consistent signs, postings, music, and visuals that mark all of its productions with a consistent voice.

## Management Processes Strategic Plan

Distance learning is a core component of First University's ability to support both the mission and vision of First Union. First University includes some key statements in its strategic plan related to the implementation of distance learning:

- Create and deliver learning technologies to support employee development
- Build the infrastructure of the University and its processes in order to strategically and tactically increase our capacity

Including these statements in our strategic plan ensures that the implementation of distance learning is integrated into our daily work environment. It is a primary accountability and commitment by the university to the corporation. It is slowly becoming a way of doing business that has been driven by the needs of both our internal university structure and our organization's environment.

Individual colleges within the university began seeking solutions to meet their challenges. Once a holistic look was taken at the challenges facing the colleges, we identified the need for a more formalized focus on the direction of distance learning.

## Infrastructure

Technology and infrastructure along with design were the two primary functions created to support a strategic plan for distance learning. Some of the staffing came from the realignment of functions in the university. Other positions were newly created, including an Interactive Distance Learning (IDL) coordinator to set the strategy for the university and an IDL manager to set the strategy for the station. The successful implementation of distance learning required the support and partnership of many groups outside the university. The purchasing of satellite, videoconferencing, and multimedia desktop equipment, for example, required the financial support of multiple business units. To ensure optimal ROI, the equipment was purchased with an implementation strategy that extended beyond the scope of distance learning. The equipment would be used for daily operating business in addition to learning. Equipment costs could not be borne by any single college or business unit. Given the high expense of equipment and maintenance, support had to be given on a central level.

First University hit on a unique and elegant solution to the idea of fiscal support for Employee Television Network's training needs. Each college gave up a percentage of its travel budget to fund ETN's initiatives. This action not only brought down the cost of training to each college but also conveyed the implied message that ETN was to be used by each college in an effort to gain return on investment.

The planning for distance education continues to be a formalized effort within the university. It is likely that we will move into an environment where distance education is not a separate mission but our standard way of doing business.

## The Anatomy of Transition: The Case of Managing Human Resources Policies (MHRP)

Like all companies, First Union is under the jurisdiction of various federal and state agencies. It also has a number of company policies that are important to the employees of the company. These policies include issues of pay, performance, time away, and other matters governing the day-to-day operation of the company. It is obvious that these policies as well as the laws governing the company be applied in a fair and consistent manner. It goes beyond the commonsense equity of fair and consistent behavior, however, because inconsistent application of policy by company officials can result in legal liability either in a civil or criminal matter. Because so many agencies can now opt for jury trials—with the concomitant risk of large jury awards against deep-pocketed companies—it is imperative that managers be given the most up-to-date information on policies and procedures and employment law. This is crucial—one jury award could dwarf the entire training budget of the university.

In an effort to mitigate this risk, a class—known by various names, but mostly as New Leader Orientation (NLO)—evolved in various units. This course was in the main taught by human resource specialists on a catch-as-catch can basis. Each unit would develop its own approach based on its current needs. Oftentimes a training specialist was involved, but used primarily as an additional delivery source. There was no standardized manual and no standardized method of delivery. Classroom delivery, when available, usually took one or two days. Those managers who could not attend were given a manual and little else in the way of training in this area. The manager would often consult with an HR generalist on a case-by-case basis and learn whatever was needed at the time of need. It was usually when an HR generalist would receive a number of these requests from a certain area that another iteration of the New Leader Orientation would be born. A lucky HR generalist might find a manual from a previous NLO class or even find a training specialist or another generalist who would act as a resource for this need.

## Traditional Classroom Challenges

Suffice it to say that this haphazard approach was faulty in several areas. One was the identification of needed classes for new managers. Another was the area of consistency of message. Third was the timeliness of information—and its correctness. All these areas were at the mercy of individual initiative. There were parts of the company doing an outstanding job at the identification and orientation of new managers and there were parts doing an adequate job. In the main, the explosive growth of the company and the constant need for experienced people in sensitive jobs made the task all the more difficult. Added to that, the eighty-plus mergers and acquisitions the company went through—and all the adjustment that repeated process entailed—made an already difficult task even more so.

New Leader Orientation began to be taught as an open-enrollment course in Charlotte, North Carolina. Charlotte is the headquarters city and the home of about fifteen thousand employees. Thus this course was regularly attended and was taught by human resource specialists. However, the course did not travel and those outside headquarters were dependent on their own HR staff for help.

This was the situation inherited by author Davis on a training team in the Consumer Banking Group College. Davis taught New Leader Orientation on demand in Charlotte, but could not usually travel to teach the class elsewhere as no budget provisions had been made. Then he took on the role of NLO project manager for Consumer Banking Group. In this area he had content responsibilities and was responsible for recruiting on-site HR specialists to teach CBG personnel at other locations. This again raised the consistency issue and made it difficult to control content and to add new content.

## MHRP Moves to Satellite

Author Stallings had been placed in the same situation about one year earlier. She was under similar constraints but did have the course as a catalog entry in the Leadership College catalog. It was Stallings who made the leap to satellite delivery, when she realized the potential of Employee Television and its ability as a training vehicle.

Stallings consulted various in-house experts and, with teammate Marty Mcchan, wrote the first satellite version of New Manager Orientation. This effort, coupled with her subsequent teaming with Davis, offers an instructional case for distance learning.

It is useful to begin with a brief tour of Employee Television Network. ETN is a division of First Union with state-of-the-art programming and broadcasting facilities. It often produces more original programming than a typical local television affiliate. The main portion of ETN is a broadcast studio with all the amenities needed for first-class video production. This lavish setup requires a large and highly skilled technical staff to operate.

In an effort to provide a more economical venue, ETN had equipped a trainer's studio that featured one camera and a desk arrangement that allowed the trainer to cut from the camera focused on the speaker to a document camera, a computer, or a VCR. This enabled a great amount of flexibility for the trainer. The studio was offered at no charge, having been funded earlier by the previously mentioned initiative at First University. It was originally equipped with a device worn by the trainer that allowed the camera to follow the trainer around automatically. This proved unwieldy and was soon dropped. A solution was provided when ETN starting offering a grip—a technician paid a daily fee, who was responsible for camera angles, audio levels, and videotaping. The grip was also a tremendous resource for first-time trainers.

The output from the trainers' studio was one-way. While this was effective in message delivery, it proved ineffective for training. The trainers' studio was therefore set up for conference-style bridgeline phone calls. This allowed the remote classrooms to talk back and gave the broadcast its needed two-way communication.

## Initial Satellite Obstacles

Early on, Stallings realized that television was not classroom. This may seem a ridiculously elementary assumption, but it is a crucial, basic tenet for all distance learning and it is far from obvious in the initial stages of planning for distance programs. At First Union, there was pressure in the various colleges of First University to migrate classes to distance learning. One of the first questions should be, Will the class translate to television? A mere reproduction of the classroom is an invitation to a mediocre program. As with all distance learning a crucial component is instructional design. It is design that makes a class work via satellite delivery. One of the first assumptions made is whether or not a class will work as a distance learning vehicle. Not all do and there must be someone to say no.

With this in mind, Stallings designed a script for the class and began to see the class not as a classroom exercise but one of distance with all its unique characteristics. However, admittedly, the early editions of New Manager Orientation were mostly one-way lecture-style classes. But as familiarity with ETN resources and comfort with delivery rose, the class began to grow from lecture to interactive.

## MHRP Growth and Enhancements

It was around this time that Davis was charged with migrating coursework to ETN. A natural alliance was formed between Stallings and Davis over the manager orientation class, now called Human Resources Policies and Procedures. Almost immediately, class sizes and number of locations rose. Stallings wanted to make the class more interactive and so she and Davis rewrote the class with an eye toward taking the class above the 50 percent interactive level. This means that half of the class interactions would be coming from the participants themselves.

## Instructional Design Improvements

Boosting the interactive aspect of the class required intense instructional design. Since locations varied from class to class and the total number of participants varied as well, interactivity had to be purposefully designed. This was done through a number of activities. First was the "call out," when the on-camera instructor would call on a specific site for a specific answer. Then exercises were designed to allow students at each site to work for a short period offline and then summarize their work online. Also, prework activities were designed both as time-savers and as immediate exercises on broadcast day. For example, participants were asked in prework to fill out a First Union time card for a fictional employee with a complicated schedule. When that portion of the class arrived, the instructor asked everyone to retrieve the exercise and then started to call out questions.

All these methods contributed to interactivity and were recognized by participants as engaging activities. However, the most engaging activity—and the one that has been the biggest boost to interactivity—has been the video role-play. Role-plays illustrated various points in the class and allowed the class sites to comment on them in the manner of a case study. Stallings developed the role-plays by asking company experts to write scripts for three- to five-minute roles that illustrated policy or legal issues. She then solicited volunteer actors and rented the main ETN studio with professional staff for a day. The outcome was a number of video scenarios that not only engaged the audience but added a modicum of entertainment as well. An additional benefit discovered in the first class with the scenarios is that the videos offered short breaks to on-camera personnel. Once the benefits of role-plays were seen, additional ones were ordered and now the day is interspersed with nineteen videos that give the participants quite a lot to ponder and comment on.

The addition of these role-plays and the aggressive nature of the on-camera experts toward soliciting responses and questions have caused the class to enjoy a factor of over 80 percent interactivity. This surpasses many classroom presentations and participants recognize that they're in a class where their participation is not only encouraged but also expected.

## MHRP, Current Environment

The class MHRP has moved to maturity. Renamed once again, to Managing Human Resources Policies, it is now taught the second Thursday of every month and is scheduled to continue on that basis indefinitely. Satellite is now the only way this class is offered. Because of its schedule and the fact that satellite is virtually unlimited in the number of seats offered, its satellite-only status has met very little resistance among the business units of First Union. Because the satellite television has 2,400 viewing sites, a class can occur virtually anywhere.

The typical monthly MHRP class now has ten sites spread throughout the United States with 150 participants. The methodology includes the satellite delivery of images to the receiving sites and the hookup of all sites to each other and the studio via telephone. There are usually three on-camera instructors, one responsible for logistics and transitions and the other two serving as subject matter experts. Also on hand is an employee of ETN, who acts as a director and does the normal tasks expected of a motion picture grip. The class is taught in one day with two breaks and a long lunch period. Assignments are given over the lunch period. ETN typically runs another broadcast on a different topic during the lunch period. Because the class is pointed to only the sites signed up, it is often called a narrowcast. However, the technology to limit the signal to the sites is expensive, so all receiving sites can receive the signal. This is not a problem, but participants and instructors are cautioned not to use real or sensitive examples to illustrate points. To help with questions that need to be answered and may be of a more confidential nature, the instructors keep the phone lines open after the broadcast, when a modicum of privacy can be offered.

The phone lines offer classes back-and-forth interaction between each site and the studio and also from site to site. There have been several occasions on past MHRP broadcasts when one site has helped another site on a specific problem. This is especially gratifying to a newly merged group, because often the problem has been recently faced and solved by the other site.

The participants not only take away knowledge gained in the class but also an extensive manual, liberally illustrated with examples for their further use. MHRP is beginning to enjoy feedback similar to that received by more traditional classroom offerings. A stated goal at the start of every broadcast is to make the technology transparent and this is usually commented on by appreciative participants.

Participants also see the advantages of being able to spend the night before a class at home, as do the facilitators. The broadcast and all its ancillary needs costs less than $1,000, which is half of what the travel and expense outlay might be to send a facilitator to a remote site. Additionally, the information is the most timely available, which is helping many in the company realize what a timely resource MHRP is. The class was the first to train managers on new policies and has been imitated for the rollout of new company human resource initiatives.

## Challenges to Sustaining Distance Learning

By any yardstick, MHRP was and continues to be a success. However there are a number of challenges still facing the class—and any other satellite-delivered class.

### Capital Expenditures

The first challenge is in the area of capital expenditures. No company wants to be extravagant with its purchases and the capital budget continues to be an issue. There are a number of technological solutions to problems but all cost money and all require a sales pitch. For example, at First Union there is a delay between the conversation on the phone line (which is virtually instantaneous) and the satellite-delivered image (which travels far enough to make a perceptible difference even at transmission speeds) of about one and a half seconds. This causes the on-camera instructors and the on-site participants to sometimes talk across one another during an interaction. This is a distraction that keeps the technology from achieving transparency. The problem can be answered with additional equipment, but does one buy this equipment for every one of over two thousand sites? The same goes for talk-back units that avoid the telephone. Again, a great enhancement for the broadcast program—but an expense that is difficult to justify when the numbers of sites are factored in.

## Inconsistent Equipment

The second challenge is the variety of equipment in the sites. Not every site has a state-of-the-art speakerphone available in the classroom. Not every site has the latest television monitor or projection equipment. Instructional designers need to take this into account, as the sophistication level of the technology must not overwhelm the least technical member of the chain.

Managing Human Resources Policies has also experimented in the area of site class management. The first experiment was in allowing individuals to join the broadcasts as a site of one. This requires that the individual be highly motivated, as it is far too easy for an individual participant to drop out of the broadcast. There was one occasion when a single participant put the telephone on hold and the entire network was treated the sound of a hold beeper tone. Because of the problems associated with experiences like this, MHRP no longer takes participants who will be alone at their site.

## Site Coordination

Another experiment was around the idea of having sites without coordinators. This is an idea that has merit—in theory, participants could do everything needed to support the program. Unfortunately, current sophistication levels among the audience are not to the point where the participants can manage the site alone. Thus MHRP uses only sites with coordinators at present and provides coaching for site coordinators.

## Managing Logistics

Another challenge for MHRP and all other satellite broadcasts is the number of participants. When the class attracts 150 participants to one broadcast, materials for 150 people have to be distributed prior to broadcast. This is no mean feat and is completely different from what many training support groups are used to. The typical face-to-face class has perhaps twenty people attending. Attempts to get prework to them before class are usually successful. And if there are changes or additions to the material, the instructor can carry replacement materials along for distribution at the site. This is not a luxury available with distance learning.

Deadlines are important as even last-minute additions are bound by express delivery schedules.

## Paradigm Shift

A final challenge is more psychological than physical. Participants are simply used to classroom training and have some inbuilt resistance to change in this area. That is why instructional design is so crucial. The natural advantages of television must be exploited. It also helps a great deal if senior leadership is sold on the concept of distance learning and pushes people to examine their prejudices. The biggest help is that distance learning be considered the primary vehicle of training delivery and that the traditional classroom be considered the alternative.

# Benefits

Now for some distance learning ancillary benefits that have been discovered with delight since the advent of Employee Television.

First is the exposure of senior management to all employees. All employees know most of the senior managers because they have embraced the coverage that ETN allows. Executives can address employees in a timely manner and give a consistent message. Also, they can do this in a comfortable, controlled environment. The studio can be made to look like a living room, a reporter's desk, a conference room, or virtually anything. It can be done with or without an audience. With or without phone calls from the field. Live or taped. All of these and hundreds of other variables can be controlled. This is not to say that smoke and mirrors will be employed but that effective messages can be gotten out to employees. Take, for example, the art of time shifting—as anyone in today's fast-paced business environment can attest, getting more than two people face to face is nearly impossible. However, with videotape, one executive live can introduce another executive on videotape. Or, as happens often at First Union, a business unit broadcast may repeat a portion of videotape of a senior executive's speech or broadcast. The use of all the modern studio equipment such as TelePrompTers, hearing devices, and camera cues all enhance a broadcast and help the participants relax.

Another benefit is the cross-sell opportunities presented. For example, on the MHRP broadcast, Stallings or Davis always promote other training programs that would be beneficial to the same audience. In addition, since content is company owned, one example may be used in another broadcast, as when MHRP uses a tape from an HR broadcast about benefits.

Still another discovery is the use of the visual to enhance participant learning or buy-in. A videotape of a senior manager endorsing a program does wonders for the program's legitimacy. In addition, illustrating an exact interaction—be it the filling out of a form, the booting up of a computer, or the treatment of a customer over the telephone—can bring realism and relevancy to the learner.

Letting employees see other employees doing the exact same function or handling the exact same problem not only is powerful for learning, it enhances a sense of community among all of First Union's employees. With seventy thousand employees, no room will hold a meeting or a social, but the creative use of the camera and studio can bring a sense of community even if it is in a virtual sense.

Eventually, training will move to on-demand desktop through a Web configuration. But where will all that video come from? Why, the ETN studio of course.

## Conclusion

Distance learning is here to stay at First Union. As with any business, distance learning still has its challenges for First Union, but its rewards far outweigh them. As customers and stakeholders continue to demand more timely response to their needs, employees will have their own timeliness needs for training and development. Satellite learning and its attributes will more than answer those needs in the near future. As for further out on the spectrum, a bigger and more prescient crystal ball is needed! Even the computer this is typed on will be obsolete long before it wears out, and who can say what we'll be using next?

CHAPTER ELEVEN

# BEYOND THE SIZZLE

## Sustaining Distance Training for Ford Motor Company Dealerships

Joan Conway Dessinger, Larry Conley

Distance training is sizzling for Ford Motor Company's Dealer Training Group. January 2000 marked the beginning of the thirteenth year of interactive computer-based training (CD-ROM multimedia or laser disc), and the seventh year of satellite-based interactive distance learning via the FORDSTAR Network. No other distance learning program does in a year what FORDSTAR does in a month, as illustrated in Table 11.1.

A FORDSTAR clone in Australia beams digital bit streams to dealers in that country. Business plans are under review for FORDSTAR clones in Europe, South America, and select Asian countries.

## Introducing FORDSTAR

FORDSTAR is a dealer communications network, funded by Ford and its dealers. While building distance learning capacity was the "sizzle" that sold Ford on the FORDSTAR Network, many other applications supported the business case for establishing the network. FORDSTAR carries both data and digital video. In addition to distance learning, all data movement between Ford and its dealers occurs over the satellite. PCs in dealerships are connected to the satellite, and all business transacted between Ford and dealers take that path. Dealers use FORDSTAR to order vehicles and parts, inquire into technical databases, submit warranty claims, register Extended Service Contracts, send e-mail, and transact business.

Ford also uses the digital video channels for *data broadcasting*, a term that means using the high-bandwidth video highway to transmit or broadcast giant data files such as service manuals and bulletins, vehicle calibration downloads, and the like to all dealership computers on the Ford LAN—simultaneously and within seconds. These giant data files make it possible for Ford dealerships to update the information in their computers.

A FORDSTAR computer in each dealership has little to do with distance learning, but deals with total communications. Support elements such as budgets, staffing, and help desk focus on the total network, not just the distance learning functions.

Ford has dedicated the FORDSTAR channels to dealer training and communication, and is very careful not to use FORDSTAR for employee training or communication. Ford was able to squeeze two extra channels out of the available satellite capacity and gave one channel to Ford Communication Network (FCN), Ford's internal network. This allowed Ford Training and Development Center (FTDC), the people responsible for Ford employee training, to use that channel to test and pilot a few courses for employees and suppliers. However, the main use of the other channel was for French-speaking automotive technical courses coming out of the United States into French Canada. These are the same courses that the English-speaking dealers in North America receive.

### TABLE 11.1. SUMMARY OF FORDSTAR MONTHLY ACTIVITY IN NORTH AMERICA.

| | |
|---|---|
| Number of courses offered | 450 |
| Hours of interactive distance learning per month | 1,450 |
| Number of dealerships reached per month | 6,000 |
| Number of dealership employees who complete classes per month | 30,000 to 55,000 |
| Number of broadcast channels | 8 |
| Number of time zones | 6 |
| Number of studios | 3 (Michigan, Canada, Mexico) |
| Satellite transmission specifications | • One-way, full-motion digital video<br>• Two-way audio |
| Geographic area | United States (including Alaska and Hawaii), Canada, Mexico |
| Broadcast focus | Technical training |

FTDC coordinated a business case to get their own transponder so that they could offer training to Ford employees. However, before their project was approved, the vendor lost control of the original satellite. As a result, FORDSTAR moved to another satellite and lost the extra transponder that had been "put on hold" for FTDC to use for employee training.

After the satellite loss, FORDSTAR made a determination to migrate to a new satellite vendor, which put the FTDC people back on square one with the need to develop a new plan if they wanted to get into distance learning.

FORDSTAR is migrating to the new satellite even as this book goes to print, and will have all dealers in North America up and running on the new satellite by the end of June 2000. The new satellite is more robust in terms of video transmission and provides FORDSTAR with sixteen channels.

## A Stage 4 Operation

FORDSTAR really is a Stage 4 operation, following the model Berge describes in Chapter Two. FORDSTAR is accepted and marveled at throughout the company. All processes (including communications, sales, marketing, and training), support functions, policies, measurements, certification programs, and so on have been institutionalized at Ford. Most Ford entities outside the United States are trying to develop a plan to cost-justify FORDSTAR as a strategic competitive advantage (Mantyla & Gividen, 1997, pp. 67–82). Decisions to use FORDSTAR have an impact on the whole relationship with dealers. The vehicle divisions (Ford, Lincoln, Mercury, Ford of Canada) have converted many communications that used to be done by field sales and service people to FORDSTAR.

Strategic planning is important at Ford, so the FORDSTAR link to Ford Motor Company's strategic issues needs to be quite strong (Mantyla & Gividen, 1997, pp. 85–90). Ford's number one goal is to become a consumer-focused company. Just as they are partners in Ford's initiatives to achieve brand preeminence, dealers are also partners in the initiative to satisfy the customer. FORDSTAR is the number one tool for coordinating Ford-dealer cooperation, training, communication, and collaboration.

Training dealer technicians is critical to Ford's goals of customer satisfaction and repeat vehicle sales. Technology-based distance learning is one of the ways Ford strives to meet these goals. Without the use of distance learning, the cost of sending forty-five to fifty thousand individuals in more than six thousand dealerships (U.S. and Canada) to forty-nine central training sites would be prohibitive, not to mention the additional cost of lost productivity during training activities.

## The Business Problem

Ford chose technology-based distance learning to meet four business needs related to training dealership personnel: the need to increase speed, reach, and interactivity, and the need to reduce variability. Each of these needs had economic and quality impacts on the company.

### Increase Speed

During the 1990s, frequent introductions of new automobile and truck models—each with new, cutting-edge technology—made it necessary to provide dealership employees with new knowledge and skills to sell and service vehicles and meet customers' needs. That required speed in cascading training, an element that a classroom delivery method could not offer. Even with 162 classroom instructors and almost fifty regional training sites, it was impossible to deliver the amount of training needed in the time allowed between new model introductions.

### Increase Reach

Approximately 34 percent of Ford, Lincoln, and Mercury dealerships are located over a hundred miles from any of Ford's training centers, making the logistics and cost of providing classroom training to all dealership employees prohibitive. On the other hand, distance training makes it possible to accomplish a number of desirable goals efficiently:

- Deliver training directly into dealership training rooms.
- Make training content available in convenient, adult-sized bites, rather than in week-long sessions at remote locations.
- Target specific individuals within the dealerships regardless of geographic location.
- Make subject matter experts available for a broadcast based on need rather than ease of access to location.

### Increase Interactivity

Training entities throughout Ford aim to create learner-centered training, that is, training that is consciously designed to benefit the learner (Ostendorf, 1997b, p. 3). Ford has found that the interactive capabilities of satellite distance learning greatly enhance the adult student's learning experience (Ostendorf, 1997a). For example, the combined capabilities of an audience response pad system and a telephone line link allow students to become actively involved in the training session by calling in to the instructor to ask or answer a question or provide information—and the whole class can hear the interaction. The instructor can also call on individual students (Ford Does Distance Learning, 1994, p. 97).

## Reduce Variability

One of the weak spots in any large training enterprise is instructor variability, or in Ford's case, the inherent variability among 162 instructors. Keeping that many instructors current and effective with emerging technology, technology that is constantly changing, is a daunting task. Keeping them all on the same page when it comes to training delivery is even more difficult. With satellite training, Ford uses the best instructors and the best scripts to help ensure that the instructional design intent is consistently carried out and all the students receive the same message.

# Desired Outcomes: Dreaming Dreams and Seeing Visions

When the Finance Committee of Ford's Board of Directors first approved the FORDSTAR Project, Tom Wagner, Ford vice president, assigned the project to Larry Conley, who headed Operations Planning and Training. The mandate was: "This was your idea, now make it happen." In order to make it happen, Conley pulled a FORDSTAR team together composed of individuals with expertise in telecommunications, video engineering, satellite technology, marketing, systems, Internet protocol, and broadcasting. Some team members came from inside Ford; others were outside vendors. For example, prime vendors supplied expertise by assigning project engineers to work with Ford's technical manager and program manager. Another vendor assigned an expert to work with Ford's video director.

Given a cross-discipline team facing many unknowns and setting out to accomplish what had never been done before, it was essential to develop a vision that would unite the team and align FORDSTAR's goals with Ford's goals. Wagner and Conley familiarized the team with the business case, provided a basic understanding of the technology that could be adapted to the project, and asked the team to produce a vision that the team, FORDSTAR, and Ford could live and thrive with. The team came up with the text of Exhibit 11.1, a statement of desired outcomes that lives today.

## EXHIBIT 11.1. FORDSTAR POSITIONING STATEMENT.

FORDSTAR is a satellite-based communication network linking the Ford Motor Company to all Ford and Lincoln-Mercury Dealers in the forty-eight contiguous United States and Canada. It will be the highest capacity privately owned satellite network in the world. FORDSTAR provides auto industry leadership in two-way communications and interactive training.

FORDSTAR will quickly, consistently, and economically link us to our Dealers without regard to their size or geographic location. FORDSTAR, a digital network that leverages state-of-the art compression technology, will be able to broadcast eight full-motion video channels simultaneously and will greatly enhance present data transmission capability.

A key FORDSTAR feature will be live, interactive Long-Distance-Learning. Distance Learning will enhance the Company's ability to deliver applicable technical and non-technical training to all dealership audiences. Like a traditional classroom, training participants will see Ford instructors, be able to speak with them, and listen to other "distant" students—all without leaving the dealership. To maximize learning, long-distance class size will be limited to enable the appropriate level of participant interaction.

A FORDSTAR Board of Governors with equal Dealer and Company representation, will establish network broadcast policies. This ensures all data and video broadcasts will be in the best interest of our Dealer customers and be consistent with our mutual goals and objectives.

FORDSTAR provides the communications infrastructure required to achieve our present and future customer satisfaction owner loyalty, and globalization objectives. The network has the capacity to be expanded to Europe, the Middle East, Central and South America. FORDSTAR provides the opportunity for immediate acceleration of Company and Dealership business process improvements and will be the foundation for future innovative applications not yet conceived.

*Source:* Prepared by FORDSTAR Marketing Launch Team, May 17, 1994, and revised through July 22, 1994.

---

# FORDSTAR Management System

A strong management system is key to sustaining distance learning (Mantyla & Gividen, 1997, pp. 91–96). Working within the parameters of the dealerships and the network, the FORDSTAR Team undertook four types of management activity: marketing, technical, program planning, and finance and administration, summarized in Exhibit 11.2.

These activities helped to launch FORDSTAR and continue to sustain FORDSTAR'S dealership distance learning programs today:

- *Marketing activities* set the foundation for the sustained success of FORDSTAR by selling the network to the dealers and by making sure that FORDSTAR de-

## EXHIBIT 11.2. FORDSTAR MANAGEMENT SYSTEM ACTIVITIES.

### *Marketing*

*Goal:*
Establish FORDSTAR distance learning as "the way we do business"; set the foundation for sustained success.
*Activities:*
- Work with Ford divisions to set up a marketing and sales plan that would "sell" FORDSTAR to dealers.
- Implement marketing and sales plan:
  - Conduct 143 sales meetings with dealers.
  - Follow up on promises made during sales meetings.
- Initiate and maintain communication with dealers.
  - Design and deliver Welcome to FORDSTAR broadcasts on how to use equipment.
  - Develop help desk standards (staffing level, response time, and so on).
  - Establish a help desk.

### *Technical*

*Goal:*
Set up the network and keep the network up and running.
*Activities:*
- Set up the network.
  - Create and build broadcast facilities.
  - Test all components.
- Maintain the network.
- Administer equipment.
  - Support all associated tools.
  - Adhere to internal and organization-wide processes.
- Design and implement customer-oriented support process for technical and process issues.

---

livered on all the promises made during the initial marketing efforts. Establishing a help desk provided a vehicle for ongoing communication with dealers.

- *Technical activities* created and built the network and the broadcast facilities and continue to keep the network up and running.
- *Program planning activities* set up operating guidelines and standards, maintain program quality, and are responsible for getting the right programs to the right students at the right time.
- *Finance and administration* activities built the financial infrastructure for launching FORDSTAR and for ongoing funding of the network. FORDSTAR's infrastructure funding was generated by cost savings; Ford and the dealers share the funding of ongoing operations. For example, dealers pay a monthly *value package* fee based on the size of the dealership and on what the dealer spent

## EXHIBIT 11.2. (*continued*)

### *Program Planning*

*Goal:*
Provide the right training to the right student at the right time according to established standards and processes.
*Activities:*
- Select class offerings based on student needs.
  - Monitor type and frequency of course offerings.
  - Analyze individualized curriculum plans.
- Maintain course quality.
- Provide internal training for instructors, instructional designers, program sponsors, and support technicians.
- Schedule and load classes.
- Communicate with training suppliers.
- Resolve conflicts.
- Nurture improvements in core and interactive technology.
- Integrate improvements into Ford's systems and databases.
- Publish and distribute monthly *StarGuide*.

### *Finance and Administration*

*Goal:*
Set standards and provide ongoing funding for development and delivery of new and existing courses based on dealer needs.
*Activities:*
- Design standards and process for funding FORDSTAR infrastructure and ongoing operations.
- Establish and maintain a Board of Governors to identify dealer needs.

---

in 1993 for soft skills training. Ford funds training that was provided by the company free of charge in 1993.

## Program Planning: An Example of How Management Systems Adapt

The program planning activity—generally called "programming"—provides a good example of the way successful management systems change over time. The activity was and is responsible for the FORDSTAR product. This includes every type of broadcast, from training to communications to collaboration. Originally, the programming activity concentrated on designing and developing the FORDSTAR product; now it focuses more on implementation activities such as selecting and scheduling broadcasts. The activity set up the operating guidelines, knocked down inhibitors, and provided training and support so potential users could get started using the network. A cross-functional team of representatives from Ford's training vendors, actual instructors, and content providers established operating guidelines and standards, addressing issues such as broadcast length, quality, evaluation, and areas specifically related to meeting learner needs. For example, one FORDSTAR guideline states that once the class schedule is distributed to the students, broadcast cancellations and changes are allowed only in extreme circumstances.

Today, the program planning activity includes something old and something new:

**Scheduling and Loading Classes.**  The program manager chooses the broadcasts that will be most beneficial to the most students in any given month, and gets the programs on the air by managing conflicts involving studios, channels, instructors, and subject matter experts. Now that individualized curriculum paths for dealership employees are combined into dealership, regional, and national composites, the program planning manager monitors this information to identify what training dealership employees currently need and what courses are available through FORDSTAR.

Scheduling has actually become easier. In the early days, the FORDSTAR used twelve transponders and four satellites to broadcast across the United States from the East to the West Coast, and it took a double bounce to include Alaska and Hawaii. Changing to a more powerful GE satellite with a bigger footprint (one that covers the entire area) made it possible to present full programming to all fifty states.

However, scheduling still involves juggling multiple time zones, time and day audience preferences, and seasonal impacts on attendance. For example, the Programming Department discovered that 1:00 P.M. is the most popular viewing time —but 1:00 P.M. occurs in up to six different times zones for the United States!

**Producing StarGuide.**  One of the FORDSTAR scheduling guidelines states that students should have access to the schedule of broadcasts thirty days prior to the broadcast date. Designed to be the one-stop-shopping source for all of a dealership student's training needs, *StarGuide* includes course and class information, help desk tips, logon instructions, instructions on how to order student materials, and training-at-a-glance management tools. While *StarGuide* will continue to report on FORDSTAR dealership training, the publication is now going electronic. The online *StarGuide* will become the information tool for all Ford training—classroom, CD-ROM, satellite, and online.

***Leading the Move to Online Training Management.*** Training management is also going online. The newest responsibility for the FORDSTAR programming manager is to spearhead the installation of a single training management system for all technical and nontechnical training throughout Ford, including FORDSTAR dealership training. This is one of the steps Ford is taking to promote the concept of one-face training to Ford and dealership employees.

# Support Infrastructure: Basic Elements

The structural elements necessary for building and sustaining the effectiveness of FORDSTAR distance learning programs are instructional development (Willis, 1993), distance learning production, and transmission of the session to the users. The FORDSTAR Team established and maintains support functions for each of these elements.

## Instructional Development Support

FORDSTAR uses the Ford Instructional Systems Design Process (Cvercko, Antonelli, & Steele, 1992) and a staff of instructional designers to make sure that all courses meet the following requirements:

- Address a training need, not just an area of poor performance.
- Target the competencies found in the learner's individual curriculum path.
- Deliver timely information to the learner.
- Involve the learner in the learning process.

In the FORDSTAR environment, applying learner-centered instructional design to take advantage of the interactive communication and learning capabilities of the network has been, and continues to be, one of the greatest challenges. For example, Ford has found that even instructional system designers with experience or academic credentials (Master's or Ph.D. level) find it difficult to creatively apply the principles of interactive learning to the adult learner through the medium of television (Ostendorf, 1997b). It has been Ford's experience that instructors who shift from the classroom to the video screen make the transition more easily than the designers do. However, instructors can only deliver what is designed into the course. To address this challenge, Ford has developed several courses for instructional designers: Learner-Centered Instructional Design for the Video Medium,

How Adults Learn, Brain-Compatible Training Design, and Delivering Distance Learning.

## Production Support

The major support for FORDSTAR production comes from equipment managed directly by the instructor. The FORDSTAR business model calls for sixteen fully automated broadcast studios called *multimedia instructional podiums* or simply *MIP desks*. Very early in the analysis phase, the Technical Team looked at the economics of distance learning and concluded that Ford could not afford a staff of thirteen or fourteen people to support the production of 450 individual broadcasts each month. Instead, Ford spent money on designing the MIP desks so that each instructor, while delivering the training, could also serve as producer, camera person, slide changer, router, and so on. Today, the only thing the instructor doesn't do is monitor the system signal to the satellite.

The MIP desk contains all program production elements, including backdrops, PowerPoint slide presentations, printed materials for the overhead camera, keypad response system controls, video controls, laser disc controls, and so forth. Each of these elements was designed to support the following goals:

- Learner-centered, interactive program design
- Lean broadcasting (simple, low-cost, reusable production elements)
- Instructor control of all production elements

Instructor-controlled MIP desks make it possible for Ford to offer a large number of programs on a very tight budget by keeping operating and production cost per-broadcast and per-student to a minimum (lean broadcasting). They also support and enhance learning by increasing learner interaction and learner input into instructional content and flow (Verduin & Clark, 1991, pp. 21–32).

Based on experience, the FORDSTAR Team determined that the minimum requirement for a one-channel network was two MIP desks. While one desk is being used for a broadcast the other desk is available for practice, backup in case of a technical problem, or quick setup when broadcasts are back to back. In the case of a network, the minimum requirement is 1.5 MIP desks for each available channel. For example, when FORDSTAR used eight channels the minimum requirement was twelve MIP desks.

The concept of simple, low-cost, learner-centered production is best represented by the MIP Scale reproduced in Figure 11.1. There are a wide range of options available to a MIP designer, and the figure illustrates possible production elements that could be included in order of cost and complexity from lowest (left

## FIGURE 11.1. MIP SCALE.

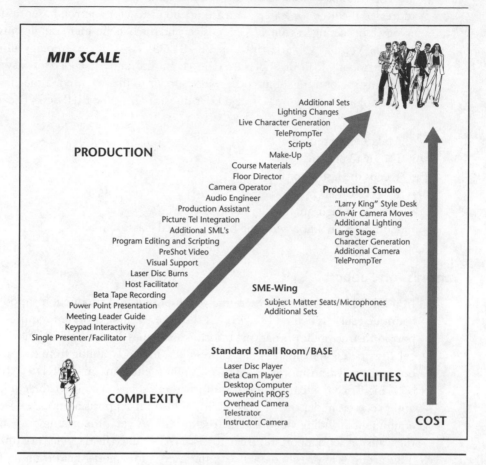

bottom) to highest (right top). A basic, yet very effective, broadcast will incorporate the bottom five or six production elements.

The types of facilities are listed along the bottom. The number of subject matter experts and the types of production items included will determine what type of MIP desk is required, or if the broadcast will need to be moved to a full-scale production studio. The important concept behind the MIP Scale is that increasing cost and complexity does not necessarily increase the quality of the broadcast. High-quality, learner-centered courses can be achieved with a minimal amount of production elements, facilities, and cost.

For example, the decision to install a laser disc player on the MIP desks addressed the need for lean broadcasting and instructor control. Laser disc technology is becoming less and less expensive, and the benefits increasingly outweigh the costs (Verduin & Clark, 1991, pp. 80–81, 95). Laser disc technology allows all required footage to be preshot, stored on a laser disc, and bar-coded for easy access by the instructor using a bar code reader similar to the one used at the checkout counter of a grocery store. Using a laser disc enhances the MIP desks because it

- Makes video reusable
- Is easy to operate
- Keeps the instructor in charge
- Is very cost-effective
- Results in high-quality digital video
- Competes favorably with the best-equipped classroom

## Transmission Support

In addition to ongoing instructional development and production support, the continued success of the FORDSTAR distance learning program requires a support infrastructure for broadcast transmission issues. Transmission is a mechanical and operational function. It requires updating and training from time to time, but essentially transmission operates with little intervention. FORDSTAR relies on a highly competent technical staff to administer and support the equipment and processes under their responsibility. This staff supports all distance learning equipment including video and instructor tools. A very important component of the transmission support infrastructure is a well-trained field service organization. This group is in direct contact with the user, and ongoing field training for replacement field technicians is a requirement.

Immediate help in identifying and resolving broadcast transmission problems is provided through a telemarketing group called Single Point Of Contact (SPOC). FORDSTAR has three levels of assistance associated with the help function:

- Level 1: All administrative and easy technical problems
- Level 2: More complex technical problems
- Level 3: More complex technical problems that require on-site assistance

SPOC usually resolves small problems (difficulty logging onto a broadcast, inability to register for class, problems with video or audio performance) within seconds. It also communicates with other support organizations and customers, escalates issues, and serves as lead for technical staff problem resolution.

# Support Infrastructure: Policy

During the development of FORDSTAR, a Board of Governors was set up and standards or policies were established to ensure that distance learning would continue to be "the quality way we do training" at Ford. Three significant policies that developed from the FORDSTAR distance learning design and delivery standards are instructor and vendor certification and student feedback.

## High-Level Oversight

Over the years Ford has broadened the responsibilities of the Board of Governors. Today, key decisions and policies related to the FORDSTAR Network are run through the Board of Governors. As issues surface, they are immediately taken before the Board for resolution. Strategic recommendations are made to the Board and Board members may accept or reject the recommendations. The board members are high enough within the company so that decisions are easily implemented and barriers are easily removed.

## Instructor Certification

Two very important and early guidelines that were developed called for each instructor to become MIP desk certified. The goals of certification is to make sure that each instructor:

- Is qualified to use the MIP desk
- Understands MIP desk philosophy
- Is able to help the students understand the dealership training equipment

Certification is obtained by attending an eight-hour course that includes instruction on the MIP desk and actual practice sessions.

In addition, the guidelines state that each instructor should have a minimum of eight hours of rehearsal for every hour on the air. Prebroadcast rehearsal gives the instructor time to practice the unique delivery components of a course and avoid some common and distracting on-air mannerisms such as the deer-in-the-headlights look. Since the instructor is always working about three or four slides ahead of the audience, on- and off-air movement requires practice to ensure a smooth on-air presentation.

## Training Vendor Certification

During the growth of the FORDSTAR Network, the FORDSTAR Team partnered with several different training vendors to provide and develop course content. The vendors attended training that Ford provided on the MIP desk, instructional design, learner-centered presentation, front-end analysis, and brain-compatible training methods. The vendors also agreed to design courses around the MIP desk philosophy of lean production.

Several vendors built their own MIP desks. Although these desks were not hooked in to FORDSTAR, they were used for rehearsal, train-the-trainer sessions, and course walk-throughs. In exchange for their investment in MIP desk design, the FORDSTAR Team made the vendors' names available to departments within Ford that needed training developed.

## Student Feedback

FORDSTAR uses an audience response pad system for student feedback, along with the call-in call-out telephone function. The system host computer enables student interaction through the keypad response system. For example, students can use the keypad to take a multiple-choice test. Each student's responses are identified by keypad number, recorded within the keypad system, and stored for downloading. The instructor can also give immediate feedback by projecting histograms showing the percentage of students who selected each response item.

As the FORDSTAR Network grew and the number of MIP desks and programs increased, the process of downloading attendance, test, and course completion information from every host computer became much more complicated. At one point it could take as long as six months to provide grades and attendance information to the students who completed a course. Clearly this was not a desirable situation.

By designing and applying the concept of a unique identifier for each and every broadcast, Ford developed a process where all course data is collected from every studio host computer each night. This data is processed through an Attendance and Grades server, all of the post-tests are scored electronically, and the attendance and grades information is automatically posted to the Training Management System each night. This provides feedback to the student within twenty-four hours after taking the course, without human intervention.

## And the Sizzle Goes on . . .

Ford does not duplicate courses, offering one course via several different delivery media. However a single dealership-training curriculum may be made up of a mix of delivery vehicles depending on the intent of the training. Although classroom training continues to play an important role in hands-on and skill-building training, FORDSTAR and CD-ROM have rapidly become the method of choice for a vast majority of courses that are completed annually by dealership employees. As Figure 11.2 illustrates, in 1994—prior to the full roll-out of the FORDSTAR satellite-based network—technology-based distance learning accounted for only 12 percent of the courses that were completed by dealership employees, and the total number of student-completed courses was 150,464; in 1997 the parallel figures were approximately 92 percent and 717,499.

### What Kept FORDSTAR Sizzling

The fact that FORDSTAR distance learning has met with continued and increasing success is due in large part to decisions made and strategies implemented during the FORDSTAR development process. Strategies that have been instrumental in sustaining the sizzle include the following:

- The *value package* provides ongoing funding for the network, removing any budget barriers that could keep training suppliers or business managers from using

### FIGURE 11.2. TOTAL NUMBER OF STUDENTS TRAINED IN FORD MOTOR COMPANY DEALERSHIP TRAINING PROGRAMS, 1994–1997.

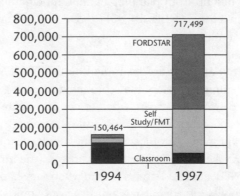

the network. Also, it allows dealerships to participate in unlimited or cafeteria-style training. Dealerships pay one price and go back through the training line whenever they have a training need.

- The network was sized and planned to be big enough. This allows FORDSTAR to provide training in the quantities needed for the whole dealership population. The network has also become the first choice for distributing information as well as learning.
- FORDSTAR User Groups meet several times during the year. This fosters the sharing of information among content providers.
- Using multiple development vendors continues to promote competition, keeps costs competitive, and provides a constant source of new and fresh ideas.
- The focus on interactivity keeps the student involved in the broadcast, checks and monitors the student's rate of learning and retention, and fosters collaboration in a safe and nonthreatening way. Interactivity also expands the use of the network to include focus groups, feedback sessions, town halls, management forums, and so on.
- Linking the scheduling and resource systems helps to avoid redundant data entry.
- Using the individual, competency-based curriculum paths to develop and schedule FORDSTAR distance learning courses has ensured that the courses meet real training needs and have business value to the dealerships.
- The media selection decision matrix (shown back in Figure 11.1) makes it easy for the designers and developers to use the right medium for the training. The MIP Scale continues to be a vital tool for developing and evaluating FORDSTAR courses.

## What Needed Fixing

Even the best up-front planning cannot anticipate all the eventualities that may arise when a network the size of FORDSTAR is implemented as a way to do the business of training.

*Registration System.* For example, the FORDSTAR Team originally designed a solid registration system that combined student registration with the planning of course delivery. However, when the no-show rate inched up to 60 percent, the FORDSTAR Team investigated and determined that if dealership employees were working with customers they could not leave the customer to attend class. By eliminating the advance registration process, the no-show rate dropped to 0 percent and students could simply attend when they had the time to take the training. The new policy did not mean that instructors would sometimes address a class with no students. Potential audiences are so large that they frequently reach the class cutoff number; the opposite, however, has not been true. FORDSTAR staff does monitor current and future business needs and forecasts a class life cycle, which means that a class is pulled when it reaches an audience saturation point.

*Network Architecture.* The network architecture also caused some problems. The technology had never been used for the purposes that Ford had in mind, nor on such a large scale—450 broadcasts per month, 1,450 hours live and interactive, as many as 45,000 students in a peak month, multiple hosts, all data traffic between Ford and dealers. With the exception of their TV and VCR, many of the initial vendor promises were not easily attained. For example, the keypad response equipment had to be reengineered to allow for multiple hosts and thousands rather than a few hundred simultaneous users. It also turned out that obtaining student information required a complete new host computer and numerous changes.

The distance learning technology was new to the original satellite provider. This factor and the FORDSTAR PC terminal forced them to greatly alter their installation skills and process.

Many of the PC systems in dealerships could not be reengineered to connect to the network. New computers were required in many cases, and computer vendors had to make in-dealership changes to connect to the network. Despite due diligence in the prior planning, the reality was a myriad of equipment of various vintages and capabilities that had to be adapted or discarded and replaced.

Additionally, Ford chose to go with OS2 because it was the only 32-bit operating system that was viable at the time. This proved to be a challenge because of difficulties toggling between OS2 and Windows for multimedia. It required users to log off and reboot before they could access the CD-ROM multimedia applications used by smaller dealers.

*Current Challenges.* Today there are still several obstacles of varying complexity that FORDSTAR must overcome to maintain the sizzle:

• Different departments operate FORDSTAR's Help Desk, Network Control Center, Video Operations Center, Registrations Systems, and Support Systems, creating a technical infrastructure split among multiple operations.

• The dealerships tend to have problems with the robustness of their equipment—for example, lack of dedicated phone lines, or nonunique phone plugs. For optimum performance, a dealership needs one dedicated telephone line that is plugged into the site controller and not used for other purposes such as fax or Internet access for laptops. The students cannot call in and the instructor cannot call out unless the phone line is plugged in properly and the instructor has the correct phone number.

- There must be enough training on the network so that the network becomes the way of doing business. It must be looked at as the key source for information. Some students don't perceive the network as being valuable, so they continue to request information over traditional methods and never turn on the set to see what's available. Also, if there are no perceived advantages for the students (who quite reasonably ask, "What's in it for me?") they tend not to take time away from their job to participate in training, no matter how "good" or convenient it is.

## Lessons Learned

The major lessons learned from the FORDSTAR experience are in the arena of finance, leadership, support, and instruction.

### Finance

Ford's cost-per-student-trained dropped dramatically, but Ford's costs actually increased because the original Value Package did not account for the significant increase in student manuals and other support costs that followed from a fourfold increase in the number of dealership employees completing courses. Significant process improvements in the electronic production of student manuals and reductions in the scrap rate of paper-based manuals almost offset the additional expense. These and other process savings have kept the Value Package cost frozen for the past five years.

The FORDSTAR plan for long-term funding, independent of the company's budget climate, has worked well to sustain distance learning. Without such a plan, year-to-year budgeting could be erratic, and a network would struggle for survival. Customer loyalty is directly related to the customer's ability to count on and plan on the continued flow of essential courses.

### Leadership

The nature of technology is constant change. Leadership is vital for execution of a technical strategy that resists unnecessary change, gains maximum value from investments made, and ensures that needed technology renewal is funded.

The role of the champion goes beyond the conception, sale, and successful implementation of the program. Because there are continuing technology developments and competing opportunities, it is necessary to continually assess new technology, rationalize its reality with the training model, and guide the organization to embrace or resist transition as it makes sense for fulfillment of the training needs.

The care and maintenance of champions is an ongoing activity. Ford's technical champions are the pushers of the envelope. These are the people who are asking for or requiring new technical innovations. They gather new ideas from the industry and have to try them out on the network. They may be difficult to please, but they continue to be a source of new and fresh ideas, keep the network looking different, and are drivers of growth. They keep the network from becoming stagnant. They keep the program from being at risk.

## Support

One strength of FORDSTAR is the close cooperation between business and technical support organizations enabled by co-location and by shared reporting relationships. Support issues arise when elements of support are independent.

## Instruction

Instructional components such as curriculum, training design, and content must constantly evolve in order to present up-to-the-minute information to the customer. The training management must understand the strengths and limitations of the technology and use it to maximum advantage.

# A Final Note—Don't Let the Sizzle Fool You

There will always be a need for strategy management of distance learning in response to outside changes that affect the system. Change is ongoing in open systems and change without change management will ultimately kill a system. Users and champions alike will not accept continual disruption due to poor or no change management, and they will abandon ship. Technology will determine whether widespread change management is necessary. Successful distance learning must have methods and processes for day-to-day operations, problem resolution (including escalation), and moves, adds, and changes.

The overall technical distance learning system employed in FORDSTAR absolutely requires ongoing change management because it is a complex system and interacts with many other changing systems. This is partly due to its coexistence with unrelated data communications applications, a coexistence that mirrors the future of communications as a convergence of applications (data, voice, video, multimedia). Unless an organization can manage the technological future it cannot manage continual process improvement.

For distance learning to succeed there must be a need, a plan, and both technology capacity and technology support. Distance learning is not something that is grafted onto a plateful of training delivery alternatives. There must be a genuine need that is recognized by the business community, as with Ford's six thousand dealerships spread all over North America and its clear perception that training to deal with new automotive technology was critical to business success—essential to satisfactory service and repair of the vehicle, and thus also essential to customer satisfaction and repeat vehicle sales.

In addition, the plan must be well thought through if it is to succeed. It is one thing to put together a proposal for $100,000,000—but ensuring a good investment that will deliver the anticipated returns requires that every element must be considered. Without a solid plan based on business needs and the technological capability to implement and support the plan, distance learning will fail. The plan was the starting point and produced the sizzle that sold Ford!

# CHAPTER TWELVE

# LEARNING TO WORK IN WEB TIME

## Evaluating Time-to-Market Instruction at Nortel Networks

Greg V. Michalski

If you build it, will they come? This variation on the famous line in *Field of Dreams* could be easily adapted by Web site developers in general and Web training developers in particular. Answers to closely related questions—for example, Who is coming and what do they expect?—constitute basic yet extremely relevant considerations in developing and sustaining Web-based distance training. An obvious reason is that—unlike the captive audiences in traditional instructor-led classroom-based sessions—users of Web-based distance training are but a mouse-click away from abandoning even the most well-planned instructional site. Given this, one aspect of sustaining Web-based training involves an accurate understanding of diverse user needs and expectations. In short, this becomes a prerequisite to delivering value to the learner.

If empirical and theoretical evaluation frameworks for evaluating Web sites are rare, those for evaluating Web-based training are even rarer. In commenting on the state of Web site evaluation, Trochim (n.d.) observed:

There is a remarkable absence of studies that examine how Web sites are conceptualized, developed, and implemented, or that look at the effects of their use. In the haste to construct the World Wide Web we have simply not had the time to evaluate and reflect on how this technology is being accomplished and the effects it is having on the way we live, perform in our jobs, and interact with our environment. We are implementing this revolutionary technology "on the fly" and with virtually no rules or theories to guide us. We are weaving this Web out of thin air. We're making it up as we go along [p. 1].

Given this underdeveloped state of Web site evaluation, a central premise of the present chapter is that Web-based training assessment and evaluation can be done most effectively through systematic efforts to describe and respond to what learners need and expect from an instructional site. Such efforts ultimately enhance decision making, affecting policy and practice as distance education becomes fully institutionalized through Stage 4 maturity (to use the conceptual framework Berge establishes in Chapter Two) within an organization.

The following discussion highlights a case example using multimedia Web-based distance training designed to promote faster product development at Nortel Networks—a global network engineering company positioned at the heart of the Internet revolution. Like other technologically advanced organizations involved in developing, deploying, and using distance training, Nortel has only recently embraced an integrated approach to assessing the needs and evaluating the results of Web-based instruction. Contrary to popular beliefs about the requirements for additional project resources needed to perform such assessment and evaluation, however, the case example provided here demonstrates how proper evaluation and assessment can be used to actually *reduce* the project schedule and cost while improving the quality of Web-based training.

## The Rise of Web-Based Training

Among the many methods and modes available to deliver distance training, the Internet (and more specifically the World Wide Web) continues grow in popularity (Driscoll, 1998; McGreal, 1997). Mortlock and Dobrowolski (1998, p. 199) enthusiastically proclaimed that "the Web is the most powerful distance-learning and education medium ever invented." As a means for instruction and learning, Schreiber (1998a, p. 402) points out, Internet-based training engages learner interaction and is flexible in facilitating constructivist learning. In terms of conceptual frameworks for distance training, Berge (1998b, p. 31) identified selected organizational factors that distinguish a constructivist (transformational), learner-centered approach from that of a more purely teacher-centered (transmission) approach (see also Chapter One). These factors include decentralization, short production runs, an intelligent organization, multiskilled workers, and a core workforce regarded as an investment (rather than a cost) by management. With continued growth in access and bandwidth capabilities expected in the near future, new opportunities to effectively use Web-based training in the business arena will continue to flourish.

## The Business Challenge to Learn and Work in Web Time

For many, increased use of Web-based technology is accompanied by aspirations to gain a competitive edge. This edge may be defined in terms of increased sales, improved productivity, or enhanced learning. As demand for effective Web applications (for example, training) increases, an expanded role for evaluation is certainly on the horizon (Bowen, n.d., p. 1).

The requirement to directly link training to business and organization goals is well established. As discussed in Chapter One, such training has been appropriately described as "just-in-time" and "just-enough." This approach serves to enhance training's relevance to the learner and the learner's motivation to engage in training. Yet exploring this concept further, it becomes evident that differential rates of change across all business sectors have led to a situation in which certain industries have less time available than others to sufficiently develop the job-related knowledge, skills, and abilities of their employees. While an accelerated pace of change is apparent across the whole business landscape—especially as accompanied by the widespread growth of the Internet—this change rate has attained unprecedented levels in the digital telecommunications and networking business sector.

### Competition and the Need for Speed in a World of Networks

New realities and challenges continue to pervade the data, voice, and wireless networking (telecommunications) industry. As a business challenge these new realities involve three major areas: markets, customers, and competition. Network and telecommunications markets are growing at a record pace. For example, the year 1996 marked the first time in history in which data surpassed voice, accounting for more than 50 percent of the traffic moving over the average cross section of North American public networks. This trend has continued and is expected to continue, with data accounting for 90 percent of network traffic within the next few years.

Amid convincing arguments that "the network is the business" (Roth, 1998) and concepts such as "business at the speed of thought using a digital nervous system" (Gates, 1999), explosive growth in the information industry has paved the way to parallel growth in consumer demand for voice and data services. The growth of the Internet has been greatly fueled by new global business opportunities, for example, e-commerce. Deregulation has eliminated traditional telecom monopolies, leading to the presence of many new network operators and services. Combined voice and data services have become increasingly important and short market windows of opportunity have created an environment in which even loyal customers cannot afford to wait for perfect product solutions. The competitive landscape has been described as a "Race to the Middle" in which previously separate industries (for example, cable, satellite, and telephone) are competing to supply total network solutions for their customers. From a business perspective, mergers, partnerships, alliances have become commonplace as the biggest players continue to jockey for position. Short product development cycles have become essential for businesses that wish to remain competitive in this environment.

But in addition to speed, the business challenge equally involves organizational knowledge. Intellectual capital has been defined simply as the sum of everything everybody in a company knows that gives it a competitive edge (Stewart, 1999). A central implication is that the collective knowledge of the organization becomes its *most* valuable asset. This is the case particularly when knowledge is properly organized. As Harreld (1998) noted, although we have an overabundance of information, *knowledge* is information that has been edited and put into useful context by knowledge workers. So speed and knowledge lie at the heart of the business challenge for technology-based firms. Particularly as networking technology advances, training delivered via the Web offers a growing opportunity to rapidly develop and use organizational knowledge.

## Nortel's Time-to-Market Challenge

With a total global workforce exceeding fifty thousand employees operating in over 150 countries and territories worldwide, Nortel Networks is a company that has worked hard to adjust and prosper in the Internet age. Founded over a century ago, in 1885, the company dates back to the era that saw the invention of the telephone. While the long history of the company is fascinating (see, for example, Newman, 1995) it takes much more than a successful past to survive in business. In fact, a long and successful past can prove blinding and ultimately even fatal to firms that once led their industry. History is littered with companies that failed largely because they did not learn as organizations (Daft & Huber, 1987).

Yet Nortel has learned and continues to do so at an ever-increasing rate. Reflecting the tag line often included just beneath its corporate logo, *How the world shares ideas*, Nortel has been heavily engaged in using the very technologies that it develops for its customers to promote learning and share ideas among its large workforce of knowledge workers. These technologies are used in a broad range of unified network products including high-speed optical, broadband, and wireless network solutions—the very stuff without which there would literally be no Internet as we know it today! As an organization that has moved well beyond the initial stages of technological capability required to support and sustain distance learning, Nortel has seen Web-based training and its evaluation become a steadily emerging component of its organizational learning strategy.

As a central player in the midst of these fast times and sweeping changes, Nortel has embraced a concept known as time-to-market (TTM) as a way to think, act, and do business in Web time by developing and introducing products faster using more efficient processes (see, for example, Bower & Hout, 1994; Meyer, 1993; Smith & Reinertsen, 1998). Web time (or Web speed) is a notion that recalibrates the traditional view of product development time into shorter cycles. According to Trochim (n.d., p. 13), "In 'Web-time' we tend to think more in terms of weeks or months than years or decades." Accordingly a "Web year" can be viewed as equal to one-quarter of a calendar year, with each calendar year containing *four* Web years. Accelerating delivery of the right product to market is a requirement to compete in the data world of short cycle time, and is critical to achieving and sustaining business profitability.

In response to internal research and benchmarking studies indicating that time to market improvements of 40 percent to 60 percent were achievable by introducing disciplined product development processes into business units, a central TTM Project objective was to cut Nortel's new product development cycle time in half. With the TTM learning initiative directed at all business units, achieving such dramatic reductions in product development time offered Nortel enormous earnings potential driven through R&D efficiency, reduced R&D spending, increased revenues, and improved product margins.

## Using Principles of TTM to Develop Web-Based Training

While the main emphasis here is on the evaluation and development of Web-based instruction, the overall development and deployment of Web-training obviously involves many technical considerations related to the information technology infrastructure and capability of an organization. These might range from graphical Web site design considerations to physical hardware and network performance constraints affecting the type and amount of multimedia (for example, streamed audio and video) that can be used to enhance learning. Although a detailed consideration of these aspects is beyond the scope of the present work, there is a growing body of traditional and on-line resources available for the interested reader (for example, B. Hall, 1997; http://www.multimediatraining.com/brandon-hall/webtraincook.html; http://www.filename.com/wbt/;http://www.dyroweb.com/).

We next turn to a consideration of the development process used to develop TTM training using its own principles. A TTM approach was used to create stand-alone Web-based distance training to introduce basic TTM concepts to all employees. The starting point for this process was learning material developed and tested in traditional instructor-led pilot sessions. In addition to the initial pilot sessions, designed to familiarize employees with TTM basics, an aggressive "Webtime" schedule was established based on seven key TTM principles. The goal was to develop and deploy a fully integrated, multimedia, instructional Web site complete with streamed audio and video available to every employee using the company's large internal network.

TTM can be summarized as consisting of seven key principles:

- *All projects are managed end-to-end.* This refers to managing work activities on a project basis rather than a functional basis and keeps the focus on the customer (internal or external) in terms of specified requirements.
- *Every project has an end-to-end accountable leader.* An accountable leader is someone who will make the project successful by driving marketing, development, operations, and other aspects, and by taking responsibility for project financials and business success.
- *Cross-functional teams have the project's business success as their only objective.* Individuals identify with the project, not their function. That is, project team members are drawn from functional groups such as design, operations, marketing, engineering, training, and others, but are assigned as full-time project members for the duration of any given project.
- *The team collects customer feedback data before launching a product.* As a result, all project plans are customer-focused and the customer is part of the development process, avoiding the pitfall of internal decisions about what a product (that is, whatever the team's goal involves—in this case, a training Web site) should or should not do.
- *Each project has a charter that defines priorities, desired outcomes, and schedules.* As a standard component of project management terminology, the project charter defines and maps project specifications and deliverables. The idea is market orientation and focus.
- *The product delivery process uses alpha and beta release control.* An alpha release is generally one designed to test acceptance by friendly customers who have indicated preliminary product interest. Beta product releases rely on customers to test the

actual functionality of a product under live conditions. Each business defines what these releases involve within its own appropriate context.

- *General managers and their cabinets are responsible for project starts, stops, and release to market based on business needs.* General managers make the business decisions to determine, for example, whether a product is at alpha, beta, or ready to ship. Further decisions involve determining whether the market is still there. These decisions require knowledge of quality metrics, customer expectations, market size, and trends.

The principle of working with customer feedback deserves particular emphasis here. Prototyping new ideas with lead customers to evaluate market acceptance and define product plans is a characteristic of successful companies. In addition to faster product development, the results include greater customer value and less wasted effort. Beyond that, customer feedback is part and parcel of evaluation of distance training of the type described in this chapter.

The TTM Web-based training case example described next illustrates elements of Stage 4 learning described by Schreiber (1998b) as well as by Berge in Chapter Two. This is exemplified by learning that has been institutionalized organizationally as characterized by policy, communication, and practice aligned to business objectives. A key to Stage 4 is systematic assessment of training events with an organizational perspective. Within the framework for sustaining distance training and education (Chapter One), the goal state of Stage 4 implementation is further characterized by management processes that reflect an integration of distance learning with the mission of the organization.

## Evaluating TTM Web-Based Training Development

The word *evaluation* generally connotes a systematic activity carried out after some event, treatment, or process to assess its impact or effectiveness. Yet information collected during the development of a Web site (before it is fully deployed) can also be useful for evaluation purposes. This is because evaluation is more than simply looking in the rearview mirror. There are two good reasons for this. First, evaluation has much to offer throughout the entire life cycle of a program. The methods that evaluators use and the perspectives they bring can greatly enhance the development of a product or program. Second, even after-the-fact evaluation will be hampered without intimate knowledge of the history and working of a program. Understanding a program in its developmental context is essential to understanding its effects and how those effects are produced (Trochim, n.d., p. 5).

In conjunction with efforts to perform such concurrent evaluation, determining the desired outcomes for any program or training intervention necessitates the involvement of multiple stakeholders (Alkin, Hofstetter, & Ai, 1998; Broad & Newstrom, 1992; Bryk, 1983; Michalski, 1997; Michalski & Cousins, 2000) to identify meaningful measures of project success. The common and competing values among all stakeholders need to be identified and developed into an appropriate set of quantitative and qualitative balanced measures. These might include data and information taken from surveys, interviews, or focus groups using various nominal group techniques, and content analyses of existing documents such as electronic communications (see Bonanno, n.d.). As a component of program management (see Chapter Two), program evaluation of distance learning programs includes a role for adult learners and other stakeholders in the evaluation. According to Alkin (1991) at least four different stakeholder roles can be identified regarding the evaluation process. These include stakeholders as primary users of evaluation results, information sources for framing the evaluation, data sources during the evaluation, and as the audience for the evaluation report.

## Determining Measures of Success

At the most general level the goal of deploying Web-based TTM training at Nortel was to make available to employees an efficient means to learn about TTM concepts and principles. As distance training, it would be considered successful if the training served to effectively and efficiently meet the needs of employees to learn about TTM as a major business strategy.

To determine project success measures, the TTM Web-training development team adapted a distance learning evaluation approach described by Simonson (1997). This approach identified the following five areas:

- *Accountability:* Did the project planners do what they said they were going to do?
- *Effectiveness:* How well was the project done?
- *Impact potential:* What potential does the project have to make a difference?
- *Organizational context:* What structures, policies, or events in the organization or environment helped or hindered the project?
- *Unanticipated consequences:* What changes of importance happened as a result of the project that were not expected?

Table 12.1 summarizes several criteria considered by the TTM Web-based training development team to be key in the success of the training beyond the beta version. As shown, accountability was described by the development team in terms of user satisfaction and practical considerations such as obtaining preliminary feedback for module improvement and meeting the development schedule for the training. Views of effectiveness included demonstrating user knowledge gain

## TABLE 12.1. PRELIMINARY SUCCESS CRITERIA.

| Accountability | Effectiveness | Impact Potential | Organizational Context |
|---|---|---|---|
| • Provide basic overview of TTM<br>• Achieve average user satisfaction rating of satisfied to very satisfied (4 to 5)<br>• Obtain useful feedback to improve future releases (formative evaluation)<br>• Meet module development schedule<br>• Meet user expectations | • Demonstrate pre- to post-test knowledge gain<br>• Provide relevant information to users (users find the information they needed)<br>• Easy to use<br>• Establish what elements of Web-based course helped or hindered learning | • Reduce volume of classroom instruction<br>• Reduce TTM training duplication<br>• Reduce uncertainty (number of questions) about TTM implementation<br>• Show usage by a range of users across various lines of business<br>• Demonstrate significant user engagement or "reach" by collecting key demographic data | • Supports business goals<br>• Addresses learning needs of multiple product development groups<br>• Addresses related issues such as individual and team rewards and recognition<br>• Conforms with relevant budget, policy, staffing |

*Source:* Adapted from Simonson (1997).

through pre- and post-testing, and the general usability of the training. Impact was conceived in terms of reductions in traditional classroom deliveries, duplication, and overall uncertainty about TTM implementation. Impact measures were also described in terms of demographic usage of the site across several lines of business. The organizational context included considerations related to integration with business goals, addressing the learning needs of multiple product development groups, related issues such as individual and team rewards and recognition, and conforming with relevant budget, policy, staffing infrastructure.

## Learner Demographics and Expectations

The assessment of user expectations should not be underestimated as a central evaluation component. In many ways the degree to which user expectations are met or exceeded will ultimately determine the success of a product or program. According to Trochim and Hover (n.d., p. 1), "One of the first and most important steps in evaluating any program or technology is to assess the expectations and assumptions that participants bring to the context. How people interact with a program is heavily influenced by their views about it, by what they expect it to be like and what they hope to get out of it. Assessing such amorphous and subjective psychological expectations poses significant methodological challenges for the evaluator."

Three evaluative components were designed and deployed with a trial (beta) version of the training: a preliminary survey intended to collect user demographics and expectations, a pre-/post-test component to assess learning, and a post-survey to assess overall user reaction. At the time of this writing, sufficient data for the second and third components were not yet available, so the following discussion focuses on the results of the preliminary survey used during the development of the training. The results are discussed in basic terms of learner demographics, rationales for engaging in the training, and expectations for the training.

## User Demographics (Who Came?)

A sample of 113 ($n = 113$) respondents was collected over a two-week period after the beta version deployment of the training. Users identified themselves according to four main categories: job function, line of business affiliation, age, and highest earned academic degree. As shown in Figure 12.1 job functions were broken down as non-manager, manager, senior manager, director, vice president, and individual contributor (specialists who have higher levels of organizational and proj-

**FIGURE 12.1. JOB ROLES OF PRELIMINARY SURVEY RESPONDENTS.**

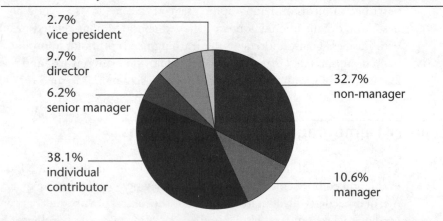

2.7% vice president

9.7% director

6.2% senior manager

38.1% individual contributor

32.7% non-manager

10.6% manager

ect responsibility but no employees reporting directly to them on a permanent basis). Approximately two-thirds of all respondents identified themselves as non-managers (32.7 percent) and individual contributors (38.1 percent). Managers at various levels comprised the balance of those responding. This included first-line managers (10.6 percent), senior managers (6.2 percent), directors (9.7 percent), and vice presidents (2.7 percent).

Figure 12.2 shows that over half of those responding identified their line of business as either carrier (57.5 percent) or carrier packet (7.1 percent) networks. Enterprise (8 percent) and wireless networks (1.8 percent) together accounted for less than 10 percent of respondents, with members from the corporate group (12.4 percent) and other lines of business (13.3 percent) accounting for the remaining respondents. The other category included internal and external services groups such as the "e-service" group, who accounted for 10.6 percent of the "other" total.

As shown in Figure 12.3, respondents ranged in age from under twenty (3.5 percent) to over fifty-five (2.7 percent) with the largest percentages of respondents identifying their age categories between these two extremes: twenty to twenty-five (4.4 percent), twenty-six to thirty (19.5 percent), thirty-one to thirty-five (17.7 percent), thirty-six to forty (28.3 percent), forty-one to forty-five (15 percent), forty-six to fifty (8 percent), and fifty-one to fifty-five (.9 percent).

Figure 12.4 shows that over three-quarters of respondents had earned at least a bachelor's (45.1 percent) or master's (30.1 percent) degree with the remaining individuals identifying themselves as having earned a doctoral (2.7 percent) or "other" degree (5.3 percent). It should be noted that among respondents who

**FIGURE 12.2. ORGANIZATIONAL LINES OF BUSINESS IDENTIFIED BY RESPONDENTS.**

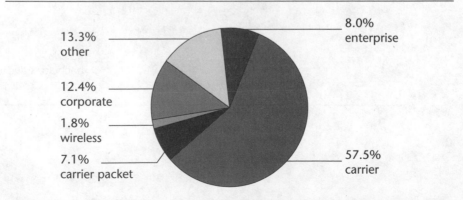

13.3% other

12.4% corporate

1.8% wireless

7.1% carrier packet

8.0% enterprise

57.5% carrier

## FIGURE 12.3.  AGE CATEGORIES OF RESPONDENTS.

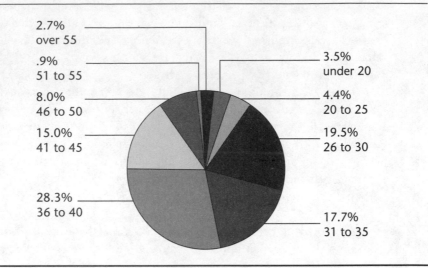

## FIGURE 12.4.  FORMAL EDUCATIONAL LEVEL OF RESPONDENTS.

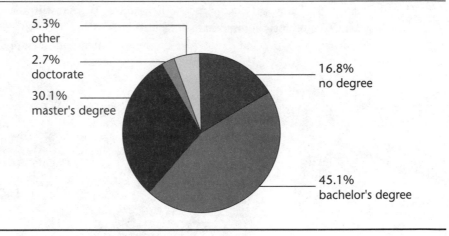

identified themselves as non-degree (16.8 percent) were individuals who were working on but had not yet formally been awarded various academic degrees. Several such individuals made this known in their written comments.

## User Rationale (Why Did They Come?)

Respondents could choose one or more predefined reasons as well as supply their own (other unlisted) reasons to respond to the survey item about rationales for visiting the Web site. Based on the intent of the site it is not surprising that the leading reason given (41.1 percent as a percentage of all responses) was "I want to improve my general knowledge about TTM." The next most often given reason for visiting the site was "I was encouraged to do so by my manager" (31.8 percent). Table 12.2 summarizes the results. Among the "other" reasons respondents wrote comments such as "We will implement TTM as part of our application development methodology," and "I am moving to a new role that will be using the TTM model."

Most respondents indicated that they had basic (35.4 percent), little (34.5 percent), or no knowledge (21.2 percent first time exposure) of TTM concepts and principles. The remaining respondents indicated that they had either a working (6.2 percent) or high (2.7 percent) degree of knowledge about TTM. Additionally, over half (52.2 percent) of all respondents indicated their "level of interest in TTM" to be high, while the rest indicated their interest level to be either moderate (35.4 percent) or low (12.4 percent).

### TABLE 12.2. REASONS PROVIDED BY USERS FOR VISITING THE TTM TRAINING WEB SITE.

| Rationale for Visit to Site | Count | Percentage of Responses |
|---|---|---|
| Improve TTM knowledge | 79 | 41.1 |
| Avoid classroom training | 9 | 4.7 |
| Curious about TTM | 19 | 9.9 |
| Curious about Web site | 8 | 4.2 |
| Encouraged by coworker | 9 | 4.7 |
| Encouraged by manager | 61 | 31.8 |
| Other | 7 | 3.6 |
| Totals | 192 | 100 |

As summarized in Table 12.3, respondents indicated a balanced variety of expectations in return for their time spent visiting the training site. This table summarizes responses to the item that asked what participants expected to be able to do after completing the presentation (for which respondents could choose one or more choices). Beyond being able to "describe basic TTM concept/principles" (22.2 percent), "answer basic questions about TTM" (16.4 percent), and "understand how TTM supports Nortel business goals" (20.7 percent), over one-third of all responses included "understand how to apply TTM knowledge to my job" (22.8 percent) or "apply what I have learned on the job" (15.3 percent).

## Preferred Learning Methods and Media

To assess their general attitude toward various learning methods and media, users were also asked to indicate their preference for a variety of learning methods and media of instruction. Using a five-point Likert scale where 1 = strongly disagree, 2 = disagree, 3 = neither agree nor disagree, 4 = agree, and 5 = strongly agree, Table 12.4 displays a rank order of preferred methods arranged from most favored to least favored as indicated by all respondents.

Exploratory factor analysis (principal components, Eigenvalues > 1, varimax rotation) further revealed that only four factors explained 68.5 percent of the variance observed. The four factors extracted involved (1) electronic but noncomputer-based media such as radio, audiotape, television, audio- and videoconference, and satellite (35.38 percent), (2) electronic, computer-based media such

### TABLE 12.3.  EXPECTATIONS PROVIDED BY USERS FOR VISITING THE TTM TRAINING WEB SITE.

| Action Expectations | Count | Percentage of Responses |
|---|---|---|
| • Describe basic TTM concept and principles | 77 | 22.2 |
| • Answer basic questions about TTM | 57 | 16.4 |
| • Understand how TTM supports Nortel business goals | 72 | 20.7 |
| • Understand how to apply TTM knowledge to my job | 79 | 22.8 |
| • Apply what I have learned on the job | 53 | 15.3 |
| • Other | 9 | 2.6 |
| Totals | 347 | 100 |

## TABLE 12.4. LEARNING MEDIA PREFERENCES INDICATED BY TTM TRAINING WEB SITE USERS.

| Rank | Learning Method | Mean | Standard Deviation |
|------|-----------------|------|--------------------|
| 1 | Web-based | 3.75 | 1.01 |
| 2 | CD-ROM | 3.63 | 1.00 |
| 3 | Traditional classroom | 3.55 | 1.24 |
| 4 | Videoconference | 3.29 | 1.11 |
| 5 | Printed (books and so on) | 3.11 | 1.06 |
| 6 | Satellite (interactive) | 3.10 | 1.10 |
| 7 | Videotape | 3.04 | 1.14 |
| 8 | Electronic Performance Support Systems | 3.00 | .945 |
| 9 | Television | 2.56 | 1.09 |
| 10 | Audioconference | 2.39 | 1.05 |
| 11 | Audiotape | 2.12 | 1.13 |
| 12 | Radio broadcast | 2.07 | .980 |

as CD-ROM, Web-based, and Electronic Performance Support Systems (EPSS) (13.63 percent), (3) classroom and videotape (10.39 percent), and (4) printed material (for example, books) (9.15 percent). These results suggest that respondents to the preliminary survey tended to rate learning media and method preferences similarly based on the technology involved. For example, respondents tended to view interactive and noninteractive broadcast audio- and video-based methods (radio, television, audioconference, satellite, videoconference, audiotape) similarly (factor 1) as distinguished from strictly computer-based methods such as Web-based, CD-ROM, and EPSS (factor 2), and more traditional methods such as classroom-based and videotape (factor 3), and printed material (factor 4).

## The Role of Evaluation in Sustaining Distance Training and Education

Viewed against the immense and growing number of topics available online (for example, the synthesized index search engine known as *Fast Search* located at www.alltheweb.com indexes over 300 million pages) as of late February 2000, the topic "Web-based training evaluation" yielded less than thirty hits using two of the more powerful search engines available (Fast Search and go2net's Metacrawler, located at www.go2net.com). By contrast searching the phrase "Web-based training" yielded nearly twenty-eight thousand hits (using Fast

Search). This result underscores an obvious fact regarding Web-based training and its evaluation: There is much more interest in Web-based training than there is in its evaluation!

But, even though they may not have been effectively combined as yet, many of the ingredients required for Web-based training evaluation already exist. These include emerging frameworks (Michalski, 2000; Simonson, 1997; Trochim, n.d.) and the definition of a set of criteria including technology, support, access, human interface, usability, and content (see http://www.nursecom.com/ncom1/ECG_WBT_ev.htm), as well as navigational flexibility, multiple representation of knowledge, and semantic network of lessons structure (see http://curricula.mit.edu/Workshop98/lab4.html). Evaluation methodologies including concept mapping, computerized methods (such as log file analysis), surveys, achievement testing, and experimental and quasi-experimental designs have also been defined (Trochim, n.d.). All of this portends a growing role for evaluation in Web-based training.

The results of Web-based training evaluation can be used to support, improve, and ultimately sustain this form of distance training by demonstrating obvious efficiencies such as reduced travel and reduced numbers of live classroom sessions. But as both Web-based instruction and its evaluation become fully institutionalized, the successful integration of an evaluation mind-set into the culture of an organization will further serve to enhance its communication and learning processes. The benefits of evaluation and the additional resources required to perform effective evaluations will be assumed as necessary conditions for doing business and competing in the Information Age. Strategic planning carried out at the organizational level will directly benefit from the aggregated results of such evaluations over time with improved decision making. Evaluation will become fully integrated into all areas of organizational life through its systematic implementation in the projects and programs that drive all business processes, including those associated with Web-based learning and instruction.

## Lessons Learned

The results of the evaluative measures introduced here are far from complete. Nevertheless, several lessons have been learned from the TTM Web-based training example at Nortel. Several of these may seem obvious, but some others are probably far less so.

In revisiting the criteria for evaluating sustainability originally defined by the TTM Web-training development team (see Table 12.1) the pre-survey results did provide user feedback to address several issues related to accountability (for example, obtain useful feedback to improve future releases; meet user expectations), impact potential (reduce volume of classroom instruction; reduce TTM training duplication; show usage by a range of users across various lines of business; collect key demographic data), and organizational context (supports business goals; addresses learning needs of multiple product development groups). But organizational context also includes questions such as, What factors aided or impeded implementation of the project?

The TTM Web-based training project was assisted by several contextual factors in the organization. First, for approximately twelve months prior to the launch of the Web-training numerous live sessions were held at several strategic geographic locations around the company to familiarize employees with TTM. Dubbed "TTM boot camps," these sessions were typically well-organized, high-energy events that served as facilitated open exchanges among TTM experts and employee groups. Designed to educate and encourage discussion on the TTM initiative, these one- to three-day sessions were typically attended by business unit implementation primes, new TTM practitioners, product development team members, and managers of all levels. The session also included a range of team-based activities that helped employees explore project plan development, effective teamwork, and project management principles and techniques.

Two other factors were seen to positively influence the initiative. These were organizational culture and leadership (Schein, 1985). The cultural impact of any change is often the most difficult aspect to quantify and can be the most challenging to deal with. TTM was introduced into Nortel during a period of sweeping organizational change. Major events of this change effort included, but were not limited to, the transformation of the R&D function from a separate large organization (formerly known as Bell Northern Research) into the product development lines, the appointment of a new CEO, and several strategic mergers and acquisitions. Amid the larger changes occurring across the telecommunications landscape, these changes had a huge impact on the organization—making it ripe for the kind of systemic change and project management fostered by TTM.

While questions related to effectiveness (and to some extent impact) will not be fully known until sufficient data are collected from pre- and post-test scores and post-engagement surveys, a few of what Simonson (1997) referred to as "unanticipated consequences" are notable. Unexpected consequences identify changes that occurred as a result of a project that were not foreseen during its planning and implementation. Internal evaluators are best positioned to observe such changes. These can provide a rich source of information about the success or failure of a project or program. The case presented provides a few examples.

The reasons provided by users for visiting the TTM training Web site presented in Table 12.2 revealed a higher than expected percentage of respondents indicating a reason for visiting the TTM training Web site as "my manager encouraged me to." The irony of this result is that, while breaking away from traditional functional hierarchy is one of the main components of the TTM approach, this very same hierarchy seemed to be an effective force in motivating employees to act (that is, visit the Web site). Perhaps those so motivated are indeed among those who stand to gain the most from learning about TTM principles.

The additional resources required to build evaluative measures into the training are also worth mentioning. In terms of the overall budget for the training development project, building the evaluation measures cost less than 1 percent of the total. Yet by using the initial results and preliminary feedback obtained, the developers were able to improve the quality of the training (based on suggested improvements provided by beta users) and deliver it a full four weeks ahead of the originally planned schedule (of twelve weeks). In this sense a little evaluation certainly did go a long way! But this is anticipated to be just the beginning of the benefits. In the longer term the pre- and post-test data accumulated with ongoing use of the training, as well as the post-survey information acquired, will contribute valuable learning to the organization as it continues to increase and mature in its capability to not only deploy but also *evaluate and improve* Web-based distance training. As active participants in the evaluation process, employees both contribute to and benefit from evaluation.

## Conclusions

As supported by the results obtained here, Web-based training users do seem to both prefer and expect value from engaging in this form of instruction. The process of planning and building simple but appropriate measures into Web-based training up front (for example, during the pilot or alpha and beta test phases) can produce highly useful information to ensure that what you finally build will attract the right clientele, at the right time, and for the right reasons.

The Web-based distance training example provided here is fully expected to be sustained for reasons that may well seem obvious. First, the training supports key strategic organizational and business goals. Second, the Internet technology involved in deploying the training is closely related to the same technology that the company develops for its own customers. In this sense it is a very comfortable fit. Third, the company has the necessary infrastructure required for this particular type of distance training to thrive. This includes sufficient budgets, a knowledgeable and well-organized staff of training and information technology personnel, and the remaining elements related to organizational management and programmatic implementation.

Finally, although Web-based (distance) training evaluation is a relatively underdeveloped area, it represents a huge opportunity for firms and organizations interested in advancing in their distance training level of maturity. Both the organizational experience of engaging in a systematic evaluation processes and the results of such efforts ultimately contribute to an improved policy, program, and project infrastructure. As models for evaluating Web-based distance training continue to emerge, the process and results of such evaluation will also continue to improve.

# CHAPTER THIRTEEN

# INTEGRATION OF INDIVIDUAL COACHING IN A DISTANCE LEARNING ENVIRONMENT

## Experiences at Cap Gemini Ernst & Young

John E. May, Jan A. de Jong

It makes sense to distinguish two kinds of distance education: group-based and individual-based. According to Keegan (1998), referring to distance (open) university training, the former is dominant in the United States, and the latter in Europe. We do not know whether these regional preferences apply to distance education in business and industry as well. In this chapter, we describe the experience at Cap Gemini Ernst & Young, a leading European management consulting and computer services firm, with individual-based distance training. The choice of an individual-based as opposed to a group-based approach is consistent with the training philosophy of Cap Gemini Ernst & Young Education & Training. Most training programs offered by the largest information and communication technology (ICT) training institute in Europe are individual-based, and thus allow for tempo and content differentiation. Another important element of the Cap Gemini Ernst & Young training programs is that coaching is provided by content experts. As Landsberg (1996) mentioned in *The Tao of Coaching*, coaching has proved to be a successful way of improving the student's performance and learning abilities.

In 1994, Cap Gemini Ernst & Young Training and Development started the first experiments with distance training. The challenge was to transfer the key elements of the individual-based Cap Gemini Ernst & Young training format to a distance learning environment. Our attempts to implement distance learning parallel to face-to-face training have not been entirely successful, but they nonetheless provide some useful insights and provided directions for current initiatives.

## Business Problem Statement

Our mission was to explore the feasibility of using distance training versions of individualized training programs taught at a Cap Gemini Ernst & Young Training Center. Exhibit 13.1 illustrates the format of the majority of programs offered by Cap Gemini Ernst & Young Education and Training.

### The Starting Point: Cap Gemini Ernst & Young Individual Training

Cap Gemini Ernst & Young Education & Training offers three hundred different ICT training courses (programming in various languages, technical and functional design, and so on) and ICT-related training courses (project management, team leading, neuro-linguistic programming, and so on), which add up to nearly 100,000 course days per year in the Benelux (Belgium, the Netherlands, and Luxembourg). Eighty percent of the courses offered are individual-based. Students who sign in for a course come to the Training Center, where they can work individually using specific computers and software and instructions on paper. The individualized format allows for custom tailoring and flexible use of the course material. The entry level of the student as well as the desired skill level are determined for all individual courses. Experienced Cap Gemini Ernst & Young consultants are employed as coaches. Usually they hold the position of coach for a few years, after which they return to their consultancy work. They offer individual coaching in their area of expertise. This coaching can be both proactive and reactive. Another important characteristic of the training programs is the use of realistic business cases. Learning by experience, as Kolb (1984) describes, the students confront live situations in business cases and apply what they have learned to those cases. These cases are developed on the basis of the practical experience of the Cap Gemini Ernst & Young consultants and are thus quite true to life. The manner in which the student approaches these cases determines the type of recommendations made to the customer organization regarding this student. In addition to a certificate, the training department can also make recommendations regarding the amount of follow-up coaching the student needs.

### Why Distance Training?

In 1994, Cap Gemini Ernst & Young Education & Training started a project in which the separate elements involved in distance training, such as videoconferencing and Internet techniques, were to be tried out and integrated in an electronic learning environment. There were several motives for starting this project. The

## EXHIBIT 13.1.  EXAMPLE OF AN INDIVIDUAL-BASED TRAINING PROGRAM OFFERED IN A CAP GEMINI ERNST & YOUNG TRAINING CENTER.

An employee goes to a manager and requests training or the manager requests that an employee follow a particular training. This can be a Cap Gemini Ernst & Young employee or an employee of one of Cap Gemini Ernst & Young Education & Training's customers.

This manager contacts Cap Gemini Ernst & Young Education & Training and is thus the customer. The training is booked, but before the training is scheduled, an intake interview is arranged with both the student and the manager. This can be in person or by telephone. During the intake interview, the knowledge and skills of the future student are assessed as well as the manager's expectations regarding the employee's ultimate level after the course. Based on this the student's course needs are determined and a personal curriculum is drawn up, consisting of various standard parts that are designed both to realize the student's personal objectives and to fit in with the student's individual learning style.

Now the curriculum can be planned. The availability of a location and of coaches for the period covered by this curriculum are examined.

On the first day of the training, the student meets the coaches for the professional area in that learning environment. One should keep in mind that the student has no fixed coach for the duration of the curriculum, but that Cap Gemini Ernst & Young Education & Training does guarantee that coaching will be available for the professional area covered by the course. The student now starts working independently and can, where necessary, request the coaches' assistance in resolving acute problems. At specific points in the material, the student will be asked to meet with a coach so that the coach can get an idea of the student's ability to apply the new knowledge and skills.

In addition, one of the coaches is appointed as the student's mentor. This coach monitors the student's progress and reports on it at regular intervals, both to the student and to the customer (generally the student's manager).

In addition to the theoretical parts, the training itself consists largely of business cases that ensure that the theory learned can be applied in practice and to give both the student and the coach insight into the student's ability to apply the material to real-life situations.

At the end of a training, one of the coaches (generally the mentor) gives the student an evaluation in the form of a certificate of skills and deployability specifying what the student has learned.

first was the expected cost reduction, in terms of both time and money, associated with student travel to and from the Training Center. The second was the expected increase in efficiency resulting from the fact that distance training course materials are accessible any time of the day. This could decrease the number days employees would be absent for learning purposes. The third motive was related to the flexibility permitted by constant availability of course materials, which could thus be provided at just the time the employee would need the new skills, making them more relevant and memorable. Since these expected advantages are relevant for anyone, the project might result in a new marketable service for external customers as well as an improvement in Cap Gemini Ernst & Young internal training.

## Target Population

Cap Gemini Ernst & Young Training & Development offers training programs to two groups of customers: internal customers and external customers. The ratio between internal participants (Cap Gemini Ernst & Young employees) and external participants (our customers' employees) is approximately 30 percent internal to 70 percent external. This allows us to be independent of our own Cap Gemini Ernst & Young organization, but Cap Gemini Ernst & Young employees constitute our largest single customer group and give us the necessary market input for course development and the incentive to experiment on new learning forms.

The Distance Training Project is meant to serve the needs of both internal and external students. It should provide an alternative route for reaching the competencies aimed for in our individual-based courses offered at the Training Centers.

### Internal Participants

Our potential internal customers are the approximately sixty thousand Cap Gemini Ernst & Young employees and new hires. These employees are specialists in two domains: redesign of business processes and application of information technology. They advise, support, and supervise organizations in improving their company operations by using information technology, and they design, build, and manage information systems. Distance learning gives the entire Cap Gemini Ernst & Young group the ability to benefit from the services of our Training Center. And the Training Center can benefit from the experiences of the entire Cap Gemini Ernst & Young group, because, as Cairncross noted in *The Death of Distance* (1997), "Communities of Practice and long-distance education programs will help people to find mentors and acquire new skills."

### External Participants

Potential external customers are our customers' (candidate) information technology specialists. Currently our customers are geographically restricted to the Benelux. Customers are the companies or departments we serve. Our contacts are generally made via the training department of the company or department. Course participants are these customers' individual employees who follow our courses. Agreements over and invoicing of the training to be followed are matters handled between Cap Gemini Ernst & Young Education & Training and the customer. The reports regarding the participants' progress go both to the individual course participant and to the customer, with additional information regarding the participant's skills, if requested. Upon completion of the course, the participant receives a Cap Gemini Ernst & Young certificate with additional recommendations regarding the level of independence with which the course participant can apply the knowledge learned, if requested.

## Outcomes Desired

To satisfy the requirements we set based on the business problem statement, our original objective was to create a product package via distance training that provides:

• Personally supervised just-for-me training
• The possibility of just-in-time training, as close as possible to the time the employee must actually perform the task
• The possibility of just-enough training, custom tailored to the individual training needs
• Ease of maintenance through modular design and reuse of the knowledge-based training available in the market
• A simple interchange between distance training and training at the Training Center
• Minimum modifications to the existing operational and administrative organization of Cap Gemini Ernst & Young Education & Training
• Enlargement of the geographical operating environment for the international Cap Gemini Ernst & Young group

In addition, our intention was to maintain Cap Gemini Ernst & Young Education & Training's values. These are the same values we maintain in our individual training centers, namely:

- Skills-based training (using Cap Gemini Ernst & Young best practices as case materials)
- Support from coaches with practical experience (professionals)
- Fast response to student questions (a maximum of thirty-minute response time)
- Regular feedback by the coach to course participants and customer
- Certification on the basis of demonstrable skills in real-life problem situations

An important feature of the distance training format to be developed is the use of distance coaching. Our positive experiences with coaching in individual-based courses in our Training Centers as well as experiences described in the literature (for example, Carnwell, 1999; Landsberg, 1996) have convinced us of the importance of the integrated use of individual coaching in a distance learning environment. Our project should provide insight into its feasibility.

## Overview of the Project History

In hindsight, the project history can be divided into three phases. In the first phase (1994–1997: Design), we experimented with various aspects of distance training, such as videoconferencing and Internet applications for document sharing, newsgroup support, chatting, GroupWare, and so on. The decision to develop a distance learning environment was made during this phase after a number of individual pilot tests with group and individual courses and the distance communication between students and coaches in those two course forms. This resulted in the design and building of this environment. Since it was not our aim to build another software package, before building we evaluated the distance learning platforms available at that time. These platforms did not support all of the principles Cap Gemini Ernst & Young Education & Training wished to maintain, so we decided to develop our own distance training environment, the Cap Gemini Ernst & Young Virtual Classroom. We did, however, use parts of third-party software that satisfied part of our functional requirements. Interfaces were developed to let software communicate that normally could not communicate. One example is a GroupWare application on the Web calling a telephone number at a particular time, which then establishes a videoconferencing session between distance locations that were not yet connected to the Internet. In addition to the third-party software and the interfaces, entirely new components were developed to satisfy the specific desires of Cap Gemini Ernst & Young Education & Training on planning, billing and registration, and tracking and tracing of students.

In the second phase (1997–1999: Implementation), we developed and implemented distance training versions of existing courses. These versions were offered as an alternative to the traditional courses. Customers could choose either to send their employees to the course as offered at the Training Center or to have them follow the same course in the distance-training version. The distance-training version was managed by the Training Center, and was subject to the same regulations as applied to the traditional course. Distance students were treated as regular students, the only difference being the location. The course materials were more or less similar. For frequently used courses we converted the content to a Web version of the course. For less frequently used courses we developed a form that incorporates both versions, partially Web-based and partially traditional. In those cases the study guide and the assignments were on the Web, but the readings were traditional. For courses with limited use we restricted ourselves to sending the traditional materials by mail and let our Virtual Classroom facilitate the communication between students and coaches.

In the third phase (1999-current: Restructuring), distance training was detached from the Training Center and more internally focused. This made us shift from a teacher-centered organization toward a learner-centered organization. The new role of Education & Training, or Cap Gemini Ernst & Young's Virtual University as it is called, would be to facilitate learning rather than simply to transmit courses. This process resembles the shifts of interactive learning Tapscott mentions in *Growing Up Digital* (1998).

## Implementation Phase: Management Processes

The preceding phase gave us a vision of how distance learning ought to operate at Cap Gemini Ernst & Young Education & Training. We suffered from the illusion that we had experimented sufficiently among our own people and that the time was ripe to enter the external market with this innovative service. As things progressed, it became apparent that the external market was not what we had expected. The majority of our customers did not have the same view of the level of their employees' individual responsibilities that we had. In hindsight, this turned out to be one of the crucial points when implementing distance learning. In the following sections, we describe separate elements of this arrangement. Exhibit 13.2 illustrates the functioning of the distance training arrangement in its initial implementation in the Cap Gemini Ernst & Young distance training environment.

## Policy

At this time it was decided that distance students would be treated just like students visiting the Training Center. They would have the same rights to access course materials or environments, as well as to use computer programs. They were

## EXHIBIT 13.2. EXAMPLE OF DISTANCE TRAINING AS ARRANGED IN THE IMPLEMENTATION PHASE.

Just as in the traditional situation, either an employee submits a training request to a manager or the manager selects a training experience for the employee. Now, however, the manager can also choose between having the student follow the training in one of the Cap Gemini Ernst & Young training centers or at a local site to be selected by the employee or manager. Assuming that the manager selects a local site, whether or not at the employee's instigation, this student will end up in the Cap Gemini Ernst & Young Virtual Classroom.

An interview will then be conducted with the employee and the manager, whether live or by telephone, in which the entry and exit levels are assessed. This results in a personal curriculum, which is scheduled based on the availability of coaching capacity. Availability of a location is no longer an issue because the student is now responsible for setting up a private learning place or a learning place facilitated by the manager. Cap Gemini Ernst & Young Education & Training just provides the specifications for this learning place. After planning, the student is scheduled for a certain number of days in the Virtual Classroom. Cap Gemini Ernst & Young issues the student a user ID and password and the training days are placed in an electronic agenda for the student. In addition, the requisite training materials are sent to the student, if they are not already on the Web.

Now the student can start studying independently. During the scheduled period, the student has the maximum freedom to work through the course materials whenever it is convenient to do so. However, coaching is available only at the times scheduled in the student's electronic agenda. Questions for the coaches are posed to the Virtual Classroom, which schedules it to the segment of the day in the agenda. This segment of the day is the time at which coaching capacity has been reserved for this student. A coach who is operating proactively will also consult the student's agenda. For technical support, however, the student has continual access to a help desk, which can assist with technical problems regarding the accessibility of the Virtual Classroom.

In terms of content, the training is identical to the training offered in one of our training centers—that is, geared toward learning by practicing with business cases. This also ensures that the procedural modifications for the coaches are kept to a minimum. However, the student now posts questions on a page in the Virtual Classroom, rather than asking the first coach who passes by in the training department. The Virtual Classroom schedules these questions based on the availability of the coaches, the availability of the student, and the number of coaches who could answer this question. These coaches see the student's questions on their personal page, after which they can contact the student. The coach chooses the form of contact that seems most appropriate for the coaching involved. This can be a telephone conversation or an e-mail message, a videoconferencing session, or a reference to a discussion forum or a Frequently Asked Questions list.

At the end of this training, the student is sent a certificate by one of the coaches (usually the mentor) that specifies the student's skills and makes a prediction about the student's capabilities in live projects.

also entitled to receive the same amount of coaching as the regular students. The ambition was to have all the courses available in a Web-based format, thus allowing for the complete integration of the management of the two types of delivery. It was expected that the organizational integration of distance training in the existing Training Center management structure would be more cost-effective than creating a new organization for the delivery of distance training. We thought we would bypass the cultural shift in going from traditional to distance training.

*Infrastructure.* We chose to have as few procedural changes as possible. But we still had to implement a Web-based environment to support both student and coach in their study annex work. This Web-based application must support the internal processes of individual training over the Web. As mentioned before, our findings in the Design phase led us to develop our own Virtual Classroom rather than use one of the available applications as a solo product. In this Virtual Classroom we combined proven technology that was suitable for supporting our individual training needs. Software we used for our Virtual Classroom includes Intel Proshare, Microsoft Internet Information Server, Microsoft Exchange, and Microsoft NetMeeting. But all this technology still had to be run. Since we are an ICT firm expertise on this subject was at hand, but for Education & Training itself it was new. We supplied all our coaches with a computer equipped with videoconferencing hardware and software, as well as with a high-performance Internet connection.

*Personnel.* There were no significant changes with regard to personnel during the second phase. In addition to the regular course participants, a coach was assigned a few distance training course participants to work with. Distance training course participants were limited to the course times that offered traditional course participants. These are fixed blocks of time—the morning, afternoon, and evening viewed from the perspective of a single time zone.

The only person that was added to this standing organization was the system manager for the Virtual Classroom Web server. From the outset, he was the most wanted (though not the most popular) person in the organization. Since most of the coaches had little or no experience with those new technologies, the technical barriers were high and the number of problems considerable. So we spent a good deal of time fixing problems with videoconferencing software on local machines or making arrangements with the local telecom operator for connecting people to the Internet.

*Budget.* The costs of Cap Gemini Ernst & Young's Virtual University can be classified into three categories: start-up costs, development costs, and exploitation costs. The start-up costs are primarily incurred during the Design phase.

In the Implementation phase, substantial costs were incurred for modifying existing courses to fit the new training model. It soon turned out that the available budget was not sufficient to develop Web-based course materials for all three hundred courses offered by Cap Gemini Ernst & Young Education & Training. In addition, there is little added value in the Web-based versions of a course compared to the traditional versions. We quickly confined our efforts to the most popular courses, making only limited changes—generally just adapting the training plan and some assignments. The majority of the materials were still traditional materials that were to be sent to the student when necessary.

The exploitation costs do not differ drastically from the exploitation costs for the courses offered in the training center. Currently the situation is such that the costs per student for managing the Internet environment are approximately equivalent to the costs for a student in one of our training locations. Eventually, we believe, the costs per Internet student will fall below those per traditional student.

## Implementation Phase: Outcomes

The implementation phase taught us a lot about the conversion of an individual training center into an individual distance training environment.

***Costs of Course Material Development.*** As Berge noted in Chapter One, Web-based training materials are time-consuming to develop. It is our experience that the development of traditional course material takes about fifteen days per course day. This includes educational design, writing, graphic design, and printing. The development of Web-based training material takes about fifteen days per *hour* of course material. The problem is that large blocks of text, which work well in traditional training, are simply not the proper way to present interactive course materials. The expert's stories need to be translated into graphical layouts and animations, and a lot of programming and graphical design work is required for just a couple of minutes of animation. This is an enormous increase in training development costs—and quickly became overwhelming when projected over the three hundred courses we currently have.

Over the long term, when the standard becomes to develop courses in Internet format (which can also be followed in a training location in the physical presence of a coach, if desired) and when a lot of reusable materials are available, including a standardized course engine and dialog layout, the total development costs will go down. Since it was currently impossible, considering the limited budget, to develop Web-based versions of all our training programs, we chose to work out several versions of distance training materials. In the first version (which was applied to the first converted courses), we developed a Web-based version of the complete course. In the second version we just converted the individual study plan and some of the assignments to a Web-based format. In the third version (which applied to most other courses), we simply sent the course materials to the student (by regular mail or electronically).

In the end, it made no difference to the student what form the course materials arrived in. The quality of the course was the same. The only minor difference was the image of Education & Training. With a glossy Web-based version of the training material available, we created a better image than by sending the traditional materials by mail. However, this did not affect the results of the individual students.

*Limited Interest.* Our customers were less eager to have their employees follow our distance training courses than we expected. Usually, the customer continued to send most of its students to follow the course at one of the training centers. Some of our customers acted as pilots for our Virtual Classroom and had one or two students follow the course in the distance training format. But usually when the pilot ended, the next student was again sent to our training centers. Thus we received no complaints over the quality of individual coaching in the distance learning environment, but the customers voted with their feet for the traditional setup.

We have tried to gain some insight into the reasons for this preference by evaluating all of our customers' pilot students and their managers (generally the training coordinator for the company or department). These are the most important reasons they mentioned:

- Managers like to have control over their employees' time. If an employee is sent to a course, the amount of time spent on the course is clear; this is less true in the case of a distance training environment, in which the employee decides how much time to spend.
- The savings in time and increase of flexibility as a result of distance training are seen by the departments of the employees but not by the training departments in the customer organizations. The latter see only an increase in educational spending, as they are responsible for the learning infrastructure in terms of the computer, Internet connection, and accommodations. So there is no real advantage to the training department in persuading the manager and employee of the advantages of distance training.
- Physical or organizational obstacles often crop up. Either the student does not have a quiet place to work on the course, or if such a place exists, the student is still close enough to the demands of regular work to be disturbed.
- Employees generally experience attending a course as a reward, well worth the investment in time and effort. They enjoy the change of pace and the hospitality offered during the course—none of which are provided with distance training. As a result, distance training does not work well in organizations where

there is a strong hierarchical culture, where a manager decides which course an employee should follow.

- Few students see the need for more flexible ways of learning. Therefore, few are willing to trade in the high quality of live communication with their coaches for the more difficult form of distance communication.

*Technological Problems.* Most of the problems encountered by our customers are organizational or cultural problems. However, technology plays an important role, too. The survey among our customers indicated the following points:

- The technical barrier for most customers is still high. Since Internet connection and videoconferencing software at the workspace is not common in most companies in the Benelux, it was a barrier when companies had to implement it for these explicit learning purposes.
- The limitations of bandwidth on the Internet cause a poor quality videoconferencing session. The technical solution we provided for improving this demands a greater than average understanding of the technology used by the student.
- Internet technology in general is not as common as we had hoped it would be. If the student has to focus on the technology instead on the content of the course, it is not seen as assisting the student in the course, but as becoming a target on its own.

*Changes in Coaching Pattern.* We also conducted a study into the changes in the training process as a result of long-distance coaching. The most important conclusion is that contacts between students and coaches became less frequent. Students tend to wait until they have several questions or are really stuck on a subject. This is compared to the traditional method where students question a coach the moment they encounter a problem, even if it is minor. This makes distance coaching more intensive.

Also, new coaches tend to use the most technically sophisticated coaching method, videoconferencing, for almost every student question. Even when a coach doubts the added value and suspects that sending an e-mail note would be a perfectly adequate way of responding to the student's question, the high-tech glamour of videoconferencing has an almost irresistible appeal. Besides the expense, this increases the amount of time spent on a single coaching session. This preference for videoconferencing usually disappears, however, when a coach is more experienced in using distance learning techniques.

Another significant aspect is that coaches tend to take a more reactive role, rather than combining reactive and proactive approaches. The coaches tend to just react to questions asked by the students instead of fulfilling their mentor role and contacting students without a student's initiating this contact. Coaches say that they have less of a bond with their students, so the proactive attitude is no longer automatic and must forced by formal procedures.

*Procrastination.* As Berge mentioned in Chapter One, some distance students tend to procrastinate. In our experience we saw two different situations. In the first situation students were studying during office hours and in facilitated, decentralized locations. In this group of students there was not much of a problem with procrastination, no more than the initial slowdown at the start of the course as they got used to using all the new communication technology. After the initial slowdown, those students tended to catch up with the regular tempo.

The other group of students where studying at their own pace on their own time (rather than during office hours). These students tended to suffer more from procrastination. This can be related to individual motivation for the courses and changing priorities in terms of study, work, and private issues. When students are not placed in a dedicated studying environment, they tend to make their own choices on how they spend their time. This gives more flexibility to the student but decreases the productivity in learning. This could lead to a delay of 50 percent to 100 percent when compared to the normal study time. This, however, does not mean that students spent that much more time on their study—they changed their priority and did not study continuously, which meant it took them twice as long to complete the course.

## Restructuring Phase: Management Processes

In evaluating the Implementation phase of the Cap Gemini Ernst & Young Virtual Classroom, we came to the conclusion that the results did not argue for large-scale implementation of distance learning for our external customers. We decided that large-scale conversion of all our lesson materials to Web-based versions is not justified at this time. However, the successes from our experiences, such as the high internal demand for Web-based courseware and the extensive internal use of it outside of office hours, did indicate that we have a clear need for distance learning within our own organization, especially for the just-in-time and just-for-me aspects. This had led to a modified implementation of distance learning with the international Cap Gemini Ernst & Young organization as the primary target group. Currently we are actively realizing this new form of distance learning for our own organization. Time will tell whether this enjoys greater success than the previous efforts and if it actually leads to a better-trained and more flexibly deployable employee. In the following sections, we describe separate elements of this arrangement. Exhibit 13.3 provides an illustration of the functioning of the distance training arrangement in the Restructuring phase of the Cap Gemini Ernst & Young distance learning environment.

## EXHIBIT 13.3. EXAMPLE OF DISTANCE TRAINING AS ARRANGED IN THE RESTRUCTURING PHASE.

In this situation, the student controls the reins. The manager is out of the picture, neither deciding to send the student to the training nor giving permission to attend. Instead, individual employees have their own annual training budget, which they are supposed to spend as efficiently as possible to ensure that their knowledge and skill levels are kept up-to-date. This stimulates each employee to get as much value from the money spent on training as possible.

The student can now decide whether to pursue an entire curriculum or just a few learning events. In choosing a curriculum, the student will put this together as a personal package, using self-awareness of personal knowledge and skill and of the desired level of knowledge and skill compatible with a specific competency within the organization. The student will try to eliminate the difference between the two using a personalized curriculum, which consists of a series of learning events.

For many learning events alternatives are available. Thus a learning event could consist of a brochure, a link on the Internet, a connection to a expert, or a Web-based training session, but it could also be a traditional classical or individual course. Thus, the learning event "negotiate" might be satisfied with a document titled "Tips and Tricks for Negotiating" or a Web-based training on "negotiation techniques" or an instructor-led class called "Negotiating." Based on the personal training budget and the desired result, the student will have to make choices regarding the learning event to follow. A student who only chooses the documents mentioned in the curriculum will not tax the training budget much, but it is arguable whether the material learned will have much practical value. On the other hand, should the student choose instructor-led training for all the learning events in the curriculum, the training budget would not begin to cover the expense.

At the end of the curriculum, the student can qualify for a new role in the organization by selecting a qualifying learning event to demonstrate capability to apply the new material in a business case. Individual coaches will guide the student on the path through these learning events and will send the student a certificate when the business case qualification process is complete.

---

*Policy.* The role of Cap Gemini Ernst & Young Education & Training has changed from simply offering training to facilitating learning—and to Cap Gemini Ernst & Young Virtual University. The student is the focal point and the area of attention has been broadened. This involves more than training; it has a close connection with human resource management and knowledge management and covers all the aspects that can be considered learning events for the individual employee. Thus in addition to traditional individual training (at a distance and in classic format), the Cap Gemini Ernst & Young Virtual University now also offers links to pages on the Internet as well as links to the expertise in our own organization and third-party technology-based training materials, as well as references to our own or third-party instructor-led training.

Earlier we made a distinction between internal and external markets. This new form of distance learning service focuses primarily on the internal market. In this context, internal training offerings have changed from a profit center to a cost center and thus are no longer responsible for contributing to the profit of the organization, but are included in the budget as a cost item.

External training offerings stayed in place as they were. Perhaps in time this distance learning service may also be offered to our customers, but it must first prove to be a success for our own employees.

*Infrastructure.*  To serve this change of objective, the infrastructure must change considerably. The previous phase only involved the processes for training to be given on the Web. In this phase, all Cap Gemini Ernst & Young Virtual University processes will be on the Web. Thus it is now possible for individual students to conduct an intake on their own, online, to assess their own knowledge and skills. In addition, all competency profiles within Cap Gemini Ernst & Young are mapped out with their associated learning invents. This is so that the employees can draw up their own curricula and can schedule the requisite learning events or access them immediately.

All these processes must be supported by Web-enabled applications. This means a shift from the traditional information systems to Web-based applications. Because most of the primary processes for training are now on the Web, security is an extremely important issue. There is a close cooperation among our system managers, developers, and the corporate security officer regarding this issue.

*Personnel.*  The role of the coach is also changing considerably. Here we make a distinction between the *coach,* who is responsible for the training processes, and the *expert,* who is responsible for the content but does not work for the training department. The coach is always the first point of contact, but can forward questions to experts who work in a particular professional area every day, and who are thus the most appropriate people to share their experiences with the students from our organization. Coaches are more difficult to schedule in this environment because employees are taking their training on an ad hoc basis more and more. This means that the organization will bear more and more resemblance to an educational call center, where the coaches do virtually all their coaching reactively. The exception will be qualifying business cases in which the coach will still play the traditional proactive role, addressing the how and why of a student's solutions.

*Budget.*  Although costs for development and exploitation of the new version of the Cap Gemini Ernst & Young Virtual University are quite high, the main costs lie in acquiring licenses for the use of third-party courseware and developing company-specific Web-based training materials. Licenses for the use of third-party courseware generally involve large numbers of courses from a supplier that are made available for all the employees in the organization. These large numbers mean high prices for the contracts, but a low price per separate course when viewed from the perspective of the number of courses and course participants. It appears that knowledge-oriented training materials are becoming more and more of a commodity. Many of them are available on the external market and their price is dropping due to stiff competition. There are even locations on the Web that offer these knowledge-oriented training materials free. The added value of a corporate university is not in developing these knowledge-oriented materials ourselves but in enriching standard training materials with the insights and experiences from our own organization or developing Web-based courses that are company specific and therefore not available on the market. The costs for creating a company-specific Web-based course are more or less comparable to a corporate license for the use of one hundred Web-based training events from a random supplier, made available for our entire population.

The costs for developing the gateway for the new Cap Gemini Ernst & Young Virtual University are considerable if you compare them to the costs for creating a Web site, but are reasonable if you consider them as realizing the information systems for the internal training processes. In any case, they are lower than the licensing costs for the use of third-party Web-based training materials.

## Restructuring Phase: Outcomes

Because we are currently in the middle of the restructuring process, it is difficult to specify definitive results. A few of the results already achieved are worth mentioning, however.

*Frequent Use of External Courseware.* The large offering of third-party training materials has been a big success thanks to the low threshold for acquiring it. The reason for this is that no booking is necessary and the cost for its use is not passed on to the individual student. This means that students using such Web-based training do not have to tap into their personal training budgets. The costs of this service are included in the budget annually.

*Changing Role of the Coach.* The role of the coach is changing from individual coach to a sort of help desk employee who deals with training questions rather than technical ones. This is not a role to which the entire current coach population aspires. This means we will lose good coaches who regard this form of student assistance as less valuable than their traditional role.

*The Expert Coach.* Since the most desired experts of the organization are of great value for their business units it is very hard to schedule them for a support role within the Cap Gemini Ernst & Young Virtual University. The time they spend to share their knowledge and experience with students could also be used to produce billable hours.

*Ad Hoc Coach Requests.* Since it is no longer necessary to schedule study times in advance, questions regarding the training topics offered come in at random times. The threshold for posing questions is quite low because there is no extra charge for this service. The students experience this as a plus, but it makes scheduling quite difficult for the Cap Gemini Ernst & Young Virtual University. Coaches must continually be available for questions that might come in. This also means that coaches must even be available for subjects for which there may be no questions at a given moment.

## Discussion and Conclusions

The most important conclusion we can draw from these three phases is that translating the existing traditional processes for individual learning has not produced the success we had envisioned. Apparently students who study via the Internet have other expectations from such training, so that long-term courses of study apparently do not adequately address these students' world of experience.

It also appears that the vast majority of current Cap Gemini Ernst & Young Education & Training customers are not adopting this new form of learning and that its implementation causes various internal organizational and cultural problems. These must be resolved before distance learning can be a success in these organizations. Once these internal problems are resolved, we will still have to deal with the question of whether these customers want Web versions of the individual training, or whether these customers will decide to use the facilitated learning model as we have chosen for our own use.

For our own organization we have decided on a knowledge management model of the "knowledge codification and coordination" type, which aims "to put organizational knowledge into a form that makes it accessible to those who need it" (Davenport & Prusak, 1998, p. 68), instead of a training center model. For the content expert involved in knowledge transfer, this model implies a second role shift. The first shift was from group-based trainer to individual coach. The second role shift is from individual coach to "expert on call." Both learning and coaching tend to escape from central planning, but they still need to be facilitated.

Those are our main lessons learned at Cap Gemini Ernst & Young.

CHAPTER FOURTEEN

# HEWLETT-PACKARD'S REGIONAL TRAINING CENTER

## Site Information & Learning Centers (SILC)

Alice Branch, Amy Lyon, Sarah C. Porten

The pace of new developments in technology is so rapid that engineers graduating from college today can expect to have most of their skills and knowledge outdated within eighteen months. For example, let's examine the technological explosion found with the Internet. The technology propelling the Internet began with Java, relentlessly marched forward to APIs, applets, and servlets, and is now moving on to "e-Speak"—a meta-technology that will assist non-Internet applications with speaking to the Internet and vice versa. "e-Speak" is a technology that did not exist before 1999. Engineers who graduated in 1996 must have studied Java and its associated parts (APIs and so on) and have a thorough understanding of NT or UNIX and any of the Web browser technologies *after* their graduation in order to make contributions to the business today.

In 1996, there were about 45 million Internet users and little in the way of Internet-based business. Recent IDC (International Data Corporation) studies have projected that by the year 2003, the number of Internet users will be in the hundreds of millions worldwide[1] and that Internet-based businesses will gross over $338 billion worldwide (Tedeschi, 2000).

Our engineers must stay on a fast track to continuous learning. Yet the cost of a technical course such as Java can range anywhere between $1,200 and $2,000. Multiply even the low end of that range by a thousand Internet engineers and a company could easily spend well over a million dollars on training in the fundamentals of just one technology. If we were to apply that to a corporation as large as Hewlett-Packard, the cost of continuous employee development could become astronomical.

Where cost is an issue for the corporation, the lack of *time* is the issue for employees—time to attend to business deliverables that are on rapid development-to-delivery cycles versus time to attend to personal technical skill development. It is often a tough call to make between a tight deadline and the need for additional training. And often, when there is a "window of opportunity" where a deadline is not on the immediate horizon, timing of available resources may be an issue; that is, there is no training event within that window of opportunity.

Hewlett-Packard (HP) is a high-tech global company that is a dominant player in the computer industry. With more than eighty thousand employees, the challenges it faces are similar to those of other companies, large and small—rapid technological change and a core of knowledge workers who, recognized as key to sustaining competitive advantage (Senge, 1990; Goldsmith, 1997; Michalisin, 1997), must stay abreast of these changes. As with many companies, over half of HP's revenue is derived from products that did not exist five years ago. Knowledge workers synthesize, integrate, and create new products and services, and the ability of corporations to support continuous learning has become another key in sustaining competitive advantage (Harrigan, 1991).

In response to the challenge of enabling a workforce to learn continuously without "breaking the bank" and of accommodating employee issues around time, various organizations within HP have launched initiatives to provide technology-based, or distance, learning to its workforce. Technology-based learning was seen as a solution to these issues because of the inherent flexibility it offered the learner and its cost-effectiveness compared to the traditional classroom for both the learner and the organization. HP's Media Solutions organization focused on the deployment of a worldwide video broadcast network that was used by HP as well as other corporations for training and special business meetings with a large, geographically dispersed audience. HP's field support organization launched a centrally managed worldwide network of self-paced training centers designed to provide technical product training to customer engineers. And many individual sites worldwide began implementing independent site learning centers focused on providing various types of self-paced training to their local employees. Though each of these initiatives remained fairly independent of the others, reflecting Hewlett-Packard's decentralized corporate structure, each was developed in response to the challenge of sustaining the knowledge worker.

## Meeting the Challenge

One such initiative stands out in that—from its inception—it was designed to be integrated within its parent organization as a viable response to the growing business challenge of sustaining education within the workforce. This initiative is identified within HP as the Site Information & Learning Centers (SILC) and was based at one of the HP campuses in Silicon Valley. Ultimately, SILC changed the way its parent organization, the Regional Training Center (RTC), approached the development and utilization of resources for the sixteen thousand employees in the San Francisco Bay Area.

### Phase 1: The Decision to Develop SILC

SILC was intended to be a major force in the delivery of training alternatives to its constituency. SILC was conceived in 1995 when an analysis of one of HP's main Silicon Valley campuses validated the need for technology-mediated education. This analysis revealed the following:

- There were many marketing operations with a critical need for information on emerging businesses and technologies.
- There were several software development labs experimenting on the "bleeding edge" of technology, and many of the senior engineers in these labs had not taken a single course in technology for several years.
- Some organizations were faced with "hire versus train" decisions regarding their workforce as new business directions were identified. The question: would it be cheaper to hire or train people to bring the necessary skills on board?
- When queried, the majority of people—from high-level managers to individual contributors—responded that they had difficulty finding large blocks of time to take courses, and that short courses, or courses that they could take when they had time, would be desirable.

As noted earlier, various organizations within HP had initiated work in the distance education arena. The types of technology used and the form of distance education delivered varied. The use of these resources by constituent departments was often sporadic. The exception was in the learning center network of the field support organization. Within that organization, the learning centers became the primary and mandatory option available to customer engineers who needed product support training, and distance education was a key and integrated part of the organization.

Although no corporate-wide initiative for distance education existed, there were informal networks within HP's internal education community that provided information and best practices to support organizations in their efforts to employ technology to deliver education. When the idea for SILC was conceived, information from these networks and the field support organization was gathered to assist in the strategic development that would ultimately become SILC. Thus, SILC, in its own way, bypassed Stage 1 of the organizational maturity model with regard to the delivery of distance education (Schreiber, 1998b; also discussed in Chapter Two of this volume) and built its foundation on successful work done by other organizations.

## Phase 2: Design and Implementation of Strategy

Phase 2 of SILC's evolution maps closely to Stage 2 of Schreiber's organizational maturity model. Shortly after the decision to develop SILC was made, the emphasis was on project management activities. These activities included laying out the strategies to establish the foundation of the organization that would sustain SILC. From these early project management activities, the emphasis shifted quickly to program development and management. The balance of this section focuses on the specific types of activities that occurred in this phase of SILC's evolution.

Several factors were considered in the design and implementation of the strategy for SILC: identify the target audience, create the organization and build shared vision, design the organizational structure to sustain distance education according to the vision, and gain management buy-in and support.

*Target Audience.* There were many professions and functions at SILC's home campus. Given the composition of the overall site, however, the initial target audience for SILC's distance education was identified as HP engineers located in the San Francisco Bay Area. This specific audience was targeted because 66 percent (or roughly two thousand) of SILC's constituents at its home campus were software development engineers. Additionally, the majority of high-quality self-paced courses available at the time (1995) for delivery via a distance education infrastructure were on technical topics. (It was only in SILC's third year of operation that high-quality self-paced products on nontechnical topics such as management and personal productivity began to appear.)

*Organization and Shared Vision.* The second element in the strategy was to form the organization and build a shared vision of what SILC would be and in becoming that vision, what SILC would provide its constituency, and how SILC would go about providing its resources. The vision selected by the team was encapsulated in the words, "learning anywhere, anytime." In that vision were glimpses of employees able to access high-quality training at their desktops, at home, or on the road. Unlike other learning centers, SILC chose to provide ubiquitous access to training and learning resources. And the training provided was to be of high quality—SILC's constituents' time was extremely valuable and the greatest accolade SILC envisioned was to have an employee state, "That was a great use of my time."

***Organizational Structure.*** Another element in the strategy was to identify the organizational structure that would best use resources to sustain a viable technology-based training delivery operation. If SILC was to realize its vision of providing ubiquitous training, its infrastructure required strong information technology systems and solutions support, expert skills in instructional design and methodology such that only the "best in class" training courses would be selected, and solid marketing plans so that organizations and employees would learn about and be motivated to try this new way of learning. Toward this end, a hub-and-spoke organizational structure was designed, based on a successful model of learning centers implemented by HP's field training organization. At the hub were the administrative functions—IT systems support and solutions, instructional design expertise, marketing, and finance; at the spokes were the on-site customer service and support that provided orientation to technology-based learning and a physical place to learn for those learners who needed to get away from their desktops or who did not have PC capabilities at home. The hub-and-spoke design allowed maximum leverage of scarce resources. (See Figure 14.1.)

***Participant and Management Buy-In and Support.*** The last and most critical element was to gain participant and management buy-in and commitment to supporting this (at the time) very new way of delivering training. Though SILC's campus constituency was highly technical in its background and thus similar to the field development engineers, few had been exposed to technology-based learning. Additionally, unlike the field development engineers, for whom the learning centers were the primary and mandated resource for product training, SILC's site constituency could select from any number of training and education options, including accredited courses through universities and colleges, external seminars, and internal instructor-led courses. For most, the idea of learning automatically conjured the image of a classroom and an instructor, of travel perhaps, and certainly of time away from the office and home. A marketing strategy was developed, including a video of SILC resources that contained testimonials from

## FIGURE 14.1.  SILC'S HUB-AND-SPOKE ORGANIZATIONAL STRUCTURE.

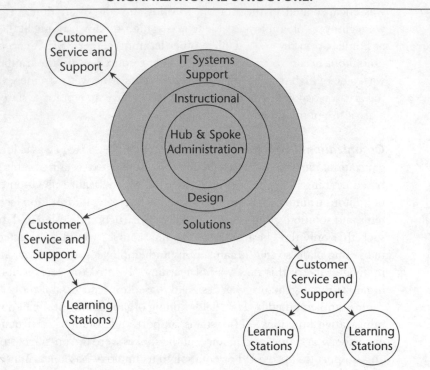

| Hub Functions | Spoke Functions |
|---|---|
| Manage and support all processes, including financial administration, strategic planning, and marketing.<br><br>Assess future and emerging technologies, and identify needed systems, applications, and utilities.<br><br>Evaluate all programs and potential learning products, and provide consulting to other education organizations.<br><br>Provide technical support, evaluate compatibility between new products and current system, and conduct capacity planning. | Provide customer service and support, including troubleshooting basic problems with remote access and assistance with course navigation.<br><br>Evaluate utilization patterns and recommend resource changes as needed.<br><br>Maintain "physical" or "brick and mortar" locations for those customers who do not wish to, or cannot, access SILC resources from remote locations. |

those who had successfully used technology-mediated education to advance their careers.

Where encouraging individuals to use technology-mediated education was the challenge among site employees, the cost of SILC operations was the major hurdle in gaining management buy-in. The typical site learning center consisted of two or three PCs with computer-based training courses on desktop applications (such as the Lotus suite and the Microsoft suite) and a few technical topics (such as basic UNIX systems administration). They were also typically not staffed and had no technical support. The operating costs of these learning centers (occupancy charges, facilities charges, and so on) were also typically subsumed within the overall budgets of their parent organizations (usually HR departments). Consequently, the visible budget for these learning centers was less than $30,000 — the cost of leasing courseware licenses for a year. SILC, on the other hand, was designed to be a major option in employee education. Staffed with dedicated IT support, customer service personnel, and instructional design, SILC needed an initial budget of around $500,000.

Research was done in a number of areas to build the case for site stakeholders that investing in SILC would be in the best interests of the organizations as well as the employees. These areas included comparisons of the cost of traditional instructor-led training in technical subjects against the cost of comparable computer-based training and a report of studies done by other corporations on the benefits of self-paced or technology-based learning over instructor-led training (for example, rate of learning and retention, cost). Through a series of meetings and conversations, key site stakeholders including the controller and the human resources managers provided their support of SILC.

Having defined the vision and received support for it, the planners went on to develop tactical implementation projects. These projects were in the realm of technological infrastructure and marketing communications. For example, if employees were to access learning from their desktops, then an IT infrastructure that maximized LAN and WAN capabilities was needed. Additionally, utilities that made this infrastructure simple and easy for employees to access were needed. A marketing strategy was defined and implemented to raise employee awareness of SILC and its resources on a continual basis, with regularly scheduled announcements, events, and newsletters.

As SILC's distance education infrastructure became established, learning resources became available to any employee located anywhere. As technologies improved the capabilities of the infrastructure, SILC expanded its use of these technologies—that is, in 1997, SILC began delivering courses over the intranet, and in 1998 it launched its "virtual classroom" consisting of mentored asynchronous, Web-enabled learning.

In this manner geographic boundaries were overridden and no longer defined the target audience. As a result more and more employees from outside the direct "target" population or audience began to use the services. Motivating factors outside of geography thus became paramount in determining future target audiences. Therefore any employee encountering the following location-independent factors could be a potential part of the target audience:

- Have a need to keep abreast of the many and varied new technological developments in the high-tech arena. This includes engineers in the research and development labs who design, develop, and implement new technology and information technology engineers who generate and support the information technology infrastructure of the company.
- Cannot afford to spend too much time away from their jobs in training classes because the competitive nature of their business environment requires employees to be highly productive.
- Have a limited budget for training. At HP all employees, with the support of their managers, put together a development plan that usually includes some form of training. Typically, the amount budgeted for employee training and development will depend on the training need and also on some other factors such as job type and organizational function. For instance, the training budget of an engineer will usually be larger than that of an administrative assistant because, typically, the cost of technical courses is greater than the cost of administrative support training.
- Be located away from main company sites and therefore have limited access to extensive training resources.

## Phase 3: Integration into Organizational Processes

The integration of distance education into organizational processes marks the third phase in SILC's evolution and maps closely to Stage 3 of organizational maturity model. SILC's parent organization was the Regional Training Center (RTC), the training and development arm of HP's centralized human resources function for the Bay Area.[2] As an organization designed to deliver traditional instructor-led training, the RTC was challenged to integrate technology-based learning as a resource into its operations that were focused on employee and management development. Resentment and resistance among the RTC staff to this new way of training were high and openly expressed. Not only did SILC offer high-quality training, it was able to offer this training at a lower cost. Technology-based learning was seen as a threat. Yet the management of the Regional Training Center clearly saw the need for an integrated learning strategy—that is, one that incorporated the strengths and benefits of instructor-led and technology-based learning.

The full integration of SILC operations into the organizational fabric of the Regional Training Center occurred over a four-year span, from 1995 through 1998. Program management was key during these years as well as "a good amount of organizational development and cultural change efforts" (Berge, Chapter Two of this volume). Each year, along with the other training functions within the Regional Training Center, SILC identified budgets, key systems investments, and breakthrough initiatives to further develop its capacity to deliver "best in class" technology-mediated training. Using a corporate-wide planning methodology in which corporate initiatives were cascaded throughout all of the organizations to the line, key initiatives were aligned with those of the parent organization, human resources, and the corporation. Each initiative was assigned to a SILC staff member, and on a quarterly basis, team reviews were conducted to validate direction, provide feedback on progress, and recognize accomplishments. As with any business operation, SILC's "numbers" (financial, utilization, customer satisfaction ratings, and so on) were reported to management, other learning center and human resources organizations, and stakeholders on a regular basis. Consequently, by the third year, a distance learning policy integrating traditional instructor-led curricula with technology-mediated training was defined, and development and delivery processes were both defined and put into place.

As stated, a considerable amount of organizational development and cultural change effort also occurred during this period. These efforts at organizational development and cultural change were part and parcel of the program management work that occurred. Weisbord (1976) proposes an organizational model with six components. For an organization to work effectively, each component of the model must be addressed and functionally in balance with the other components. Operating as a dimension within these six components are two subsystems: the formal, or "work to be done" system, and the informal, or actual "process of working" system. Weisbord's model, known as the "Six-Box Organizational Model," offers a basis from which to examine and summarize the integrated program and organizational and cultural development work that occurred with SILC and the RTC during this period.

Using Figure 14.2 as the basis for discussion, we note that the six boxes of the model are Purposes, Structure, Relationships, Rewards, Leadership, and Helpful Mechanisms. The work that occurred with each of these boxes during this stage is summarized as follows:

***Purposes.*** The formal and informal systems were aligned with each other in two ways. First, goals that integrated traditional instructor-led classes and technology-mediated training were defined through group processes. Then, to gain goal

## FIGURE 14.2. WEISBORD'S SIX-BOX ORGANIZATIONAL MODEL.

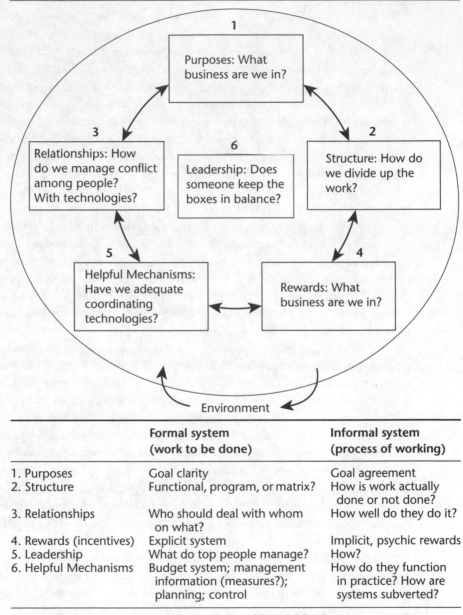

|   | Formal system (work to be done) | Informal system (process of working) |
|---|---|---|
| 1. Purposes | Goal clarity | Goal agreement |
| 2. Structure | Functional, program, or matrix? | How is work actually done or not done? |
| 3. Relationships | Who should deal with whom on what? | How well do they do it? |
| 4. Rewards (incentives) | Explicit system | Implicit, psychic rewards |
| 5. Leadership | What do top people manage? | How? |
| 6. Helpful Mechanisms | Budget system; management information (measures?); planning; control | How do they function in practice? How are systems subverted? |

*Source:* Weisbord, 1976. Reprinted by permission of Sage Publications, Inc.

agreement, assignment to the initiatives supporting these goals was based on individual interest and passion for the subject.

***Structure.*** The RTC was restructured to align with its financial and business model, with those engaged in revenue-generating activity focused on delivery only. Those who conducted needs analyses, QA, and administration were removed from activities focused on generating revenue. Work teams were aligned across the organization, so that individuals in revenue-generating activities were supported with information and processes from those not directly involved in teaching or delivering training. These activities removed the pressure on content managers to focus on instructor-led training, since they were no longer measured on the number of seats filled in the classroom—the primary revenue generator for the RTC.

***Relationships.*** The entire RTC staff (including SILC staff) was engaged in workshops on interpersonal communication and conflict resolution, as well as group activities to align the informal with formal system.

***Rewards.*** A formal "awards and recognition" program that complemented HP's corporate awards and recognition structures was defined with the assistance of the entire staff. Because HP does not offer incentives to non-sales personnel, all focus in this supporting structure for organizational alignment was placed on recognition. Once again, there was focus on alignment between formal and informal systems. Specific elements within this program included peer-to-peer recognition and group recognition for teamwork. To ensure consistency in recognition for outstanding performance relative to key business initiatives, management discussed and evaluated each result using predefined criteria for formal recognition. Employees were awarded stock options and other commendations in recognition of innovations in distance education and education programs integrating technology with the traditional classroom. Some of these initiatives included the following best practices—all of which were subsequently adopted by other HP training and education organizations:

- Widespread implementation of LAN-based delivery of CBT
- A carry-and-learn program consisting of portable PCs with preconfigured courses, which allowed employees to learn while traveling or at home, if home PCs were not available
- An interactive Web-based course catalog and registration system that reduced customer calls by 50 percent
- Delivery of mentored asynchronous courses over the Internet

• A career self-reliance program integrating instructor-led classroom training, online self-assessment tools, and distance one-on-one coaching

***Leadership.*** Leadership activities within the RTC and SILC were compatible from early in SILC's development. Focus was more on "post-heroic leadership" (Huey, 1994), where the leaders embraced two fundamental tasks of this type of "transformational leadership." First, they focused on developing and articulating exactly what the organization was trying to accomplish for and within employee development, HR, and the corporation. Second, they focused on creating an environment in which employees were empowered to figure out the specific "what" and "how" of reaching business objectives. Management focus remained on managing the "white space" (Rummler & Brache, 1995) and facilitating the success of employees.

***Helpful Mechanisms.*** SILC leadership created an environment in which individual contributors were encouraged to lend their expertise in determining needed helpful mechanisms. In this way, SILC was able to acquire and maintain state-of-the-art technologies for delivering education. Informal alignment was supported and encouraged through peer feedback mechanisms. Again, alignment of the organizational structures according to the business and funding model ensured proper alignment between helpful mechanisms and the work that needed to get done.

## Phase 4: Distance Education Institutionalized

By late 1998, SILC had clearly established itself as a leader in distance education, and the RTC's efforts with distance education had become institutionalized. Further development of the technological capabilities included the provision of mentored asynchronous education over the intranet and programs that provided training leading to certification in Microsoft office applications and systems administration. Mapping closely to the organizational maturity model, "effective strategic planning to guide cultural change and resource reallocation for success" (see Chapter Two) marked the focus of activities for the Regional Training Center. SILC, as a fully integrated entity of the RTC, was quickly losing its identity as a functional structure and the RTC, instead, was being seen as a provider of integrated curricula for employee and management development.

At the end of its third year of operations, SILC was more "virtual" than not, with over 85 percent of all utilization occurring from remote locations. That is, learners were availing themselves of SILC's courses via the intranet and the LAN.

For learners requiring orientation and course navigation assistance, as well as a physical place in which to learn, SILC maintained its "brick and mortar" locations.

Strategic planning activities for the RTC in 1999 included the further expansion of technology-mediated education as a key initiative was identified to integrate video broadcasts. This particular initiative was selected so that the RTC could provide a broader range of education opportunities to its constituency. With video broadcasts, the RTC could deliver synchronous interactive education across a wide geographic region. Early forays into this arena were very well received.

And, finally, by the end of its third year, SILC's infrastructure, or rather the RTC's capacity to deliver and sustain distance education, was fully integrated into business operations as witnessed by the following:

***Fully Developed Tracking and Delivery Systems.*** SILC's tracking and delivery systems were key to providing the technical infrastructure for the delivery of online training and tracking employee progress, and by the end of the third year, tracking included the delivery of classroom instruction. Tracking systems were selected or developed based on their ability to gather utilization metrics required for the statistical analyses critical to ensuring stakeholder support and buy-in. SILC's tracking and delivery systems ran on pervasive hardware platforms and operating systems to reflect the diversity in the equipment used by the target population. These systems were also compatible with the databases of corporate information and training management systems; this compatibility supported SILC's ability to identify users as HP employees and to track student activity records for employee files. And finally, SILC's delivery systems were flexible enough to launch and track Web-based and computer-based courses from multiple vendors. By the end of the third year, SILC's systems infrastructure was able to provided customized access to specific targeted resources by other HP divisions and sites, including Corvallis (Oregon) and San Diego.

***Needs Analysis.*** The goal of any corporate training organization, regardless of the form of delivery, should ultimately be to enhance and optimize employee performance. Needs analysis can help to achieve this goal by seeking out gaps between current and optimal performance, determining the nature of those gaps if and when they exist, and defining interventions to close said gaps. Training and learning can often, though not always, provide the appropriate intervention to close performance gaps and ultimately optimize employee performance. The RTC, reflecting its approach to integrating learning, initiated a performance needs analysis of the Bay Area in late 1999.

*Integrated Curricula.* One course, learning event, book, or other learning resource is not always sufficient. A path of study made up of different learning experiences is often necessary to thoroughly cover a topic or skill. Hence, robust and well-formed curricula are essential in sustaining distance education. Once the gaps between actual and optimal performance were determined and training deemed the appropriate intervention to close performance gaps, employee needs were translated into suitable paths of study, or curricula. Designs for curricula considered the specific learning needs including subject matter, learning media, and learning environment.

*Marketing.* Constant marketing is another critical element to sustaining distance education. Marketing helps ensure that all employees know of available training opportunities. The pressures of the business environment often mean that employees may not pay attention to something unless it is directly under their nose — or in their face, as it were. As a result, even though we know employees have a burning need to learn, we understand that they will usually pursue only those options that they hear about on a regular basis. If employees are not made aware that training is available they will not always seek it out for themselves. Furthermore, it was our experience that marketing must not only be constant but provide similar messages via multiple channels. For example, a new course may be marketed via e-mail, flyers, posters, and on the organization's Web site. Additionally our experience was that employees much prefer to receive marketing messages that are consolidated by topic and not by delivery channel. So, for instance, an employee looking to learn the C++ programming language would like to receive information about all the training options on that topic — including all training delivery modes such as classroom, video, books, audio, Web-based training, computer-based training, and so forth — in one place, rather than having to look up C++ under each of the available channels.

*Vendor Management.* Managing vendor interactions including contract negotiations and monitoring of ongoing relationships was very important, especially since all of SILC's offerings were produced by vendors. Key processes were put into place to evaluate content for technical accuracy as well as sound instructional design for the medium. Other vendor management processes to ensure solid content that met learner needs included monitoring for timely updates to technical training, ease of access to learning modules and navigation within courses, and so on. On a quarterly basis, vendor performance was also evaluated on timely customer support. And, finally, vendors became strong partners in assisting the organization with keeping abreast of changes in technology and the impact of such changes in the learning environment.

***Employee Support.*** Human interface to the employees to help them understand what is available to them and how their needs may be met were key in SILC's initial success, and through its history, SILC retained personnel dedicated to customer support and service. Distance education can often make learners feel isolated, unlike a classroom environment where there is always the opportunity to ask questions. More and more distance education is synchronous, providing the opportunity for learner and instructor interaction. It is critical to have in-depth knowledge of the courseware and the delivery system when consulting with employees who are customers of the program. It has been our experience that the more people know about the courseware prior to taking the course the more comfortable they become.

***Instructional Technology and Design Expertise.*** A major part of meeting customer needs is to understand how people like to learn, that is, their learning style and what kinds of delivery best suit their work and business environment. With valuable information from the constant needs analysis described earlier, we are able to match learning styles and needs based on business environment with the availability of new and innovative alternative learning technologies. This further ensures that customer needs are met. For example, it was clear that SILC customers wanted the flexibility of learning independently at their desks or at home. However, much of the self-paced computer-based learning provided initially at SILC left people feeling isolated. Customers often asked, "Well, what if I have a question?" This crucial classroom element—namely, the ability to interact with instructors and peers—was missing. As Internet technology developed it became clear that the communications elements of the Internet such as chat, threaded discussion, and e-mail could help to solve this problem. Course vendors began to use these elements to develop an integrated approach to learning over the Internet and many created mentored synchronous and asynchronous courses. Using principles of instructional technology and design and zeroing in on customer needs, SILC designed a strategy for learning over the intranet that included this type of learning.

Instructional design expertise is also critical for evaluating and selecting high-quality third-party vendor courses to meet customer needs. As mentioned earlier, most SILC courses are produced by and purchased from third-party vendors. SILC has chosen to rely on off-the-shelf courseware as opposed to developing it in house because customer needs are mostly generic and not company specific.

It is therefore more cost-effective and time-efficient to purchase a course on a generic topic than to develop it ourselves. The quality of available courses has improved immensely over the past five years. Courses are moving more and more away from static "page turning" to interactive and engaging formats that will also accurately measure student learning. Pre- and post-assessments are becoming standard, allowing learners to gauge their knowledge level at the outset and create a customized learning path concentrating directly on the areas within which they specifically need to build competency.

## Conclusion: The Future of Distance Education at HP Beyond SILC

Sustaining distance education can be a major challenge—no matter how successful the organization and how well integrated into its parent organization. In 1999, HP's human resources function along with other infrastructure functions underwent massive restructuring—first to remove redundant structures and second as a consequence of the decision to split the corporation into two companies: Hewlett-Packard and Agilent Technologies. Management of the Regional Training Center underwent realignment along with all other internal education delivery organizations in the United States. SILC was subsequently subsumed under another site's learning center outside Silicon Valley. The future of SILC remains in question.

The future of distance education at Hewlett-Packard, however, is not in question and actually is very compelling. Two large-scale initiatives, in fact, are currently under way. The first, led by Global Learning for Performance, is focused on supporting employee development. Like SILC, this initiative is focused on implementing e-learning strategy and suitable infrastructure that will make personalized and collaborative learning and knowledge management resources available, via a global learning portal, to every employee with access to the intranet. The second initiative is focused on external customers. Led by HP's customer education organization, this initiative has implemented an Internet resource that provides interactive real-time training (with an online instructor) as well as access to asynchronous self-paced training. As a component of the corporation's e-services strategy, HP Education's e-learning resources are poised to provide business-to-business as well as end-user training.

If we were to step back and, using the organizational maturity model, examine the corporation as a whole, it is clear that HP's efforts overall in the realm of distance education have evolved through the four stages. Stage 1 is reflected in the work done by various organizations, or divisions, across HP. Stage 2 is reflected in the work done by organizations such as the field support organizations and SILC. Stages 3 and 4 are reflected in the integration of e-learning into the corporation's e-services initiative—for both internal and external customer education.

## Notes

1. As reported by *Internet Business News*, Coventry, on May 11, 2000; April 6, 2000; and February 6, 2000.
2. HP's human resources functions in Silicon Valley were centralized in 1993 under a major initiative to reduce costs and redundancies. Major HR functions, such as records and benefits, staffing, compensation administration, and training were centralized, while management support functions such as liaison and organizational effectiveness remained at each of the various businesses and sites in the Bay Area.

PART FOUR

# ACHIEVING ORGANIZATIONAL GOALS

CHAPTER FIFTEEN

# BUILDING MOTIVATION FOR DISTANCE LEARNERS IN PUBLIC HEALTH

Barbara Polhamus, Anita M. Farel, Tim Stephens

*Healthy People 2010*, the nation's health goals for this decade, calls for ensuring the highest quality of health care through the development of data monitoring and evaluation tools and a public health workforce that has the training needed to use information technology systems to improve public health practice (U.S. Department of Health and Human Services, 2000). Distance training can provide an effective and economical means for professional staff to advance their skills while continuing to meet their extensive work-related responsibilities.

Enhancing Data Utilization Skills through Information Technology (EDUSIT) is a distance education project that trains Maternal and Child Health (MCH) professionals in state and local health departments to collect, analyze, and interpret data via a Web-based course. The course is offered through the Department of Maternal and Child Health in the School of Public Health at the University of North Carolina (UNC) at Chapel Hill in collaboration with the School's Center for Distance Learning.

The overall goal of the project is to train MCH professionals to apply data analysis skills and information technologies to improve access to health care services for mothers and children. This goal is being pursued by developing and implementing a yearlong six-module course presented in a self-paced Web-based format. Participants are expected to complete the entire course. Six hours of graduate credit is being offered as an incentive for participants to complete the course.

EDUSIT is funded by a grant from the Health Resources and Services Administration, Maternal and Child Health Bureau (MCHB) in the U.S. Department of Health and Human Services. MCH programs are required to document health status problems at the state and local level, defend spending priorities, and address an array of public health concerns. This case study of a project to help MCH programs meet these requirements illustrates the organizational and management systems involved in designing and implementing this initiative and highlights features for motivating participants.

## Problem Statement

Motivating professionals to engage in training opportunities, without the attendant rewards of a trip out of town and time away from the office, is a challenge for distance training initiatives aimed at the public health workforce. Funding at the local, state, and national levels, although limited, continues to support training for public health professionals through workshops and conferences. In recent years interest in examining the potential of information technology for meeting training needs has generated new initiatives such as EDUSIT that focus on training the professional workforce at a distance.

Over a decade ago, the Institute of Medicine's recommendations regarding the government's public health obligation emphasized knowledge development and dissemination through data collection, research, and information exchange (Institute of Medicine, 1988). The need to enhance the knowledge base of public health professionals through on-the-job training and continuing education programs continues to be critical (Roper, Baker, Dyal, & Nicola, 1992). However, the financial constraints of government at all levels in the 1990s strained existing resources and limited the funding available for training. Additionally, reduced staff in many programs limited the feasibility of training that requires staff to be away from the job. Consequently, there is an urgent need to close the gap between state-of-the-art Web-based instruction and those training programs typically available to public health service agencies (Maibach & Holtgrave, 1995).

In 1993, the Centers for Disease Control and Prevention began providing training to public health professionals through the Public Health Training Network (http://www.cdc.gov/phtn/), a distance education system that uses a variety of instructional media ranging from print-based to videotape and multimedia. The focus has been on topical issues rather than skills development.

## Population Served

The EDUSIT initiative is a pilot project targeting employees in state and local MCH programs in the southern region of the country. A regional approach was taken because of strong existing relationships between the UNC School of Public Health and state health departments in this region. Thirteen state health departments are participating in the project: Alabama, Arizona, Georgia, Kentucky, Mississippi, North Carolina, South Carolina, Tennessee, Virginia, Maryland, Arkansas, Louisiana, and New Mexico. Teams with at least two professionals from each state were originally formed, with a few teams consisting of up to five members.

Forty participants enrolled in the course. Participants were older than average (82 percent are forty years or older), well educated (67 percent have master's degrees or higher), and in most cases their last degree was awarded more than ten years prior to the project. Most participants (90 percent) work at the state rather than the local level. As a cohort, this group had positive attitudes about using data and technology although their confidence in their abilities to use data and demonstrate technology skills was low.

Currently thirty participants are in the course. Ten people dropped out because they left their agency, moved to a different position in the health department and the course did not fit into their new job, or picked up added responsibilities on the job that did not leave time to complete assignments.

## Outcomes Desired

At the outset of the project, three primary outcomes reflecting the overall goal of the project were identified: motivating participants to complete the full yearlong course, improving information technology literacy among participants, and improving data collection and analysis skills among participants. The achievement of these outcomes was dependent on developing an interesting and appealing interactive Web-based course.

## Description of Management Processes

Since the grantee had no experience in the area of distance education prior to obtaining funding for this project, the Center for Distance Learning (CDL: http://cdlhc.sph.unc.edu) has been a critical collaborator in the project and funding for its participation was written into the grant. The success of the EDUSIT project is the result of collaboration within the School of Public Health and support from the university. The CDL provides technical support from various staff members including the center director and assistant director, an instructional designer, a webmaster, and other technical staff such as audio assistants and software specialists. Academic Technology and Networks, the university technology support office, provides consultation and training for the software used to administer the course.

Webster and Hackley (1997) identify four categories of influence on distance education outcomes: technology, course, instructor, and student characteristics. We have adapted this model to discuss the management process and to examine factors that motivated and deterred participation in EDUSIT. Student characteristics were described in the "Population Served" section.

## Technology

The Center for Distance Learning (CDL) within the School of Public Health was established in 1996 to bring a policy and operational focus to the School of Public Health's educational outreach efforts. The CDL incorporated responsibility for continuing education (the school has the largest program of all accredited U.S. schools of public health), technical management of distance learning technologies, and meeting management services.

Since the founding of the CDL, the school and university have progressively built their procedures and policies for supporting distance learning. For example, in 1997, action was taken to begin development of a strategic plan to guide the university in prioritizing information technology needs, allocating resources for this purpose, and developing or expanding information technology–based services. Included in the plan were recommendations for distance education (Roadmap to the Future, 1999). The university has instituted base funding for distance degree programs in line with residential degrees, leading to programs' being funded through the appropriations process rather than fees and grants. The CDL has staffed the committees involved in these processes, and is assigned the role of assuring the technical competence of the school to deliver its distance learning programs.

Greater accountability for program outcomes (and for budgeting within these programs) has been implicit in the funding shift. To this end, the school developed policies related to admissions, faculty selection, technology support, financial feasibility, and evaluation of distance degree programs. These policies were summarized in a document adopted by the school's Academic Programs Committee (Distance Learning Subcommittee of School of Public Health, 1999).

The document is grounded in assumptions that outcomes and quality should be the same for distance education courses as for residential programs, but that specific procedures are necessary to ensure this in context. The CDL has a role in ensuring that there is consistency at least at the level of the technology employed in delivering these programs. As a result, the center manages the technology assets of the school and the employment of the specialists (instructional designers, multimedia developers, and Web programmers) who interpret and facilitate the use of technology.

Since 1993, the CDL and its predecessor organizations have managed the school's interactive video classrooms. Over the years, programming in these rooms has expanded to 1,300 hours a year. Since 1996 the CDL has managed its own Web servers for online course development and delivery. CDL has also developed courseware in video and CD-ROM formats, but has not invested in these technologies.

CDL depends on grants and contracts for funding. While funding is not institutionalized, the center has been able to sustain and support the rapid growth in staff that occurred in 1998, when it jumped from three full time equivalents to twelve. Since then, it has turned over new grants, extended contracts, and developed new alliances that have allowed it to stabilize its staff and define its core services. In the past six months it has received its first state appropriation for staffing via a new $10 million legislative appropriation for distance education.

CDL staff participated with EDUSIT in the initial design discussions about the appropriate delivery method. Decisions about the appropriate technology to deliver this program were based on the geographic distribution of the audience and characteristics of the learners as indicated by an initial survey. Videoconferencing, the technology the CDL had the most experience supporting, was quickly eliminated because the audience was so dispersed and unlikely to be able to meet simultaneously. Video and CD-ROM were not considered, because of the emphasis on being able to manipulate data and the need to revise and update materials in response to learner needs. Consequently, the course is entirely Web-based. One instructional designer was assigned to the project.

Potential learners were provided a description of the technological capacity including software they needed to participate in the course. The description was derived from criteria the CDL had been using in other programs it supported.

During the development phase of the course, weekly meetings were held between EDUSIT and CDL staff involved in the project to ensure that both content and technology were on track.

Since the beginning of the EDUSIT project, the CDL has evolved into a center that develops and supports numerous Web-based courses within the SPH. At the beginning of this project, CDL's primary experience was in supporting videoconferencing within the state of North Carolina. It now supports twelve Web-based courses including all core public health courses for the school's MPH programs, both distance and residential.

## Course

The EDUSIT course has four components:

- Precourse technology skills training
- Six password-protected, Web-based modules focusing on quantitative and qualitative data collection, analysis, and interpretation in the context of maternal and child health
- Application of data skills to a significant health status problem selected by each state team
- Evaluation

The following sections discuss each course component and management strategy in turn.

*Precourse Skills.* To successfully participate in Web-based distance training, learners need access to appropriate technology—and the skills to use it. Baseline survey data revealed wide variation in EDUSIT participants' technology skills. For example, some participants had never been connected to the Internet while others were very comfortable using it. Because of this wide variation, follow-up phone interviews were conducted to explore this variation in more depth. Interviews revealed that technology experience and confidence were notably more variable than anticipated. One participant remarked that she was concerned that she had taken on more than she could handle since she had never even used e-mail, while another indicated that she was looking forward to making discoveries in a new frontier.

As a result of these interviews, a decision was made to present skill-building activities to ensure that all participants started the course with a set of basic technology skills and that participants had the needed software on their computers.

To promote success and motivate participants, precourse technology training needs were identified. Ten Internet skill-building activities that related directly to the skills and modes of electronic communication needed for the course were developed. Because the course had been well defined, we were able to identify the specific technology skills needed and then provide training and practice to develop them. Both usefulness and ease of use have been identified as central variables in motivating users of information technology (Davis, 1989). Consequently, when the course began, the focus was on course content rather than on the technology. Training activities included using e-mail and its various features, completing an efficient Internet search, downloading Adobe Acrobat Reader and RealPlayer, participating in discussion forums, and subscribing to mailing lists. We monitored participation by building in a task that required an answer to be submitted by e-mail.

At the completion of these activities, participants were required to pass a short technology skills test to obtain a password to the course. This test was adapted from one that CDL had developed so learners could assess their hardware and software, and their own ability to navigate, copy, and paste—that is, to confirm they had the tools and skills needed to cope with the coursework.

By providing technically appropriate training prior to the course, we prepared participants to be successful learners. Skills training is a means for increasing participants' self-efficacy, a variable identified in the literature as critical for motivating adult learners (Compeau & Higgins, 1995). Assessing participants' technology skills and subsequently developing prerequisite technology training are key factors for successful implementation of distance training for public health professionals (Hillman, Willis, & Gunawardena, 1994). The following quote from a participant sums up the importance of preparing the learner: "I can truly say that without these activities, the convenience of e-mail and the use of the Internet would still be giant mysteries and monsters to me! Now I feel comfortable with both. Thank you."

***The Six-Module Training.*** The content for the online course emerged from experiences in traditional training initiatives conducted by the Department of Maternal and Child Health and from recommendations from program directors in the states participating in the EDUSIT project. Content focuses on quantitative and qualitative data collection, analysis, and interpretation. The following modules were presented in the listed order. A new module begins every other month:

- Basic epidemiological and statistical concepts
- Qualitative data collection and analysis
- Measuring social inequalities in health
- Developing data collection instruments and planning data analysis
- Economic analysis
- Using EPI INFO and Geographic Information System software

Various presentation modes were used throughout the modules, including online tutorials and slides with audio and video. Interaction was encouraged through online discussion forums, chats, and presentation space for participants to post written assignments and for faculty to give feedback. Online self-tests and quizzes with instant feedback were available.

Each module took approximately fifteen to twenty hours to complete. To ensure that material and assignments could be completed within that time frame and that material and instructions were clearly written, the modules were field-tested by graduate students and then modified based on field testers' evaluations before being released for training. This was a valuable step in the development of the course since significant changes were made in many of the modules based on field test results.

The course has been designed in WebCT, a software package used as the instruction management system by the School of Public Health. The advantages of using this software include the ability to track participation and grade quizzes with immediate programmed feedback. The primary disadvantage is the time initially required to learn the system interface and to navigate the course.

**State-Specific Health Status Problem.** Practical application of skills learned in training is important for developing confidence with the particular skill. In each state, participants work in teams to apply the skills they learn to a health status problem that is significant in their state. The rationale for requiring teamwork to complete a final product for the course was stimulated by research about the impact of social networks on reinforcing use of technology (Fulk, Schmitz, & Steinfield, 1990).

Participants are developing reports on their state-specific health status problems and publishing them on the Internet. Reports cover a variety of topics with Web page designs that range from simple to complex. For example, one group is presenting a two-page report summarizing state and local data on childhood asthma in their state with two links to relevant resources. Another is presenting a report on sports- and recreation-related injuries with links to twenty Web pages containing relevant data, recommendations, and conclusions.

**Evaluation.** The evaluation model, including formative, summative, and impact measures, is implemented at various points in the course. The distance learning literature describes the importance of knowing the learners' needs, their characteristics, and their environment or circumstances (Granger & Benke, 1998). Initially, participants completed a baseline survey assessing their data and technology knowledge, beliefs, self-efficacy, and current practices, as well as agency factors and demographic characteristics. At six months after completion of the training, the survey will be readministered to determine if change in knowledge, attitudes, and use of computers and information technology occurred.

The formative evaluation consists of qualitative and quantitative measures and is administered after each module to determine what worked and what did not. Participants rated the value of each topic in a module using a Likert scale, indicated successes and limitations, and offered recommendations that are considered in the development of subsequent modules. Phone interviews were conducted with each state team midway through the course to discuss course progress and use of technology, and to elicit recommendations.

The summative evaluation consisted of pre- and post-tests for each module that included questions related to knowledge of the module content, beliefs about topic usefulness, self-efficacy, and current practices. The data are analyzed to compare changes from the beginning and the completion of the module. All questionnaires and evaluations are available online.

The final evaluation focuses on the impact of the initiative and the benefits of training to the state health departments, skills developed, directors' willingness to institutionalize training into their program, and benefits to community-level programs.

The overall project evaluation is based on a model for changing the behavior of health professionals involved in continuing education that was derived by Umble, Cervero, Langone, Lincoln, and Smith (1996) and is grounded in prominent health behavior theories. The model postulates that training influences knowledge, beliefs, and both self-efficacy and intention to perform the behaviors. Actual adherence to the behavior requires adequate skill, support from peers and supervisors, and continued belief in one's efficacy to perform the behavior.

## Faculty

Faculty were selected for their expertise in teaching specific data skills in traditional classrooms or through consultation venues. A different faculty member developed each module and none had experience with Web-based training. Several reported anxiety about teaching via the Internet. One faculty member who reluctantly agreed to teach in the course said, "If I don't do this, I feel the train will leave without me."

To facilitate understanding of the Web-based format and to develop faculty expertise with various approaches, training was provided through a faculty Web site and meetings. The Web site was used to present examples of previously developed Web-based courses at UNC and to facilitate the exploration of numerous Web-based technologies. For example, guidelines were posted on how to successfully monitor a discussion forum since each module had a least one forum. Meetings were held throughout the development phase of the project. Since the faculty were scattered in different geographic areas, conference calls were used simultaneously with online material posted at the faculty Web site. During these meetings, information about what worked well in the course and what had not was discussed.

A survey of faculty experiences teaching in the course revealed that faculty could not rely only on material developed for the classroom but needed to develop and organize new material for their modules. Faculty for all but one module reported that considerably more time than anticipated was needed to develop their traditional material for a Web-based format. Completing material within the scheduled time frame was critical since the material was turned over to the instructional designer who put the course on the Web. This included designing the layout and activating all quizzes and interactive segments. Faculty were dependent on the instructional designer to help them organize their material for the Web. The instructional designer guided faculty in deciding about the most appropriate format to use for various topics, augmenting print material, making their material more interactive and appropriate for a Web-based format, developing slide presentations, and developing useful examples. In addition to the expertise of an instructional designer, faculty needed administrative assistance obtaining copyrights and scanning articles and maps, as well as technical assistance for recording the audio portions of their modules.

Several important lessons were learned during the development phase of the modules:

- Allow plenty of time for development—consider doubling initial estimates to make sure that materials are completed on time.
- Involve an instructional designer from the beginning to the end of the development phase to reduce the number of unexpected problems.
- Give faculty with no experience teaching online the time and the skills training to learn how to be effective instructors when using the Internet.

## Motivating Professionals

Much of the literature about motivating adult learners in distance education programs describes academic students seeking college degrees or professionals meeting continuing education requirements (Leidner & Jarvenpaa, 1995; Livneh & Livneh, 1999). We describe the adaptation of these experiences for motivating participants in EDUSIT. Many of the features of the project that enhance motivation include support that is built into the course at the university setting (technology training, responding to inquiries, streamlining administrative processes) and support that is provided for the learners in their work environment.

In interviews, participants indicated various reasons for taking this course—feeling a need to update skills to keep up with the changing work environment and to be assured of staying competitive in their position, wanting to learn the skills to improve their knowledge base for personal growth, wanting course credit toward another degree, converting credit to Continuing Education Units, and anticipating taking a distance education degree program in the future and wanting to test their self-discipline to complete this course. All of these reasons affect motivation to complete the EDUSIT course.

One of our first steps to motivate participants was to create an online community of learners through a Web site for participants. The Web site included an overview of the course, a course user's manual, photos and biographical sketches of course faculty, project staff, and participants, a bulletin board for activities and updates, and a list of resources. The password-protected course and its newsletter (inaugurated with a prize for the participant who came up with the best name) were accessible from the Web site. The idea of creating a Web site with all of these components was to provide a classroom-type atmosphere and a site where all course information could be obtained.

Because we surveyed learners at the beginning of the project and identified the wide variation in their basic computer skills, we were able to develop technology skills training needed for the course. The training was highly successful and learners were immediately engaged since they could use the skills they learned on the job and were viewed by coworkers and associates as having desirable skills that others wanted to learn.

Technical assistance for participants through phone or e-mail five days a week was another motivating feature. The program assistant provided immediate consultation, taught technology skills, and reinforced confidence and feelings of competence. Questions or issues that could not be tackled at this level were referred to CDL staff, who then worked with participants or program staff to resolve the issue. We assisted in forging a relationship between the agency Local Area Network (LAN) manager and the participants so on-site technical assistance was available when needed.

The opportunity for participants to engage with faculty who were nationally recognized experts in particular topic areas (for example, geographic information systems and cost analysis) was another mechanism to motivate participation. Experts were available for individual consultation and group discussion as well as course interaction.

We elicited ongoing feedback from participants through module evaluations and by creating an atmosphere where any comment could be made. We responded to participant suggestions for changes to make the course more appropriate for the intended audience. For example, the original syllabus was not useful to participants, who suggested that a list of activities and tasks for each module would be more appropriate. Consequently, a checklist was added to the syllabus. The ability to be flexible and change directions when necessary appeared to be an important factor in participants' continued investment in the course.

Since distance learners do not necessarily have the experience of group interaction, we included activities that would bring participants in contact with other learners. For example, by requiring participants to work in teams on a health issue of relevance in their state, we gave them an opportunity to discuss course content with colleagues and to apply what they had learned to an actual problem. Another activity required participants to work in teams with learners from other states and complete a group assignment that involved developing a budget for a specific scenario within a health department. Participants were randomly assigned to one of three groups. They then had to communicate with each other via e-mail, phone, or chat to complete the assignment. We used several opportunities for face-to-face gatherings at regional and national meetings attended by participants to initiate discussion about the project and to provide an opportunity for participants to meet each other.

## Successes and Failures

Paramount among training needs in public health is the development of skills in collecting, analyzing, and reporting data to generate sound public health policies and programs. Thus the successes of the initiative we describe in this chapter include launching the Web-based course that provides an opportunity to improve data skills and to increase information technology literacy. Successful features of the course include development and implementation of the precourse technology training and the content of the six-module course, provision of ongoing consultation about specific content and technology concerns of participants, and acquiring valuable information about the needs and norms of the public health workforce. We know from participants that both the precourse training and several of the modules provide opportunities for the application of new skills on the job. However, the implementation of the course revealed limitations that provided important lessons for future work.

For several reasons, a yearlong course was not an appropriate model for training the target population. First, the public health workforce is constantly changing. Professional staff move in and out of the system at both the state and local levels. Thus, efforts to build a training community within a cohort of participants were consistently undermined. Second, as in any business, the health care work-load ebbs and flows. Professionals have more leisure at one time than at another to complete course-related assignments. Even though directors had given their support—and in some cases attempted to protect time for staff to complete course-related activities—the immediacy of day-to-day tasks took precedence over coursework. Thus, supervisory support for training in the workplace was tempered by realities of the job. Finally, not all data skills modules were of equal interest or provided new material to all participants.

The characteristics of the work environment need careful consideration. Modules were too long and lacked natural stopping points, so they were disruptive to the flow of normal work responsibilities. Shorter modules taking two to four hours to complete that are "just in time" (Hudspeth, 1992) would be more appropriate for training professionals in the workplace. They would meet more immediately the diverse needs of public health professionals. Shorter modules that are self-contained would make it possible for professionals to have a successful training experience and support their continued engagement with this technology while fulfilling their responsibilities in the workplace.

Offering graduate school credit for the training was initially perceived to be an incentive for participants to complete the course. However, ultimately it turned out to undermine the implementation of the program, which would have been more appropriate for professionals had it not been designed within the constraints of an academic model. The criteria for graduate credit necessitated that the volume of material and assignments meet specific guidelines that increased the amount of time required to complete the modules.

## Discussion

In planning for training via the Internet in the workplace, the shift in the cost and responsibility for technology support must be considered. In the traditional classroom and in satellite and videoconferencing programs, the providing institution bears the greatest cost while learners have responsibility of arranging for free time and traveling to a site. In using the Internet for training, responsibilities shift. For the learner, the freedom of scheduling a convenient course time comes at the price of having to secure and maintain an operating computer system. To the learners this may seem like piling the responsibility for infrastructure onto their shoulders, but this does not mean that the provider institution is immune from costs and responsibility in this area. For the provider, the control over designing a common space (classroom) is replaced by the need for a support system for learners who work increasingly at nontraditional times. For example, twenty-four-hour help desks that run seven days a week have become common elements of distance education programs.

Our experience with EDUSIT illustrates this shift in responsibility when providing a Web-based course. Even though states were given a list of hardware requirements needed to complete the course, numerous participants discovered through precourse training activities (or when taking the technology skills test) that their computers were not equipped with the necessary system configuration. For example, some participants discovered they could not play audio and had to install sound cards. Others found they were unable to engage in discussion forums or chats. A technical expert from the CDL worked with the university computing services and the state LAN managers to identify the problem.

It turned out that there was a firewall around agency computing systems to deter outsiders from getting into the data files. The university computer was using a nonstandard port number to provide access to discussion forums and chats, and the firewall interpreted this as something like a hacker attack and blocked all access. The outcome was a partial solution. Participants were able to engage in discussion forums when the agency used a third-party site to shift the port number to a standard one that the firewall would let through. Participants behind the firewall were never able to get into the chats. However, contents of the chats were archived as the chat occurred and later saved to an independent location by project staff. Participants unable to participate could at least access the files and read the contents.

Other learners who had never been hooked up to the Internet realized the very slow speed at which they were able to access information from the Web. In this case, learners had to negotiate with their supervisors to get a faster machine or work from home if they had a computer with the needed capacity. Although the ultimate responsibility was left to the participant, project staff with backup from technical experts were able to answer questions that allowed participants to obtain the needed hardware.

Planning for staffing for a distance education project must include not only the consultation of experts for course content but also the expertise of an instructional designer and other technical experts. The instructional designer's involvement in the development of our six-module course was critical to the look of the course, the layout of individual modules, and the interactivity within each module. In using course content material that has been used in a traditional classroom, it is easy to make the mistake of putting volumes of text on the Web with no consideration of appropriately adapting the material to the medium. The involvement of an instructional designer in the course design enabled us to avoid this pitfall.

To sustain the EDUSIT training, we are considering several alternatives. Since the EDUSIT course has been implemented with time-limited federal funding, we have had to consider other funding sources. We obtained state funding to revise existing materials and implement a two-credit Web-based course for human services professionals in North Carolina. This course is offered through the university system and thus generates tuition. In the short term, continued outside funding is a means of securing funds necessary to continue to refine and implement the material to ensure that the training continues to be available to public health professionals. Since we are in an academic setting that is continuing to expand and develop distance education, we have continued access to opportunities to compete for funding. In the long term, the course may become self-sustaining.

CHAPTER SIXTEEN

# SUPPORTING AN ENTERPRISE DISTANCE LEARNING PROGRAM AT NYNEX

Barry Howard

The promise of distance learning remains unfulfilled in many organizations. In spite of many good intentions, extensive pilots and trials, and a great deal of perception-building efforts, these organizations fail to recognize some key planning and implementation steps that can make the difference in sustaining distance learning. It is the intent of this chapter to focus on a number of organizations, documenting their good intentions but noting where their efforts fell short of the critical mass needed to make the distance learning stick.

I was the director of distance learning for the NYNEX, now Bell Atlantic Corporation, until 1997. During my last ten years at NYNEX I had the opportunity to observe many other organizations through a succession of speaking opportunities at corporate training conferences. Since 1997, as the senior distance learning consultant for QED Consulting, I have been able to extend that observation process. This chapter represents all those experiences, as well as my observations on the plans, events, and projects that did *not* happen.

It is hoped that this chapter, read by the corporate manager intent on making a change in training delivery that is truly sustainable, can provide some key issues to be included in a distance learning plan and some key dead ends that need to be avoided. It addresses some of the technology—and a great deal of the culture and the politics of the corporation. As such, it is really intended for the corporate reader more than the government and academic reader, who may have to contend with a different set of rules and culture.

This experience is only one person's efforts, one vantage point on this vast field. It does not pretend to be the ultimate guide for sustaining distance learning. Hopefully, the experience of reading the entire book with its many vantage points will provide that guidance.

## NYNEX History

Bell Atlantic purchased NYNEX in 1996. A regulated telephone company, NYNEX was the combination of two AT&T subsidiaries, New York and New England Telephone. This fact is more than just history. At the time that NYNEX began its distance learning transformation it was also struggling with the still incomplete process of merging two different companies and cultures. In many ways merging different cultures was an obstacle for distance learning planning as well as an opportunity for some significant and unexpected distance learning value.

### Industry Background

The AT&T divestiture in 1984 had a significant impact on distance learning in all parts of the company. The general departments AT&T had set up in Basking Ridge, New Jersey, were populated with bright, well-trained, and experienced staffs that could not be maintained at any one of its subsidiaries. This shared resource was frequently cited by operating companies in testimony to public service commissions as the reason for substantial payments back to the home company. That center of expertise was most obvious in the centralized training departments (each discipline had its own training department, Business Office, Field Technicians, Sales, Operator Services, and so on). By hiring experts in cognitive learning processes and learning program design, AT&T could fund research and development and then amortize the cost across many operating companies.

On the day of divestiture, all that expertise and support ended. Although some of these experts were able to return to their operating companies, most of the operating companies had to create new staffs from scratch. In that process, the critical skills needed for the new distance learning development were lost as the operating companies chose subject matter expertise or operational management over cognitive learning design skills for their training teams. When learning technology finally came of age, most of the companies were not ready to capitalize on it.

AT&T also created another legacy that made sustaining distance learning more difficult. In the mid-1970s, the education experts, without personal computers to play with, created a great deal of what was then called "programmed learning" on paper. Applied to business office training, operator services training and other key entry-level positions, this student-centered, self-paced reading and learning effort failed badly, leaving many line managers going into the divestiture period with a very bad taste for self-paced anything.

My early CBT efforts crashed right into some of the people who had felt misled with the programmed learning process that had been sold to them by the old training department. I can still remember a vice president's cringe when I announced self-paced CBT and he remembered another trainer's sales pitch that resulted in many unhappy employees—it was a painful process I would much rather have avoided.

## Training Organization and Needs

NYNEX went through divestiture and created a training department. This highly centralized organization absorbed trainers previously spread throughout New York and New England Telephone, many reporting to local managers in specialized disciplines. Training fiefdoms allowed trainers to form a bench of highly skilled subject matter experts to be drawn upon when service conditions dictated, postponing their training duties. Populating the training organizations with individuals who were superb practitioners but not necessarily course developers or deliverers created a force that feared distance learning. They were not comfortable with the technology and had limited cognitive learning skills to apply to make it work. As I tried to take the early programs from pilot to large-scale implementations, this group became one of the significant obstacles. As I found with many distance learning clients, this pattern of subject matter expert use in training departments for training and operational reasons was common.

The training reorganization merely consolidated the diverse teams, creating an organization that, with few exceptions, maintained discipline expertise as the prime organization driver. Geography formed the next strategy and then training function formed the last. Course development skills were based on organization strategy, subordinate to geography and target discipline. The rare developers skilled in Web-based training in one discipline would have had to move and learn another target discipline to find more content for their skills to process. Loyalty was always to the department, rarely to any learning process. A few college-trained educators could be made to feel like outcasts in the training department as they pursued learning over department rules.

## Client Needs: The Business Problems

NYNEX's training clients, like many other clients, thought they were strapped for training time long before the technology came along as a potential magic pill. Especially with the frequent diversion of training hours to support operational needs (as noted in the preceding section), training itself tended to be a one-time event—initial training. After that, training became a much more haphazard process. Middle and senior managers rarely went back for classes, postponing professional development forever.

As business needs increased, training clients needed more training and yet had less available time for the event-driven process of the past. Training clients found themselves under even more pressure. The new product cycle was producing new items to sell or implement. This required more training. Process reengineering created more multiskilled jobs, requiring even more training. Globalization added more fuel to the fire, and consistency in training became as big an issue as volume. Competition, especially in the once regulated corporations, added an urgency to the training process.

The major symptoms of this malaise were clear if you looked for them:

- Centralized training classes were running with a high degree of absenteeism.
- Centralized course development demands required rapid turnaround.
- Shelf life of courses was becoming shorter.
- Trainers were burning out on the road.
- Clients were building their own classrooms.
- Clients were starting to build their own distance learning systems.

## The Clients Served

The early start for distance learning came from the information technology groups. With their comfort with workstation interaction, constant shortage of time, and egos that fit the self-study mode, the early CBT students were taking courses on mainframes using crude languages and blue screens to transfer knowledge on new rules of COBOL. As the PC replaced the workstation and found its way onto more organization desks, the target population shifted to managers who needed to understand the very tool that would become the teacher. By this time PC-CBT and multimedia had displaced mainframe learning tools. Learning Centers expanded the learning population to the subordinates of those managers. The PC—emulating an old 3270 display workstation—arrived on the desks of the call centers and other line functions, providing the opportunity to expand the potential learner client base to clerical and sales staffs, bringing with it courses in generic selling skills and practices. Electronic Performance Support Systems (EPSS) took advantage of the new tools to bring learning along with new and old mainframe systems. With employees' buying their own computers for home use, the target population included everyone in the organization from CEO to janitor.

## Early Solutions

I was appointed director for information technology training in 1987. This position gave me the perfect platform for building the distance learning infrastructure for the organization. Placed organizationally within HR (not IT), I was able to hear the pain from other training managers. Through successive downsizing, the existing staff was threatened. Outsourcing was growing because the IT tools were changing too fast for an in-house staff.

### The Technology-Based Steps

There were some bright trainers and developers who were ready to take their IT skills and transform them into distance learning skills, focused on more than just the IT client. As many organizations have taken similar approaches, I have documented those early steps, even though some did not grow beyond the pilot stage.

*Early Disk CBT: Generic.* The first distance learning project involved off-the-shelf programs. With relatively low cost and proven results with other clients, these generic products were easily applied to the growing personal computer user community. The disks allowed individuals, for the first time, to choose an alternative to classroom training that had more interaction than a reference book.

*Early Custom CBT.* Once the generic CBT demonstrated real value to the organization, clients began asking for courses that reflected NYNEX products and procedures. Early custom CBT used authoring tools like Phoenix and then grew through 10Core to Toolbook and similar tools.

*Multimedia.* With the success of disk-based CBT, multimedia added the sophistication of audio and full-motion video. While few users were equipped with CD drives and sound cards at their desktops, many had them at home, allowing the training organization to deliver training at home with almost zero job cost to the business. With video vignettes, soft skills could now be part of the learning offering.

*Learning Centers.* As the users realized the value of self-paced learning, they struggled between the learning process and the interruptions of a busy desk. Learning Centers, built in the back of the room or down the hall, satisfied the need for learning events that would use brief sessions in the middle of a workday. The separate environment also supported combined self-paced and group-paced workshop efforts.

**Video Broadcast.**  New product or process training required large audience coverage in a short time. Business Television was the solution for that need. Using land or satellite facilities, this high-production-value learning tool allowed learning to reach wide audiences with limited feedback requirements. Knowledge transfer worked well. Development of site competition tools increased interaction and impact.

**Videoconference for Learning.**  NYNEX built its fifty-odd videoconference sites to reduce travel costs, but distance learning became the largest single user of the system. Videoconferencing, with its two-way audio and video, allowed an incredible student-centered learning experience, passing the mantle of instructor from facilitator to student at multiple sites.

**Web-Based Training.**  Success of these self-paced learning tools created a demand for learning events that avoided the distribution effort required of disk and CD-ROM packages. The Web offered that capability as a minimum. Student tracking, multiple feedback systems, and rapid updates added value to the learning process without additional cost.

## The Pilot Strategy

One of the most common corporate strategies for new organization tools, especially new technology, is the pilot test. In concept, the pilot test is used to prove the overall concept before major investments are made.

My experience with virtually all of my Learning Technology clients includes some sort of pilot. The best are well structured, well funded, strongly supported and deeply evaluated, and have goals that are clearly defined and met. The worst are haphazard efforts designed to satisfy the manager who wants to do something, but isn't sure how to get started. The results are rarely conclusive, requiring a real stretch to sustain the process.

Virtually every organization I have worked with has used a cautious pilot-test strategy without realizing that there are risks associated with this limited approach. Before electing this strategy, the user should carefully consider the pros and cons listed here.

**The Pro of Pilot Tests.**  There are some undeniable advantages to this approach:

*Reduced Risk.*  The pilot strategy reduces individual, department, and corporate risk. Careful pilot test construction can help to define issues on a small scale. The small scale ensures that the organizational focus can be maintained. Issues that could potentially be lost in a large implementation are attended to.

*Reduced Exposure.* Along with reducing risk comes the limited organizational exposure. A failure of a pilot test allows the proponents to try another tool or technique without the losing interest and funding from the overall organization.

*Reduced Cost.* Pilot tests can be relatively inexpensive in terms of costs of implementation. The limited scale reduces out-of-pocket expenses, although the learning processes can be as large as an entire implementation.

*Reduced IT Engagement.* Information Technology (IT) is usually a key player in distance education, sometimes becoming the primary approver of many projects. This is especially true with intranet projects—in which IT usually owns the intranet. A pilot test can be attempted with an Internet solution, bypassing the IT concerns for a short time.

**The Con of Pilots.** Despite their advantages, pilot tests are not assured of success. There are a number of intrinsic disadvantages:

*Minor Impact.* Pilot tests have little impact by definition. Many of my clients have approached me with a fistful of pilot test results and a frustration that little bottom-line impact was accomplished. The pilot test, successful or not, never gets to the major organizational training needs, denying the promise that was probably included in its justification. Internal costs (for example, for training staff supporting trials) can easily approach the cost of the entire implementation.

*Difficulty of Expansion.* Because the pilot test is usually safe, perhaps easy, perhaps limited to a friendly audience, it can solve inconsequential problems while leaving the mainstream training applications untouched.

*Reduced IT Integration.* Bypassing the IT department, while convenient, denies the distance learning application the chance to integrate itself with the major IT game plan. When that game plan controls budgets, desktop software, intranet bandwidth, server platforms, firewall restrictions, network expansion, and so on, the pilot program could find itself with no place to go.

*Enterprise Issues.* With more applications bridging the entire enterprise (for example, SAP or PeopleSoft) pilot tests can miss the opportunity to be embedded within these major efforts, failing to obtain the budget, employee awareness, support, and headcount that could have made the jump to "Enterprise Learning" easier.

## Initial Training Opportunities

The disadvantages of a cautious, small-scale pilot strategy severely limit its actual usefulness, tempting as it seems at first glance to go very slowly at first. Although it is far more comprehensive and risky to target initial training and then move on to the entire enterprise, the rewards make this approach well worthwhile.

In many organizations initial training is the largest training segment. Focused at line workers in the field or call center, this training load increases with mergers, acquisitions, product expansion, turnover, and *churnover* (where employees move out of the field up the career path to other jobs, departments). Because this can be 60 – 80 percent of the entire training department workload, timid practitioners usually avoid this major impact area for trying out distance learning. What a mistake!

Another element that makes initial training a significant distance learning target is the potential application of EPSS. Many initial training program operators, fearing that they will never see the students again once they have been imprisoned by the field organization, attempt to teach students 100 percent of their skill requirements even though the students may only need 20 percent of the skills and knowledge to perform 80 percent of their function. The unused material is forgotten quickly after initial training, evaporating in cold storage. EPSS can bring just-in-time learning to those rarely used subjects, allowing the employees out in the field to request mini lessons that explain any unfamiliar screens, forms, or fields they encounter. This allows people to learn just what they need when they need to use it, which both improves the likelihood that the information will stick for another time and reduces the potential for damage if the information does not stick— after all, the mini lesson is still there and can be repeated as often as needed until an employee internalizes its content.

# Enterprise Planning

To ensure that the distance learning plan will be sustained, I have helped every one of my clients create an enterprise-training plan (ETP) that creates a new learning architecture that will be implemented over a number of years. Pilot tests can then be designed with the overall plan in place, allowing the successful ones to grow into to the long-term plan.

## Basic Elements

The following is a sample template that I have used to obtain the funding, commitment, and energy of the organization in support of distance learning goals:

*The Mission.* This is the corporate mission, not the departmental or training mission. The mission statement ensures that the distance learning plan, within the overall training plan, perhaps embedded in an HR plan, is clearly in line with the overall corporate mission. Where distance learning can be used for training of customers in addition to internal training, the linkage with the mission is even more critical.

*The Macro View.* This defines the overall corporate situation surrounding the training environment and includes those issues that may be driving the training volume upward while reducing the amount of available time that individuals can devote to attending traditional training sessions.

*The Current State.* This section is a definition of the current state in terms of performance goals, skills needed, courses, students, learning activities, locations, and current distance learning activities. Listing them here ensures that all are included in the final plan. Done correctly, this section includes a comprehensive inventory of courses with cross-indexed matrices of topics, skill linkages, position linkages, size of the training universe, number of individuals requiring training, learning processes, potential distance learning tools, and so on. Outside help is useful for gathering this information in an unbiased manner.

*The Future State.* This section, frequently the result of a middle-level plan, describes the vision of how the organization would like its training to be. Continuous lifelong learning concepts, linked to corporate goals, performance goals, and career planning, are found here. A facilitated group meeting can be used to develop this portion of the plan quickly.

*The Gaps.* This section defines where there is a need for the learning organization and an equivalent learning architecture. It describes the learning and support systems to bring the current state to the future state.

*The Alternatives.* There is rarely a single solution, nor should there be. Here the author shows all the potential opportunities from doing nothing through minimal plans to full-scale, multi-tooled applications. Outside learning technology experts who can describe the best practice in the field are valuable here.

*The Plan.* The author has the opportunity here to recommend one of the alternatives to fill the gap and reach the future state. The author can use this section to sell a preferred choice. I have used this section with my clients as an educational section explaining the tools, their applications, and the benefits.

*The Issues.* This section lists and explains all the organizational, budgetary, cultural, political, and related issues that could stand in the way of creating a sustainable plan.

*The First Steps.* The author uses this section to describe the potential first steps that would follow approval of the overall plan. The same outside experts can make this process more effective. See next section.

## Creating the Enterprise Plan

The Enterprise Plan template is useful, but there's a good deal of work involved in applying it. There are also many choices as to approach to the job.

*Do It Yourself.* While having a plan may seem obviously desirable, few training managers have the time to create one. In addition, if this long-range planning process is not a part of the regular job, it may be the function that will get done "when there is time"—and that time rarely comes. In addition, the creation of the plan needs input from many industry stakeholders, not often found at the behest of the training practitioner. Senior management would do well to consider bringing in other sources to support the manager in creating a "best practices" view for the organization. Doing it yourself may not be the best way to ensure its success.

*Consultants.* Distance learning consultants represent an ideal source for assistance in creating a long-term plan that will sustain the distance training effort. Those drawn from the ranks of practitioners bring many years of experience in the training trenches. Those with a strong IT background are helpful. Those with strong links to the industry, the vendors, and other sources of expertise are a real plus.

The senior manager considering the aid of a consultant might choose one of the following strategies:

- *Minimal immersion:* Internal team produces the entire plan. Consultant provides an over-the-shoulder comment and critique that ensures that the plan has no major failings.

- *Moderate immersion:* Consultant is used as part of the team in the development of the plan, ensuring that all the best practices are included.
- *Maximal immersion:* Consultant leads the internal team, drawing on the team's resources to adapt the best practices plan to the organization.

**University Involvement.**  Creating a plan for sustaining distance learning requires a strong mixture of practical best practices and cognitive learning processes well documented for adult learners. A university could be considered as a partner to build the long-term plan. Senior managers will need to find a partner that can step out of the box of the usual academic life and into the crazy world of business to make it work. This requires flexibility on both sides. Some of these partnerships have worked well (Northwestern University is a good example in its partnership with Anderson Consulting), but both players should be clearly focused on their true objectives and goals. The benefits are many, including those that go beyond the creation of the plan itself (internships, externships, research, product creation, and so on).

**Vendors.**  Vendors are the most common partners in the creation of a long-term plan. Most will exchange free consulting effort for the sale of the vendor's product both now and in the future. Maintaining the balance between helping and selling bias is difficult even when time permits detailed cooperation with client staff. When senior managers are preoccupied, this balance can shift toward the vendor. If the guardians of client-vendor balance (corporate purchasing) note this shift, the training manager can lose control of the very process that is needed for the long-term plan creation.

**Peers.**  Although peers have their own problems to contend with, the popularity of distance learning conferences proves the value of the peer relationships that can help the novice create the long-term plan. On Line Learning, Tech Learn, ASTD, ISPI, Performance Management, Support Services, and many other related forums provide a mixture of peer conference rooms, vendor exhibits, and keynote speakers designed to attract practitioners and help shape their plans. Web-based discussion groups and list servers can expand the forums right at your desk. Local chapter meetings (the American Society of Trainers and Developers, the International Society for Performance Improvement, and others) can also provide the networking that helps in the first step to long-term planning.

**Competitors.**  While individual competitors are rarely a source of help, industry associations often attack common training needs and share the costs across all of their members (who are competitors but nonetheless have strong mutual interests). Given industrywide applications and skill needs, these associations can provide a lower-cost solution to creating the plan by yourself.

## Support Systems

The long-term plan for distance training and the tools for accomplishing the transformation of instructor-led classes to technology-based equivalents are two legs of a three-legged stool—a stable platform needed for a sustained process of distance learning. Support systems are the third leg. The items listed in this section constitute some of the support systems that will maintain the process while business needs and technology continue to change.

*Performance Goals.* Performance goals for individual positions should always have been a part of the human resources arsenal, but they are especially important when the expertise of the in-class teacher is spread across the distances, integrated in the software, or hidden behind a network communication system. This change should force the trainer to look for operational goals as the proof of the value of distance learning. Cycle time, sales volume, speed of response, and other operational measures linked to the overall corporate mission have always been better goals than sheer volume of students by the hour, the day, or the pound. With operational measures defined earlier in the transformation and operational systems that provide ongoing measurement, the training manager can track the impact of learning before, during, and after a distance learning intervention.

*Competency Analysis.* Sustaining distance training is linked to the organization's awareness of its performance goals and the distance that the organization has to go to obtain the skills and knowledge necessary to achieve mission objectives. This is the basic platform that builds to the current state objectives in the distance learning plan mentioned earlier. As an ongoing process, competency analysis fuels the distance learning program by redefining the organization's goals after a change in structure, ownership, or product focus. This process is not a simple one, even though the distance learning program itself appears to be an ideal vehicle for gathering the requisite data (for example, by online testing). Sources of competency analysis can include the following:

*Certification.* Individuals are measured against goals using tests or processes that have been normalized across a large group to ensure validity (that is, to make sure that the tests or processes predict successful performers). The certification process is frequently job enabling, compensation affecting, or has a significant impact on work assignments. Organizations will need to be prepared to defend these tests in the face of lawsuits, union or group concerns, and even the reluctance of managers to agree to use the results. Using products developed by outside organization that can support the findings is frequently a way to avoid liability.

*Noncertified Assessments.* Simple knowledge or skill testing that merely points to deficiencies is valuable in ensuring that individuals know where they need more training and where in the distance learning plan they can go for assistance. Such tests can provide a customized course or module roadmap that can generate learning activity into the future. Because they are not certified, however, the data must be carefully protected, ensuring that the information is not abused by managers or supervisors. A simple process of providing only aggregate data to managers will give the organization the information it needs but prevent managers from using the test as a substitute for competent appraisal processes.

*360-Degree Processes.* These processes provide the individual with information from peers, subordinates, and supervisors. They can be an ideal source of competency analysis and can also link to a development plan to direct the individual to specific opportunities in the distance learning program.

**Alternative Selections for Development.** Sustaining the overall distance learning program requires that the results of the competency analysis drive the employee toward ways of solving any competency shortcoming. There is no simple or single solution, however. As stated earlier, this author has used a wide spectrum of tools to provide a number of choices to the trainer and the individual. They include matching the learning objectives, the employee's learning style, the infrastructure available, and the delivery location desired to the specific technology tool. Table 16.1 indicates some of the potential tools for each choice.

**Measurement Systems.** Sustaining the distance learning process requires a change in the way the training organization measures its processes. In many corporations that measurement has been linked to cost (budget) and benefit (student days).

*Cost.* The budget historically has been supported by a chargeback process (pay as you go), a corporate resource funded at an overall corporate level, or some combination of both. In my experiences with this type of major change in process, the

## TABLE 16.1. ASSESSING DISTANCE LEARNING TOOLS.

| Distance Learning Tool | Learning Objective | Learning Styles | Infrastructure | Location |
|---|---|---|---|---|
| Self-paced, network delivered | Knowledge transfer, skill building | Ideally, can be adapted for individual left-brain or right-brain learners by using adaptive testing or student selection. | Bandwidth limitations can create limits on full-motion video, audio, and animation for learning. | Delivery via intranet frequently limits locations to those at work. Internet delivery can extend delivery to home or on the road. |
| Group-paced, network delivered (two-way) | Knowledge transfer with experience sharing | Requires facilitator to sense and understand the learning styles of the students. | Bandwidth can allow a full range of tools from text and graphics (chat rooms) to audio graphic to videoconferences adapted for learning. | At work is the most common location. On the road or home reduces (though doesn't eliminate) the opportunity to use real-time video. |
| Broadcast (one-way) | Knowledge transfer | Requires facilitator to sense and understand the learning styles of the students. | Can use new streaming tools for video. Audio (telephone) and text and graphics (Internet) can use public facilities. | Video only at job site. Audio almost anywhere. Text and graphics only where computers and networks are available. |
| Collaborative learning | Peer learning | Peer exchanges are either text or audio depending on the tools used. | One or more networks are needed (Internet, audio bridge, and so on). | Audio and text can reach virtually any location with a phone and a PC. |

budget strategy needs to be modified to reflect the maturity of the change explained in the following three-step process:

- *Initial Introduction:* During this period of pilot tests and trials, the buyer (manager) should not be penalized (charged) for using the new distance learning tools. Rather that manager should be rewarded by allowing as much exploitation of the distance learning tools as the workload will permit. Failing to use this budget strategy could doom the change and all the future benefits it could provide.
- *Ramp-Up Period:* During this time a minimal chargeback to cover some costs should be used, allowing new students and organizations to share in the value but still maintaining the momentum.
- *Mature—Production Delivery:* At this time the full chargeback system can be implemented. The organizations that use the services will pay for them once they're sure of the value.

*Benefits.* As indicated earlier, measuring benefits in terms of student days has little real value to the organization and the managers who are responsible for training. Most important, the key drivers of the training, the performance goals, can be overlooked just because they are difficult to measure or merely inconvenient. Not trivial is the fact that distance learning requires new measuring tools just to make them equivalent to student days. In my experiences at NYNEX I found that many courses could not be tracked (students passed disks to one another without bothering to notify anyone else), took very short intervals of time (EPSS systems provide lessons as short as five minutes), or included a duration in which training was a small percentage of the total elapsed time (a three-hour Web-delivered CBT course taken over a period of weeks).

Selecting performance goals linked to the introduction of distance learning requires the participation (and hopefully the leadership) of the line managers in selecting the measurements that will change as a result of the training intervention. Ideally this would be a measurement that was already being monitored by the line organization. Any change would provide immediate feedback to the line managers, ensuring their support for more distance learning. Frequently, the measurement has to be created to reflect the impact of the training intervention. For example, when we installed an EPSS that allowed call center personnel to obtain information about unfamiliar fields, the unit supervisor stopped being dragged away from other work to provide short-term training. When we created a facilitated multimedia center, we reduced the amount of time it took to create a specific report. In both cases, the time savings were measurable—but they were in areas that simply weren't being measured at all before.

Training has many side benefits that are difficult to measure, one of which is improving the quality of life in that corporation. When we implemented a self-service computer-based training solution for retail workers, we selected retention as the measurement for tracking the impact of training—on the assumption that workers who could take control of what they needed to know would be happier on the job and more likely to stay with it than those who couldn't.

Note that the measurements discussed thus far only reflect traditional training values, the improvement of human capital. Distance learning adds to this measurement the value of reduced cost in lost on-job time, reduced cost of commutation for learning, and reduced instructor and facilitator costs.

**HRIS Links.** For organizations without Human Resources Information Systems, paper tracking may suffice for distance learning courses. Once a formal HRIS has been adopted (PeopleSoft, Oracle, SAP, or one of the others), distance learning courses, with their computer-tracked events through learning portals, may be easier to integrate.

**Evaluation.** Evaluation is one of the specialized measuring tools long used by trainers. Donald Kirkpatrick (1994) has provided a convenient measuring system that describes the depth and impact of the course on the students. It can be applied to distance learning courses as well.

*Level 1.* Level 1 usually found as end-of-course evaluations. Sometimes unaffectionately called "smile sheets," these tools measure student satisfaction with the course. With instructor-led courses these documents are rarely of value as a result of the students' desire to leave the classroom quickly and their concern that their relationship with the instructor could be damaged with a bad report.

Distance learning systems have an advantage in the Level 1 evaluation process. Though they are mostly electronic interfaces, students could provide traditional ratings and comments as a part of the learning experience itself, keying them at the end of the course. As a result, the process of entering and automating the gathered data becomes simplified. Without an instructor looking over the student's shoulder, an objective process is supported.

But why stop there? When you're implementing network-delivered courses, it is easy to provide evaluation notes as a part of every page of the course, allowing the student to enter comments that could subsequently be harvested by the course designer to improve the course in real time.

*Level 2.* Level 2 measures what the student learned. Distance learning systems again have the advantage of a multitude of testing devices from simple true-or-false to drag-and-drop exercises and then scenario-based testing techniques. By increasing the frequency of testing, developers are able to test the student module by module, directing the student to remedial work as required. In Web-based learning this has great value in charting a student's progress through the class. However, it only shows that something was learned, not that performance was changed as a result.

*Level 3.* Level 3 measures the impact on the job. While still at NYNEX I directed the development of a novel Level 3 tool that provided a rich mixture of student's impressions of the course and what they saw as its impact on their job performance. I recognized that transitional evaluations, even if we completed them, could not adapt to this new learning architecture. When distance learning moved the classroom out across the organization footprint, with outsourced facilitators and teachers and classes being provided at all hours of the day or night, our team came up with an interesting tool. A voice mail (IVR—Interactive Voice Response) computer was pressed into service as a communication and evaluation tool.

Here is how it worked:

- On a sampling basis (usually one per day per class) a student would fill out a self-addressed company mailing envelope.
- Thirty days after the class, the student received the envelope back. Inside was a one-page instruction to call a toll-free number. The sheet described what the student should expect during the call. It promised anonymity.
- The toll-free number linked to the voice mail system that was being used for traditional operations.
- After a brief introduction from me, the IVR machine—using my voice—asked the student six questions. These questions, similar to those used on end-of-class forms, asked the student to enter a numerical rating (0 to 9) for that item. Most of the questions focused on the impact of the course on the individual, as perceived thirty days later. Following the six questions came two narrative questions asking the student to verbally describe the class's impact on their job and how the material could have been improved. The voice mail machine easily picked up the student's entire response.
- The evaluation ended with a thank you from me.
- The aggregated numerical data for the six questions were put onto a disk, moved to my PC, and then summarized using Microsoft Excel and Access. The resulting graphs demonstrated changes in the data over time (for a particular site or facilitator) and the impact of managerial intervention (a change in food policy for example).
- I listened to all of the narrative responses. Because all managers could be reached through the voice mail network, I could send the student's responses

to whoever would find them useful—the delivery manager, the development manager, even managers in other disciplines. (I did not send them to the students' own managers, however, as I had promised anonymity.) The narrative was rich and tough; you could hear the emotion of the students when they praised or complained about the job impact of the course. Many students filled up the full two and a half minutes that we allotted to the narrative questions.

• The narrative was forwarded to my administrative assistant for paraphrasing and summary. That summary was sent to training managers.

This distance learning evaluation system allowed me to monitor the far-flung, time-shifted, modularized distance learning program in an effective and exciting way. Students responded very favorably and managers knew that I (the director of learning technology) was personally engaged in the evaluation process.

*Level 4.* Level 4 is designed to describe the ROI of the distance learning effort. I never completed one for the entire program, but did complete them for individual projects after the pilot was concluded. The impact of demonstrating a very positive ROI for these distance learning projects, primarily through job time saved, allowed the continued expansion of the program.

**Distribution.** While many distribution issues are absorbed by the newer network delivery systems, group-paced systems (such as videoteleconference for learning or synchronous Internet) frequently require the distribution of collateral material to support the class. Student workbooks, tests, reference guides, and so on need to be in the students' hands prior to the class itself. Downloaded files and faxed materials frequently filled this requirement. If the material was too bulky for electronic transfer, company mail and occasionally overnight mail took care of the load.

Dealing with global clients, I smile when I remember talking to an employee in southeast Asia who realized that he didn't have to wait on his company's snail-slow mail system to bring the next course in his development. His Web-based system made him the controller of distribution, a fact that was not lost on him.

**Training Help Desk.** As more subjects are delivered to the student without benefit of a live subject matter expert (SME), each CBT development required a process to identify an individual to take student calls, respond to e-mail, monitor a chat room, or maintain a bulletin board to provide the support that the student usually received in the classroom. FAQ files were also valuable.

As more subjects fill the distance learning servers, there will be a larger need for offline SMEs to handle the questions. Some could easily come from the instructors of traditional courses in that discipline.

*Outsource.* Outsourcing is already common for instructor-led training, and it is far more prevalent in sustaining distance learning. Expertise, available time, and skills make the outsource (consultant, vendor, and so on) a valuable way to get started and maintain momentum. We used a pool of vendors to manage or support our distance learning projects.

Unless distance learning is your core business, outsiders can easily provide the fast track for your program with a minimum cost and risk. The successful result of a well-managed outsourcing strategy can be a rapid and effective transition to distance learning.

*Senior Management Engagement.* Any organization program benefits from senior management engagement. While distance learning will probably not be used to train many senior managers themselves, creative approaches to reach them through their families or secretaries can frequently bring them closer to the overall distance learning plan. I remember a number of very aloof senior managers who became engaged in distance learning via stand-alone multimedia when we gave their children copies of the courseware. Only one convert is required to create a senior advocate who can be counted on to carry the distance learning to the conference tables where the future of the plan will be decided.

*Middle Management Engagement.* I found middle managers, next to the trainers themselves, most difficult to engage in distance learning for their own education. Unlike first-level line managers who soon observe the value of distance learning with their working teams, middle managers need more selling, more support. It is worth the effort. The converted middle manager will become a champion of the distance learning concept for you.

I can still see the virtual light bulb go on when a middle manager realized that he was the beneficiary of distance learning—not the training department.

*Promotional Programs.* Sustaining the program requires a major promotion effort at the beginning of the project. Over the years I have used a variety of tools effectively:

- Open houses (for Learning Centers)
- Articles in organizational newsletters (when a new milestone has been reached)
- Learning technology fairs with demonstrations and speakers—and popcorn
- E-mail promotions for pilot test segments
- Flyers and wall posters to announce the availability of new tools, courses, and programs
- Management and team briefings (when a pilot test or program begins)

- Distance learning tools combined with all of these promotions wherever possible

***Reuse of Media.*** Earlier in this chapter I advocated for multiple tools to satisfy the learning goals, styles, infrastructure, and locations needed by the distance learning program. One effective tool to sustain initial programs is to reuse materials between delivery media as follows:

- Creating libraries of shared learning objects for CBT stored in learning repositories
- Recording major video events and then pressing them to searchable, random-access CD-ROM formats
- Using successes to create standards for new development efforts
- Reusing learning actors (cartoons, personalities, people) in a variety of courses to create a familiar setting for learning
- Reusing navigation steps and the general look and feel across all similar media

***Stakeholder Issues.*** As with any major organizational program, the distance learning plan needs a champion prepared to defend and advocate to many potential stakeholders. The list includes but is by no means limited to the following:

- *Board of Directors:* Can assist in driving the effort.
- *Stockholders:* Can participate in distance learning programs designed to identify and explain corporate direction, products, and so on.
- *Unions:* May have concerns about job content but could be advocates for their members' educational concerns.
- *Community Relations:* Can see value in sharing distance learning programs and facilities with local communities and disadvantaged groups.
- *Regulators:* Will want to include their agenda in classes for employees.

## Future View

I am very excited about this field and the potential for the future.

My experiences at NYNEX and Bell Atlantic, and with my current learning technology clients, have demonstrated that getting the right tools is only the starting point for a distance learning program. Sustaining that effort requires a wide range of fundamental plans, support systems, and a high level of awareness of the selling process.

As new tools and new techniques enter the industry, it will be harder and harder to pick out the important drivers of the long-term, high-impact plan. Managers will have to draw their line in the sand to get the process started—and will need to find qualified, concerned, and enthusiastic partners. And they will need to look at their existing teams to help them mold their new careers in the distance learning arena.

Failing to understand the entire playing field could result in a fragmented, pilot-filled frustration that never delivers for senior managers. As the industry matures, the tolerance for that kind of failure will be reduced, raising expectations that distance learning will improve both the internal and external skills sought by the organization within the new global information revolution.

CHAPTER SEVENTEEN

# THE U.S. POSTAL SERVICE'S INTEGRATION OF DISTANCE TRAINING AND EDUCATION INITIATIVES TO MEET ORGANIZATIONAL GOALS

Mary Jane (Molly) Wankel

How does the Postal Service keep improving its delivery of hundreds of millions of pieces of mail every day, handling 41 percent of the world's volume? How do we train our almost 800,000 career employees (making us the one of the nation's largest civilian employers) who work on three tours (shifts) around the clock around the nation? How do we train drivers of our 200,000 vehicles (making us the owners of the largest fleet of vehicles in the world)? The answer to these questions—in part—is training.

The challenge in providing such training is threefold: cost, limited resources, and consistent message. The cost of sending employees to a central location to

*Note:* A special word of thanks to the following people for their input and help in preparing this chapter: Earl Artis, Corporate Relations Manager, Southeast Area, Memphis, Tennessee; Ross Caroland, Producer, Tennessee District, Nashville, Tennessee; Larry Dingman, Southeast Area Satellite Network Manager, Memphis, Tennessee; Sara Giballa, HR Communications, Employee Resource Management, Washington, D.C.; Glen Hubbel, Distance Learning Coordinator, National Center for Employee Development, Norman, Oklahoma; Olaf Jaehnigen, Multimedia Specialist, Employee Development, Washington, D.C.; Livio Linares, Supervisor, Media Productions, William F. Bolger Center for Leadership Development, Potomac, Maryland; Gordon McGraw, Training Development Specialist, Employee Development, Washington, D.C.; John Mitschell, Training Specialist, National Center for Employee Development, Norman, Oklahoma; Carrie Nivens, Customer Relations Specialist, Cardova, Tennessee; Deborah C. Smartt, Communications, Assistant/Photographer, Tennessee District, USPS, Nashville, Tennessee; Bill Stefl, Manager, Employee Development, Washington, D.C.; Bill Sweitzer, HR Manager, Tennessee District, Nashville, Tennessee.

attend classroom-based instruction is growing, making this option sometimes unfeasible. Even narrowing the scope by limiting the offerings to only the eleven areas or eighty-seven districts becomes difficult because instructors or facilitators often must travel for months to offer the needed message in all these locations, thereby being unproductive at their home base.

The second part of the challenge is that our two national training centers have limited resources. These are fixed-size facilities with limited space, equipment, and instructors. There are more employees who need training than the national facilities can realistically accommodate.

The third part of the challenge is getting a consistent message (whether training or information) uniformly applied to all plants and post offices throughout the Postal Service. For example, one of the districts had tried three methods for communicating information:

- Managers would write a memo and make 645 copies to send to all plants and post offices in their district. When they tested this approach, the district managers found that it did not always work. The message might not get passed on to other employees or the message might be misunderstood by those delivering it, and therefore would not always be communicated correctly to employees.
- The district would hold cluster meetings during which the district manager would talk to the group of direct reports, hoping they would tell their direct reports who would in turn tell their direct reports. Again, this communications process did not deliver a consistent message, nor did it consistently reach most of the district's employees.
- The district tried using telephone chains in hopes of getting the message to all employees in a consistent fashion, but district management found those attempts were not always as successful as they had hoped they would be. The message that reached the end of the chain tended to differ from the one that started the trip.

Thus a system for communicating messages and delivering training and education programs in a more cost-effective manner with limited resources and in a consistent fashion was needed.

## Population Served

If you count both full-time employees and the varying but always large population of casuals (temporary employees) and contractors, any training program the Postal Service offers potentially can reach over a million people. Postal Service employees work in the following functions:

- Maintenance
- Operations and processing
- Delivery
- Customer Service
- Transportation
- Logistics
- Postmasters
- Supervision
- Management
- Executive leadership

Postal Service employees work all over the country from the bottom of the Grand Canyon in Arizona to deep in the Arctic Circle in Barrow, Alaska. We even deliver mail by boat to communities in the Puget Sound. We have people at work twenty-four hours a day, seven days a week.

Because of the large and widely dispersed population needing information, training, and education delivered in a consistent, cost-effective fashion, distance training is a viable option. The Postal Service has been in the business of offering distance training since 1986 with the Postal Audiographics Teletraining Network (PATN), and we expanded in 1990 to live, interactive courses via the Postal Satellite Training Network (PSTN). Besides these two networks, we currently offer training via five other methods:

- PBS The Business and Technology Network, another satellite distance training and education vehicle
- Videotape
- CD-ROM applications
- Web-based training (WBT)
- Performance support tools

## Types of Training

Nationally, satellite distance training and education programs are offered primarily to two large segments of the population: maintenance, through courses offered via PATN and PSTN, and management, via PSTN and courses offered by a major vendor, PBS The Business and Technology Network.

### Postal Audiographics Teletraining Network

PATN started out as a simple teleconferencing medium. People called in with a telephone while running through a set of numbered slides in a slide carousel with a portable slide projector that had been sent prior to training. Thus people could hear the instructor over the telephone for the audio part of the instruction and use the slides for the visual part of the course. The first course was MultiPosition Letter Sorting Machine, which taught maintenance and upkeep of this piece of equipment using the comfort of the student's local surroundings and familiarity of their home office as an instructional advantage. Again, all student materials needed for the course had been sent prior to the date of training—references, manuals, drawings, and Learning Activity Packets containing the procedures and activities for learners to apply on the machine after the module. The instructor would tell everyone which slide to project and then what page in the schematic to look at in the appropriate drawings. This was a use of teleconferencing by telephone as an instructional methodology.

Then PATN advanced by using the Optel Audio-graphics system, which uses a software package to control the screen and display of the student site via a modem. This feature allowed the developer to create and convert standard PowerPoint slides and use them instead of the old 35mm slides. This system also gave the instructor full control over the graphic environment and solved the problem of ensuring everyone was looking at the same picture. PowerPoint gave the instructor the ability to add text, pictures, and line drawings to the slides. In addition, the program allowed instructors to draw on the screen from the originating location and have everyone see the drawing live on their screens.

## Postal Satellite Training Network

As noted earlier, the Postal Service is divided into eleven areas and eighty-seven districts. One of the areas serves as an exemplary case study of the organization's use of PSTN distance training. The Southeast Area consists of nine districts: Miami, Tampa, Orlando, and Jacksonville, Florida; Macon and Atlanta, Georgia; Birmingham, Alabama; Nashville, Tennessee; and Jackson, Mississippi. The Southeast Area has been offering a wide-reaching service to potentially 100 percent of its population, longer than any other area in the Postal Service. They have been providing these services in addition to the PTSN programming since 1995.

Working with staff from headquarters, from the area level, and from the nine districts comprising the Southeast Area, the area found it had the best of all possible worlds. It could offer all these services:

- Headquarters programming, including Postal Vision, a program that runs each workday and provides information regarding international and postal news.
- Maintenance training for craft employees out of Norman, Oklahoma.
- Area broadcasts for employees in the entire Southeast Area.
- Production facilities to each district for producing their own broadcasts. Some are monthly broadcasts that are individualized and produced especially for that district.

The Southeast Area has provided each facility of fifty employees or more with a satellite dish with which to receive live or rebroadcast programming. The area bought TVs and VCRs for its smaller facilities, thereby ensuring 100 percent saturation for some programs. Programming is received either by satellite, fiber optic, or tape.

## PBS The Business and Technology Network

Employees have access to five hours of quality distance training and education programs, five days a week, via PBS The Business and Technology Network. This initiative, implemented across the nation, offers all Postal Service employees the opportunity to select from over eight hundred additional course offerings—1,200 hours of satellite-delivered programs, including live, interactive seminars featuring top business experts. These and dozens of how-to programs and executive education courses can be applied to fulfill each year's Strategic Focus training goals.

By expanding technology-assisted learning, the Postal Service offers employees more job-related and personal growth opportunities. The USPS and PBS The Business and Technology Network partnership helps fulfill the continuing mission to improve customer service and productivity systemwide. This means that more people can learn more things, consistently, accurately, cost-effectively, throughout the entire organization.

PBS The Business and Technology Network offers programs in change and innovation, computer skills, customer service, employment law, executive education, health and safety, and interpersonal skills. In addition to these skill-building programs, there are live events designed to give access to leading business thinkers and timely topics. Plus, Postal Service employees have access to executive education programs from institutions such as the Massachusetts Institute of Technology that allow them to obtain full college credit without leaving their work site.

The Postal Service Web site offers information about PBS The Business and Technology Network including a course catalogue and available dates and times of selections. Coordinators of the program can access the network's home page and download advertising materials to copy and distribute to the workers in their facility.

## Videotape

The Postal Service uses videotape to distribute training, information, and corporate messages. Postal employees communicating postal ideas and information on videotape is a very powerful tool. An example of the most pervasive use of corporate communications in the Postal Service is "Strategic Focus," a videotape that is sent out each year for each employee to view. "Strategic Focus" is the national

Voice of the Employee (VOE) training and corporate initiative that requires all career employees to receive training in the principles of the *CustomerPerfect!* system. For more information about this system, see the "Description of Management Processes" section later in this chapter.

*CustomerPerfect!* is a performance management system, based on the Malcolm Baldrige Award criteria. The goal for this initiative is to improve employee and organizational effectiveness by having the right people in the right place with the right tools at the right time to consistently provide superior customer value and ensure commercial viability in a dynamic market. "Strategic Focus" builds on the preceding years' VOE training experience, incorporating lessons learned from implementing past programs, and redirecting efforts to achieve maximum organizational impact.

The Malcolm Baldrige National Quality Award was created by law in 1987 and named for Malcolm Baldrige, who served as Secretary of Commerce from 1981 until his tragic death in a rodeo accident in 1987. The purposes of the award are to promote an understanding of the requirements for performance excellence and competitiveness improvements and to promote sharing of information on successful performance strategies (Russo, 1995, p. 11). For more information about the Postal Service's alignment of our management philosophy with the Baldrige criteria, see the "Description of Management Processes" section later in this chapter.

## CD-ROM Applications

Several departments within the Postal Service are using CD-ROMs to distribute training materials to the Field. One such course, the new Orientation for New Employees (ONE), was revised due to the result of the Baldrige June 1998 recommendation to improve orientation, education, and training of people joining the Postal Service. New with this edition of ONE is an Administrator's Guide. This instructional guide focuses on how to make orientation an enjoyable experience rather than an information dump. There are also vibrant new slides and a video montage that should be used before orientation begins and during breaks. The course takes about eight hours to go through. It is the first product to be packaged in its entirety on a CD-ROM (Administrator's Guide, Facilitator Guide, Participant Workbook, video montage, and PowerPoint slides).

Another course that incorporates CD-ROM applications is Safety for Postal Leadership. This two-day course provides leaders with information and techniques to identify safety problems and prevent accidents. The course also underscores the critical role of leaders in promoting safety. All instructor materials are on a CD-ROM. The CD contains PowerPoint slides the instructor uses in the classroom and contains motion video segments the instructor shows learners of examples of proper safety techniques—and what happens when proper safety techniques are ignored.

## Web-Based Training

Most of the USPS WBT courses can be taken for credit or viewed randomly without credit. Once learners have successfully completed the course, they may print a Certificate of Completion to take to their managers or training coordinators for entry into the training documentation and record keeping computer system.

The following are examples of courses offered via the Web at the Postal Service:

- *TIMES*

The Transportation Information Management Evaluation System (TIMES) allows headquarters to monitor the movement of all trucks in the field. To accomplish this, a communication network was established to collect the data from the field sites. Integral to the collection process was the input devices used on the back dock of every facility. The maintenance of this equipment was important, and training was required. A maintenance training course was developed and conducted. At first, the TIMES course was taught on PATN via the Audio-graphics system. The developer took the graphics from the Audio-graphics system and converted them and the text to HTML files. Audio was added using compressed audio files but was still limited to small sound bites. Because it was short course with small files, TIMES did not weigh down the LAN, and it was thus suitable for offering on the Web. All documentation for the course was made available on the Web so it could be downloaded as well.

- *Lockout / Tagout*

This course was very similar to the TIMES course in that it had been offered on PATN, then converted to HTML. The WBT course used the same graphics as the PATN course, but no audio. This course was selected for offering on the Web because of its importance to the field. All operators and maintenance people have to be trained in Lockout / Tagout—a target population so large that the class loads could not be handled by conventional instructor-led, classroom-based training. This has been an effective use of the Web for training many people on the same material in a systematic, standard fashion.

- *Personnel Selection Methods*

The purpose of the course is to offer consistent, easily accessible training for the 79,000 EAS employees who have responsibility to serve on selection committees, review job applications, or serve as a selection official. The previous training consisted of instructor-led, classroom-based sessions using an eight-hour videotape; or a self-paced workbook and the same videotape. The workbook and video were outdated and there was a need for consistent, standardized training for many people around the country. Given today's budgetary constraints, the request from the client was to provide this training via the Web. This approach enables newly promoted EAS personnel to take the required course, and also allows current staff members to go on the Web to review materials prior to serving on a review board.

This WBT course has proven to be cost-effective in that any of the tens of thousands of employees who need the training can take the course online at once, and not wait for an instructor-led course to be offered or have to travel to take the course. The course provides timely materials on an as-needed basis because employees can download the materials when they prepare to serve on review committees. The course allows employees to work at their own pace, repeat modules as needed, or quickly refresh themselves on areas of concern. The WBT course incorporated interactive practice exercises and a post-course test to measure achievement. The WBT course was developed in Authorware 4.0. The Appendix at the end of the chapter shows the flowchart of the overall course design, lessons within a module, and samples of screens with their storyboard frames of the Personnel Selection Methods WBT Course.

- *Injury Applications System (IAS) CBT*

IAS is a forty-five-minute course using a mix of hypertext markup language (HTML) and audio without other plug-ins. The course offers an overview and a tutorial about IAS, a system that combines mainframe functions, such as injury compensation and workers compensation, and payroll applications together into a single Windows application in a way that lets employees work more easily and productively.

- *RTR Processing System CBT*

Retirement, Thrift Savings Plan & Reduction in Force (RIF) is a thirty-minute course about the RTR Processing System, a Windows 95–based PC application that allows service history to be entered, provides reports on service computation dates and other data calculated by RTR, and performs calculations for over a half dozen other determinations. The course explains how to use the system and introduces its benefits: the way it eliminates manual calculations and errors that might result, uses consistent edits to ensure accurate and complete data entry, and reduces costs and liability by ensuring correct retirement plan codes and other information.

- *Legal Coursework*

There are several courses the Law Department offers via the Web that offer a course book (electronic textbook) with interactive case studies that provide feedback for correct and incorrect answers. These are some of the course titles:

- Accidents and the Claims That Follow
- Financial Conflicts of Interest

- Discipline for Misconduct
- Duty to Provide Information to the Union in Grievance Matters
- Family and Medical Leave Act (FMLA)
- Ethics of Outside Employment
- Performance Management Plans (PIPs)
- Reasonable Accommodation
- Sexual Harassment and Inappropriate Conduct

## Performance Support

The Postal Service is implementing a pilot maintenance support system in processing plants in two Florida sites whereby technicians use a device that can be handheld or worn on the hip much like a cellular phone to troubleshoot equipment malfunctions. The device is known as System Integrated Maintenance Online (SIMON) and combines the wearable computer with a cellular LAN. Instead of receiving a call from an operator about a malfunctioning piece of equipment, the technician hears about the fault directly from the malfunctioning equipment. The technician, already knowing what the fault is, can review the corrective procedure on SIMON. The technician also has access to online documentation such as manuals, references, and illustrations, and can even order replacement parts through SIMON. Thus SIMON allows for greater productivity by troubleshooting the problem, providing direct access to reference manuals, and allowing for direct contact to the parts department.

# Description of Management Processes

In 1992, the Postal Service began a transformation toward a more businesslike, customer-focused organization. We restructured, cut bureaucracy, expanded our marketing efforts, and increased resources to address customer needs. In 1993, we began to adapt our management philosophy to align with the Baldrige criteria. There are seven categories that Baldrige applicants must address (Russo, 1995, p. xii):

- Leadership
- Strategic Planning
- Customer and Market Focus
- Information and Analysis
- Human Resource Focus
- Process Management
- Business Results

In 1994, we conducted—with the help of senior Baldrige Examiners—our first organization-wide assessment, and developed action plans for improving what we do and how we do it. This work culminated in 1995 with the creation of *CustomerPerfect!*—our version of the Baldrige model—a systematic, integrated way of managing our business, focused on serving customer needs. Internally, the Postal Service refers to its three broad, corporate goal categories as *voices*. The Voice of the Customer (VOC) centers on customer satisfaction and the achievement of superior customer value in targeted markets. Performance goals include providing timely delivery and consistently accurate service that is affordable and easy to use. The Voice of the Employee (VOE) focuses on organizational and individual effectiveness, aligning human resources with business objectives by having the right people in the right place with the right tools at the right time. The Voice of Business (VOB) focuses on financial performance to ensure commercial viability and bottom-line results. Bill Henderson, Postmaster General and CEO (USPS, 1999), has professed in numerous speeches that strengthening the employees' voice is the vital to improving the business and customer satisfaction. Clarence Lewis, executive vice president and chief operating officer (U.S. Postal Service, 1999), also has expressed the same sentiment many times: listening to Postal Service employees' feedback, concerns, and suggestions not only will improve our bottom line, but our entire system of processing mail, delivering parcels, and serving customers at the window.

## Outcomes Desired

There are four major desired outcomes for using distance training and education initiatives at the Postal Service. The first is to use training and education resources more cost-effectively. The second is to reach a broader audience more easily. Another is to keep Postal Service employees better informed and updated in a more timely fashion about operations and automated equipment. The last is to share information by providing opportunities for interaction with employees.

### Headquarters Plans

In order to achieve the desired outcomes of providing training and information cost-effectively to a broader audience and in a more consist fashion while promoting two-way communication, all levels within the Postal Service have had to develop management processes. At the headquarters level, we devised a distance training and education business plan. The business plan provided a breakdown of the issues affecting implementation of distance training and education initiatives, and recommendations and specific action items for addressing the issues. The issues addressed were goals, the pros and cons of various methods of delivery, course selection for distribution, content generation, administration, marketing and communication, desktop publishing, and internal staff development.

## Southeast Area Plans

The degree to which the areas are using distance training and education initiatives affects the level of their management processes instituted. The shining example at the Postal Service is the Southeast Area's development of policy and standard operating procedures as suggestions for use by satellite broadcast producers. This information is compiled into one binder that includes everything a producer needs to know about this form of distance training. The information includes the mission statement as well as lists and examples for every aspect of setting up a satellite broadcast facility from suggestions for show formats and roles and responsibilities to how to design sets, place studio equipment, and work with technical staff, hosts, and guests. The information also includes the use of TelePrompTers, scriptwriting, visual aids, storyboards, lighting, and editing—all delivered in a light-hearted, visually interesting fashion.

The Southeast Area also created standard operating procedures for prospective television production vendors, specifying much of the same kinds of information as for producers internal to the Postal Service. In addition, this product offers information specific to vendor contracting officers and describes other requirements specific to vendors.

Moreover, the Southeast Area developed a complete information package to send to managers in other areas who are researching the possibilities of satellite communication. The package offers four packets consisting of a booklet and a CD-ROM (and a videotape with the same content as the CD) that provide step-by-step instructions on everything one needs to know for installing a similar satellite distance training system. The first packet provides a brief overview and the features and benefits of initiating or expanding distance training offerings. The second packet expresses the rationale for choosing satellite communication technology over other technologies for the Postal Service. The third packet is tailored to informing the creative and implementation teams about formats, topics, visuals, training requirements, and other production issues. The last packet describes follow-up procedures and next steps.

## Tennessee District Plans

Because of its heavy use of distance training and education activities, the Southeast Area's Tennessee District has created its own policies, processes, and procedures tailored to its specific needs. The district even built its own studio after years of using a local Public Broadcasting Service–affiliated TV station for the

uplink and production equipment needed. Now the Tennessee District is building a new professional-quality studio that has a three-camera setup. Its development staff are enhancing their use of motion segments with posters used as displays
for education, training, and information-sharing purposes. In the Southeast Area,
this is a fully integrated, widely accepted communication, training, and education tool.

## Return-on-Investment Measures

One way to ensure the longevity of distance training and education programming
is to provide more return-on-investment (ROI) information to senior officials. The
Southeast Area has instituted another management process to do just this. An automated system surveys employees after every broadcast to measure participant
reactions. Survey results indicate that employees want information regarding

- How the organization is doing
- The newest technology and how they may be affected by this technology
- Training for craft employees
- What the district manager thinks

Ask the Boss programs, call-in sessions during which employees in each district
can ask their district manager any questions they wish, are especially popular.

# Outcomes Attained

The Postal Service has experienced myriad successes in achieving its desired outcomes for distance training and education at every level in the organization.
Postmaster General (PMG) and CEO Bill Henderson and other managers are delivering monthly broadcasts via PSTN. When PMG Henderson testified before
Congress recently, employees were able to watch rebroadcasts of the testimony.

## Headquarters Programming

At headquarters, we produce many regularly scheduled programs:

- *Training Update*, a monthly Employee Development (ED) program that reaches
  all Human Resources employees at headquarters, at our two major training
  centers in Potomac, Maryland, and Norman, Oklahoma, and all managers of
  training and their staffs at all area and district offices
- *Human Resources Quarterly*, which provides information about upcoming personnel programs and initiatives to HR managers, HR specialists, and other HR
  personnel in all eighty-seven districts

- A quarterly program for *Delivery* that explores best practices for managers, customer services supervisors, and their people in all eighty-seven districts
- A *Stress Management* course offered by ED that has been broadcast for the last year and a half and will continue through fiscal year 2000

Distance training and education initiatives at the headquarters level offer

- Programming for the twenty-hour annual training requirement for Postal Service managers
- Programming to meet the eight-hour annual training requirement for craft units
- Programming to meet the corporate requirements for sexual harassment, diversity, and other subject areas
- Management and executive development opportunities

Other successes at the national level include our use of distance training for craft employees outside the eight-hour requirement. In terms of maintenance training, distance training is the prevalent means of delivery. As graphed in Figure 17.1, participation in distance training courses has exceeded classroom participation since the early 1990s, and the margin is continuing to increase.

Moreover, as discussed earlier, the Postal Service initiated its first major Web-based training (WBT) course through its intranet. The course, Personnel Selection

### FIGURE 17.1. GROWTH IN USE OF ALTERNATIVE DELIVERY METHODS FOR MAINTENANCE TRAINING AT THE POSTAL SERVICE.

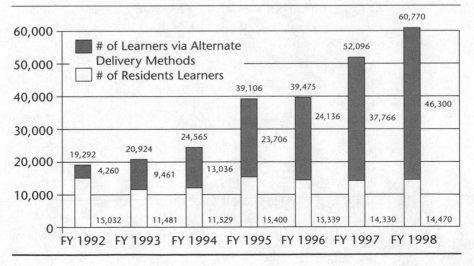

Methods, offers procedures and tips for selecting and interviewing job candidates. This course is offered online, just-in-time, and allows Postal Service employees to complete the training (or to just check out the course and its associated "textbook") any time convenient to them.

## Southeast Area Programming

The Southeast Area offers special programs to achieve the desired outcome of interacting with employees that have been especially popular:

- Managing Your Money, a program to address employees' personal budgeting needs draws a regular audience.
- A panel with members from credit union and local utilities answered questions about Y2K issues.
- The area also offers "commercials" that show employees modeling exemplary behavior.

The Southeast Area expanded its offerings by broadcasting from two major mailers' facilities to show Postal Service employees how important they are to customer success. Chief executive officers from both mailer companies and the Postal Service participated in the broadcasts.

Moreover, each district in the Southeast Area has a coordinator who delivers a monthly address concerning new developments in the district. This monthly program involves one-way communication. Information-sharing involving two-way communication is very important to district managers, but it is difficult to accomplish with over twelve thousand employees. At the district level, there have been two very successful information-sharing programs: one on retirement issues and the other on workplace environment issues. Both sessions were by invitation only and had relatively small audiences (150 compared to 12,000 total audience members). Both had very lively discussions by the participants.

## Tennessee District Programming

In terms of measuring the success of distance training and education programs, the Tennessee District wanted to get the biggest ROI of training dollars by using distance training measures to reduce travel expenses and time employees spend away from their facility. Three offices in Tennessee alone computed that they saved $2.7 million by not sending people for maintenance training at the national training facility in Norman, Oklahoma. Using PSTN, every Postal Service employee can receive information as needed, twenty-four hours a day. This service is not just a one-way channel from management to the employees. Instead, it is a total communications and distance training and education vehicle. This medium enhances employees' ability to do the job. This is a total integrated package of communications vehicle to get communications messaging and a call to action to all employees.

## Evaluation of Distance Training and Education Programs

Another area of success in the Postal Service's use of distance training and education measures is found in a study that assessed the effectiveness of one of the satellite training programs (Whetzel, Felker, & Williams, 1996, p. 5). The study measured the achievement of various learning requirements that ranged from simple recognition and recall of information to the performance of a specific job procedure. This study also compared satellite training with traditional classroom-based instruction using scientific methodology (pre-test and post-test with control groups) using the same material being taught via both delivery methods.

The study addressed the first three of four levels of Kirkpatrick's model of evaluation (Kirkpatrick, 1994, p. 21): reaction, learning, and behavior. Table 17.1 describes the four levels of Kirkpatrick's model (Kirkpatrick's title for each level is in parentheses).

Results of the study indicate that learners' reaction (Level 1 of Kirkpatrick's model) to the satellite training program was favorable; most found it to be an acceptable delivery method. The study showed that learning was slightly greater in the courses delivered via satellite than in classroom-based instruction (Level 2). Findings also showed that post-test performance on some complex job tasks was

### TABLE 17.1. THE KIRKPATRICK MODEL OF EVALUATION.

| Level | Type | Example Description |
|-------|------|---------------------|
| 1 | Learner Reaction (Reaction) | Use questionnaires that yield quantitative and qualitative data to determine how well learners liked the course or performance support item. |
| 2 | Learner Achievement (Learning) | Use test items derived from performance objectives to assess achievement. |
| 3 | Performance Improvement (Behavior) | Use an experimental control group method to determine if any improvements were made on the job. |
| 4 | Organizational Impact (Results) | Again, use an experimental control group method to evaluate results of the course or performance support item. |

significantly better after satellite-delivered instruction than after classroom-based instruction (Level 3). Coupled with the lower costs and logistical ease associated with satellite-delivered training, this becomes an extremely desirable medium with which to deliver training, education, and information programs (Whetzel, Felker, & Williams, 1996, p. 17).

## Words of Advice

*Using Training Resources.* As budgets decrease, we will need to examine how the Postal Service uses its training resources. Conventional training is not going to fulfill our needs unless we increase the amount of classroom space and the amount of equipment made available to student use. This is a relatively unpalatable investment, because conventional training at our national training centers also requires money to be spent on travel and time spent away from the job.

*Improving Saturation.* The Postal Service is one of the leaders in the use of distance training and education technology. Our satellite network is available up to twenty-four hours every day. However, not every post office or processing plant has direct access to the satellite network. We own almost seven thousand buildings, and do not yet have satellite downlinks everywhere. We can improve saturation by increasing the number of downlinks we provide. We can also help our areas and districts to improve saturation by reminding them of the benefits of the technology (reduced travel time and dollars spent, consistent message, and so on) and by providing programming, technical, and consultation assistance in using the technology. The Southeast Area is helping other areas to develop their own networks to achieve 100 percent saturation by offering their information packets to distance training and education producers.

We could also improve saturation rates by simply getting employees to turn on their monitors to tune in to training courses or information-sharing opportunities. Using by-invitation-only small group audiences greatly increases the likelihood that employees will participate. They feel honored to be invited and are more likely to take the opportunity to do so. Moreover, using videotapes of live broadcasts offers programming that is apt to be more engaging than a carefully staged studio performance, while allowing employees to watch the tape at their convenience.

*Addressing Workers' Issues.* As deliverers of distance training and education programming, we suggest to those who are just starting out that they avoid the tendency to oversell and underdeliver—and that they address workers' issues. There is a pitfall that is easy to fall into: to think that just because you are interested in something, all other employees find that topic of interest, too. When the Tennessee District first set up its network, it promoted the delivery method, but failed to ask employees what their needs were in terms of distance training and education programming. Some of the early programs were not very successful. After learning that lesson, Tennessee District Managers now hold eight to ten Town Hall Meetings each year. During these meetings, employees sit at tables of about seven each. The managers go from table to table to listen to employees' concerns and to discuss upcoming issues affecting workers. Managers are able to hear potential topics for distance training and education programs. One such topic was that employees wanted to learn about our competitors' activities; some of the best-received programs have been about our competition. We've found it very powerful to present craft employees telling stories to their peers about how the Postal Service beat out the competition.

***Stressing ROI.*** We in the training function realize the value and need of distance training and education offerings. The real challenge is to be able to justify the costs of these offerings to senior officers. We need to prove cost effectiveness and the return on investment of training dollars, and sell the fact that distance training and education offerings have a significant ROI. With increasing competition for all resources including training initiatives, we have to highlight this delivery method and its cost-effectiveness. Thus we must continue our ROI measurements and communicate our findings during the budget process.

# Summary

Distance training and education efforts—initiated in 1986 and expanded over the years—play an integral role in meeting the goals set forth for the Postal Service's three voices. By offering training via PSTN and the intranet directly to retail centers, we give our customer services employees tools and processes to improve their work, which addresses our Voice of the Customer goals. Our Voice of the Employee goals also can be met using distance training and education offerings in that employees are provided training at their job site. Employees can access the training when they need it. Offering training via our intranet on an as-needed basis to our retail centers enhances productivity as customer services employees are taught how to use the new hardware and software recently installed around the nation, thus addressing our Voice of the Business goals. Since 1995, using distance training and education activities to address the goals of our three voices has led to greater operational efficiency, three years of profits that have reduced by half the accumulated losses of two decades, unprecedented stability in postage rates, record levels of first class mail performance, stricter standards for priority mail and first class mail, and greater customer satisfaction.

We are positioning ourselves now through our partnering effort with the PBS The Business and Technology Network and through other distance training and education initiatives to give our employees even more opportunities for training over the next twelve months. This is certainly an innovative approach to increasing employee efficiency, and we welcome the challenge. Our employees can expand their opportunities for personal and professional growth. We believe that well-trained people do a better job—and that when people do their best, they are happier. And that's what we're striving for in the new millennium: people who will do their best. If we can measure our ROI and develop long-range budget planning, we will enhance our chances of meeting the goals of using training resources more cost-effectively, reaching a broader audience more easily, keeping Postal Service employees better informed in a more timely fashion, and sharing information by providing opportunities for dealing with the constant obstacles of cost, limited resources, and consistent message. With all this, we will improve our ability to meet the organizational goal of delivering the mail better.

## Appendix: Personnel Selection Methods Course

### A: Sample Flowchart of Course Modules

# Course Map

Module 1
Importance of Selection

Module 3
Behavioral Examples

Module 5
Application Review

Module 2
Past Behavior Predicts
Future Performance

Module 4
Personnel Selection

Module 6
Consensus Building

Module 8
Interviewing

Summary

Module 7
Interview Preparation

Quit

## B: Sample of Lessons Within a Module

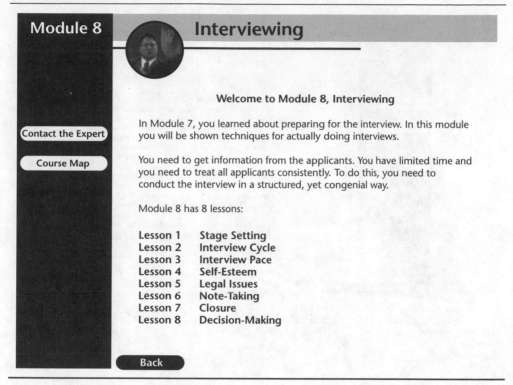

**Module 8**

# Interviewing

Contact the Expert

Course Map

**Welcome to Module 8, Interviewing**

In Module 7, you learned about preparing for the interview. In this module you will be shown techniques for actually doing interviews.

You need to get information from the applicants. You have limited time and you need to treat all applicants consistently. To do this, you need to conduct the interview in a structured, yet congenial way.

Module 8 has 8 lessons:

| | |
|---|---|
| Lesson 1 | Stage Setting |
| Lesson 2 | Interview Cycle |
| Lesson 3 | Interview Pace |
| Lesson 4 | Self-Esteem |
| Lesson 5 | Legal Issues |
| Lesson 6 | Note-Taking |
| Lesson 7 | Closure |
| Lesson 8 | Decision-Making |

Back

## C: Sample Lesson Screens with Storyboard Frames

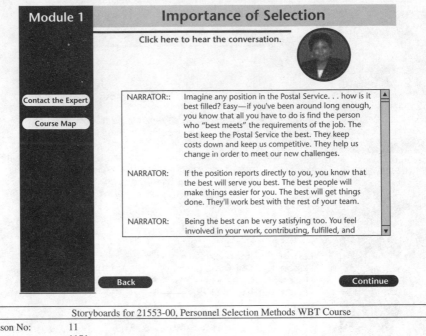

Storyboards for 21553-00, Personnel Selection Methods WBT Course

| | |
|---|---|
| Module/Lesson No: | 11 |
| Frame Name: | 11S1 |
| Next Frame: | 11I1 |
| Input Data: | |
| Touch Zone: | Y |
| Music: | |
| Graphic: | |

Text:      Click here to hear the conversation.

Audio:

NARRATOR:      Imagine any position in the Postal Service. . . how is it best filled?  Easy if you've been around long enough, you know that all you have to do is find the person who "best meets" the requirements of the job.  The best keep the Postal Service the best.  They keep costs down and keep us competitive.  They help us change in order to meet our new challenges.  If the position reports directly to you, you know that the best will serve you best.  The best people will make things easier for you.  The best will get things done.  They'll work best with the rest of your team.  Being the best can be very satisfying, too.  You feel involved in your work, contributing, fulfilled, and successful.  Having the best person in every position is most rewarding for everybody.  That's why filling these vacancies with those who can best meet their responsibilities is so important.  Choosing less than the best can cause all kinds of problems.  If the position reports to you, your job becomes harder, your team less effective.  It can be hard on the misplaced person, too.  And imagine the cost of poor selection decisions to the Postal Service.

Text:      Press [CONTINUE] to learn about potential consequences of poor selection decisions.

| Module 1 | Interviewing |
|---|---|

**Click here to hear the conversation.**

CARL: Welcome. Did you drive up?

TRISH: I did, yesterday. and it was a super day for a drive like that.

CARL: You were in town then, last night?

TRISH: Yeah, it's my first time here, believe it or not.

CARL: Do you prefer "Patricia" or "Trish"?

TRISH: I've been going by "Trish" for almost 20 years now. Though I still put "Patricia" on most official forms.

CARL: You can call me "Carl" - and you've met Barbara and Al.

Contact the Expert

Course Map

Back          Continue

---

Storyboards for 21553-00, Personnel Selection Methods WBT Course

Module/Lesson No:      81

Frame Name:      81S1

Next Frame:      Depends on learner input

Input Data:      Y

Touch Zone:      Y

Music:

Graphic:

Text:      Click here to hear the conversation.

Audio:

CARL:      Welcome. Did you drive up?

TRISH:      I did, yesterday. And it was a super day for a drive like that.

CARL:      You were in town then, last night?

TRISH:      Yeah, it's my first time here, believe it or not.

CARL:      Do you prefer "Patricia" or "Trish"?

TRISH:      I've been going by "Trish" for almost 20 years now. Though I still put "Patricia" on most official forms.

CARL:      You can call me "Carl" - and you've met Barbara and Al.

Text:

Question: Why is it important to establish rapport with applicants?

a. 81S1WA1: Discussing personal information at length with applicants allows you to get friendly and empathic with the person. NFID: 81S1WA1F1: Incorrect. Discussing too much information not relevant. . . . You will learn in this lesson about how to properly establish rapport with applicants. NFID: 81S1CA1F2.

b. 81S1CA1: Establishing a conversational style for the interview allows you to put applicants at ease. NFID: 81S1CA1F1: Correct. After greeting the applicants, start by. . . and should help to put them at ease. NFID: 81S1CA1F2.

c. 81S1WA2: Obtaining details about applicants now allows you to "nail" them later on in the interview. NFID: 81S1WA2F1: Incorrect. Don't think you're going to be able to trick applicants into divulging potentially negative information for which they may be "nailed" later on in the interview. . . . You will learn in this lesson about how to properly establish rapport with applicants. NFID: 81S1CA1F2.

81S1CA1F2: Goes back to question frame (81S1) with a check mark beside 81S1CA1. NFID: 81I1.

CHAPTER EIGHTEEN

# TeleEDUCATION NB

## Problems with Integrating Technology into a Provincewide Distributed Distance Learning Network

Rory McGreal

TeleEducation NB (TENB) is a provincewide distributed distance learning network that assists educational institutions and private sector companies in delivering distance education in New Brunswick, a small maritime province on the east coast of Canada. TENB provides an open network of distance learning centers that assist course delivery from different provincial institutions using audiographic teleconferencing, computer-based training (CBT), and the Internet. Over six years, the network has facilitated the delivery of more than eight hundred courses to over fourteen thousand students.

What kind of technology and network infrastructure is needed to sustain the TeleEducation NB operations?

The TeleEducation NB infrastructure consists of a geographical network of sites, an electronic network for data, a voice network, and access to the Internet using the provincial telephone lines or the government intranet. Different networks facilitate the delivery of courses and network management. TENB is not committed to any specific technology or delivery medium; it takes a pragmatic approach, adopting technology based on pedagogical and management principles.

---

*Note:* Research for this unit was originally conducted as part of a doctoral dissertation at the School of Computer and Information Sciences, Nova Southeastern University.

# Geographical Network

The TeleEducation NB logistical or operational network consists of seventeen regional distributed learning centers. Each regional center is coordinated by a site facilitator. Eleven of the sites are designated English-speaking and three are French-speaking. Three other sites are designated bilingual. There are thirty-eight electronic classrooms at these sites. The site facilitators also support twenty-nine other community sites with thirty-two classrooms (see Table 18.1).

TENB sites are located in community centers, schools, university or community college campuses, adult literacy centers, libraries, and hospitals. These community sites are facilitated by volunteers. The regional site facilitators work closely with them to ensure the smooth functioning of courses. The increased number of classrooms at sites results when there are multiple demands for space at the same time. Host institutions and communities are usually accommodating, finding space when it is needed.

### TABLE 18.1. TeleEDUCATION NB DISTRIBUTED LEARNING SITES SHOWING LINGUISTIC SUPPORT.

| Regional Site | Language | Classrooms | | Other Sites in the Region |
|---|---|---|---|---|
| Bathurst | B | 4 | – | – |
| Blackville | A | 2 | 1 | Doaktown |
| Campbellton | F | 3 | 2 | Dalhousie, Saint-Quentin |
| Dieppe | B | 2 | 2 | Moncton, Sackville |
| Edmundston | F | 2 | 3 | Université de Moncton, St-François |
| Fredericton | A | 3 | 4 | University of New Brunswick, Stanley, Harvey |
| Grand Falls | B | 1 | – | – |
| Grand Manan | A | 1 | – | – |
| Minto | A | 1 | – | – |
| Miramichi | A | 2 | 5 | Douglastown, Baie-Ste-Anne, Rogersville, Newcastle |
| Perth-Andover | A | 3 | 4 | Plaster Rock, Bristol, Centreville, Wicklow |
| Rexton | A | 3 | 3 | Bouctouche, St-Louis-de-Kent |
| St. Stephen | A | 2 | 4 | McAdam, St. Andrews, Campobello |
| Shippegan | F | 3 | 3 | Caraquet, Paquetville, St-Isodore |
| Sussex | A | 4 | – | – |
| Woodstock | A | 2 | 1 | Nackawick |
| TOTAL | | 38 | 32 | 70 classrooms in all |

*Note:* A = English-speaking (anglophone) B = Bilingual F = French-speaking (francophone)

These virtual classrooms are situated in communities in all areas of the province. The majority of sites are in rural areas (Figure 18.1). There is a site within a half-hour drive of anyone living within the province. More than 56 percent of students travel less than 10 km and only 11 percent travel as much as 30 km (Labour Market Analysis Branch, 1996).

TENB is a bilingual (French/English) network and must ensure that all citizens receive adequate service in the official language of their choice. To ensure this, sites have been designated bilingual, francophone, or anglophone (as shown in both Figure 18.1 and Table 18.1). Site facilitators must speak the official language of their region. In some sites, the site facilitators must be bilingual to serve a mixed population. In primarily French-speaking regions, the English-speaking minority lack access to learning opportunities other than through distance edu-

## FIGURE 18.1. NB SITE MAP.

### TeleEducation NB

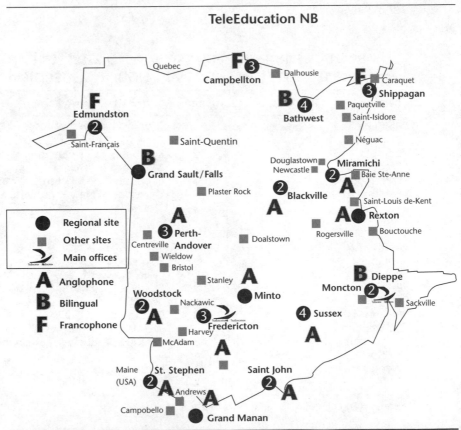

cation. This is doubly true for French-speaking minorities in English-speaking areas.

To ensure that members of both linguistic communities had access to learning opportunities in their own language, the majority of facilitators chosen were bilingual. Unilingual facilitators were hired only in regions where the population was more than 90 percent English or French. In these areas, the unilingual facilitators were partnered with bilingual facilitators in other areas to ensure that even there, students, instructors, and administrators were guaranteed service. This was accomplished over the telephone, with the bilingual facilitators serving as interpreters, or during teleconferences, where a bilingual facilitator was always present.

# TeleEducation NB Technological Network

The present physical network that interconnects computers and peripherals for exchanging information is made up of three independent networks, which operate through NBTel, the local telephone company. There are separate networks for audio (voice), data (Smart 2000 audiographic teleconferencing), and computer-mediated communications (CMC).

Audiographic teleconferencing (also known as electronic whiteboarding or data conferencing) involves the use of ordinary telephone lines for voice and data communications between remote sites. An electronic tablet and stylus plus voice communication enable participants in different locations to take part in educational activities. This electronic environment simulates a chalkboard, an overhead projector, or a slide projector. Recently, the Internet and intranets have been used to enable data and some voice connections.

Computer software sharing allows users at multiple sites to access and manipulate software applications together in real time. CMC involves asynchronous communications using mailing lists, newsgroups, and discussions using Web-based conferencing software. Synchronous conferencing is also possible using IRC (Internet Relay Chat).

## Technology and Network Details

The audiographic data connections are made through two separate Smart 2000 bridges located at the TeleEducation NB office in Fredericton. The bridges are accessed by a dial-up connection using an ordinary telephone line. There are fifty-six ports. Sites can also connect through the Internet with the TCP-IP protocol.

The voice connections are made through NBTel over standard telephone lines to two MultiLink digital, full duplex audio bridges, one with 144 ports and the other with 96 ports that serve the Atlantic region of Canada from Saint John. Special codes that are given to users for each course to ensure that billing is directed to TeleEducation NB at the special rate that was negotiated.

The different connections are made at the same time and are normally not discernible to the instructors and students who are using the network. To them, it is one system. An example of a course using the audio and data network is shown in Figure 18.2.

The CMC connections are made through NBNet, the local Internet Service Provider, to a TeleEducation NB server in Fredericton.

The minimum hardware configuration for each site is regularly reviewed. These specifications have been updated from their original configuration—based

### FIGURE 18.2. GRAPHIC CONFERENCE MAP.

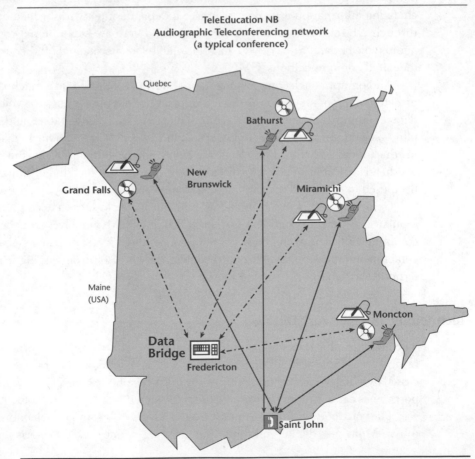

TeleEducation NB
Audiographic Teleconferencing network
(a typical conference)

on a 33MHz 486 processor—to the Pentium II. The minimum specification is updated every two years and consists of hardware, peripherals, software, and audio teleconferencing equipment including a PC system, a graphics tablet, Smart 2000 software, and an Office suite. Teleconferencing equipment includes a half-duplex teleconferencing convener with microphones.

Access to common office equipment such as a fax machine, a photocopier, and a printer as well as to a television, a VCR, and an audiotape player is normally the responsibility of the participating institution or community (see Figure 18.3). Furthermore, participants provide the room and facilities for both delivering and receiving courses at their sites. Their contribution is valued at over C$12,000 (US$7,920) for equipment as well as over C$4,000 (US$2,640) per year for use of their facilities at each site.

TeleEducation NB supplies the computer teleconferencing equipment and software needed for course delivery, and also provides initial staff training and ongoing support. TENB also arranges for two lines that are billed at a special rate negotiated with NBTel, to be described later. A third line is provided for administrative purposes at most sites. Some of the more disadvantaged communities

## FIGURE 18.3. TYPICAL TeleEDUCATION NB SITE CONFIGURATION.

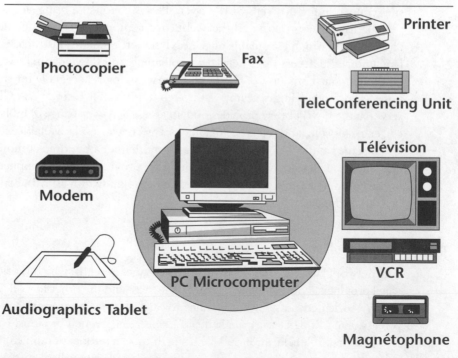

without learning centers cannot be expected to have equipment available. In these cases, a wider range of necessary equipment is being supplied. The communities are still responsible for providing the facilities. Some communities are also providing volunteers who are working in cooperation with the regional site facilitators.

This minimal buy-in from communities is considered essential. Some communities that have approached TENB to set up a site have proposed to charge rent for space and requested that TENB install all the equipment free of charge and with no obligations. All such solicitations have been refused on the assumption that the community is not yet·ready. The act of contributing signals that a community understands its need for the network and is willing to support it. Without this support, the local community site could not be sustained. A number of site installations were delayed because of the insistence on community contributions. However, no community requesting a site has refused to contribute eventually. When a community contributes, it takes responsibility for the site. When a community gets something for nothing, it does not perceive the value.

## Computer-Mediated Communications

CMC is achieved through NBNet using a 10Mb intranet connecting community college campuses, the campuses of the universities, and some high schools. Other sites connect using NBNet's SLIP server. This is conducted using simple e-mail, mailing lists, newsgroups, and the WebBoard computer-mediated conferencing environment, which is available on a TENB server. Students, instructors, and site facilitators also access the Internet for uploading and downloading assignments and other course materials. The UNB library catalog is accessible for study purposes (as are other library catalogs through the Internet gateway). A CD-ROM server at the UNB library provides student access to a wide range of bibliographical, encyclopedic, and reference databases. Internet access is available to students and teachers at the TENB sites as well as at more than a hundred community access sites in small towns and villages around the province. TENB supplied routers to the community college system to ensure high-bandwidth (10Mb) connections between campuses.

## World Wide Web Site

The network has two Web sites, one for TeleEducation NB, which is oriented toward provincial course developers and deliverers, and the other for TeleCampus, which is oriented outside the province toward distance education students and professionals. Both sites are available in English and French versions.

The first TeleEducation NB Web site (http://teleeducation.nb.ca) has been available since 1994 (see Figure 18.4). This site is used primarily by instructors and

## FIGURE 18.4. TENB WEB SITE.

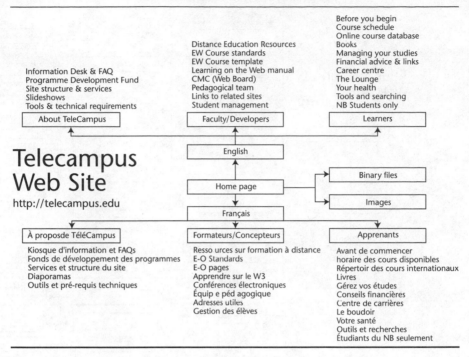

Information Desk & FAQ
Programme Development Fund
Site structure & services
Slideshows
Tools & technical requirements

**About TeleCampus**

Distance Education Resources
EW Course standards
EW Course template
Learning on the Web manual
CMC (Web Board)
Pedagogical team
Links to related sites
Student management

**Faculty/Developers**

Before you begin
Course schedule
Online course database
Books
Managing your studies
Financial advice & links
Career centre
The Lounge
Your health
Tools and searching
NB Students only

**Learners**

## Telecampus
## Web Site
http://telecampus.edu

English

Home page

Binary files

Images

Français

**À proposde TéléCampus**

Kiosque d'information et FAQs
Fonds de développement des programmes
Services et structure du site
Diaporamas
Outils et pré-requis techniques

**Formateurs/Concepteurs**

Resso urces sur formation à distance
E-O Standards
E-O pages
Apprendre sur le W3
Conférences électroniques
Équip e péd agogique
Adresses utiles
Gestion des élèves

**Apprenants**

Avant de commencer
horaire des cours disponibles
Répertoir des cours internationaux
Livres
Gérez vos études
Conseils financières
Centre de carrières
Le boudoir
Votre santé
Outils et recherches
Étudiants du NB seulement

administrators who want to find information about the network, including reports, strategic plans, community site maps, staff listings, service offerings, and audiographic course offerings within the province. There is also a database of reports and manuals as well as links to distance education resources found elsewhere, including other organizations, institutions offering courses, papers and journals on distance education, and Web course development. The site provides links to the TeleCampus. Other useful tools for instructors include a Web instructors' manual, templates for constructing courses, example online course modules, and standards guidelines.

The other Web site, TeleCampus (http://telecampus.com, shown in Figure 18.5), serves distance education students and delivering institutions by providing a student support environment. The TeleCampus site is centered on the TeleCampus Online Course Database, which is a comprehensive listing of more than twenty-eight thousand exclusively online courses. It is sponsored by Industry Canada, the Office of Learning Technologies, the World Bank, the Commonwealth of Learning, Le Centre international pour le développement de l'inforoute en français, and other organizations. The site also provides internal and external links to many different student support sites such as libraries, dictionaries,

**FIGURE 18.5. TELECAMPUS WEB SITE.**

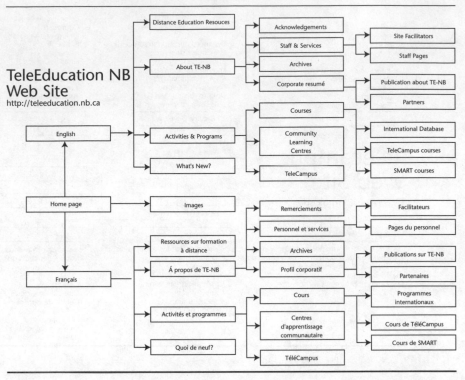

bookstores, career centers, study skills and financial information sites, and other sites of interest to students. The TeleCampus also supports computer-mediated conferencing, mailing lists, and discussion groups.

The TENB technology has been selected to be capable of supporting the growing infrastructure. The TENB Internet server farm is made up of servers used for supporting both audiographic teleconferencing and online course delivery modes. A server also hosts WebBoard, the bilingual CMC system. A third server is reserved for backups and hosting NetMeeting sessions. Other servers are used for functions such as hosting e-mail accounts for students, developing online databases, and conducting office business.

## Technical and Network Problems

Problems identified by institutional users, students, and staff include the high cost of telephone long-distance charges, the NBTel billing system, meeting the technical demands of users at short notice, and keeping the equipment in the disparate locations in good repair and up to date. Technical breakdowns, which plagued the network in the first year, became manageable in the second year. The maintenance of the Web sites is also a challenge.

The most frequently cited obstacle for institutions using the TENB network is the telephone long-distance charges (Edgett, 1995; Labour Market Analysis Branch, 1996; McGreal, 1998b, p. 252). Although the costs are reasonable for two telephone lines to anywhere in the province, the outlay still represents a significant expenditure for delivering institutions. TENB understood this and negotiated a special rate with NBTel before the start-up of the network.

NBTel charges 1.5 times the single-line rate for two telephone long distance connections, using the preferred government rate. This provides users with a discount of more than 70 percent off line charges and bridging fees. An overall payment is made by TENB on a monthly basis for the use of the bridge and lines at the different sites.

Even though these rates are quite reasonable, users still find the costs too high to maintain. TENB is continually searching for ways to reduce or eliminate this cost. Presently, a growing number of users are transmitting their audiographic data via the Internet, but voice over Internet is not yet clear or robust enough for TENB to recommend switching. TENB is monitoring Internet telephony closely. TENB is also promoting more use of asynchronous conferencing either for an entire course or to replace parts of teleconferencing courses to cut costs.

Another related cost is that of maintaining at least two telephone connections in every electronic classroom. These costs are assumed by the network and are ongoing monthly charges of approximately C$28.00 (US$18.65) per line. With up to eighty sites, monthly maintenance costs can exceed C$2,000 (US$1,320). This problem has been addressed through negotiations with NBTel. When lines are not being used, they are turned off and TENB is not charged for them.

In addition, the billing system that NBTel provides to TENB is complex. It is very difficult to determine the correct amounts to be charged back to institutional users. As TENB is benefiting from overall charges based on a network of only thirty sites, it has never been a top priority to clarify the situation. (TENB pays an amount based on the usage of only thirty of the more than eighty classrooms in the network.)

This agreement came about when NBTel realized that the success of the network was utterly dependent on low line charges to institutions. In the negotiations with NBTel, TENB stressed that it would have to install a network that worked on only one telephone line (rather than two for the present audiographic system) and limit the network to fifteen sites if the telco could not bring down the line charges. TENB proposed that it would take a risk and contract for thirty sites up front if the telco would agree to limit its pricing to an overall total based on the existence of only thirty sites. This gave TENB an incentive to increase the number of sites—and it gave NBTel a rationale for providing the discount. It was agreed that after two years, both sides would revisit the agreement and renegotiate the charges based on usage patterns. Subsequently, the two sides agreed that even with eighty sites, less than thirty were using the phone lines at any one time and that the agreement could therefore be maintained as originally negotiated.

The geographical network spreads around the province. Usually, when a group of learners in a community that does not have a TENB site wants to access a course there, they contact TENB or the institution delivering the course. Sometimes the approach is from community leaders who express an interest in joining the network. TENB negotiates an arrangement with them. These agreements differ from community to community, but generally include the community's providing space, furniture, and some equipment as well as naming a volunteer. Site facilitators in each region must then work with the technical personnel to help install equipment and telephone lines.

As new sites are added to the network, some of the old ones are removed when there is no longer a demand. For example, in one very small community (Black's Harbour, population less than 750), three students needed to take nursing courses for a specific upgrading requirement. Once this course was completed, the demand for the network fell off and the site was closed. This process of adding and removing sites occurs in most semesters in one or two locations. Usually, requests come in at the last minute, just as courses are getting under way in the busiest periods of September or January. TENB views this as a natural process and recognizes that these months are going to be hectic. Technical staff try to do their best to accommodate requests, and apart from delays of a week or sometimes two weeks, all requests are accommodated.

Every semester, faulty equipment must be repaired or replaced. Special equipment and software must be installed at specific sites for classes that request it. In addition, there is an orderly process of updating equipment by removing the oldest units and replacing them with newer models.

This process places major demands on the technicians, particularly during the start-up periods. Although they can fix most problems by talking facilitators and volunteers through the problem on the telephone, they still must travel extensively around the province to do installations and repairs, often at very short notice.

TENB had discussions with the assistant deputy minister responsible for the community college system and requested that technicians at the community college campuses be made available to help in making repairs to equipment, installing software, and ensuring robust Internet connections. This was agreed to, but further problems were encountered when community college technicians did not respond to requests in a timely fashion. Timely responses are crucial in a distance education network. Further negotiations are under way, aimed at ensuring that responses to TENB requests are a top priority for community college technicians.

When TENB first started, the equipment used was state of the art. The network was among the first created using Windows. Staff and students felt that they were using the most sophisticated technology available—and they were not mistaken. Now, although some of the equipment has been upgraded and the network runs on Windows 98, the Smart 2000 system has not been upgraded. (The company no longer supports the software.) Many staff members feel that the network is no longer on the cutting edge, and this has serious consequences for staff morale.

TENB technical and pedagogical staff continue to experiment with new delivery media and have taken a leadership position in their investigations. As mentioned earlier, TENB produced a report for Industry Canada (Gram, Mark, & McGreal, 1997), published the results of an investigation (McGreal, 1998a), and maintains a comprehensive listing of links to integrated distributed learning environments (available online at http://direwolf.teleeducation.nb.ca/distanceed/).

TENB staff do not yet feel that a robust replacement is available for Smart 2000. To date, other online products either lack the features of Smart 2000, do not work well in a multipoint environment, or are not reliable.

During the start-up period of TENB, there were serious problems with the software and the equipment. In particular, TENB technical staff had to work very closely with Smart Technologies, the company that sold the Smart 2000 audiographic software, to eliminate problems relating to the data bridge freezing, problems with software sharing at multiple locations, and other glitches. These were compounded by problems using NBTel's audio bridge and noise on the audio line during bad weather conditions. One administrator referred to this as a period "when the bridge did not work and there were many breakdowns" (McGreal, 1998b, p. 252).

Course deliverers and students were very patient. Instructors were advised to keep back-up plans, so that lessons continued with audio only when data transfer problems occurred. The inexperience of the instructors and facilitators compounded the problems. They had a great deal to learn along with their students. Administrators, students, instructors, and site facilitators all commented on the problems that occurred in the initial years. The bridge seized up regularly and telephone lines did not work, but everyone involved concurs with the student who noted, "In the past year or two, the system hasn't had any problems" (McGreal, 1998b, p. 259). This improvement in network reliability was also noted in the Program Review (Labour Market Analysis Branch, 1996).

The TENB network consists of the geographical network of sites and three distinct physical networks for voice, data, and the Internet. Every semester new instructors and students unfamiliar with the equipment, procedures, protocols, and limitations of the infrastructure must be trained and helped through their initial classes. The local site facilitator plays an important role in guiding neophytes during the introductory period, knowing when glitches can be handled locally and when to call for the help of technical personnel. There are minor problems with the overbooking of sites and the bridge at the beginning of each semester, but these are normally resolved within the first few weeks as courses are added and dropped.

Administrators complain about the long wait for a response to requests for software upgrades and hardware fixes. A staff member felt that the delay in solving some of the equipment and software glitches was the most serious technical problem. "Two weeks for the instructor and students while they are waiting is way unacceptable for a network" (McGreal, 1998b, p. 259). Site facilitators, administrators, students, and instructors also felt that TENB must ensure that the distance education system is dependable and always working when needed (per TeleEducation NB internal surveys).

The Web environment poses two significant obstacles: maintenance of robust Internet connections and maintenance and updating of the Web content on a regular basis. Until recently, the TENB servers were behind the government firewall and used a shared line with all the community colleges and the department. This line connected with the main government server, which was shared by all government departments. This caused problems when courses using shared software applications were blocked by the firewall. Real-time applications could not be used. TENB now has established its servers outside the government and departmental firewalls and is able to offer these features to users of the network. The TENB Internet specialist ensures the robustness of the servers and the connections as well as the security and integrity of the data through regular backups and offsite storage.

Updating of content is always difficult. The first TENB Web site was established in 1994 at Mt. Allison University. At that time, the site offered some basic information about TENB and distance education. As the World Wide Web grew, the site picked up useful links to other distance education organizations and reports on distance education. Now the Web is becoming a key part of the strategy of TENB, hosting the TeleCampus as an online environment for provincial course deliverers and acting as a center for marketing New Brunswick courses offered on the Web. The importance of the Web means that more attention must be paid to regular maintenance and updating of the site. This was addressed by hiring an Internet specialist and through the training of TENB personnel in how to use the Web. Contracts were awarded to companies to help in the redesign of the site.

The billing process inherited from the old department operates on three separate systems that are quite old and cannot work together. This is presently being changed to fit the processes of the new Department of Education (DOE). As of December 1998, the TENB financial officer must maintain all three links to ensure the efficient processing of bills and invoices. Now that TENB is integrated with the DOE, this system is under review and major changes are expected. TENB works within the department and government to promote the establishment of an integrated, digital billing system.

## Discussion

In summary, the network and technical infrastructure of TENB is based on computer technology using audiographics. This technology was chosen because it promotes the role of teacher as facilitator and introduces instructors to computers and multimedia. The system chosen was easy to learn and operate as well as being reasonably priced. As a result, as Figure 18.6 illustrates, there has been significant growth in the numbers of students, teachers, and administrators who are comfortable using computers in a distance education environment.

The willingness of different institutions to collaborate and share each other's facilities in a provincewide network is a major contributor to the success of TENB. Different universities, community colleges, and private sector businesses

**FIGURE 18.6. TeleEDUCATION IN NB GROWTH, 1993–1999.**

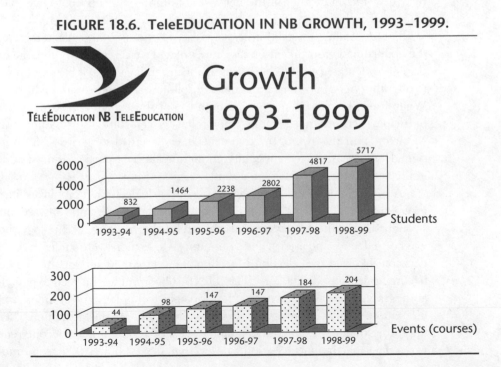

mutually share resources that TENB and its partners make available. In addition, these entities offer complementary rather than competing courses. They have also made progress in mutually accepting credits earned by students participating in the distance education endeavor regardless of which institution granted them. This credit acceptance includes courses delivered by some community colleges and all universities in the Atlantic region (Newfoundland, Prince Edward Island, New Brunswick, and Nova Scotia).

This willingness to collaborate extends to the communities with TENB sites. All these communities provide space and furniture, make available computer and office equipment, and provide software and services. This active support demonstrates the extent to which the community endorses the TENB network.

TENB quickly established convenient access to courses in every corner of New Brunswick. TENB established a very tight and self-imposed deadline for establishing the first distance education sites, within months of hiring the first staff and site facilitators. New sites were established as quickly as possible thereafter, and a critical mass of sites became available to institutions and students. The ubiquity of the network is a major factor in the success of the initiative. Because sites are available within a short drive for anyone in the province, there are few obstacles to participation. Courses normally need a minimum of ten to fifteen students to provide cost recovery. The more sites in the network, the more students could take part in courses, thereby making TENB a viable entity.

Paradoxically, the establishment of extra classrooms in larger centers increases the opportunities for students in the more isolated rural regions. With large numbers of students accessing a course at major urban locations, it becomes possible to offer the course. Without a minimum enrollment, the course cannot be offered. When it can be offered, the smaller numbers of students in rural areas can also participate. For example, a course might have seven students in Bathurst, six in Moncton, and only two or three students in each of two rural sites. TENB is designed for increasing access in small communities, and the participation of students at the larger urban centers is an essential success factor.

A key technological success factor was the early decision to not invest heavily in video teleconferencing equipment, computer hardware, and software, but to strongly support the development of content. Furthermore, the technology chosen was cost-effective and used in any community where there were students. Another decision involved the selection of technology that would support instructors in becoming learning facilitators. The TENB subcommittee on technology chose audiographic teleconferencing as the principal technology in the initial implementation. Besides its pedagogical function in promoting the facilitation of learning rather than the lecture model, the low cost of audiographic teleconferencing was a major factor in its selection. For less than C$1,500 (US$990), communities were equipped with tools for delivering and receiving courses. In addition, since each audiographics site can deliver and receive courses, instructors can teach at any participating site. This flexibility allowed for a democratic network. Teachers from small communities could participate on the same basis as those in larger centers. Audiographic teleconferencing is simple and reliable, and it supports synchronous learning, which is based on the creation of a common meeting time to create a community of learners, paced by the instructor.

The success of the audiographics network also depended on the negotiation of a contract with the local telco for low long distance charges. TENB was only able to move forward with an advanced audiographics system because of the special arrangement with NBTel that substantially reduced long distance costs of using two telephone lines.

Today, institutions are using audiographics over IP on the Internet or on the community college intranet for the data connections. Telephone lines are used for data connections only with particularly isolated communities that have unreliable Internet access. There are few of these now and TENB expects every community in the province to be able to transmit and receive data over IP this year.

The principal problem preventing the audiographic network from going over completely to IP is the low quality of multipoint voice connections. Point-to-point voice over IP connections seem to have adequate quality, and some deliverers are satisfied users, particularly those using the community college intranet. However, once multiple sites are added the voice quality deteriorates and is not yet acceptable. Another technical problem is enhancing the microphones and audio speakers so a group of learners can communicate using one computer.

TENB upgrades part of the network hardware every year, rather than all at once. This gradual approach to introducing new equipment and phasing out older equipment keeps the network up to date. For example, in 1995, twenty-five new 66MHz Pentium workstations replaced older 486 PCs in one-third of the electronic classrooms. In 1997, 133 MHz PCs were put in a third of the classrooms. In 1999, twenty-five electronic classrooms received 300MHz Pentium PCs.

Another key technology and human success factor is the simple act of informing instructors and students of the potential for logistical and technical glitches. When students expect glitches and they happen, they are prepared and patient. Instructors are advised to always have a backup plan in case of technical problems.

A typical backup plan for teachers is to ensure that audiographic slides are available on the computer and in print form at the different sites. That way, if there is a data communications problem, the students can still access the images and follow a discussion or lecture. Plans might also include reference to a Web site where lectures and discussions are stored in text, audio, or video formats.

## Conclusion

In conclusion, the experience gained with the integration of technology into the TENB network points to the following recommendations for those working in similar distributed learning networks:

- Implement the project, even if you do not fully understand what is happening or if you are still not in possession of all the facts. Just do it.
- Be nonthreatening if possible and work within existing structures. When TENB was created, participating partners insisted that it be noncompetitive with existing institutions.
- Be neutral—and be perceived as being neutral. The trust built up by TENB is considered a principal asset. TENB is accepted by educators, administrators, and practitioners as a neutral agency that does not play favorites.
- Collaborate and share costs with others. TENB is built on the principle of sharing with participants. All institutions share one network. Communities participate in collaboration with other communities and with TENB.
- Ensure that communities and institutions buy in to the network. When institutions provide services and space or pay part of the costs, they become committed.
- Move quickly in establishing sites to open access to users.
- Establish a critical mass of sites. The viability of courses depends on the participation of a minimum number of students. With more sites, more potential students can access courses.
- Include larger centers. The greater number of students available in the larger centers makes course delivery to rural sites cost-effective and therefore viable.
- Choose technology based on pedagogical considerations but also consider price, ease of use, and other features.
- Take an incremental approach to purchasing hardware and software. If you buy everything at once, all components will become outdated at the same time, making another large purchase necessary. If you buy in stages, then as the oldest equipment becomes outdated, you can buy newer equipment to replace it.
- Avoid using the very latest technology. For pedagogical purposes, the bleeding edge can be disastrous. Use a technology that has been tested and achieved some maturity.
- Keep delivery and development costs down so that institutions and students can afford to participate.

CHAPTER NINETEEN

# FROM TRAINING ENHANCEMENT TO ORGANIZATIONAL LEARNING

## The Migration of Distance Learning at the American Red Cross

Nadine E. Rogers, Sandra L. Becker

Efforts to bring the American Red Cross into alignment with current training technologies have been successful. For this large organization, distance learning has come to rely on two technologies: interactive satellite-based television courses (teletraining) and Internet-based learning (online learning). American Red Cross units can now link up and participate in roundtable discussions, town hall meetings, and training courses from anywhere across the business television network via a television set. A personal computer and Internet connection are all that are needed to access career development tools, courses, and discussion forums. This chapter describes the evolution of distance learning at the American Red Cross from initial attempts to enhance training to its current position as an essential strategy for achieving organizational results.

## Background and Context

American Red Cross workers are a sociable collective. They enjoy the camaraderie of getting together. Training events provide some of the best opportunities to get to know each other. One may argue that the social nature of the American Red Cross workforce is connected closely to the team nature of disaster relief and community-based service efforts. The implementation of satellite-based, keypad-enhanced courses interfered with this culture in an unexpected way. With two-way audio and one-way video, we were suddenly pushing the workforce toward "virtual socialization." Although American Red Cross workers have become more comfortable with this way of learning, it did not happen as quickly as we wanted it to.

Moreover, American Red Cross workers began to ask, "How will this help me meet my unit's goals?" If they could not readily see the connection, they surmised that they did not need the course. The emphasis was not on learning for individual and organizational growth, but rather on completing the training requirements to perform specific tasks. Moving American Red Cross workers along a continuum toward self-directed learning proved challenging but not impossible. Additionally, it required the Red Cross to be more purposeful and strategic about how this was made to happen. At the Red Cross, we needed to make clear links between organizational goals and learning opportunities and we needed to deemphasize the technology and focus on learning. For example, during the early design stages of one telecourse, we convened an advisory council of stakeholders and members of the target audience. The advisory council then determined the bottom-line business goal driving the course and derived course objectives and content that were directly tied to the bottom line. This approach placed less initial emphasis on the technology and focused on business needs.

Additionally, it was clear that the social culture of the American Red Cross would require that we provide a variety of approaches to learning that included technology-based, self-paced, and face-to-face delivery methods. Currently, we are offering courses via a combination of Internet, intranet, and interactive television as well as more traditional delivery mechanisms. This chapter describes the process, including the difficulties, of how we got from where we were to where we are today.

## Business Problem Statement

The American Red Cross needed a way to distribute learning opportunities across a wide network of paid and volunteer staff. The strategy for making this happen had to encompass the organization's mission, vision, and several business goals that were identified as critical to continued organizational success. The American Red Cross mission is essentially, "to provide relief to victims of disasters and help people prevent, prepare for, and respond to emergencies," while its vision is to be, "always there, touching more lives, in new ways, under the same trusted symbol." Due to the highly social nature of the American Red Cross workforce, the distance learning strategy—while intended to support change—still had to fit into the existing culture. In addition to the learners' need for interaction and socialization, the American Red Cross faced issues at the learner, unit, and organizational levels.

*Learner-Level Issues.* As with those in other organizations, American Red Cross workers have varying learning needs and learning styles. Traditionally, the focus on education at the American Red Cross has been instructor-led skills training. As such, the target audience was not all at the same point along the learning continuum. In a recent article, self-directed learners were described as those "who identify, assess, and select appropriate learning resources; are able to identify criteria for assessing learning; critically question information and circumstances of rules and procedures; [and] adjust the circumstances of learning experience to maximize learning potential" (Confessore & Kops, 1998, p. 367). Some American Red Cross workers—closer to this description—were ready to be self-starters, others needed guidance. Therefore, the strategy had to ensure the greatest possible learning success for all learners.

*Unit-Level Issues.* The long-term strategy for distance learning at the American Red Cross had to account for varying levels of technological capability at American Red Cross units. Although some larger units were readily able to purchase the keypad responders and satellite technology or install networked computers, some smaller units remained at a disadvantage. It is possible that the initial cost-recovery strategy, which required units to buy keypad responders, served as a barrier to the ready adoption of the technology.

The American Red Cross is essentially a crisis-response organization. We promise that when disaster strikes, we'll be there. Consequently, American Red Cross workers are time-challenged and are always responding to the community's needs. Additionally, some American Red Cross units operate twenty-four hours a day, seven days a week, which results in shift schedules. Learning opportunities have to be modular, just-in-time, and highly relevant to compete with fundraising, blood collection, disaster-response, and community activities. The just-in-time approach to learning ensures that information and knowledge resources are available to learners at a time and place that is convenient to them—this approach is very much the direction of the twenty-first century (Christensen & Cowley-Durst, 1998).

Initially, the American Red Cross attempted to use the satellite-based delivery mechanism for global training messages such as diversity. However, we realized that with limited time, staff only wished to participate in learning opportunities with an immediate impact on their ability to do their job. Consequently, we changed our strategy to address field operations issues such as market analysis, volunteer and staff recruitment, and time management. Finally, the American Red Cross strategy for the successful maintenance of distance learning also addressed elements of the organization's culture such as the value of learning, individual career design and management, and the role of leadership. In response to this need, we built messages about learning, continuous development, and leadership into the course content. We determined that change was in part tied to consistent yet subtle messages. For instance, in a course about volunteer and staff recruitment, we addressed the issue of encouraging internal staff to develop knowledge and skills in areas of organizational need.

## Population Targeted and Served

The business of the American Red Cross is saving lives. This business is achieved through the work of several lines of services including Biomedical Services, Disaster Services, and Health, Safety, and Community Services. The range of work assignments involves a variety of professions such as nurses, medical technicians, emergency response professionals, community organizers, health educators, and fundraisers. Consequently, the American Red Cross workforce includes a very broad spectrum of occupations, for both paid and volunteer staff.

The initial implementation of distance learning at the American Red Cross was in Biomedical Services, where blood and tissue products are collected, tested, processed, and distributed. Distance learning efforts began with interactive television. Due to the nature of the work in Biomedical Services and the need for precision, learning events were targeted at a variety of populations based on the business need. The result was unwittingly egalitarian and exposure to distance learning was not based so much on rank as function. For example, courses were tied to the Blood Services Directives that guide and ensure quality in the blood manufacturing process, and learners registered for class based on their technical role in the manufacturing process. Tying the course offerings to bottom-line business needs (particularly in a regulated environment) ensured that interactive television quickly became an essential element of the learning continuum in Biomedical Services.

After two years of delivering satellite-based training in Biomedical Services, a strategy for expanding distance learning to the entire Red Cross was needed. The broader implementation of distance learning at the American Red Cross had to be much more specific and targeted than in Biomedical Services to be successful. The size of the population as a whole (1.3 million volunteers and 33,000 paid employees) and some of the driving business needs such as financial stewardship and market analysis indicated that the initial focus of the broader implementation should be on managers and supervisors. However, managerial schedules and the nonmandatory nature of the courses influenced the number of participants that attended these initial satellite-based offerings. American Red Cross chapters have a franchise-like relationship with the national headquarters and are not required to attend all the learning opportunities offered to them. In Biomedical Services, because of the regulatory nature of the subject matter, certain training courses were mandated. In chapters, there is no legal requirement for training. Consequently, we had to focus on promoting the courses and the value that they added rather than requiring attendance as we did in Biomedical Services. Over time and with the implementation of online learning via The Learning Community, the population served is broadening beyond managers and executives to all who want the opportunity to learn.

## Outcomes Desired

Continuous learning is central to the future of the American Red Cross. Our vision and business goals—which at the time were growth, innovation, learning, and employee satisfaction—are evidence of the organization's commitment and belief that a focus on learning will result in significant organizational performance gains.

How does distance education fit in the organization's strategy as the American Red Cross prepares for the year 2000 and beyond? In part, our strategy and focus has shifted from training technology to learning and performance—where technology has become a means to an end rather than the end itself. In fact, at the American Red Cross, satellite-based training and online learning are not referred to as *distance learning* per se; rather they are considered part of the larger menu of learning opportunities.

With all learning solutions including those delivered via technology or other delivery strategies, our desired outcome is improved performance in support of the organization's goals. With technology, we are seeking growth and the ability to touch more lives in new ways. To achieve this growth, the American Red Cross has several goals to leverage technology for the year 2000 and beyond. Our goals include working to

- Provide access to learning opportunities to the entire American Red Cross.
- Evaluate the transfer of learning to the job, and ultimately, measure increases in performance.
- Create a broad-based curriculum of learning opportunities so that learners can customize and build individual learning and development plans.
- Expand our online capability to include more informal learning opportunities in addition to courses.
- Increase learner involvement in creating technology-based learning opportunities.

How will we achieve these goals? By seeking ways to

- Integrate complementary technologies.
- Outsource generic skills-based training.
- Develop customized learning solutions to meet business needs.
- Involve employees and volunteers in creating learning opportunities.
- Ensure that supporting performance systems complement learning solutions.

Success in achieving all these goals depends on continual investment in technology, but equally important are effective management systems and processes and organizational commitment. The development of technology capability within an organization takes time, resources, and sustained effort. In the next section, we describe how the American Red Cross has developed significant organizational capability to deliver technology-based learning to achieve its organizational goals.

## Development of Technology Capability at the American Red Cross

The development of technology capability for distance learning is not an overnight process. During the past several years, the American Red Cross investment in distance learning has resulted in the growth of organization capability, moving from individual programs to systems that support ongoing delivery of distance learning opportunities and toward strategically aligned distance learning.

Using Schreiber's Stages of Organizational Technology Capability for Distance Learning (1998b), we would position the American Red Cross as moving from Stage 3 toward Stage 4. If we examined different technologies individually, we might find that they are at different places along a continuum. Specifically, systems supporting interactive satellite-based training have been in place longer than Internet- and intranet-based learning at the American Red Cross. However, steps have certainly been taken to propel us beyond the dissemination of a policy and move us toward institutionalizing distance learning. Interactive teletraining is now being used to train new chapter board members; Health, Safety, and Community Services is now committed to using interactive teletraining to support new product roll-outs; and the Internet and intranet approach is being used for course delivery, distribution of course materials, and ongoing instructor support.

The evolution of technology-based learning at the American Red Cross has taken several years. Through this transition, the American Red Cross has shifted its focus from individual projects and programs to a more strategic focus, leveraging technology to achieve organizational results. In terms of programmatic implementation, there are systems in place for instructor training, participant materials distribution, marketing programs, and evaluating programs. The bridge to a more strategic focus is apparent in budgeting, infrastructure, staffing, and policy decisions. Today, innovation and learning are key to our organizational strategy. This shift correlates with the progression of the American Red Cross through various stages of organizational technology capability over a five-year period. Table 19.1 highlights key organizational policies, the distance learning focus, capacity-building strategies, and the programming for each year of the five-year transition period.

## Year 1: Initial Organizational Commitment to Leverage Technology

During this first year, the acting president of the American Red Cross, Gene Dyson, issued a technology policy memo that outlined a plan for the technological advancement of the entire organization. The memorandum contained a proposed timeline for rolling out technology in incremental phases. By the summer of 1995, the American Red Cross launched its first interactive teletraining program, a new employee orientation program for Biomedical Services employees. The American Red Cross first established its business television network in 1989. The addition of interactive keypad technology was part of a strategy to take advantage of the existing business television network for learning.

Subsequent teletraining programs employed the interactive keypad technology at all Biomedical Services downlink sites (approximately sixty sites, roughly half of the American Red Cross TV network of downlink sites). The existence of experienced American Red Cross television and video professionals, including site coordinators at every downlink site, and the American Red Cross studio, network, and other infrastructure made the transition to interactive satellite-based learning much simpler for the American Red Cross than many other organizations have found the process. However, the organization had much to learn in terms of overall effective distance learning. Continued delivery of distance learning programs required systems, processes, and shorter life cycles. We had to learn how to design and deliver for this medium at the same time that we were required to produce viable courses. To do this, the Red Cross formed highly skilled work teams with the authors as team leads. The teams shared lessons learned on a routine basis and functioned in a truly democratic way. As a result, team members with technical skills and instructional design skills all had a voice in the project planning and the course design and development. This strategy ensured that every team member knew what the course was intended to achieve and what their own contribution meant for its success. While we made some mistakes, this team approach to design and implementation ensured that mistakes were caught early and their impact minimized.

**TABLE 19.1. EVOLUTION OF DISTANCE LEARNING AT THE AMERICAN RED CROSS.**

| | Year 1 (1995) | Year 2 (1996) | Year 3 (1997) | Year 4 (1998) | Year 5 (1999) |
|---|---|---|---|---|---|
| Policy and Organizational Strategy Level | Acting Red Cross president issued a policy memo, outlining a plan for technological advancement organization-wide. | Cross-functional team prepared a proposal, *Recommendations for Using Technology to Enhance Training and Education at the American Red Cross.* | Senior leadership approved four areas of strategic focus, including learning and innovation. Red Cross COO introduced *The Learning Initiative* in an ARC-TV broadcast. This includes mandate to invest 2 percent of budget in learning. New corporate training department established. Interactive keypad technology introduced organization-wide. | Corporate Services aligned to enhance cross-functionality (training and intranet). Corporate training department created strategic business plan to link learning to organizational strategic goals. | Corporate training department reorganized in support of business plan. New team dedicated to technology and research established within the training department. |
| Distance Learning Focus | Interactive, satellite-based teletraining for Biomedical Services. | Interactive, satellite-based teletraining for Biomedical Services. | Interactive satellite-based teletraining *organization-wide.* | Interactive satellite-based teletraining organization-wide; The Learning Community created on the intranet. | Leveraged the most appropriate technologies to achieve organizational goals—including ARC-TV, intranet, and Internet. |

| | | | | | |
|---|---|---|---|---|---|
| Systems, Processes, and Strategies to Build Distance Learning Capacity | Existing Red Cross business television network leveraged. Training on designing interactive distance learning (IDL) delivered for Biomedical Training staff. | Communication, marketing, and distribution systems in place for tele-courses. First series of technical training tele-courses delivered. | Training on designing interactive distance learning delivered to a cross-functional group from across the organization. Instructor training course developed and delivered. | Communication, marketing, and distribution systems move to the intranet and e-mail. Ongoing instructor training. IDL process becomes standardized. "Early adopters" support new learning opportunities database on The Learning Community. Regular ARC-TV programming using ARC-designed and third-party programs. The Learning Community site used mostly as an information source. | Published *Interactive Distance Learning Process Guide*, containing standards, templates, and tools. Training department develops in-house capability to design and code Web sites. |
| Programs and Learning Opportunities | First interactive teletraining programs delivered. | First ARC-TV management training program. | First organization-wide teletraining courses planned for ARC-TV. | | Continued program, including third-party programming. First offering of third-party online courses. First Learning Community online forum for leaders. |

## Year 2: Leveraging Technology for Learning

Shortly after the presidential memorandum was issued, a cross-functional team of training and technology professionals began working on a proposal to take advantage of technology as a training delivery mechanism across the organization. The proposal included two primary strategies, one to use the existing interactive satellite-based television network and a second strategy to launch Internet-based training.

The second year saw the successful implementation of teletraining with keypad technology in the Biomedical Services (for a full discussion, see Klueter & Kalweit, 1998). During this year, various programs were delivered using the interactive satellite network, including the first series of related technical training programs and the first program targeted toward American Red Cross management. Additionally, systems for communication, marketing, and distribution of materials were put in place to support interactive distance learning programs via the TV network. See Exhibit 19.1 for a sample program bulletin. Supporting materials and job aids were designed to assist learners in using the technology. All of the programs delivered via ARC-TV were evaluated.

Up to this point, intranet technology was being developed within the organization. However, lack of standardization of the technology and lack of internal capability to design and deliver online learning were barriers to moving ahead more quickly with the strategy for online learning. The need for more flexible learning to meet the needs of diverse American Red Cross populations ultimately led to the development of The Learning Community in year 3.

## Year 3: Strategic Focus, Investment on Learning, and Transition

Year 3 marked the beginning of the shift in the focus on distance learning as an organizational strategy. Success with teletraining over the preceding year resulted in the organization's investment in interactive keypad technology to support the business television network beyond the Biomedical Services sites. The expansion of the interactive keypad system to the broader network marked an essential transition point for the American Red Cross.

The investment in technology coincided with the introduction of several organizational goals, which included continuous learning and innovation. In support of the continuous learning focus, the American Red Cross introduced The Learning Initiative. This initiative marked the first time the organization had proposed a minimum level of investment in learning for all units (that is, 2 percent of the unit's compensation budget).

## EXHIBIT 19.1. SAMPLE PROGRAM BULLETIN.

### *PROGRAM BULLETIN*

Thursday, Friday                                                     One Touch Broadcasts
November 14 &15

## CHARLES DREW BIOMEDICAL INSTITUTE
**Advanced Deviations Training**

| | | | |
|---|---|---|---|
| Nov. 14 | North Central, South Central, and Western Areas | 12:00 PM–3:00 PM ET<br>ARC Receiver/IRD: Channel 21 | Program #559 |
| | North Atlantic, Southeast, North Central, South Central, and Western Areas | 5:00 PM–8:30 PM ET<br>ARC Receiver/IRD: Channel 11 | Program #560 |
| Nov. 15 | North Atlantic, Southeast Areas and National Headquarters | 9:00 AM–12:00 PM ET<br>ARC Receiver/IRD: Channel 11 | Program #561 |
| | All NTL's | 1:00 PM–4:00 PM ET<br>ARC Receiver/IRD: Channel 21 | Program #562 |

Ku-Band: Galaxy 4                     Network: BioLink                     Encrypted: **YES**

**For complete breakdown of satellite time (listed above) and other pre- and post activities, refer to** *Administrative Guide.*

Who Should Watch: Biomedical staff responsible for leading activities throughout the deviations management process.

**Advanced Deviations Training** has been designed to provide ARCBS personnel with additional tools and techniques for handling investigational deviations, and developing effective preventive actions. Because of the significant competitive edge afforded our viewers, this broadcast or any taped version must be restricted to ARCBS personnel.

The host instructors for the teleclass are Area Training and Education Directors, Louise Eisenbrey and Deb Brown, who are accomplished trainers in the ARCBS system, have sound knowledge of the deviations process, and are experienced in problem-solving methods.

Barbee Whitaker, QAO National Headquarters Quality Assurance will also be available to help debrief difficult questions and clarify any areas of confusion. She has presented the current revision of BSD92.103T, **Deviations,** to the FDA, Area Vice-Presidents, and end-users in the field.

## THESE PROGRAMS ARE INTENDED FOR RED CROSS INTERNAL USE AT BIOMEDICAL ONE TOUCH LOCATIONS, AND VIEWING SHOULD BE LIMITED TO ARCBS STAFF.

The initiative also coincided with the creation of a new Corporate Education and Training division dedicated to serving departments and units organization-wide with a mandate to leverage technology. To support organization-wide distance learning efforts, the authors transferred from the Biomedical Services training division to the newly formed Corporate Education and Training as part of the expansion. Over the course of the next several months, other technical and support staff migrated from Biomedical Services to Corporate Education and Training. The reconnecting of this highly competent team facilitated the rapid deployment of interactive teletraining.

The first organization-wide teletraining courses were planned for delivery via ARC-TV. In addition, Biomedical Services continued to offer targeted technical training courses and expanded the viewing audience to include American Red Cross customers and partners when appropriate.

The newly formed Corporate Education and Training led the effort to expand the organization's capability to design and deliver interactive distance learning via satellite. Instructional designers, training developers, and managers from throughout the organization were trained in the unique considerations for this medium by experts in designing instructional programs for satellite-based delivery. A separate training program to prepare instructors for satellite-based training delivery was created and taught by Corporate Education and Training instructors. To accelerate the expansion, Corporate Education and Training aligned with renowned industry experts in interactive teletraining and Web-based delivery. We codesigned and cotaught with these experts, thereby increasing our velocity and quality, and reducing our time to delivery.

## Year 4: Expanding Technology Capability and Planning Strategically

During year 4, Corporate Education and Training focused much of its human and financial resources on delivering regular programming via ARC-TV to help sell the new way of learning to American Red Cross chapters. Even though we were into our fourth year of the distance learning initiative, the need to convince stakeholders and potential learners of the value of this approach to learning was still strong. Prospecting for supporters and selling distance learning remained a major element of the expansion effort. The staff of Corporate Education and Training designed, delivered, and supported nine teletraining courses on a variety of management topics. To complement American Red Cross–designed programming, Corporate Education and Training spearheaded the broadcasting of a series of third-party management programs, also on basic management topics.

To build organizational capacity, experienced interactive distance learning program managers and technical experts consulted with other American Red Cross units to deliver additional programming. Partnerships were formed with Human Resources, Diversity, Disaster Services, and Health, Safety, and Community Services to provide design support and coaching of designers and instructors. Instructor training was regularly offered to expand the number of skilled ARC-TV instructors. Partnering with other units helped build sponsorship for the initiative and increase usage of the technology. Work accomplished in this year formed the foundation for the templates, project management tools, and work samples that were published at the start of year 5.

In addition to using ARC-TV, Corporate Education and Training launched The Learning Community—a section of the American Red Cross intranet dedicated to learning. The initial site served primarily as an information resource. A key section of The Learning Community dedicated to business and management skills also went live that year. This portion of The Learning Community contains an online database of internal and external learning opportunities linked to competencies. Critical to the success of this site was the involvement of "early adopters" who assisted in the review and creation of the business management site.

A second component of The Learning Community was an online magazine, *Community Voices,* dedicated to learning, leading, and working in the American Red Cross. The stories and themes of the magazine addressed key organizational issues and the changing perspective of learning. In fact, one column was dedicated to "learning how to learn."

This year also marked the integration of technologies. Old paper-based systems for the communication, marketing, and distribution of materials for ARC-TV were replaced with online postings, e-mail, and automated fax systems. Special articles in *Community Voices* were published online to correspond with ARC-TV broadcasts. Corresponding vendor training courses, books, and articles were included in the business management site and linked to online promotions of ARC-TV programs.

The successes in interactive distance learning via ARC-TV and the launch of The Learning Community were impressive, but perhaps the most important work accomplished by the Corporate Education and Training division was the creation of a strategic business plan to link learning to organizational strategy. It is difficult to comprehend that all this work was done without a formalized business plan. However, the demand for rapid implementation of distance learning kept all resources thoroughly committed for quite some time. Additionally, the business plan that eventually emerged was a reflection of the collective experience gained during the implementation period.

## Year 5: Linking Learning to Organizational Strategy

The year 1999–2000, year 5, marks the year of greatest change. During this year, there was a shift from training technology to learning linked to organizational results. Corporate Education and Training has reorganized in support of the division's strategic business plan. The newly organized unit has dedicated internal consultants responsible for identifying learning and development needs based on organizational goals and strategic initiatives. Additionally, a new team within the department is dedicated to technology and research, as well as evaluating the results of learning.

Continued programming via ARC-TV is on the schedule for this year. For example, teletraining such as the Chapter Board Orientation orients new chapter board members on their roles and responsibilities and provides an unprecedented opportunity for volunteers to share best practices across the chapter network. Additionally, other customized interactive teletraining courses are slated with an eye to meeting the specific business needs of the lines of service.

Corporate Education and Training is in the pilot test phase of a new online learning curriculum. The audience for the online learning pilot test is 250 manager-level paid and volunteer staff. This strategy again applies the concept of early adopters—who are present in encouraging numbers; within several business days of posting the opportunity to participate, we had all 250 slots filled.

# Management Processes

The evolution of distance learning at the American Cross reveals key shifts in organizational policy and structure, distance learning focus, and distance learning capacity. Ultimately, as illustrated in Table 19.1, these shifts have resulted in the progression from isolated distance training programs to strategically focused learning opportunities employing complementary technologies. The transition was dependent upon the development of systems and processes, as well as strategic focus and commitment to change the learning culture of the organization.

## Systems and Processes

In the process of planning and delivering these programs, we began to develop templates, processes, and ultimately systems to enhance the quality and reduce the cycle time of each product. These include project management tools, instructor training, participant materials, program marketing, and program evaluation.

## Strategic Focus and Commitment to Change

The development of technology capability at the American Red Cross is marked by several strategic decisions, as well as changes in the way the organization operates. Key strategic decisions included the initial memo to leverage technology from the president's office, the proposal to employ technology for learning, the creation of a new corporate training program with a designated budget and a mandate to deliver distance learning programs, and the Corporate Education and Training strategic business plan designed to ensure that all learning initiatives—whether delivered via technology or face to face—are aligned with strategic initiatives and produce measurable results.

A critical part of the shift from programmatic focus to strategic focus involved positioning distance learning activities within a longer-term strategy and using complementary technologies to provide multiple ways of accessing information. We are moving away from holding one-time events. For example, as part of an organizational initiative to foster innovation, a multi-session conference was held in Wilmington, Delaware; a section of the intranet was dedicated to best practices; an issue of the online magazine *Community Voices* was dedicated to innovation; resources on innovation were added to the online database on The Learning Community; and an interactive distance learning broadcast was delivered. More informal learning has been encouraged to support innovation and other initiatives through the creation of online discussion forums. The innovation initiative required cross-functional collaboration—a second critical aspect necessary for building distance learning capacity.

Schreiber writes that successful distance learning efforts require that "traditional corporate hierarchy evolve into a more flexible institution that facilitates teamwork, collaboration with business partners, and distributed decision-making" (Schreiber, 1998b, p. 11). Clearly, at the American Red Cross, these strategic decisions and initiatives alone could not singularly effect the change in culture and the way of operating required for successful implementation of distance learning.

The first partnership was formed when a cross-functional team of training and technology professionals collaborated to create the proposal to leverage technology for learning. As the need for and value of distance learning has grown, dedicated positions have been created across the entire organization, forming a decentralized but interdependent network of distance learning and technology

professionals. Additionally, the American Red Cross has formed external partnerships with distance learning experts and vendors to build the overall organizational capacity to deliver distance learning.

Finally, the efforts around the launch of The Learning Community illustrate
the importance of recognizing that successful distance learning requires a partnership with participants and end users as well. Much of the success of The Learning Community and online learning can be attributed to the involvement of early
adopters in the development and evaluation of various distance learning strategies.
Involvement of early adopters was critical at both the information-only phase and
after we began to deliver learning opportunities via online technology. Working
with early adopters made it possible for Corporate Education and Training to
complete and evaluate a pilot test of online curriculum in the area of business
management. The audience for this pilot test was staff at the entry-level management and mid-management levels. Pilot participants were recruited voluntarily
from all over the organization.

## Outcomes Attained

The fusion of distance learning technologies with strategic initiatives has been successful at the American Red Cross, and we've learned some important lessons
along the way.

### Successes

American Red Cross workers are beginning to embrace technology-based learning and are actively applying it to such business problems as ethics, diversity, nursing, health, safety, community services, and disaster services. Communities are
beginning to take shape at the American Red Cross that cross organizational, hierarchical, and geographical boundaries. American Red Cross workers are now
coming together for learning around critical subject matter versus the function-
driven approach of the past.

Corporate Education and Training has been able to deliver a variety of
needed learning opportunities that is closely aligned with the mission and direction
of the organization. Continued growth is occurring as the American Red Cross
moves to offer new types of products and services, including community health
education using distance learning technologies.

## Lessons Learned

Of course, there are some challenges associated with this kind of change effort. During this five-year period, we learned some lessons that are critical to the current strategic thrust. For instance, the sluggish adoption of the keypad technology led us to work first with the early adopters when launching the intranet site. In addition, the cost and time sensitivity of building the internal teletraining design capacity led us to work with vendor-developed materials when pilot testing online learning.

The desired speed with which the organization hoped to ramp up the initiative threatened some fundamental instructional design tenets. Without time for a thorough needs analysis, we attempted to offer generic, one-size-fits-all learning opportunities. In some instances, this approach caused us to miss the mark. In the process, we tarnished our credibility by coupling new technology with new curriculum. A more strategic approach might have been to repurpose some existing mission-critical courses to avoid simultaneous experimentation with content and medium.

The organizational decision that required chapters to pay for the necessary hardware turned out to be counterproductive. While the underlying strategy was based on the idea that chapters would value the system more if they had an actual stake in it, this approach had the opposite effect. Chapters already on a tight budget could not make educational technology a priority without some clear indicators of success. It might well have been more effective to convert several instructor-led courses to distance learning and show chapters how they could save time and money before asking them to invest in the system. Essentially, we needed to give the technology away in order to ensure a smoother initiation.

Another critical lesson learned was that once we generated a need for distance learning among American Red Cross workers, we did not have the internal infrastructure to keep pace with the demand. While we successfully ramped up designers, instructors, and technical support, the cost of internal development soon outweighed its value. In addition, the cycle time was too slow. The strategy employed with The Learning Community, which used vendor-produced materials for the pilot test, has allowed a faster delivery of ready materials and has enabled us to focus on learner needs.

In the final analysis, as a not-for-profit organization, the American Red Cross is challenged by learner availability and cost considerations. We need learning initiatives to work on their first attempt and in record time. As we learn more about how a learning organization can be supported by distance learning technologies, we are becoming smarter about our strategic approach. As educators across the organization gain greater credibility for the early success of our distance learning efforts, we are being engaged earlier in the process and allowed to make more strategic decisions. We can expect that further advances in distance learning will emerge from our ability to guide educational strategy.

## Discussion

To sustain a distance learning initiative in a large nonprofit organization requires considerable planning and mobilization of resources. Always conscious of the way donated funds are used, the American Red Cross cannot take innovation for granted. It is important for us that initiatives are carefully assessed for feasibility, planned, executed, and monitored to ensure that our investments are solid. The distance learning effort has become integral to the organization's strategic plan. Learning opportunities that focus on much-needed skill areas such as project management, market analysis, finance and accounting, grant writing, and customer service directly support the transformation of the American Red Cross workforce into one that is ready to meet the challenges of the new millennium.

Distance learning technology at the American Red Cross is enabling self-directed career assessment and planning. Learners can now download career assessment and planning tools from The Learning Community and then determine the appropriate training and learning opportunities to help them meet their goals. Although still a leader among the businesses of the heart, the American Red Cross faces many business challenges similar to our counterparts in the for-profit world. Change is certain and American Red Cross workers need to be able to retool and redirect their career activities easily and smoothly.

The connection between growth and innovation is critical to the American Red Cross, because we need to create solutions to urgent business problems and to distinguish our products and services from those of other providers. Distance learning is emerging as a significant tool for enabling discussions, sharing sessions, and delivering coursework on innovation. Nationally recognized leaders in the field of innovation have become easily accessible to the entire American Red Cross network because of distance learning technologies. Additionally, learning opportunities that highlight successful American Red Cross units as they share how innovation has improved their operations are available both by teletraining and by intranet.

The bottom line seems to be that the long-term survival of distance learning efforts hinges on how quickly and how well they are integrated into the organization's overall strategic plan. At the American Red Cross, mapping out a plan for implementing and maintaining a distance learning program involved the highest level of leadership. This involvement immediately gave the program visibility and sponsorship. While keeping leadership involved has been challenging at times, we continue to benefit from executive input and support. As we progress toward Stage 4 of Schreiber's model (institutionalization of distance learning), our greatest challenge will be how to assess the transfer of learning and its impact on organizational performance.

PART FIVE

# SUMMARY

CHAPTER TWENTY

---

# TOOLS FOR CHANGE

---

## Linking the Organizational Perspective with Distance Training and Education Programs

Zane L. Berge

K ey to the success of sustaining initiatives in technology-enhanced learning and distance education is the commitment and support of the organization's top leaders (Berge & Smith, 2000). These leaders will need to exhibit enthusiasm for, champion, and allocate resources to these programs while encouraging and rewarding instructor cooperation. Such leaders can build credibility for distance education, maintain currency in the field, and gather support and partners inside and outside the organization.

The most important function of organizational leadership may be to create a shared vision that includes widespread input and support from the instructors and managers, articulates a clear training or educational purpose, has validity for stakeholders, and reflects the broader mission of the organization. Both top-down and bottom-up support are needed for successful, sustained distance training and education at the higher stages of organizational capability. In addition to the establishment of a vision, leaders link strategic planning and specific program implementation and monitoring using such tools as budgeting, infrastructure development, communication, workforce development, and policy revision.

## Establishing a Budget

Providing funding support as a budget item from the central resources of the organization firmly establishes technology-enhanced learning as part of the organizational landscape. The organization's leaders must decide what equipment and resources are considered infrastructure and what are to be considered operational expenses. A review of cost analyses for other organizations' distance education and training programs may show that a program will appear to lose money if technology infrastructure costs are included in the program budget. Still, a program budget, to give a true indication of costs, must cover all areas including support services provided (instructional development, registration, library services) as well as infrastructure and faculty development.

## Determining Functional Infrastructure

Some infrastructure resources and functions should be common across all distance program locations, and others are more useful if they are decentralized. Although decentralization may appear to unnecessarily duplicate efforts and costs, it may more closely align local expertise with local program needs. A centralization of services may allow managers of all distance education and training programs more direct access to top decision makers and encourage a more efficient use of resources, but there is risk in overburdening individual programs with bureaucracy and overhead while not meeting specific program needs. Generally, to help eliminate duplicate efforts, centralization is favored for the following functions: marketing and communication, instructional design and development support, technology help desk, development of instructors, and tracking participants.

## Communication

Part of the communication function could be considered as necessary internal marketing. The assumption made throughout most of this book is that training will be done internally to the organization and is designed for the use by the employees, rather than as courses or programs to be sold to persons outside the organization. Even so, in large organizations, marketing and sales to internal business units who are likely to have needs for which the program is being developed is critical—often the departments who need it most do not know that it is available!

A significant part of communication should support documenting and sharing knowledge in a community of learners. Xerox models "Ten Domains of Knowledge" (CIO.com, 1999) that give structure to the activities around which knowledge management plans are built:

1. Promoting knowledge sharing and best practices
2. Making that sharing an enterprise-wide responsibility
3. Capturing and re-using past experiences
4. Embedding knowledge in their products, services and processes
5. Knowledge as a product
6. Building and mining customer knowledge bases
7. Mapping the knowledge of experts
8. Mixing explicit and tacit knowledge to achieve innovation
9. Manage intellectual assets
10. Measure the value of knowledge in all its forms

Of course, it takes a particularly well-designed and implemented knowledge-management database to accomplish all this. The Xerox effort was also aided by a culture that sees value in becoming a knowledge-sharing community on a global basis.

## Workforce Development

It is hard to imagine anything more important to program implementation than recruiting and retaining expert delivery and support staff. Are all instructors and trainers equally suited to teach in distance education programs? The answer is generally no. Would it be wise to begin with a small group of willing instructors? Time and energy spent in training this cohort—and support for its development and implementation—is an investment that will be multiplied many times throughout the organization. In some organizations an initial group of enthusiastic instructors have been trained in effective distance teaching methods, and the individuals comprising the group then become mentors for the next group of instructors. Ongoing support should be given to these initial instructors through workshops, online discussion groups, and feedback. Occasionally, an instructor works as an apprentice to a practitioner who is teaching a distance course, and during a subsequent session is mentored while practicing the new skills. Broader workforce development —including provision and facilitation of the technical and pedagogical competencies needed to operate effectively in a distance training environment—is probably one of the most crucial determinants of success and ultimate movement into more mature stages of capabilities for distance education.

Articulating a provisional timeline is helpful to new distance education teachers as they begin to conceptualize their tasks. Answers to the following questions, and the availability of specific training as needed, will go a long way toward retaining new distance educators.

- At what point should the syllabus be in place?
- What materials need to be developed and tested?
- Is the hardware and software already in place and functional?
- What are the options when something goes wrong?

## Revising Policy and Procedures

Essentially, organizational policies and procedures are tools to direct members of the organization to do what is thought to be right, and to do those things the right way. Several critical issues unique to program planning for distance education emerge. It is clear that organizational policy and procedures need to be reviewed to remove potential barriers to the success of programs delivered at a distance.

Beyond that, however, it should be noted that part of the cultural change is an extension of the flattening of the organization—the reduction in hierarchy. Technology gives the freedom to work anytime and anyplace with anyone, anywhere. Where traditional organizations have been rule-governed, with behavior defined by policies and procedures, trust and empowerment are terms that take on new significance in organizations where flexibility rather than adherence to set policies is required (Flynn, 1999).

## Further Research

As with almost any large research effort, many new questions were raised along those that were answered. For instance, I noticed that the authors in each of the three major divisions of this book emphasized different tools for change as they described their organizations. In the section on how distance training is being used to help meet the challenge of uncommon organizational change, the authors emphasized infrastructure, communication, and cultural change for the most part. Those informants whose chapters are in the section of this book devoted to setting the competitive standards through distance training also focused on communication, but they emphasized workforce development and budget as tools to implement sustained distance training. Finally, in the section of this book on achieving organizational goals using sustained distance training, the contributors focused their discussion on workforce development, infrastructure, and budget. Why? And why was policy not emphasized by authors in any of these areas? This is only one mystery for which we can speculate and conduct further research in understanding organizations better. I would like to spend the remaining space in this book to discuss a couple of things that are clearer to me after analyzing the cases in this study.

## Conclusions: Access, Quality, and Acceptance

A lot of the challenge for distance training and education has to do with access to resources. Going almost without saying is the bedrock reality that quality must be present regardless of the delivery format. The tools for organizational change have to do with *acceptance*—by learners, instructors, and other stakeholders. In thinking about budgeting, workforce development, policies and procedures, infrastructure, and communication, some of the barriers to acceptance include

- Learner motivation
- Reasons for participating
- Timing, location, length of the event or program
- Marketing, communication, promotion of the event or program
- Incentives
- Level of support for learners and instructors
- Physical learning environment

The checklist in Exhibit 20.1 points to items important to your organization as you build the capabilities for sustaining access, quality, and acceptance of distance training and education.

Changes in society and the marketplace demand changes in the workplace, including a shift in the focus of distance training and education from *instructing* to *learning*. These changes affect the expectations, roles, and responsibilities of instructors, students, and managers as the organization builds capacity for technologically enhanced learning. If distance learning is to become part of the organization's profile, there must be an integration of project and program management, change management, and strategic planning. This type of sustained effort usually requires cultural change driven by mission-critical needs and opportunities.

## EXHIBIT 20.1. CONSIDERATIONS WHEN LINKING THE INSTRUCTIONAL PROGRAM PERSPECTIVE WITH THE ORGANIZATIONAL PERSPECTIVE REGARDING DISTANCE TRAINING AND EDUCATION.

1. Program Perspective
   - ✓ Exercise professional responsibility.
   - ✓ Engage relevant contexts.
     - ☐ Conduct market analysis of specific proposed programs and summarize for assessment purposes.
   - ✓ Design the program.
     - ☐ Plan the formative and summative evaluation and other feedback regarding the program.
     - ☐ Make explicit to instructors and learners that the quality of training and education is design dependent more than technology dependent.
     - ☐ Media selection.
   - ✓ Manage administrative aspects.
     - ☐ Conduct a walk-through of instructor, learner, and administrative support services:
       - ☐ Registration
       - ☐ Admissions
       - ☐ Advising
       - ☐ Computer and technology access
       - ☐ Materials resources support; online and offline library
     - ☐ Provide technical support services for instructors and learners.

2. Organizational Perspective
   - ✓ Integrate technology-enhanced learning initiatives with the organizational mission and strategic planning process.
     - ☐ Formalize measurement and evaluation of programs.
   - ✓ Integrate guiding beliefs and principles.
     - ☐ Gain widespread commitment, education, and experience with distance education.
     - ☐ Address stakeholders' personal concerns.
   - ✓ Make an external environmental scan.
   - ✓ Utilize internal organizational strengths.
     - ☐ Make an existing resources inventory and plan for improvements in such things as
       - ☐ Distance delivery technologies (hardware and software)
       - ☐ Technical support staff

    ☐ Administrative support staff

    ☐ Instructional development support staff

    ☐ Related projects and programs already started and being maintained

  ✓ Conduct an environmental scan, benchmarking, and market assessment for distance education initiatives.

3. Tools for Linking the Two Perspectives

  ✓ Provide funding support as a line item from the central resources of the organization.

    ☐ Implicit in such budgets is measurement of success in terms such as return on investment, and reduced costs.

  ✓ Determine the infrastructure and functions that are common across all programs.

    ☐ Plan for what technology is needed, and how often to update.

    ☐ Plan functions that are best centralized and those that are best decentralized.

    ☐ Leverage technology for more efficient processes and reduced costs.

  ✓ Focus on communication that supports documenting and sharing knowledge in a community of learners.

    ☐ Provide the infrastructure to support sharing of knowledge across the organization.

    ☐ Use internal communication to promote distance education efforts.

  ✓ Plan, recruit, administer incentives, and determine how to retain instructors, support staff, vendors, and administrators who are experienced in distance education.

  ✓ Conduct a review of the fit of the proposed programs with regard to existing policies and procedural changes needed for success.

  ✓ Conduct an assessment of how much roles or philosophy may need to change across the organization for distance education to be effective, accepted, and sustained.

# CASE STUDY RESEARCH METHODOLOGY USED FOR THIS BOOK

As noted in the Preface, while reviewing hundreds of cases involving distance training and educational technology, I have noticed some patterns and commonalties that I believe will be useful to those persons involved in such endeavors. I entered this research with the goal of refining a model and framework for sustaining distance training and describing the essential elements in that model, using multiple cases to illustrate.

## An Explanation of the Methodology

Given my research goal and the context I wish to study, I have taken a qualitative approach using a multiple case study strategy. A case study, for research purposes, is an empirical inquiry that "investigates a contemporary phenomenon within its real-life context, especially when the boundaries between phenomenon and context are not clearly evident" (Yin, 1994, p. 13). This can involve a single case or multiple case studies. Case study strategy uses "unobtrusive data collection methods" (Webb, Campbell, Schwartz, & Sechrest, 1966) within an organization to discover the natural flow of events and processes. This type of data collection is one of the significant characteristics that differentiates qualitative research strategies from quantitative research. This chapter presents a description of my research plan and how I designed, conducted, and extended the research to overcome the traditional criticisms of case study strategy, while keeping in mind what Bogdan and Biklen (1998) cautioned about qualitative research: "Qualitative researchers avoid going into a study with hypotheses to test or specific questions to answer. They believe that shaping the questions should be one of the products of data collection rather than assumed a priori. The study itself structures the research, not preconceived ideas or any precise research design. Their work is inductive" (p. 49).

## Research Method

Robert Yin (1994) states that different research strategies—case studies, surveys, histories, and experiments—can be used for any research purpose: exploratory, descriptive, or explanatory. What distinguishes these strategies are three conditions: the type of research question posed, the extent of control an investigator has over actual behavioral events, and the degree of focus on contemporary as opposed to historical events. He goes on to say, "Case studies are the preferred strategy when 'how' or 'why' questions are being posed, when the investigator has little control over events, and when the focus is on a contemporary phenomenon within some real-life context" (p. 1). This clearly describes my research questions and the context in which I want to study them. Studying organizational and management processes, in which the investigator wishes to retain the holistic and meaningful characteristics of those real-life activities, is a situation where case studies are typically used as a research strategy.

## Case Study Design

*Study Questions.* I have observed that there are many distance training efforts that are isolated from the mainstream efforts of the organization, or can be characterized as functioning separately from the way that training is normally done in the business unit under study. There is nothing inherently wrong with these events-driven efforts; many are, in fact, very successful. However, for an organization to move beyond this level of participation in the design and implementation of distance education requires a different level of capability. The capabilities needed for such integration across the organization involve changes in many factors, such as the infrastructure, policies, and at some point, the very culture of the organization. The investment is high, so integrating and sustaining distance training requires significant business reasons.

 This book presents a framework that explains how training at a distance can be sustained within an organization, describes distance training in a naturalistic way, and indicates the level of organizational maturity necessary for distance training to be integrated to the extent that it is part of that organization's profile. The organizations in this study are for-profit, nonprofit, and government, including the military. Educational institutions were specifically excluded. While the principles are the same, this book is designed for use in business and industry, where training activities are seen as sharply different from those occurring in educational institutions. Nonetheless, this book contains two cases that do involve educational organizations. Chapter Fifteen, Building Motivation for Distance Learners in Public Health, is included because it describes a strong partnership developed with public health professionals in state and local health departments in the southern regions of the United States. Chapter Eighteen, TeleEducation NB, describes a provincewide governmental agency that happens to work in education, but could have been in another business just as easily.

***Propositions.*** Propositions state why the researchers believe as they do about the phenomenon under study (Mertens, 1998). I started with the following propositions:

- When you find an organization that has developed the capabilities for widespread integration of distance training throughout the organization, meeting business needs and goals are the cause. In other words, the organization's strategic plan determines how diffuse within the organization the capabilities for distance training will be and this drives the organizational perspective concerning distance training.
- Regardless of the organization's stage of technological capability for distance training, it needs effective program or project management to maximize the chance for success for each project and program.
- When organizations have a need to increase their technological capabilities and to integrate distance training into the matrix of organizational training, there is a concomitant change in the culture surrounding training. Effective change management leads to success in such organizational change.
- Executives and managers support, encourage, evaluate, and otherwise manage the various distance training programs or projects and align them with the strategic plan of the organization through the use of tools and processes such as budgeting, infrastructure building, policy development, and staffing.

After I reviewed the first chapter drafts, I developed an additional proposition to explain distance training as it occurs in the sites selected and to frame the reporting of the data in this study:

- Significant change occurs in an organization when enough pain is felt by the CEO. Said another way, significant change only occurs within an organization when it becomes more painful to stay the same than it is to change. The cause of such pain has several sources—competition, awareness of important opportunities missed if there is no change, mergers, and mandates.

*Unit of Analysis.*  This study's unit of analysis is the organization and the relationships among the business processes with regard to distance training.

*Logic Linking Data to Propositions.*  Among other questions, I asked each contributor, What support is there for analyzing, designing, developing, implementing, and evaluating instructional programs, regardless of the content of any particular program? What structural support elements are in place that are necessary in an organization that is beyond needing a champion for distance education projects? What systems and processes are necessary for an organization where, through strategic planning, distance education has gone beyond needing widespread change management and has established itself within the organization as successful?

I also requested each contributor to supply descriptions within their organizational setting that included:

• Introduction to the context
• Business problem statement
• Population served and targeted
• Outcomes desired
• Description of management processes
• Outcomes attained, successes, failures, words of advice to others, and so on
• Discussion and conclusion regarding sustaining distance training and education

Using these guidelines for authors allowed me to relate the data collected to the theoretical propositions.

*Criteria for Interpreting Findings.*  No statistical tests were used to compare the statements self-reported by the contributors of each case, nor would statistical analyses have been appropriate.

I compared the descriptions written by the case authors—essentially informants in this research—with the tentative model I had developed before data collection. As Merriam (1998) points out, deriving a theory from the data involves both the integration and the refinement of that data with the model. As this process continued, modifications became fewer, with later modifications mainly bearing out predictions in the literature: "clarifying the logic, taking out non-relevant properties, integrating elaborating details of properties into the major outline of interrelated categories" (Glaser & Strauss, 1967, p. 110; cited in Merriam, 1998, p. 191).

After modifications to the model, the comparisons I made of each case to the model show support for the claim of replication.

## Purposeful Sampling

Purposeful sampling allows a researcher to select information-rich cases for in-depth study. The idea is to choose a case or cases that will increase understanding of the phenomenon being studied. (This is in contrast to *probabilistic sampling*, where the goal is to sample in ways that will increase the generalizability of the sample to all similar cases.) "The power and logic of purposeful sampling is that a few cases studied in depth yield many insights about the topic, whereas the logic of probability sampling depends on selecting a random or statistically representative sample for generalization to a larger population" (McMillan & Schumacher, 1996, p. 397).

*Site Selection.* Essential in purposeful sampling is a clear definition of the criteria for selection. The organizational perspective on distance training within each organization (and specifically excluding institutions involved strictly in education), was the focus in this study. As stated in the descriptive materials that accompanied the call for chapters, for purposes of this study the focus is on "distance training in the workplace, not in education. The workplace, for my purposes here, is mainly concerned with for-profit business and industry, but also includes non-profits and government agencies." An organization "means the entire organization, not just individual projects by some individual or group. In the case of a large, multinational corporation, it may mean the activities of a division rather than the entire enterprise." Thus the organizations selected for this study were ones in which "a distance learning policy and planning has been established. This means a stable and predictable process is in place to facilitate the identification and selection of technology to deliver distance training . . . [that] has been institutionalized in the organization as characterized by policies, communication, and practice all being aligned so that business objectives are being addressed. The business unit has established a distance learning identity and conducts systematic assessment of distance training events from an organizational perspective."

Prospective authors needed to demonstrate that their cases met at least three criteria. First, the authors had to be in a position within the target organization to observe firsthand the organizational perspective that was a focus of this study. Second, the case could not be focused on an trainee audience at an educational organization. And third, the authors needed to present résumés that showed sufficient writing and communication skills to effectively investigate and present each case selected. Each of the sixty-one proposals and their respective authors were reviewed by at least two reviewers using these criteria. To be selected for this study, the case had to be approved by two reviewers.

*Sample Size.* The authors of nineteen cases were finally invited to submit draft chapters for inclusion in this study. After further discussions with contributors, seventeen usable first drafts were received, describing how distance training is sustained in as many organizations. The decision to use cases to illustrate my proposed framework and to disseminate the results in a book had occurred before the other design of the study was decided, and was significant in determining how many cases would be used. I believe more cases were needed for the content of this book than would have been necessary for me to modify the model and disseminate the results in other than this book format.

## Data Collection and Analysis

*Planning.* Consideration of my research question and purpose guided the development of the call for proposed chapters. In part, the call described the kind of site that would qualify and what would be required of each contributor. This led to the guidelines for purposeful sampling and selection of cases in the following way:

> The purpose of this book is to describe the infrastructure and support needed by businesses as they apply education and training at a distance to meet business goals. . . . Your proposal should identify a business problem(s) that involves teaching and learning at a distance, briefly set the business context, show how technology-mediated learning significantly helped meet your instructional goals and solve the problem and then focus on what is needed to sustain your distance training efforts. It is implicit in this request that the organization has been using distance training for some number of years, and has experience in sustaining such delivery. The interest in this book is ultimately for each author to describe in a very rich way, his/her perceptions of the barriers encountered in sustaining the training and the solution within the organization, the limitations, pitfalls, and false-starts of the solution, along with the successful results, lessons learned, and future directions that are recommended for such support.

This call for chapters was widely distributed electronically in the training and distance education communities.

*Data Collection.* To begin data collection, contributors whose proposals were accepted were sent guidelines (see http://www.gl.umbc.edu/~berge/authgdsdt .htm). Additionally, a brief description of the phenomenon under study and a working model of the relationship among project management, change management, and strategic planning was sent to the authors (see http://www.gl .umbc.edu/~berge/sust_des.htm). This was viewed more as a working hypothesis, knowing that refinements were expected as data was collected (Bogdan & Biklen, 1998).

*Analysis.* I compared the descriptions written by the case authors with the model I had derived from the literature and previous cases. Dimensions of special interest when analyzing the cases were project or program management, strategic planning, change management, budget, infrastructure, communication, workforce development, and policy.

## Reducing Threats to Reliability and Validity

While the case study is a distinctive form of empirical inquiry, many research investigators nevertheless have viewed case studies as "a less desirable form of inquiry than either experiments or surveys" (Yin, 1994, p. 9). Probably the biggest reason for this has been a lack of rigor in case study research. It must be remembered that research bias can enter any research strategy if care is not exercised to eliminate or reduce it. To help overcome these concerns, I will document how I addressed the common concerns in case study research: strategies to enhance internal validity, strategies to enhance external validity, and strategies to enhance reliability (McMillan & Schumacher, 1996).

*Internal Validity.* Internal validity deals with the question of how research findings match reality. This study used several strategies to enhance internal validity. The authors had instructions to review the tentative model and framework while working on their first drafts. In fact, several authors asked clarifying questions and pointed out apparent contradictions in their cases that helped me to refine the framework. They had access to the framework, assumptions, and theoretical orientation I took for this study. Each author had instructions to review the modified models and framework while working on their final chapter drafts. At least one of the authors for each chapter had to be an employee of the target organization— someone who was in a position to access internal documents and had access to executives to supply a holistic, rich, accurate study. The publisher reviewed the first draft and had three outside reviewers comment on the draft manuscript. An additional triangulation strategy (Stake, 1995) involved the permissions require-ment by the publisher. An authorized agent of each organization had to sign off on the case. This occasionally produced inquiries to the author that required clarifi-cation or modification and thereby increased the accuracy of the case, as judged by the case study subjects.

*External Validity.*   External validity is concerned with the extent to which the find-ings of one study can be applied to other situations—how generalizable the results of the research study are. In experimental and correlational studies, the ability to generalize to other settings is ensured "through a priori conditions such as assumptions of equivalency between the sample and population it came from, control of sample size, random sampling, and so on" (Merriam, 1998, p. 207). In qualitative research, this type of random, statistical sampling is not used. Rather, a purposeful, small sample is used precisely to understand the particular event in depth. There are several ways of viewing generalizability. I particularly like one of Merriam's descriptions: "Think in terms of the reader or user of the study. *Reader or user generalizability* involves leaving the extent to which a study's findings apply to other situations up to the people in those situations. . . . This is a common practice in law and medicine, where the applicability of one case to another is determined by the practitioner" (p. 211).

Of course, it was still important for this research to report rich, thick descrip-tions, providing the readers with enough detail to determine how closely their sit-uations matched the research cases. Readers also need descriptions of how sites were selected so these too can be used for comparing case sites to their own, and discussions of the use of multiple sites to show the diversity of practices for sustain-ing distance training.

*Reliability.*   Reliability refers to the extent to which research findings can be repli-cated. If the study is repeated by another researcher in other circumstances, will the results come out the same? While this may be assumed in the natural sciences, qualitative research is not conducted to find and isolate the laws of human be-havior. Merriam (1998) points out that what is being studied

> is assumed to be in flux, multifaceted, and highly contextual, because informa-tion gathered is a function of who gives it and how skilled the researcher is at get-ting it, and because the emergent design of a qualitative case study precludes a priori controls, achieving reliability in the traditional sense is not only fanciful but impossible. . . . Since the term *reliability* in the traditional sense seems to be something of a misfit when applied to qualitative research, Lincoln and Guba

(1985, p. 288) suggest thinking about the "dependability" or "consistency" of the results obtained from the data [p. 206].

Therefore, rather than the benchmark's being that outsiders obtain the same results, the researcher seeks outsiders who can agree that, given the data collected, the results make sense—they appear to be dependable and consistent. While this has been done to a limited degree during the data collection and reporting of this study, I hope that by explaining here such things as the assumptions and theory behind the study, the basis for selecting informants and describing them, and the criteria for case selection, the reader can also make informed judgments about the consistency and dependability of the study.

# GLOSSARY

**Analog technology.** A technology type that is based on continuous measurement. For example, sound is continuously varying air vibrations, and is converted into analogous electrical vibrations resembling the original sound. Current TV and radio signals are analog, as are many telephone lines. Analog technology is now being replaced by digital technology.

**Asynchronous.** Transmission by individual bytes, or packets of bytes, not related to specific timing on the transmitting end. Often used for low-speed terminal links. When the term is used to describe computer-mediated human interaction, it indicates that communication can take place without both parties being logged on at the same time, as messages can be left for subsequent reading.

**Audio bridge.** Telephone connection among many sites, allowing all sites to hear all other sites.

**Audioconference.** Two-way electronic voice-only interactive conference among two or more groups or three or more sites. A conference call using regular phone lines. Generally, this medium is best used for short (up to two-hour) meetings or training sessions. Audioconferences may be supplemented with previously distributed handouts or with interactive graphics.

**Audiographic conferencing.** Technology allowing computer links between sites so that a presenter can speak to conference or training participants and present interactive graphics on a computer screen for all participants to view simultaneously. Connection of graphic display devices to allow participants to view high-resolution, still-frame visuals (including facsimile, slow-scan television, and 35 mm slides) at different sites. In more sophisticated systems, participants can manipulate and change the visual as well as view it, or collaborate on the development of new files or documents.

**Authorware.** A term for commercial software packages such as Authorware Professional, Quest, or Toolbook that permit persons with little or no computer programming knowledge to create CBT courses using drag-and-drop technology.

**Bandwidth.** Derived from the traditional term used to describe the size or "width" of the frequencies used to carry analog communications such as TV and radio, bandwidth (for purposes of the Internet) is essentially a measure of the rate of data transfer. It is best visualized using the "pipe analogy"—the bigger the pipe, the more fluid you can put through it in a specified period of time. Internet service providers are essentially bandwidth retailers—they buy large bandwidths wholesale and then resell that bandwidth in smaller widths to multiple individual users. Bandwidth is usually stated in bits per second (bps), kilobits per second (kbps), or megabits per second (mps). A full page of English text is about 16,000 bits. Full-motion full-screen video would require roughly 10,000,000 bits per second, depending on compression. A rule of thumb is that the higher the bandwidth, the better the video looks, the better the audio sounds, and the faster data load and transfers.

**Bridge.** Device that interconnects three or more telecommunication channels, such as telephone lines. A telephone conference audio bridge links three or more telephones (usually operator-assisted). A meet-me audio bridge can provide teleconference direct dial access number. Both connect remote sites and equalize noise distortion.

**Broadcast site.** The site from which the instructor is transmitting. For the students at this site, it is viewed as their classroom site.

**B-roll.** Videotape (prerecorded footage) rolled into a live production. ("A-roll" is the tape recording the live or primary production.)

**Bulletin Board System (BBS).** A type of electronic communication using the Internet or an intranet whereby messages can be posted and read over a period of time. Usually BBSs focus on a theme and facilitate debate and discussion.

**Business Television (BTV).** Typically one-way video broadcast via satellite from corporate headquarters to branch offices. Primary applications of BTV include information dissemination (critical, just-in-time, or need-to-know) and motivational presentations.

**CD-ROM training.** CBT courses contained on one or more CD-ROMs. Advantages are that the student does not need to have access to the Internet or an intranet and that CD-ROM courses can incorporate dynamic video and audio elements to add interest and fun. Disadvantages are that students must have a computer powerful enough to run CD-ROM programs, and such programs can be very expensive to develop—and once a CD-ROM is produced, it cannot be changed. CD-ROM courses are often appropriate when subject matter is stable (for example, project management skills or quality analysis principles). Internet-based courses are appropriate when subject matter changes frequently.

**CD-ROM.** Compact Disc—Read Only Memory. A storage medium. These discs can store a variety of data types, including text, color graphics, sound, animation, and digitized video that can be accessed and read through a computer. A disc can store up to 600 megabytes of data, much more information than can be stored on a 3.5-inch computer disk, which holds up to 1.4 megabytes. This makes CD-ROM an inexpensive medium for storing large amounts of data. Digitized, full-motion video requires even more space than a disc can hold, however, so compression technology is important in compressing data to fit on a disc and then decompressing data for playback. (Note: A CD provides enough storage for five encyclopedias on a 4.75-inch disc and is read by laser technology.)

**Codec.** Acronym for coder-decoder, the hardware that codes outgoing video and audio signals (converting and compressing analog information into digital form) and decodes incoming ones (decompressing the digital information and re-coding it into analog form).

**Compressed file.** A file in which wasted space has been removed by using a computer application that replaces current bits and bytes with new ones. The process is called *compression*. Formulas or algorithms allow duplicate or empty space removal, and also permit reconstruction of the original file identically (lossless compression) or nearly identically (lossy compression).

**Compressed video.** When the vast amount of information in a normal TV transmission is squeezed into a fraction of its former bandwidth by a codec, the resulting compressed video can be transmitted more economically over a smaller carrier. *Compressed digital video (CDV)* transmits live video and audio simultaneously over special phone lines (Integrated Services Digital Network—or ISDN lines), switched-56 kilobit lines, or T1 lines (large "pipes" consisting of twenty-four 64-kilobit channels). The interactive communication between sites is two-way audio and two-way video. No special production studios, equipment, or satellites are required.

**Computer conferencing.** A distance learning method using computers. Computer conferencing participants leave messages for each other (asynchronously) and do not usually access the conference at the same time (synchronously).

**Computer-Assisted Instruction (CAI).** See computer-based instruction (CBI).

**Computer-Assisted Learning (CAL).** See computer-based instruction (CBI).

**Computer-Based Instruction (CBI).** Refers to using computers to instruct human users. CBI includes computer-assisted instruction (tutorial, review and practice, simulation, and so on), computer-managed instruction (diagnostic and prescriptive testing functions), and electronic messaging (which is generally associated with networked computer classrooms).

**Computer-Based Training (CBT).** The use of interactive computer or video programs for instructional purposes. Often refers to the actual instructional materials delivered as CD-ROM or Web-based programs. Any training course in which the student receives the course content and responds to that content (for example, exercises and tests) using a computer terminal. Most CBT training courses are now Windows-based, allowing for relatively easy integration of text, graphics, animation, video, and sound. One advantage of CBT courses is that trainees may proceed through the material at their own pace. One disadvantage is the generally high development cost and lengthy development time to produce a good course. Generally, CBT can be divided into two categories: Internet (or intranet) training and CD-ROM training.

**Computer-Mediated Communication (CMC).** Refers to the entire range of electronic networking activities and includes electronic mail, computer conferencing, informatics, and computer-based instruction. See computer-based instruction (CBI).

**Desktop conferencing.** Using a desktop computer to send and receive video, audio, and text in real time via the Internet. Most appropriate for small groups or individuals. Many desktop conferencing systems support document sharing. Desktop conferencing that includes live two-way video transmission is often referred to as *desktop videoconferencing*.

**Digital technology.** A form of information (discrete bits) that is represented by signals encoded as a series of discrete numbers, intervals, or steps, as contrasted to continuous or analog circuits. This method allows simultaneous transmission of voice and data. Can be sent through wire or over the air.

**Distance education.** A formal process of distance learning with information being broad in scope, such as whole college courses.

**Distance learning.** The acquisition of knowledge and skills through mediated information and instruction, encompassing all technologies and other forms of learning at a distance.

**Distance training.** Business practitioners' reference to distance education. A more customized or targeted learning experience; content is focused to facilitate performance outcomes that meet business needs.

**Document sharing.** A computer program feature supported by many desktop videoconferencing systems that allows participants at both ends of a videoconference to view and edit the same computer document.

**Downlink site.** A training site where students view the instructor via monitors. Oftentimes referred to as the remote site. The instructor is located at the broadcast site.

**Drag and drop.** Use of the computer mouse to choose a function from a toolbar and to insert the function or item into your Authorware course. For example, one option might be to click on a screen *button* (a small picture representing a function) and drag the button down to a position in your course. Trainees could click on the button to view a brief video clip or to open a pull-down set of options.

**DVD (Digital Versatile Disc or Digital Video Disc).** A type of high-capacity, dual-sided CD-ROM that holds 4.7 gigabytes per side, enough for a full-length movie. As with other media, DVD capacity may increase as the technology improves.

**Electronic education.** Similar to distance learning; a broad concept implying distance learning that employs multiple and diverse forms of technology to meet education and training needs at a distance. See Chapter Sixteen, the NYNEX case study by Barry Howard.

**Electronic mail (e-mail).** A means of sending text messages to individuals or groups of individuals using a computer network. The sender inputs a message to the computer via a terminal, and the receiver also uses a terminal to read and respond to messages. This is one method of transmitting information in distance learning.

**Electronic Performance Support System (EPSS).** An integrated computer program that provides any combination of expert system, hypertext, embedded animation, CAI, and hypermedia to an employee to enhance performance with a minimum of support and intervention by others. Examples include help systems, electronic job aids, and electronic expert advisers. See also performance support systems.

**Extranet.** A Web site that is made available to external customers or organizations for electronic commerce. Although on the Internet, it generally provides more customer-specific information than a public site. It may require a password to gain access to the more sensitive information.

**Feedback.** A high-pitched whine, sometimes caused by the need to adjust equipment volume, often caused by a microphone in the receiving (downlink) site being too close to the TV monitor from which the sound is coming. Alternatively, replies from students or others affected by a program or action, indicating their responses to it.

**Fiber optics.** The technology that transmits voice, video, and digital information using light waves through thin glass strands. Fiber optics uses a fraction of the space and energy required by conventional copper cable. A strand of fiber-optic cable has a bandwidth of about 2 billion hertz, versus twisted pairs of copper wire, which have about 500 hertz.

**HTML (Hypertext Markup Language).** The language used to code text files with links and formatting commands for use with Web browsers.

**HTTP (Hypertext Transfer Protocol).** Text linked so that the user can jump from one idea to another, usually by clicking on underlined or highlighted text items or pictures.

**Hyperlink.** A highlighted word or picture within a hypertext document that when clicked takes you to another place within the document or to another document altogether. Text that includes links or shortcuts to other documents, allowing the reader to easily jump (browse) from one point in the text to another, related point, and consequentially from one idea to another, in a nonlinear fashion.

**Hypermedia.** A program that links different media such as text, graphics, video, voice, and animation under learner control in a way similar to hypertext linkage of text. For example, a hypermedia video link allows the learner to choose to see a related video sequence and then return to the program.

**Integrated Services Digital Network (ISDN).** A digital telecommunications channel that allows for the integrated transmission of voice, video, and data at speeds up to 128,000 bits per second over regular phone lines. It is anticipated that ISDN technology will become increasingly important in distance learning and may replace current telephone lines.

**Interactive Distance Learning (IDL).** A mode of delivering distance learning and distance training that involves one-way video satellite transmission and two-way audio via telephone lines. IDL may include an automated electronic input device (such as the ONE TOUCH system) to accommodate participant responses.

**Interactive graphics.** A set of slides, charts, or other computer-generated visuals that can be displayed simultaneously to several sites during an audioconference. Normally, an Internet or intranet site is used. Audioconference participants log in to the site and view the graphics, which are controlled by the presenter.

**Interactive Multimedia (IMM).** A multilevel multimedia presentation that allows access to information randomly and nonsequentially. IMM often involves sophisticated, large-memory computer-based training programs.

**Interactive Television (ITV).** A mode of delivering distance learning and distance training that employs one-way video satellite transmission and two-way audio via telephone lines. ITV may also include an automated electronic input device (such as the ONE TOUCH system) to accommodate participant responses.

**Interactive video.** A mode of delivering distance learning and distance training that employs two-way video transmission between two or more sites. (Two-way audio is included.) Transmission can be via either satellite or compressed technology.

**Internet.** An electronic data network that enables infinite numbers of computers to send text and graphics to one another over phone lines. A worldwide network of networks that all use the TCP/IP communications protocol and share a common address space. First incarnated as the ARPANET in 1969, the Internet has metamorphosed from a military network to an academic research network to the current commercial network. It commonly supports services such as e-mail, the World Wide Web, file transfer, and Internet Relay Chat.

**Internet or intranet CBT.** A student logs in to a site or home page for training. Options include enrolling, receiving content, and completing individual lessons by computer as well as communicating with a distant instructor. An advantage of Internet and intranet courses is that they may be changed and updated quickly in one central location. A disadvantage is that bandwidth compression reduces the amount of video and audio options that may be included because they take too long to download and be manipulated. Such courses, therefore, tend to be more heavily text-based than CD-ROM courses.

**Intranet.** A private network that uses Internet-related technologies to provide services within an organization. Always lowercase except at the beginning of a sentence, to differentiate it from the Internet, which is one specific entity. Compare extranet.

**Job aid.** A tool that assists an employee in completing a task. Examples are paper references or computer help options in software packages such as Word or Lotus. Job aids are also called performance support systems. Job aids can be used instead of formal training if employees must have access to a body of information or a process but do not need to remember it.

**LAN (Local Area Network).** A group of computers at a single location (usually an office or home) that are connected by phone lines or coaxial cable. This represents a private transmission network. Similar terms: *MAN (Metropolitan Area Network); WAN (Wide Area Network)*.

**Laser disc.** An optical disc used for full-motion video. Laser discs have been used for interactive training as well as for home theater, where the higher resolution is noticeable on larger screens. For the most part, CD-ROMs have replaced laser discs for training, and it is expected that DVDs will replace the laser disc as well as VHS tape for movies.

**LISTSERV.** The registered name of one of the major programs for managing a computer mailing list, "LISTSERV" should not be lowercased or used as a generic term.

**Mailing list manager.** A software program that manages electronic discussion groups or computer conference distribution lists. These discussion groups are often called "lists" because the mailing list manager programs use what is called a "mail exploder" and a subscription list of electronic mail addresses to send messages directly to the electronic mailboxes of many subscribers. Participants subscribe by sending a message to the mailing list software hosting the list of interest. LISTSERV, majordomo, and Listproc are the most commonly used programs of this type.

**Malcolm Baldrige National Quality Award.** Created by law in 1987 and named for Malcolm Baldrige, who served as Secretary of Commerce from 1981 until his tragic death in a rodeo accident in 1987. The purposes of the award are to promote an understanding of the requirements for performance excellence and competitiveness improvements and to promote sharing of information on successful performance strategies. There are seven categories that applicants must address: Leadership, Strategic Planning, Customer and Market Focus, Information and Analysis, Human Resource Focus, Process Management, Business Results.

**Multicast.** See Streaming.

**Multimedia.** Any training course delivered through a combination of media such as text, sound, video, and animation. Often presented on CD-ROM.

**Multipoint conference.** Interactive videoconference or teleconference in which more than two sites are linked.

**Multipoint.** More than two linked sites that can collaborate on an activity, connected by a computerized bridge to allow full interactivity.

**Online training.** In technology-based learning, information currently available for direct access. Usually implies linkage to a computer.

**Originator site.** See Broadcast site.

**Performance support systems.** Any tool made available to assist an employee in completing a task (for example, answering inquiries or completing a procedure such as processing a case). The simplest example is a written job aid. Performance support systems may also be electronic; a good example is the "Help" option available in most word processing programs such as Word or WordPerfect. Instead of developing and delivering a training class in the expectation that the trainee may need the skills at a future time, developers of performance support systems eliminate the need for training by providing the employee only what is essential to know at exactly the right time.

**Protocol.** A formalized set of rules governing the format, timing, and error control of transmissions on a network. The protocol that networks use to communicate with each other. *TCP/IP* is an example of a network protocol.

**Remote access.** The ability to access one computer from another, from across the room or across the world. Remote access requires communications hardware, software, and an actual physical link—at least a telephone line.

**Remote site.** The training site where students are viewing the instructor via monitors or desktop. Also called downlink site, especially if satellite communications are involved. The instructor is located at the broadcast site.

**Satellite communications.** A *satellite* is an electronics retransmission device placed in orbit around the earth in a geostationary orbit for the purpose of receiving and retransmitting electromagnetic signals. It normally receives signals from a single source and retransmits them over a wide geographic area. Domestic communications satellites operate on two frequency ranges designated C- and Ku-band. Each requires specific electronic equipment. C-band is less expensive and operates at 4 kHz. Ku-band operates at 12 kHz.

**Satellite teleconferencing or teletraining.** A meeting or training event conducted using a satellite telecommunication system.

**Special Interest Group (SIG).** A subset of a larger group that brings together members who have common interests and backgrounds. Some groups get together to learn new skills or sharpen existing ones. Others focus on keeping up with state of the art in a particular field or discipline.

**Streaming.** A technology to hear and view media over the Internet without having to wait for a large movie or sound file to download to your computer. For example, when you click on a video it copies the beginning to your computer and starts to play while it copies the rest to your computer. You are able to watch or listen to a larger portion of media without having to wait for the entire file to download. Two primary types of streaming include unicast and multicast applications. *Unicast* is a one-to-one delivery method by which each user is served individually (that is, the server streams requested files to each user so that a hundred requests result in a hundred separate streams). Applications might include shared learning or virtual classroom environments. Many organizations provide primarily unicast service with supplemental "cache servers" in key locations so users can stream their content from the nearest server to enable the highest quality service possible. *Multicast* is a one-to-many delivery method in which a single server streams one file to multiple requesting sites. This streamed file can then be replicated and redistributed by local servers to save bandwidth. Applications might include lectures, presentations, meetings, news headlines, and weather updates. Both unicast and multicast streaming techniques rely on the steadily increasing speed and bandwidth that are at the heart of Internet growth.

**Switcher.** A special effects generator in a studio that allows the operator to switch between two video camera signals.

**Synchronous.** Data communications in which transmissions are sent at a fixed rate, with the sending and receiving devices synchronized. Synchronous human communications involve two or more users speaking and listening to one another in real time.

**T1 line.** A high-speed, high-bandwidth leased line connection to the Internet. T1 connections deliver information at 1.544 megabits per second.

**T3 line.** A high-speed, high-bandwidth leased line connection to the Internet. T3 connections deliver information at 44.746 megabits per second.

**Telecommuting.** Working at an alternate site instead of commuting in the traditional style. The alternate site may be the worker's home. Typically involves the use of a computer for communications with the organization and transmission of work.

**Teleconferencing.** Two-way electronic communication between two or more groups, or three or more individuals, in separate locations. Includes group communication via audio, audiographics, video, and computer systems. Loosely, a meeting where the participants are at separate locations. A telephone call with three parties would be a very simple teleconference.

**TelePrompTer.** A device for displaying a moving, magnified script in front of a presenter in the studio.

**Teletraining.** Teletraining is a human performance system that integrates telecommunications into planning, designing, and delivering training programs. Methods may include one or all of the following techniques: audio-only, audiographic, computer conferencing, one-way video broadcast, one- or two-way video with audio interaction, and desktop videoconferencing. (See interactive television [ITV] and interactive video.)

**Unicast.** See Streaming.

**Uplink site.** Also known as the originator site or broadcast site. The term refers to the uplinking of a program to a satellite for subsequent transmission to the receiving or downlink sites.

**Videoconferencing.** Communication across long distances with video and audio contact that may also include graphics and data exchange. Often this communication is via satellite. Also, meeting involving at least one uplink and a number of downlinks at different locations. Communication is often one-way video and two-way audio.

**Video roll-in.** See B-roll.

**Videoteleducation.** Similar to videoconferencing, employing one-way video and audio via satellite and two-way audio via telephone.

**WAN (Wide Area Network).** A private long distance network, typically the intercity network that covers an area larger than a single building or campus and uses leased lines to connect computers or LANs. A MAN (metropolitan area network) generally covers a city or suburb.

**Web-Based Training (WBT).** Computer-based training delivered via the Internet.

**World Wide Web (WWW; the Web).** A distributed information system created by researchers at CERN in Switzerland. It allows users to create, edit, or browse hypertext documents. Different systems highlight hyperlinks differently—some put a link in boldface or in color, others underline the link. The clients and servers using the Web are easily accessible and available.

**Contributing resources for this glossary:** Berge and Collins, 1995; Brooks, 1997; Picard, 1996; Portway and Lane, 1994; Schaaf, 1997; Schreiber, 1995; and the IRS *Staff / Volunteer Development Newsletter.*

# REFERENCES

Alkin, M. C. (1991). Evaluation theory development: II. In M. W. McLaughlin & D. C. Phillips (Eds.), *Evaluation and education: At quarter century* (pp. 91–112). Nineteenth Yearbook of the National Society for the Study of Education, Part II. Chicago: University of Chicago Press.

Alkin, M. C., Hofstetter, C. H., & Ai, X. (1998). Stakeholder concepts in program evaluation. In A. Reynolds & H. Walberg (Eds.), *Advances in educational productivity,* 7 (pp. 87–113). Greenwich, CT: JAI Press.

AQP (1998). Fall 1997 Conference Upper Left Corner Chapter draft report: The power of collaboration: Summary of participants' work. [Online]. Available: http://upperleft.aqp.org/draft.html

Bandura, A. (1971). *Social learning theory.* New York: General Learning Press.

Bandura, A. (1997). *Self-efficacy: The exercise of control.* New York: Freeman.

Bassi, L. J., & Van Buren, M. E. (1998). *Sharpening the leading edge.* American Society for Training and Development (ASTD). [Online]. Available: http://www.astd.org/CMS/templates/template_1.html?articleid=20940

Bent, F. T., & McLean, J. E. (1958). Teaching methods: Course instruction. In S. B. Sweeney (Ed.), *Education for administrative careers in government service,* p. 76. Philadelphia: University of Pennsylvania Press.

Bentley, M. L. (1993). *Constructivist pedagogy.* [Online]. Available: http://www.chias.org/www/edu/crcd/crcdcon.html

Berge, Z. L. (1996). Changing roles in higher education: Reflecting on technology. *Collaborative Communications Review,* annual (pp. 43–53). McLean, VA: International Teleconferencing Association.

Berge, Z. L. (1998a, Summer). Barriers to online teaching in post-secondary institutions. *Online Journal of Distance Learning Administration, 1*(2). [Online]. Available: http://www.westga.edu/~distance/Berge12.html

Berge, Z. L. (1998b). Conceptual frameworks in distance training and education. In D. A. Schreiber & Z. L. Berge (Eds.), *Distance training: How innovative organizations are using technology to maximize learning and meet business objectives* (pp. 19–36). San Francisco: Jossey-Bass.

Berge, Z. L. (1998c). Technology and changing roles in education. In Z. L. Berge & M. P. Collins (Eds.), *Wired together: The online classroom in K–12. Volume 1 of 4: Perspectives and instructional design* (pp. 1–13). Cresskill, NJ: Hampton Press.

Berge, Z. L., and Collins, M., Eds. (1995). *Computer mediated communication and the online classroom.* Cresskill, NJ: Hampton Press.

Berge, Z. L., & Schrum, L. (1998). Strategic planning linked with program implementation for distance education. *CAUSE/EFFECT, 21*(3), 31–38.

Berge, Z. L., & Smith, D. (2000). Implementing corporate distance training using change management, strategic planning, and project management. In L. Lau (Ed.), *Distance learning technologies: Issues, trends and opportunities.* Hershey, PA: Idea Group Publishing.

Bogdan, R. C., & Biklen, S. K. (1998). *Qualitative research for education: An introduction to theory and methods* (3rd ed.). Needham Heights, Mass.: Allyn & Bacon.

Bonanno, D. (n.d.; accessed February 22, 2000). *Evaluating electronic communication patterns over a semester: A qualitative content analysis.* [Online]. Available: http://trochim.human.cornell.edu/WebEval/webcomm/webcomm.htm

Bowen, K. A. (n.d.; accessed February 23, 2000). *Website evaluation: Experimental and quasi-experimental design issues.* [Online]. Available: http://trochim.human.cornell.edu/WebEval/webexper/webexper.htm

Bower, J. L., & Hout, T. M. (1994). Fast-cycle capability for competitive power. In K. B. Clark & S. C. Wheelwright (Eds.), *The product development challenge: Competing through speed, quality and creativity* (pp. 43–58). Boston: Harvard Business Review.

Broad, M. L., & Newstrom, J. W. (1992). *Transfer of training: Action-packed strategies to ensure high payoff from training investments.* Reading, MA: Addison-Wesley.

Brooks, D. W. (1997). *Web-teaching: A guide to designing interactive teaching for the World Wide Web.* New York: Plenum Press.

Brown, T. L., LeMay, H. E., Jr., & Bursten, B. E. (1997). *Chemistry: The central science* (7th ed.). Upper Saddle River, NJ: Prentice Hall.

Brush, D. J. (2000). *Program analysis and summary: Prepare a quality deficiency report (QDR).* Internal report available from the USAIC Distance Learning Office, ATTN: ATZS-CLD, Fort Huachuca AZ 85613-6000.

Bryce, H. J. (1987). *Financial and strategic management for nonprofit organizations.* Upper Saddle River, NJ: Prentice Hall.

Bryk, A. S. (Ed.). (1983). *Stakeholder-based evaluation.* New Directions for Program Evaluation, no. 17. San Francisco: Jossey-Bass.

Bryson, J. M. (1988). *Strategic planning for public and nonprofit organizations: A guide to strengthening and sustaining organizational achievement.* San Francisco: Jossey-Bass.

Cairncross, F. (1997). *The death of distance: How the communications revolution will change our lives.* Boston: Harvard Business School Press.

Carnwell, R. (1999). Distance education and the need for dialogue. *Open Learning, 14*(1), 50–55.

Christensen, H., & Cowley-Durst, B. (1998). Thoughts on distance learning: An interview with Alan Chute. *Performance Improvement, 37*(9), 30–32.

CIO.com. (1999, September 15). Knowledge management: Big challenges, big rewards. CIO Special Advertising Supplement. [Online]. Available: http://www.cio.com/sponsors/091599_km_1.html

Collins, A. (1991). Cognitive apprenticeship and instructional technology. In L. Idol & B. F. Jones (Eds.), *Educational values and cognitive instruction: Implications for reform*. Hillsdale, NJ: Erlbaum.

Compeau, D., & Higgins, C. (1995). Computer self-efficacy: Development of a measure and initial test. *MIS Quarterly, 19*(2), 189–211.

Confessore, S., & Kops, W. (1998). Self-directed learning and the learning organization: Examining the connection between the individual and the learning environment. *Human Resource Development Quarterly, 9*(4), 365–375.

Curtin, C. (1998, May/June). Tools to develop and manage Web-based training and support. *CBT Solutions* (pp. 25–27).

Cvercko, S., Antonelli, M., & Steele, J. (1992). *Ford instructional systems design process*. Dearborn MI: Ford Motor Company.

Daft, R. L., & Huber, G. P. (1987). How organizations learn: A communication framework. *Research in the Sociology of Organizations, 5*, 1–36.

Davenport, T. H., & Prusak, L. (1998). *Working knowledge*. Boston: Harvard Business School Press.

Davis, F. (1989). Perceived usefulness, perceived ease of use, and user acceptance of information technology. *MIS Quarterly, 13*(3), 319–339.

Distance Learning Subcommittee of the School of Public Health Academic Programs Committee. (1999). *Recommendations for approving degree-granting distance learning programs*. Chapel Hill: School of Public Health, University of North Carolina.

Driscoll, M. (1998). *Web-based training: Using technology to design adult learning experiences*. San Francisco: Jossey-Bass.

Duncan, W. R. (1996). *Guide to the project management body of knowledge*. Project Management Institute Standards Committee, 130 South State Road, Upper Darby PA 19082 USA.

Edgett, J. (1995, June 30). *Distance education project report*. Fredericton, New Brunswick: Office of the Auditor General.

Ellsworth, J. B. (1995). Planning for success: Considerations for managing the dissemination of training technology. In M. Simonson & M. Anderson (Eds.), *Proceedings of the 1995 annual national convention of the Association for Educational Communications and Technology, Anaheim, Calif., 17* (pp. 136–146).

Ellsworth, J. B. (1998). Factors affecting participant reactions to new training devices. *Dissertation Abstracts International, 59*(08), 2938A. (University Microfilms No. AAI99–03405)

Ellsworth, J. B. (2000). *Surviving change: A survey of educational change models*. Monograph. Syracuse University: ERIC Clearinghouse on Information and Technology.

Ely, D. P. (1990). Conditions that facilitate the implementation of educational technology innovations. *Journal of Research on Computing in Education, 23*(2), 298–305.

ES Revitalization Project. (n.d.; accessed June 14, 2000). A six-step training process prepared as a companion to "The Workforce Development Staff Skills and Training Challenge" Report. [Online]. http://www.icesa.org/articles/template.cfm?results_art_filename=sixsteps.htm

Espinoza, S., Whatley, S., & Cartwright, C. (1996). Online courses—the 5 W's and 2 perspectives. [Online]. Available: http://www.coe.uh.edu/insite/elec_pub/html1996/16teless.htm#espi

Feretic, E. (1999, September). A common language. *Beyond Computing, 8*(7), 6–8.

Flynn, J. (1999). Communication effectiveness in the virtual environment: Implications for distance learning in management education. *Business, Education and Technology Journal.* [Online]. Available: http://internet.ggu.edu/~bfulkerth/journal4.html#commnication_effectiveness

Ford does distance learning by the numbers. (1994, October). *Training, 31*(10), 97.

Formby, S., & Ostrander, G. (1997, August). Managing change the project management way. *PM Network* (pp. 32–34).

Friend, N. S. (1997). *Ethics in the workplace: Summative evaluation for CBT, instructor-led and information package delivery methods.* Irving, TX: SBC Communications, Center for Learning.

Friend, N. S. (1999). Case study: Distance learning at the SBC Center for Learning. *Performance Improvement Quarterly, 12*(4), 33–44.

Fulk, J., Schmitz, J., & Steinfield, C. (1990). A social influence model of technology use. In J. Fulk & C. Steinfield, (Eds.), *Organizations and communication technology* (pp. 117–141). Thousand Oaks, CA: Sage.

Galusha, J. M. (n.d.; accessed June 14, 2000). Barriers to learning in distance education. [Online]. Available: http://www3.ncsu.edu/dox/NBE/galusha.html

Garland, M. R. (1993). Student perceptions of the situational, institutional, dispositional and epistemological barriers to persistence. *Distance Education, 14*(2), 181–198.

Gates, W. H. (1999). *Business @ the speed of thought.* New York: Warner.

General Accounting Office, Office of Information Management and Communication. (1996). *Videoconferencing Technical Guide.* Washington, DC: General Accounting Office.

General Accounting Office Training Institute. (1995). *Video teletraining: A guide to design, development, and use.* Washington, DC: General Accounting Office. [Also online]. Available: http://www.gao.gov/special.pubs/publist.htm

General Accounting Office Training Institute. (1999, June). *Annual training and education report.* Washington, DC: General Accounting Office.

Glaser, B. G., & Strauss, A. L. (1967). *The discovery of grounded theory.* Chicago, IL: Aldine.

Goldsmith, M. (1997, November). Retain your top performers. *Executive Excellence, 14*(11), 10–11.

Gram, T., Mark, T., & McGreal, R. (1997, March). *A survey of new media development and delivery software for Internet-based learning.* Sackville, NB: Mount Allison University, Centre for Learning Technologies.

Granger, D., & Benke, M. (1998). Supporting learners at a distance from inquiry through completion. In C. C. Gibson (Ed.), *Distance learners in higher education: Institutional responses for quality outcomes* (pp. 127–137). Madison, WI: Atwood.

Grundy, R. R., & Grundy, W. N. (n.d.; accessed January 25, 2000). Diffusion of innovation: solar oven use in Lesotho. [Online]. Available: http://www.accessone.com/~sbcn/lesotho1.htm

Hall, B. (1997). *Web-based training cookbook.* New York: Wiley.

Hall, G. (1978). Implications for planned dissemination, implementation, and evaluation revealed in the SRI/NDN evaluation and levels of use of the innovation studies. Paper presented at the annual meeting of the American Educational Research Association, Toronto, Ontario, Canada.

Hall, G., & Hord, S. (1987). *Change in schools: Facilitating the process.* Albany, NY: State University of New York Press.

Harreld, J. B. (1998). Building smarter, faster organizations. In D. Tapscott, A. Lowy, & D. Ticoll (Eds.), *Blueprint to the digital economy* (pp. 60–76). New York: McGraw-Hill.

Harrigan, K. R. (1991). Knowledge workers: The last bastion of competitive advantage. *Planning Review, 19*(6), 4–10.

Hawkins, B. L. (1999). Distributed learning and institutional restructuring. *Educom Review, 34*(4), 12–15.

Hillman, D., Willis, D., & Gunawardena, C. (1994). Learner-interface interaction in distance education: An extension of contemporary models and strategies for practitioners. *American Journal of Distance Education, 8*(2), 30–42.

Hinnant, E., & Oliva, L. (1997). Strategies for the integration of technology into teaching. In J. Morrison (Ed.), *Technology tools for today's campuses* [CD-ROM]. Redmond, WA: Microsoft.

Hirumi, A. (1995). *Systems theory lesson.* [Online]. Available: http://ide.ed.psu.edu/change/lessonoutline.html

Hudspeth, D. (1992). Just-in-time education. *Educational Technology, 6,* 7–11.

Huey, J. (1994). The new post-heroic leadership. *Fortune, 129*(4), 42–50.

Institute of Medicine. (1988). *The future of public health.* Washington, DC: National Academy Press.

Irby, A. J. (1999, March/April). Postbaccalaureate certificates: Higher education's growth market. *Change, 31*(2).

Jackson, T., Lorenc, D., & Iorizzo, L. (1997). Interactive distance learning over the Internet: A hybrid solution. *Journal of Instructional Delivery Systems, 11*(3), 24–29.

Jonassen, D. (1991). Objectivism vs. constructivism. *Educational Technology Research and Development, 31*(3), 5–14.

Joyce, B., & Weil, M. (1996). *Models of teaching* (5th ed.). Needham Heights, MA: Allyn & Bacon.

Kaye, T., & Rumble, G. (1991). Open universities: A comparative approach. *Prospects, 21*(2), 214–226.

Keegan, D. (1998). The two modes of distance education. *Open Learning, 13*(3), 43–47.

Kirkpatrick, D. L. (1994). *Evaluation training programs: The four levels.* San Francisco: Berrett-Koehler.

Klueter, L., & Kalweit, E. (1998). Disseminating time-sensitive information: Using interactive distance learning (IDL) to deliver training and education with the American Red Cross Biomedical Services. In D. A. Schreiber & Z. L. Berge (Eds.), *Distance training: How innovative organizations are using technology to maximize learning and meet business objectives* (pp. 115–136). San Francisco: Jossey-Bass.

Knowles, M. S., Holton, E. F., III, & Swanson, R. A. (1998). *The adult learner* (5th ed.). Houston: Gulf.

Kobulnicky, P. J. (1999). Critical factors in information technology planning for the academy. *CAUSE/EFFECT, 22*(2), 19–26.

Kolb, D. (1984). *Experiential learning: Experience as the source of learning and development.* Upper Saddle River, NJ: Prentice Hall.

Kubala, T. (1998, March). Addressing student needs: Teaching on the Internet. *T.H.E. Journal, 25*(8), 71–74.

Labour Market Analysis Branch. (1996, March). *TeleEducation NB: Program review.* Fredericton, New Brunswick: Department of Advanced Education and Labour.

Landsberg, M. (1997). *The Tao of coaching: Boost your effectiveness at work by inspiring those around you.* London: HarperCollins.

Lebel, C. (1989, April). *Le support à l'étudiant en enseignement à distance* (Student support in distance teaching). In *Student handbook.* Quebec: Télé-université.

Leidner, D., & Jarvenpaa, S. (1995). The use of information technology to enhance management school education: A theoretical overview. *MIS Quarterly, 19*(3), 265–291.

Lewis, J. H., & Romiszowski, A. (1996). Networking and the learning organization: Networking issues and scenarios for the 21st century. *e-Journal of Instructional Science and Technology, 1*(4). [Online]. Available: http://www.usq.edu.au/electpub/e-jist/vol1no4/article1.htm

Lincoln, Y. S., & Guba, E. G. (1985). *Naturalistic inquiry.* Thousand Oaks, CA: Sage.

Livneh, C., & Livneh, H. (1999). Continuing professional education among educators: Predictors of participation in learning. *Adult Education Quarterly, 49*(2), 91–106.

Maibach, E., & Holtgrave, D. (1995). Advances in public health communication. *Annual Review of Public Health, 16,* 219–238.

Mantyla, K., & Gividen, J. R. (1997). *Distance learning: A step-by-step guide for trainers.* Alexandria, VA: American Society for Training and Development.

McConnell, S. (1996). *Rapid development: Taming wild software schedules.* Redmond, WA: Microsoft Press.

McGreal, R. (1997). The Internet: A learning environment. In T. E. Cyrs (Ed.), *Teaching and learning at a distance: What it takes to effectively design, deliver, and evaluate programs* (pp. 67–74). New Directions for Teaching and Learning, no. 71. San Francisco: Jossey-Bass.

McGreal, R. (1998a, Spring/Summer). Integrated distributed learning environments on the Internet: A survey. *Educational Technology Review,* (9), 25–31.

McGreal, R. (1998b, October). *A learning history of TeleEducation NB.* Fredericton, New Brunswick: TeleEducation NB. [Online]. Available: http://teleeducation.nb.ca/

McMillan, J. H., & Schumacher, S. (1996). *Research in education: A conceptual introduction.* White Plains, NY: Longman.

Merriam, S. B. (1998). *Qualitative research and case study applications in education.* San Francisco: Jossey-Bass.

Mertens, D. M. (1998). *Research methods in education and psychology: Integrating diversity with quantitative and qualitative approaches.* Thousand Oaks, CA: Sage.

Meyer, C. (1993). Fast cycle time: How to align purpose, strategy, and structure for speed. New York: Free Press.

Michalisin, M. D. (1997). In search of strategic assets. *International Journal of Organizational Analysis, 5*(4), 360–387.

Michalski, G. M. (1997). *Stakeholder variation in perceptions about training program results and evaluation: A concept mapping investigation.* [Online]. Available: http://www.conceptsystems.com/papers/paperusr/michalsk/aea51.htm

Michalski, G. M. (2000, April 10–14). Evaluating Web-based learning and instruction (WBLI). Paper presented at the International Society for Performance Improvement meeting, "Papers in Performance Technology," Cincinnati, OH.

Michalski, G. M., & Cousins, J. B. (2000). Differences in stakeholder perceptions about training evaluation: A concept mapping/pattern matching investigation. *Evaluation and Program Planning, 23*(2), 211–230.

Miles, R. E., & Snow, C. C. (1995, Spring). The new network firm: A spherical structure built on a human investment philosophy. *Organizational Dynamics* (pp. 5–18).

Miller, N.A.S. (1992). Toward a common vision: The change process in practice. *Educational Technology, 32*(11), 58–62.

Moe, M. T., Bailey, K., & Lau, R. (1999, April 9). *The book of knowledge: Investing in the growing education and training industry.* Report #1268. Merrill Lynch & Co., Global Securities Research and Economics Group, Global Fundamental Equity Research Department.

Mortlock, M., & Dobrowolski, E. (1998). Reskilling employees for competitive advantage: Reinventing learning at Unisys Corporation. In D. A. Schreiber & Z. L. Berge (Eds.), *Distance training: How innovative organizations are using technology to maximize learning and meet business objectives* (pp. 187–200). San Francisco: Jossey-Bass.

New Brunswick Telephone Company Ltd. (1998). *Standard rate chart.* Fredericton: Author.

Newman, P. C. (1995). *Nortel: Past, present, future.* Brampton, Ontario: Nortel Networks.

Noblitt, J. (1997, May-June). Top-down meets bottom-up. *Education Review, 32*(3), 38–43.

Norris, D. M., & Malloch, T. R. (1997). *Unleashing the power of perpetual learning.* Ann Arbor, MI: Society for College and University Planning.

Ostendorf, V. A. (1997a). *Response systems in distance learning.* Littleton, CO: Virginia A. Ostendorf, Inc.

Ostendorf, V. A. (1997b). *Teaching through interactive television.* Littleton, CO: Virginia A. Ostendorf, Inc.

Palloff, R. M., & Pratt, K. (1999). *Building learning communities in cyberspace: Effective strategies for the on-line classroom.* San Francisco: Jossey-Bass.

Picard, D. (1996, November). The future in distance training. *Training,* pp. s5–s10.

Portway, P., and Lane, C. (1994). *Teleconferencing and distance learning* (2nd ed.). Livermore, CA: Applied Business Telecommunications.

Powers, B. (1992). Strategic alignment. In H. Stolovitch & E. Keeps (Eds.), *Handbook of human performance technology: A comprehensive guide for analyzing and solving performance problems in organizations* (pp. 247–258). San Francisco: Jossey-Bass.

Roadmap to the future: The UNC information technology strategy—a report to faculty, staff, students, trustees and friends of the 16 campuses. (1999, October; accessed February 22, 2000). [Online]. Available: http://www.ga.unc.edu/its/netstudy/ roadmap/ ITS_ROADMAP.html

Rogers, R. (1995). *Diffusion of innovations* (4th ed.). New York: Macmillan.

Roper, W., Baker, E., Dyal, W., & Nicola, R. (1992). Strengthening the public health system. *Public Health Reports, 107*(6), 609–615.

Roth, J. (1998). The network is the business. In D. Tapscott, A. Lowy, & D. Ticoll (Eds.), *Blueprint to the digital economy* (pp. 283–297). New York: McGraw-Hill.

Rothwell, W. J., & Cookson, P. S. (1997). *Beyond instruction: Comprehensive program planning for business and education.* San Francisco: Jossey-Bass.

Rummler, G. A., & Brache, A. P. (1995). *Improving Performance: How to manage the white space on the organization chart* (2nd ed.). San Francisco: Jossey-Bass.

Russo, C.W.R. (1995). *ISO 9000 and Malcolm Baldrige in training and education: A practical application guide.* Lawrence, KS: Charro.

Sachs, S. G. (1999). The mature distance education program: Who are we now? *Performance Improvement Quarterly, 12*(2), 66–83.

Scardamalia, M. (1997). Networked communities focused on knowledge advancement. Paper presented at the 1997 American Educational Research Association (AREA) Meeting. Chicago, March 24–28, p. 16.

Schaaf, D. (1997, October). D.T. comes home. In Distance Training, a special editorial section in *Training*.

Schaffer, R., & Thomson, H. (1992, January-February). Successful change programs begin with results. *Harvard Business Review*, pp. 80–89.

Schein, E. H. (1985). *Organizational culture and leadership*. San Francisco: Jossey-Bass.

Schreiber, D. A. (1995). *Introduction to distance learning*. Washington, DC: AARP/ Learning Center.

Schreiber, D. A. (1998a). Best practices of distance training. In D. A. Schreiber & Z. L. Berge (Eds.), *Distance training: How innovative organizations are using technology to maximize learning and meet business objectives* (pp. 393–409). San Francisco: Jossey-Bass.

Schreiber, D. A. (1998b). Organizational technology and its impact on distance training. In D. A. Schreiber & Z. L. Berge (Eds.), *Distance training: How innovative organizations are using technology to maximize learning and meet business objectives* (pp. 3–18). San Francisco: Jossey-Bass.

Schreiber, D. A., & Berge, Z. L. (Eds.). (1998). *Distance training: How innovative organizations are using technology to maximize learning and meet business objectives*. San Francisco: Jossey-Bass.

Senge, P. (1990). *The fifth discipline: The art and practice of the learning organization*. New York: Currency Doubleday.

Senge, P. M., Kleiner, A., & Smigh, B. (1994). *The fifth discipline fieldbook: Tools, techniques, and reflections for building a learning organization*. New York: Doubleday.

Shenk, D. (1997). *Data smog: Surviving the information glut* (Rev. ed.). New York: HarperEdge.

Sherritt, C. A. (1992). Forum: The hidden agendas of distance education. *Journal of Adult Education, 21*(2), 31–35.

Sherry, L. (1996). Issues in distance learning. *International Journal of Distance Education, 1*(4), 337–365.

Shklanka, O. (1990). Off-campus library services: A literature review. *Research in Distance Education, 2*(4), 2–11.

Simonson, M. R. (1997). Evaluating teaching and learning at a distance. In T. E. Cyrs (Ed.), *Teaching and learning at a distance: What it takes to effectively design, deliver, and evaluate programs* (pp. 87–94). New Directions for Teaching and Learning, no. 71. San Francisco: Jossey-Bass.

Smith, P. G., & Reinertsen, D. G. (1998). *Developing products in half the time* (2nd ed.). New York: Wiley.

Spodick, E. F. (1996). The evolution of distance learning. [Online]. Available: http://sqzm14 .ust.hk/distance/idstance6.html.

Stake, R. E. (1995). *The art of case study research*. Thousand Oaks, CA: Sage.

Stansell, J. C. (1997). Mentors and mentoring: Reflections of a circle with/in circles. In J. L. Kincheloe & S. R. Steinberg (Series Eds.) & C. A. Mullen, M. D. Cox, C. K. Boettcher, & D. S. Adoue (Vol. Eds.), *Counterpoints: Studies in the postmodern theory of education: Vol. 55. Breaking the circle of one: Redefining mentorship in the lives and writings of educators* (pp. 121–144). New York: Peter Lang.

Stewart, T. A. (1999). *Intellectual capital: The new wealth of organizations*. New York: Currency Doubleday.

Surry, D. W. (1997, February 20). Diffusion theory and instructional technology (pp. 1–11). [Online]. Available: http://intro.base.org/docs/diffusion/

Systemic Reform. (1994, September). Perspectives on Personalizing Education. [Online]. Available: http//www.ed.gov/pubs/ EdReformStudies/SysReforms/stiegel7.html

Tapscott, D. (1998). *Growing up digital*. New York: McGraw-Hill.

Tedeschi, B. (2000, May 22). Internet business may find the global village dauntingly native. *New York Times*.

Tobin, D. R. (1998). *The knowledge-enabled organization: Moving from "training" to "learning" to meet business goals*. New York: American Management Association.

Toffler, A. (1980). *The third wave*. New York: Bantam Books.

Trochim, W. (n.d.; accessed February 22, 2000). *Evaluating websites*. [Online]. Available: http://trochim.human.cornell.edu/WebEval/webintro/webintro.htm

Trochim, W. & Hover, D. (n.d.; accessed March 14, 2000). *Mapping student views of the benefits of a course website*. [Online]. Available: http://trochim.human.cornell.edu/WebEval/mapuser/mapuser.htm

Tucker, G., Gunn, C., & Lapan, S. (Eds.). (1998). *Technology, integration, and learning environments: CEE monograph: The NAU Centennial Year of Education* (Monograph Series No. 5). Flagstaff: Center for Excellence in Education, Northern Arizona University.

Turcotte, L. H., Ellis, M. G., & Iorizzo, L. J. (1994). *Distance learning: The continuing evolution of the digital army classroom*. Vicksburg, MS: Information Technology Laboratory, U.S. Army Corps of Engineers Waterways Experiment Station.

Umble, K., Cervero, R., Langone, C., Lincoln, R., & Smith, S. (1996). *Evaluation of the epidemiology and prevention of vaccine-preventable diseases PHTN distance learning program: Proposal and theoretical framework*. Unpublished manuscript. Atlanta, GA: Division of Media and Training Services, U.S. Centers for Disease Control and Prevention.

U.S. Army Intelligence Center. (1997). *Intelligence training xxi: Ready now*. Fort Huachuca, AZ: Author.

U.S. Department of Health and Human Services. (2000, January; accessed February 22, 2000). *Healthy People 2010*. [Online]. Available: http://www.health.gov/healthypeople/Document/HTML/Volume1/Opening.htm

U.S. Postal Service. (1999). *Strategic focus '99: We deliver better!* (Videotaped program). Washington, DC: Author.

Vazquez-Abad, J., & Winer, L. (1992). Emerging trends in human performance interventions. In H. Stolovitch & E. Keeps (Eds.), *Handbook of human performance technology* (pp. 672–687). San Francisco: Jossey-Bass.

Verduin, J. R., & Clark, T. A. (1991). *Distance education: The foundations of effective practice*. San Francisco: Jossey-Bass.

Vygotsky, L. S. (1962). *Thought and language* (E. Hanfmann & G. Vakar, Ed. & Trans.). Cambridge, MA: MIT Press.

Vygotsky, L. S. (1978). *Mind in society: The development of higher psychological process* (M. Cole, V. John-Steiner, S. Scribner, & E. Souberman, Trans.). Cambridge, MA: Harvard University Press.

Wagner, E. (1992). Distance education systems. In H. Stolovitch & E. Keeps (Eds.), *Handbook of human performance technology* (pp. 513–525). San Francisco: Jossey-Bass.

Webb, E. J., Campbell, D. T., Schwartz, R. D., & Sechrest, L. (1966). *Unobtrusive measures: Nonreactive research in the social sciences*. Chicago: Rand McNally.

Webster, J., & Hackley, P. (1997). Teaching effectiveness in technology-mediated distance learning. *Academy of Management Journal, 40*(6), 1282–1309.

Weisbord, M. R. (1976). Organizational diagnosis: Six places to look for trouble with or without a theory. *Group and Organizational Studies, 1*, 430–447.

Whetzel, D. L., Felker, D. B., & Williams, K. M. (1996). A real world comparison of the effectiveness of satellite training and classroom training. *Educational Technology Research and Development, 44*(3), 5–18.

Willis, B. (1993). *Distance education: A practical guide.* Englewood Cliffs, NJ: Educational Technology Publications.

Yin, R. K. (1994). *Case study research: Design and methods* (2nd ed.). Thousand Oaks, CA: Sage.

Zaltman, G., & Duncan, R. (1977). *Strategies for planned change.* New York: Wiley.

Zellner, L. (1997). Four recipes (scenarios) on mentoring: Or, how I became an e-mail mama. In J. L. Kincheloe & S. R. Steinberg (Series Eds.) & C. A. Mullen, M. D. Cox, C. K. Boettcher, & D. S. Adoue (Vol. Eds.), *Counterpoints: Studies in the postmodern theory of education: Vol. 55. Breaking the circle of one: Redefining mentorship in the lives and writings of educators* (2nd ed., pp. 35–51). New York: Peter Lang.

# INDEX

## A

Acceptance, 142–143, 355

Access: analyzing, in MCI World-Com case study, 82; as classroom learning obstacle, 165–166; ensuring, in MCI World-Com case study, 77–78, 84; in FORDSTAR case study, 181, 186; in Hewlett-Packard case study, 241–242; in TeleEducation NB case study, 317–318, 326

Accommodation, 8

Accountability: as criterion for Web-based training, 206, 207, 215; policies and, 258–259; for spending, 152; for time-to-market (TTM) project, 204

Activities, in satellite television class, 172

Activity-centered programs, 18

Adaptive learning model, 35–36

Administrative Corporate Education System (ACES), 133

Administrative support, 20–21; for FORDSTAR, 184–185

Adult learners, 5, 6–7

Agenda items, for organizational strategic planning, 151

Agilent Technologies, 250

Ai, X., 206

Alignment mechanisms, 246

Alkin, M. C., 206

Alpha product release, 204

Alternative delivery systems, 3, 52

Alternative media, defined by SBC Center for Learning, 52

Alternatives section, of enterprise-training plan, 278

American Council on Education, 152

American Red Cross, 329–347; background and context of, 329–333; Biomedical Services training of, 332–333, 335, 338, 339, 340; business problem statement of, 330–332; collaboration in, 338, 343–344; commitment to change at, 343–344; Corporate Education and Training division of, 340–341, 342, 343, 344; cost issues of, 345–346; distance learning

focus of, 336; evolution of distance learning at, 334–342; evolution of distance learning at, overview, 336–337; expanding technology capability of, 340–341; goals of, to leverage technology, 333–334; growth and innovation at, 346; integration of technology at, 341; learner-level issues of, 331; learning approaches of, 330; Learning Community of, 338, 341, 344, 345; The Learning Initiative of, 338, 340; learning strategy of, 333; lessons learned from, 345–347; management processes of, 342–344; organizational commitment to leverage technology at, 335; organizational maturity of, 334, 347; organizational strategy linkage of, 342; outcomes of, attained, 344–346; outcomes of, desired, 333–334; policy and organizational strategy of, 335, 336; programs and learning opportunities of, 337; sample